National Basketball Association Franchises

National Basketball Association Franchises

Team Performance and Financial Success

Frank P. Jozsa Jr.

LEXINGTON BOOKS
Lanham • Boulder • New York • London

Published by Lexington Books
An imprint of The Rowman & Littlefield Publishing Group, Inc.
4501 Forbes Boulevard, Suite 200, Lanham, Maryland 20706
www.rowman.com

Unit A, Whitacre Mews, 26-34 Stannary Street, London SE11 4AB

British Library Cataloguing in Publication Information Available

Library of Congress Cataloging-in-Publication Data

Includes bibliographic reference and index
ISBN: 978-1-4985-4799-4 (cloth : alk. paper)
ISBN: 978-1-4985-4800-7 (electronic)

™ The paper used in this publication meets the minimum requirements of American National Standard for Information Sciences—Permanence of Paper for Printed Library Materials, ANSI/NISO Z39.48-1992.

Printed in the United States of America

To basketball fans, especially from Indiana

Contents

Abbreviations

AAA	American Airlines Arena
AAC	American Airlines Center
ABA	American Basketball Association
ABL	American Basketball League
ACS	Auto Club Speedway
AD	Atlantic Division
AHL	American Hockey League
AOL	America Online
BAA	Basketball Association of America
BCBS	Blue Cross and Blue Shield
BET	Black Entertainment Television
BLF	Bankers Life Fieldhouse
CD	Central Division
CEA	Chesapeake Energy Arena
CEO	Chief Executive Officer
CNN	Cable News Network
DAL	Delta Air Lines
DCR	Digital Content Repository
D/V	Debt-to-Value
EC	Eastern Conference
ED	Eastern Division
ESPN	Entertainment Sports Programming Network
FCE	Forest City Enterprises
FCI	Fan Cost Index
FFBP	Fall Fast Break Pass

FSF	Fox Sports Florida
GR	Gate Receipts
HB2	House Bill 2
I-4	Interstate 4
IHL	International Hockey League
ISU	Iowa State University
LED	Light-Emitting Diode
LGBT	Lesbian Gay Bisexual Transgender
LLC	Limited Liability Corporation
MBA	Masters of Business Administration
MIT	Massachusetts Institute of Technology
MJ	Michael Jordan
MLB	Major League Baseball
MLS	Major League Soccer
MLSE	Maple Leaf & Sports Entertainment
MSG	Madison Square Garden
MVP	Most Valuable Player
MWD	Midwest Division
NA	Not Applicable
NBA	National Basketball Association
NBL	National Basketball League
NCAA	National Collegiate Athletic Association
NCAs	Nuggets' Community Ambassadors
NCRM	National Civil Rights Museum
NESN	New England Sports Network
NFL	National Football League
NHL	National Hockey League
NLL	National Lacrosse League
NWD	Northwest Division
OI	Operating Income
OTT	Over-the-Top
PBF	Professional Basketball Franchise
PCI	Partners for Community Impact
PD	Pacific Division
PE	Players Expenses
PGA	Professional Golfers Association
QLA	Quicken Loans Arena
QSR	Quick-Service Restaurant
R	Rank

RDA	Redevelopment Agency
RSN	Regional Sports Network
SED	Southeast Division
SKC	Smoothie King Center
SLI	Sports Loyalty Index
SWD	Southwest Division
TMR	Team Marketing Report
TNT	Turner Network Television
TSN	The Sports Network
TWCA	Time Warner Cable Arena
UC-SD	University of California-San Diego
US	United States
USC	University of Southern California
VSHA	Virint Smart Home Arena
WC	Western Conference
WD	Western Division
WGU	Western Governors University
WNBA	Women's National Basketball Association
W%	Win-Loss Percent
YES	Yankee Entertainment Sports
YHP	Youth Hoops Program

Acknowledgments

While organizing, writing, and editing the manuscript for this book during 2016, a few individuals provided information for it and thus helped me in different ways. Most important to my project, Pfeiffer University's library director and assistant professor of library science Lara Little found numerous readings about *National Basketball Association Franchises* from such publications as *Business Week*, *Forbes*, *Fortune*, *SportsBusiness Journal*, and the *Wall Street Journal*, and then promptly forwarded them to me. I appreciate Lara's professionalism and her commitment to spend time and obtain articles, reports, and studies for me regarding the business, economics, finance, and operations of teams in the sport. Surely, Lara is a superstar librarian for the university's administration, faculty and staff, and especially for the school's undergraduate and graduate students.

Besides Lara, another contributor was University of Michigan professor of sport management and codirector of the school's Center for Sport Management Rodney D. Fort. He forwarded me information and a website regarding payrolls of NBA teams. The coauthor of the book *Pay Dirt*, Professor Fort provides business and other historical data on professional sports teams at https://sites.google.com/site/rodswebpages/cod.

Former Loras College economics professor Laddie Sula offered advice and spoke with me about the NBA including his views of teams and their players. While at Loras, Laddie had a great career playing on the basketball team. As a result, he was inducted into the school's Sports Hall of Fame.

Forbes sports editor Kurt Badenhausen directed me to some websites regarding the business and history of the NBA and its teams and their coaches and players. According to Kurt, the files on these websites are accurate and reliable. He also answered my questions about financial amounts reported in articles such as the magazine's "The Business of Basketball." Player's expenses, for example, are altered to account for benefits, costs, insurance money teams get back for injured players, draft picks sold, amnestied players, and other things. Special thanks to Professor Fort, Laddie, and Kurt.

My fiancé and best friend Maureen Fogle allowed me to use her computer to organize and write a manuscript for this book. Despite spreading books and files on the carpet in our office and also needing time to research, rewrite, and edit copies of chapters, she understood how important this project was for me to complete and then submit a professional copy of it to Lexington Books on or before the due date. Once again, thanks to Maureen for her cooperation and patience particularly since my retirement as a business/economics professor from Pfeiffer University in 2007.

Frank P. Jozsa Jr.

Introduction

The most prominent and successful organizations in American professional team sports emerged, developed, and matured during different but distinct periods. When named, these different groups—from most to least experienced in each sport as of their 2015 season—include 140-year-old Major League Baseball—officially the American League in 1901 and National League in 1876—and then the ninety-nine-year-old National Hockey League, ninety-four-year-old National Football League—named American Professional Football Association in 1920–21—sixty-seven-year-old National Basketball Association (NBA), and twenty-year-old Major League Soccer.

Despite *internal* problems as executives' conflicts and players' injuries, and also such *external* issues as economic recessions and government legislation, teams within the NBA have performed in regular-season games. Then if qualified, they competed against each other in various types of playoff series including division semifinals and finals, and league semifinals and finals in the 1949–50 season through the first round of the playoffs, Eastern Conference (EC) and Western Conference (WC) semifinals and finals, and the league finals in the 2015–16 season.

To organize and schedule games in each of its regular-seasons and postseasons, the NBA encouraged and promoted its teams to exist for years and even decades within their small, midsized, large, or very large metropolitan area and appeal to fans in local, regional, national, and even international sports markets. Essentially, professional basketball teams perform to provide entertainment for spectators and on television networks by competing in home and away games at new and/or renovated arenas while also operating as franchises or commercial enterprises in order to earn maximum profits with sufficient amounts of cash inflows and revenues.

For various reasons, however, some teams previously located in metropolitan areas of America ultimately folded because they had financial problems; inferior owners, coaches and/or players; apathetic hometown fans; and/or simply underachieved for periods while playing rivals primarily in their division and conference.

PURPOSE

From researching such sport-specific sources as books and articles in journals, newspapers, and websites on the Internet, and studying demographic, economic, and financial data, and other information in the literature, *National Basketball Association Franchises* focuses on and analyzes fifteen each EC and WC teams' historical regular-season and postseason performances, and also provides a recent financial profile of them while being competitive and profitable or unprofitable but also well-publicized enterprises. Certainly this is an important, newsworthy, and unique topic for different audiences because it includes existing NBA clubs and reveals how effectively each of them competed and also operated, survived, and prospered or not prospered from a business perspective.

BOOK OVERVIEW

After the front matter, which includes acknowledgments, abbreviations, and an introduction, *National Basketball Association Franchises* consists of six chapters followed by a conclusion and appendix, bibliography, and index. As such, the following describes the organization of these chapters and also facts about their contents.

While the acknowledgments and abbreviations are self-explanatory, each chapter discusses five NBA teams within a division. Besides two major sections—Team Performances and Franchise Business—there are subsections in the chapters. Sequentially, these focus on each team's early history and historical performances, its principal owner, financial data, amounts of players' payrolls, its arena including its amenities and entertainment value, fan cost index at home games, and important business news.

More specifically, the chapters denote when, where, and how effectively fifteen EC teams and then fifteen in the WC had performed and their financial status and significance as members of the world's most competitive and popular professional basketball organization. Readers learn, for example, which of them won division and/or conference titles while owned by an individual or group; age, construction cost, and economic value of their arena; amounts fans spent for tickets and other items to attend hometown games; teams' market value, revenue, operating income, gate receipts, and other financial information including their payrolls; and a few interesting but important topics and local activities, events, and projects that influence them as franchises. The contents also explain why some teams have succeeded more than others based on such things as attendances at games in their arenas and also win-loss records, market size, and estimated net worth.

Within chapters, franchises are compared to current rivals in their division like the Boston Celtics and New York Knicks in the EC's Atlantic Division, Chicago Bulls and Cleveland Cavaliers in the Central Division, and Miami Heat and Orlando Magic in the Southeast Division. Furthermore, their performances and financial results are ranked to others in their and the other conference—EC or WC.

Teams whose name did not change after switching from the American Basketball Association (ABA) are included in the analysis but not those who formally existed at prior locations. For example, there is the EC with a chapter containing the former ABA Indiana Pacers and current Washington Wizards, but not the Baltimore Bullets; and the WC with another chapter that discusses the former ABA Denver Nuggets and current Oklahoma City Thunder, but not the Seattle SuperSonics. In other words, this book answers questions regarding the history, productivity, and prosperity of NBA's least, average, and most prominent clubs as of their 2015–16 or simply 2015 season.

Among its audiences, *National Basketball Association Franchises* was written and published for current and prospective owners and executives of NBA franchises and potential investors in these organizations; the NBA commissioner and his staff; practitioners and scholars who research the sports industry; college and university professors who teach undergraduate and graduate students majoring in sports administration, business, economics, history, management, and/or marketing; and especially for basketball fans of today's EC and WC teams.

Part I

EASTERN CONFERENCE

Chapter One

Atlantic Division

Established in 1970 by the National Basketball Association (NBA), the Atlantic Division (AD) of the league's Eastern Conference (EC) included the Boston Celtics, Buffalo Braves, New York Knicks, and Philadelphia 76ers. The AD changed, however, when the New York Nets joined in 1976, Washington Bullets in 1978, Charlotte Hornets in 1988, Miami Heat in 1989, Orlando Magic in 1991, and Toronto Raptors in 2004, and also when the Braves withdrew in 1978, Hornets in 1997, and the Washington Wizards (former Bullets), Heat, and Magic in 2004.

Given these changes in structure, this chapter discusses the historical development and highlights business news and the financial facts of AD teams based in Boston, Massachusetts; Brooklyn, New York; New York City, New York; Philadelphia, Pennsylvania; and Toronto, Canada. Which of them, for example, had won the fewest division titles and championships? What were their market values, revenues, gate receipts, and ticket prices in the league's 2015–16 or simply 2015 season? Who have been the least and most successful owners among the five clubs? How do their arenas rate in capacity and entertainment among fans? The answers to these and other questions are covered in the chapter.[1]

TEAM PERFORMANCE

Boston Celtics

During June 1946, a group of eleven prominent men—who owned large arenas and/or ice hockey teams—met and formed a new professional basketball league and named it the Basketball Association of America (BAA). Among the men was businessman Walter Brown, who owned the Boston Garden Corporation. To play in the new league, Brown organized a team—Boston Celtics—which identified with the legacy of a barnstorming club that helped spur the growing popularity of basketball during the 1920s and 1930s in the country's northeast region.

On November 5, 1946, the Celtics made their debut at the Boston Garden before 4,329 fans. The game, however, was delayed an hour when the wooden backboard on the court was damaged by a player's practice dunk during warm-ups. After the backboard was repaired, the Celtics lost to the Chicago Stags by a score of 57–55 and finished their inaugural season with a 22–38 record and tied with the Toronto Huskies for last place.[2]

Historical Results

From the BAA's 1946–47 to 1948–49 season and NBA's since 1950–51, the Celtics were a member of the EC. During this seventy-year period, they won almost 59 percent of their total games including thirty division and nine conference titles and seventeen league championships in fifty-three playoff appearances. Among fourteen other EC teams as of 2015, Boston ranked first in winning percentage and also in number of total titles and playoffs (table A1).

Compared to other NBA clubs as of their 2015–16 season, the Celtics were fourth all-time in winning percentage (.588) following the Western Conference (WC) San Antonio Spurs (.621), Oklahoma City Thunder (.616), and Los Angeles Lakers (.613), first in division titles, championships, and playoffs, and second in number of conference titles after the Lakers. Based on these results, Boston's professional basketball team has been outstanding, popular, and well-known while performing for seven decades in the league.

Performance Highlights

Remarkably the Celtics were in consecutive playoffs during NBA seasons 1950–1968, 1971–1976, 1979–1992, 2001–2004, 2007–2012, and 2014–2015. Besides being led by such successful coaches as Red Auerbach, Tommy Heinsohn, Bill Fitch, K. C. Jones, Chris Ford, Jim O'Brien, and Doc Rivers, some of the team's greatest players included Ed Macauley, Bob Cousy, Bill Russell, John Havlicek, Larry Bird, Robert Parish, Kevin McHale, and Paul Pierce. Because of their talent and accomplishments, a few coaches and several Celtics players are in the Naismith Memorial Basketball Hall of Fame or Hall of Fame.

For various reasons, however, the club did not appear in playoffs in back-to-back seasons of 1948–1949, 1969–1970, 1977–1978, 1995–2000, and 2005–2006. Because of major and minor problems like ownership issues, coaching mistakes, injured players, retirement of the team's superstars, and competition from the division's Bullets, Nets, Knicks, 76ers, and Raptors, Boston had more losses than wins these years and failed to qualify for the conference's playoffs.

In a recent study, the Entertainment Sports Programming Network (ESPN) ranked the 1960, 1961, 1964, 1965, and 1986 Celtics teams in the top twenty of all-time. Led by Coach Jones and small forward Larry Bird, center Robert Parish, and power forward Kevin McHale plus guards Dennis Johnson and Danny Ainge, the 1986 club had a .817 winning percentage and won the league championship by defeating the Houston Rockets in six games.[3]

Based on their record in regular seasons and postseasons and other factors, the Celtics are the first or second greatest franchise in NBA history. The club was dominant especially from the mid-1950s to late 1960s, early 1970s to 1990s, and 2007 to 2012, and except for the Lakers, has been the most popular, prominent, and well-respected organization in the league.

Brooklyn Nets

After its 1976–77 season, the New York Nets were renamed New Jersey Nets. Combined, they played 2,904 games and won 41 percent of them including four division and two conference titles in sixteen playoffs. After finishing between second and fifth in the AD since 2006, playing their home games before small crowds at the Prudential Center, and failing to secure financing for a new arena in Newark, New Jersey, the Nets moved to Brooklyn, New York in 2012 and renamed Brooklyn Nets. The 18,200-seat Barclays Center became their new home in Brooklyn.

Regarding the club's relocation, Nets' principal owner Mikhail Prokhorov and Barclays Center developer and majority owner Bruce Ratner jointly issued the following statement:

> We would like to express our heartfelt thanks to [NBA Commissioner] David Stern and the NBA team owners for their role in making the Nets' move to Brooklyn a reality. Barclays Center will give the Nets a state-of-the-art new home and, together, we will give Brooklyn the great sports and entertainment experiences it so deserves. We are [look] forward to the opening of the Barclays Center on September 28 [2012] and to the start of the next NBA season as the Brooklyn Nets.[4]

Historical Results

While the New Jersey Nets were in consecutive playoffs during seasons 1981–1985, 1991–1993 and 2001–2006, they lost games in the EC's first round series or semifinals, and/or in the NBA championship. The club won its division four times and established a .634 winning percentage in 2001–2 but was eventually defeated by the WC's Los Angeles Lakers in the league's final series. During this period, their most successful coaches included Larry Brown, Stan Albeck, Chuck Daly, Byron Scott, and Lawrence Frank, and such players as Buck Williams, Derrick Coleman, Richard Jefferson, and Vince Carter. Former Nets players such as Alonzo Mourning, Bernard King, and Drazen Petrovic are in the Hall of Fame.

As a member of the conference's AD in the 2012 to 2015 seasons, the Brooklyn Nets had a .463 winning percentage and appeared in but lost too many games in three playoffs. In their division, they finished second twice, but also third and fourth, each once. The team's most important coaches were Pete Carlesimo, Jason Kidd, and Lionel Hollins, and such players as point guard Deron Williams and center Brook Lopez (table A1).

Performance Highlights

The Brooklyn Nets' best and worst seasons were, respectively, 2012–13 and 2015–16. In the former period, they won forty-nine regular-season games and qualified for the playoffs but lost in the conference's first round to the Chicago Bulls. Besides Williams and Lopez, shooting guard/small forward Joe Johnson scored more than 1,000 points and also 400 field goals. In contrast to 2012–13, the club struggled again in 2015–16. Because of players' injuries, wrong decisions by coaches Hollins and Tony Brown, and simply lack of talent, they won only twenty-one games and finished fourth in the division with their home attendance ranked twenty-seventh in the league.

In projections of where all NBA teams will be placed over the next three years [2016–2018 seasons], ESPN sports analysts Chad Ford and Kevin Pelton ranked the Nets thirtieth as they have for three straight editions of the Future Power Rankings. Ford and Pelton, who accurately predicted the club's debacle in 2015–16, are not optimistic or have much hope for Brooklyn for three seasons. In fact, they also rated the team last in quality of their current players and future draft picks.[5]

According to them, however, there are two positive things about the club. First, the Nets fired the general manager that got them into this mess, Billy King, and replaced him with Sean Marks. While Marks is inexperienced, he comes to Brooklyn from the San Antonio Spurs and is highly regarded around the league. If he instills discipline, a winning culture, and a more process-oriented approach, Brooklyn should be better off in the long run. Second, the Nets, for the first time in a while, are not in salary cap purgatory. Being ranked fifth among all NBA teams in this category, even if the club spends money efficiently, its roster score could dramatically increase. Despite relatively low attendance and also television ratings, Ford and Pelton believe fan enthusiasm will emerge if the Nets start looking respectable in games.

New York Knicks

In the early to mid-1940s, basketball was a growing and increasingly profitable sport in New York City. Although professional ice hockey was another popular and profitable sport, the teams' arenas were not used very often. After New York sportswriter Max Kase became sports editor at the *Boston American* in the 1930s, he met Boston Garden owner Walter Brown and developed the idea of an organized professional basketball league to showcase college players upon their graduation.

Being intrigued by the opportunity for additional income when ice hockey teams were not playing or on the road, Brown met with several arena owners. During June 1946, Kase and Brown and a group of seventeen others assembled at the Commodore Hotel in New York City and formed the BAA in which charter franchises were granted to major cities throughout the country. Meanwhile college basketball promoter, retired sportswriter, and president of Madison Square Garden (MSG) Ned Irish joined the group.

Kase originally planned to own and operate the BAA's New York franchise and approached Irish with a proposal to lease the Garden to him. Irish explained that the rules of the Arena Managers Association of America stated that MSG was required to own any professional teams who played in the arena. On the day of the meeting, Kase made his proposal to other owners. They, however, were more impressed by Irish and his vast resources. As a result, Kase relented and the league's franchise was awarded to Irish.

Irish wanted a distinct name for his basketball team, that is, one that represented New York City. After tallying the votes of his staff, it was named Knickerbockers or simply Knicks. That came from the pseudonym used by Washington Irving in his book *A History of New York*, which applied to the descendants of the original Dutch settlers of what later became New York, and then by extension to New Yorkers in general.[6]

Historical Results

From the league's 1946 to 2015 season the Knicks had a .493 winning percentage and in forty-two playoffs, they won eight division and four conference titles and also two NBA championships. Among fourteen other EC teams, New York ranked eighth in winning percentage and also second in number of playoffs, tied for sixth with the Philadelphia 76ers in division titles, sixth in conference titles, and tied for fifth with the 76ers in league championships. Thus, this is a large-market and above-average franchise based on its performances during a seventy-year period (table A1).

Compared to other NBA teams as of their 2015–16 season, the Knicks were sixteenth in win-loss percent, third in number of playoffs, tied for eighth in both division and conference titles, and tied for seventh with three different clubs in number of championships. Relative to all members of the league, New York has performed above average partly because of its attendances and popularity at home games, and its competitiveness, location, and rivalries with the division's Celtics, Nets, 76ers, and Raptors.

Performance Highlights

The Knicks were in consecutive playoffs during seasons 1946–1955, 1966–1974, 1987–2000, and 2010–2012. From 1969 to 1973, for example, they appeared in three finals series and won two of them. During various postseasons, the club's most outstanding coaches were Joe Lapchick, Red Holzman, Pat Riley, Jeff Van Gundy, and Mike D'Antoni. After Holzman's team finished 60–22 in the regular season and won a championship, he was NBA Coach of the Year in 1970. Twenty-four years later, Riley also received the award.

Some players had memorable performances for the franchise. To succeed in many games at their positions on the court, Harry Gallatin, Walt Bellamy, Willis Reed, Walt Frazier, Patrick Ewing, and Carmelo Anthony scored enough points and/or out-rebounded their opponents. Excluding Anthony, these players are in the Hall of Fame along with, for example, Dick McGuire, Richie Guerin, Dave DeBusschere, Bill Bradley, Earl Monroe, Tom Gola, and Spencer Haywood.

For various reasons, Knicks teams failed to qualify for the playoffs in such consecutive seasons as 1959–1960 to 1965–1966, 2004–2005 to 2009–2010, and 2013–2014 to 2015–2016. During these periods, the Celtics, Nets, and/or 76ers—and Raptors since the mid-1990s—had more talent and simply out-coached and performed better than New York in their home and away games.

According to points assigned in one online study, the Knickerbockers fell just outside the top ten franchises in NBA history in terms of performances per year. Their points-per-year average was just short of the top ten cut-offs even though the franchise had much success during its history. As of 2016, the club had won two league championships, a whopping four conference titles, and eight division crowns. Even though this New York-based franchise lacked consistency for quite a while, another championship would certainly vault it into the top ten of all-time.[7]

Based on different factors and other facts and information about the franchise, the 1969–70 and 1972–73 Knicks teams were their two best of all-time. Besides an NBA championship, they each won more than 69 percent of their regular-season games, featured several Hall of Famers, and dominated rivals on offense and defense. In fact, players Bradley, DeBusschere, Frazier, and Reed were role models and superstars on those teams while coached by Holzman and his staff.

Philadelphia 76ers

After Italian immigrant Daniel Biasone sent a $5,000 check to the National Basketball League (NBL) offices in Chicago in 1946, the Syracuse Nationals became the league's largely Midwest-based and easternmost team which existed in upstate New York. With NBL clubs mostly located in small Midwestern towns, the Nationals had a 21–23 record and finished in fourth place in their first season, but then defeated in the playoffs by upstate neighbor Rochester Royals in four games. In their second season (1947–48), the Nationals struggled to finish in fifth place with a 24–36 record. Even so, the team made the playoffs but then were swept by the Anderson Duffey Packers in three straight games. Despite a winning record and making the playoffs the next season, Syracuse lost again to the Duffey Packers.

Being one of seven NBL teams that combined with some from the BAA to form the NBA in 1949, the Syracuse Nationals played fourteen seasons in the league and during those years finished first in their division three times and won a league championship in 1955 led by Coach Al Cervi and such players as Dolph Schayes and Billy Gabor. Nevertheless, the club's playoff overtime loss to the Cincinnati Royals on March 26, 1963 proved to be its last game as investors Irv Kosloff and Ike Richman purchased the team from Biasone for approximately $500,000 and then moved it to Philadelphia.[8]

Although Syracuse was the last of the midsized cities to host an NBA team, it was apparent that central New York's population was no longer large enough to support and sustain a professional basketball franchise. Thus, the NBA returned to Philadelphia one year after the city's Warriors relocated to San Francisco.

A contest was held to decide on an original nickname for Philadelphia's team. The winning entry, chosen by basketball fan Walter Stalberg, was 76ers. Newspaper writers welcomed the name because it easily shortened to Sixers in news headlines. Consequently, the shorter name was accepted by the team for marketing purposes and for most of the last half-century as 76ers and Sixers becoming interchangeable with each other.

Historical Results

From the 1963 to 2015 NBA season, the 76ers played 4,291 games and achieved victories in approximately 50 percent of them. During the period, they won eight division and five conference titles, and also two championships in thirty-three playoffs. Among fourteen other EC teams as of 2015–16, Philadelphia ranked sixth in winning percentage, tied for fourth with the Detroit Pistons in number of playoffs, tied for sixth with the Knicks in division titles and for fifth in league championships, and tied for third with the Pistons and Miami Heat in conference crowns. Given these results, the 76ers have been competitive and above average while performing as a franchise in the NBA's EC (table A1).

Relative to the all-time performances of twenty-nine other clubs following the league's 2015 season, Philadelphia was fourteenth (winning percentage), tied for sixth (playoffs), tied for eighth (division titles), tied for fifth (conference titles), and tied for seventh (championships). Thus, the 76ers are in the upper third of all NBA clubs based on these statistics and the franchise's records in regular-season games and postseason series since 1963.

Performance Highlights

Philadelphia appeared in consecutive playoffs during seasons 1963–1970, 1975–1986, 1988–1990, 1998–2002, 2007–2008, and 2010–2011. Besides Dolph Schayes and Alex Hannum, the team's most prominent coaches included Jack Ramsey, Gene Shue, Billy Cunningham, Jim Lynam, Larry Brown, and Doug Collins. In 2001, Brown was NBA Coach of the Year because his team won more than 68 percent of its games, finished first in the AD of the EC, but then was defeated in the NBA Finals by the WC-champion Lakers.

Through the years, several players contributed their skills and talent to 76ers' victories. Other than Cunningham and Collins, some of them were Hal Greer, Wilt Chamberlain, Julius Erving, Charles Barkley, Moses Malone, Alan Iverson, and Andre Iguodala. For the franchise, Chamberlain won three Most Valuable Player (MVP) awards and Erving, Malone, and Iverson one each. Most of these players and Chet Walker, Bailey Howell, Bob McAdoo, and Dikembe Mutombo are in the Hall of Fame.

For sure, the two best 76ers teams played in the league's 1966–67 and 1982–83 seasons. They each won more than 79 percent of their regular-season games and also the EC and NBA Finals. Coached by Alex Hannum and then Billy Cunningham, respectively, the first club featured NBA all-star and MVP Chamberlain who averaged both twenty-four points and rebounds per game while center Malone led the champion 1982–83 team in scoring and rebounds. Three other competitive 76ers clubs also won division titles in 1977, 1978, and 1990.

The Sixers, however, performed dismally and thus failed to qualify for the playoffs consecutively in its 1971–1974, 1991–1997, 2005–2006, and 2012–2015 seasons. Too much competition from such rivals as the Celtics,

Nets, Knicks, and Raptors, some players' injuries and poor performances, coaching problems, and perhaps ownership issues during these years caused Philadelphia to lose a majority of games in its division and against several other teams in the conference.

In a recent analysis published online, Philadelphia (including the former Syracuse Nationals) ranked seventh all-time among NBA franchises. According to the study's author:

> The 76ers [franchise] boasts an incredibly impressive resume for a team that not everyone typically associates with great success. But this franchise has seen a plethora of success in its 68 years in the NBA. It's won *only* five division championships but also an incredible nine conference championships. It has also won three NBA championships in its history, too. The 76ers' fans should be incredibly proud of their place on this list and their overall history.[9]

During 2013–2016, the Sixers tanked at the end of their seasons in order to obtain a high draft pick. Their plan was to collect as many assets and draft picks as possible, and one day group together the right core of young superstars to dominate the league for the foreseeable future. Thus far, that strategy has not been successful.

While impossible to judge the results as of mid-2016, the 76ers have little to show for it. The club still has loads of future draft picks to find the next great superstar, but their plan also has one big roadblock that seems questionable. Part of the Sixers' plan hinges on the belief that they can draft young players, develop them, and then retain their rights for years to come in hopes of building a championship contender. However, that logic assumes that players will remain with the 76ers long enough for that part to pan out.

Toronto Raptors

It seemed appropriate that the city of Toronto hosted the first game in BAA history on November 1, 1946, since James Naismith—the inventor of the sport—was a Canadian. The Toronto Huskies lost that game to the New York Knickerbockers 68–66. The Knicks would go on to be a cornerstone of the league that soon would become the NBA while the Huskies folded after one season with a 15–45 record. Thus, the NBA did not return to Canada for nearly fifty years.

During April 1993, Professional Basketball Franchise (Canada) Inc. (PBF) officially applied to acquire an NBA team. The application was made by John Bitove—president of a financial services company—and a group that included former Ontario Premier David Peterson and Detroit Pistons star Isiah Thomas, who later became the Toronto Raptors' vice president.[10]

Three months later an NBA expansion committee traveled to Toronto, where the PBF group presented their plan for a downtown arena site near the city's subway line. In September 1993, PBF was conditionally awarded a franchise for the league's 1995–96 season and become its twenty-eighth team for a record expansion fee of $125 million. According to the agreement, Toronto would play its first two seasons at the SkyDome while its arena was being completed.

During 1994, fans submitted their preferences for the team's name. These included Dragons, Hogs, Scorpions, T-Rex, Tarantulas, and Raptors. Influenced by the popularity of the Steven Spielberg film *Jurassic Park* and a logo featuring an aggressive dinosaur dribbling a basketball, the team's new moniker—Toronto Raptors—was unveiled in mid-May on Canadian national television and then its logo a few days later.

Historical Results

As a member of the EC's AD from the 1995–96 to 2015–16 seasons, the Toronto Raptors played 1,674 games and had victories in 734 of them. During the period, they won four division titles but zero conference titles and league championships in eight playoffs. Among teams in its division as of the NBA's 2015 season, the club ranked fourteenth in both winning percentage and number of playoffs, twelfth in division titles and also tied for twelfth with three other teams in conference titles, and tied for tenth with the Nets and four other clubs in championships. As such, Toronto has performed below-average relative to its competitors in the EC since 1995 (table A1).

Compared to twenty-nine other NBA teams, the Raptors placed twenty-sixth (winning percentage), tied for twenty-sixth (playoffs), tied for twentieth (division titles), and also tied for twenty-first (conference titles) and tied for sixteenth (championships). Based on these results and other information, Toronto has been an inferior performing club because of such things as its mediocre coaches, lack of enough talented players, ownership issues, fan apathy, and too much competition from the division's Celtics, Nets, Knicks, and 76ers.

Performance Highlights

The Raptors were in successive playoffs of the conference during the 1999–2001, 2006–2007, and 2013–2015 NBA seasons. Within this period, their coaches included Butch Carter, Lenny Wilkins, Sam Mitchell, and Dwane Casey. While each of them also had losing seasons, so did coaches Brendon Malone, Darrell Walker, Kevin O'Neill, and Jay Triano. Regarding the group of them through 2016, they did not win an NBA Coach of the Year award for the franchise.[11]

Some of Toronto's players were very competitive and made a difference in games by scoring points and getting rebounds and/or assists and effectively guarding their opponents. More specifically, Vince Carter, Chris Bosh, Jose Calderon, Amir Johnson, Kyle Lowry, and Jonas Valanciunas had memorable performances for the franchise. Carter and Bosh were particularly good offensively and thus on several NBA all-star teams

Other than losing games six times in the EC's first round and once each in the semifinals and finals, the Raptors failed to qualify for the playoffs in the league's 1995–1998, 2002–2005, and 2008–2012 seasons. Simply put, the club experienced problems with inept performances of its coaches and players because of their bad and ill-timed decisions, inability to compete and win games as a team, lack of motivation, and significant challenges from division rivals.

Ahead of such opponents as the Charlotte Hornets, Memphis Grizzlies, Minnesota Timberwolves, Los Angeles Clippers, and New Orleans Hornets/Pelicans, the Raptors ranked twenty-fifth among NBA teams in a 2014 study. According to its author,

> The Raptors, Canada's only current NBA franchise, has seen some success in its 19 years in the league. Two times the Raptors have won their division but they've failed to go further than that, yet. Toronto can't feel too bad about its position on this list considering their age. They haven't had quite as much time to rack up points as others, but then again they haven't been particularly great.[12]

In a recent analysis published online, Toronto placed fifth in a preseason report for 2016–17. Regarding specific categories, the club's rating was fifth on offense and eleventh on defense. The Raptors finished with a winning record in the 2015–16 NBA season against each of the other conference playoff teams and were the only one in the league with a better record against teams over .500 than against those .500 or below. In other words, they have the resume to make a deep run in the playoffs and their defense is much better than it was a year ago (in 2015–16). But can they adapt when the opponent takes away their initial offense?[13]

Based on their winning percentages and number of playoffs and titles, the Celtics have the most impressive all-time performances among the EC's AD teams followed by the Knicks, 76ers, Raptors, and Nets. While a few of the club's coaches and many of its players are in the Hall of Fame, Boston is a great sports town for Celtics fans who, in turn, attend home games and enthusiastically root for their team particularly against rivals and during the playoffs.

Regarding the performances of other teams in the division, the Knicks have been successful at qualifying for the playoffs but less so at winning conference titles and championships. Although the Sixers have played on average above .500, they were better in the 1960s and late 1970s to the early 1990s than in the past twenty-five regular seasons. Lastly, the Raptors have never won a conference title as of 2016 while the Nets are the youngest team in the league and need additional talent and also experienced and successful coaches to become consistent contenders in their division.

FRANCHISE BUSINESS

Given the performances of them as teams, this section focuses on and examines the commercial aspects of NBA franchises including their principal owner or ownership groups and also various facts and other details in tables about each team's arena, differences in costs for families to attend home games, current and important financial data, and yearly trends in players' payrolls. In part, this information reveals why some franchises are more valuable and wealthy than others and therefore how successful or unsuccessful historically while being business enterprises in the sports industry.[14]

Boston Celtics

Born in Worcester, Massachusetts, in 1961, Wycliffe "Wyc" Grousbeck graduated from the Noble and Greenough School in Dedham, Massachusetts. He continued his education at Princeton University, where he received a Bachelor of Arts degree in history in 1983. While there, he rowed on the 1983 undefeated lightweight crew team that claimed the Ivy League title and national rowing championship. Three years later, Wyc received a law degree from the University of Michigan and then in 1992, a Master of Business Administration (MBA) at the Stanford Graduate School of Business.[15]

After spending seven years as a partner at the venture capital firm, Highland Capital Partners, Grousbeck—along with his father H. Irving Grousbeck—founded Boston Basketball Partners, a Limited Liability Corporation (LLC). During 2002 that group of investors, which included venture capitalist Steven Paglicua, acquired the Boston Celtics franchise and a rent-free lease to the FleetCenter for approximately $360 million from Paul Gaston. In addition, they also bought a 48 percent stake in the team owned then by a publicly traded limited partnership.

In 1986, Gaston and fellow owners Paul Dupree Jr. and Alan Cohen had sold 40 percent of the Celtics for $18.50 per share as the novelty of owning the team began to subside for them. As the club faded into mediocrity during the mid to late 1990s, its stock declined to about $11. As a result, Gaston and his syndicate accepted the Grousbecks' offer to purchase their franchise.

Since 2002, the Celtics have won six division and two conference titles and one NBA championship in eleven playoffs. Compared to other owners and performances of their teams in the EC, Boston tied for third in winning division and conference titles and also championships. Among all franchise owners in the league, the Celtics were, respectively, tied for fifth (division and conference titles) and for sixth (championships). Based on these results the Grousbecks, particularly Wyc, have been superior owners of the club for fourteen years by improving its record in regular-season games and in postseason series (table A2).

Ranked by basketball sportswriter Josh Hill as the eighth best owner in the NBA, Hill stated online that:

> Wyc Grousbeck is a much more reserved and lesser known owner than many of his counterparts in the NBA, but he's nonetheless a massive influence in the Celtics success. He's [pieced] together a front office and deals that sped up the rebuilding process to bring a title to Boston. You may credit [director of player personnel and president of basketball operations] Danny Ainge with the moves the Celtics make, but it's Grousbeck who deserves the credit for putting the pieces in place so that the Celtics don't become a train wreck like their cross-country rivals have become over the years. There's a way to own a successful franchise and not be the face of it—and Grousbeck has managed to find the balance.[16]

Team Financials

Besides performing as teams in regular-season and postseason games, NBA franchises are also commercial enterprises. To that end, their economic objective is to earn maximum revenue and obtain the greatest amount of profit on a fiscal basis from their operations. Although they share revenue with each other from such sources as national television contracts and other deals, it is important for them to efficiently allocate resources, determine and distribute payrolls, set non-premium and premium ticket prices, and schedule investments in short- and long-term assets. To reveal and manage these activities, this section focuses on different parts of the Celtics franchise's business environment and how well its organization succeeds or not succeeds from a financial perspective.[17]

Periodically sportswriters at *Forbes* magazine research and publish financial information about teams in professional sports leagues including the NBA. According to data as of the league's 2015–16 season, the Boston Celtics' estimated market value was $2.1 billion, revenue $181 million, operating income $57 million, gate receipts at home games $56 million, debt-to-value ratio 8 percent, and players expenses $69 million. Within its division, the team's amounts were second or third to those of the Knicks except for players expenses and the debt ratio (table A3).

Among EC clubs as of early 2016, the team ranked third in value and operating income following the Knicks and Bulls, fifth in revenue and gate receipts, and twelfth in both its debt-to-value and players expenses. Compared to amounts of twenty-nine other NBA teams in 2015, Boston's market value ranked fourth, revenue eighth, operating income tied for fifth with Golden State Warriors, gate receipts tenth, debt ratio tied for twenty-first with the Dallas Mavericks, and players expenses twenty-fifth. Based on these results, the Celtics are a lucrative, profitable, and rich franchise with a relatively high net worth, sufficient revenue and income to continue operations, and comparatively low debt and players expenses.

Besides market size, salary inflation, and other factors, an NBA team's annual payroll partly reflects its commitment to players and their current and potential contribution individually and as a group to winning games in regular seasons and postseasons. From 2011 to 2015, for example, the Celtics' payroll among fourteen EC teams ranged in rank from first in 2011 ($78.7 million) to eleventh in 2014 ($61.9 million). Compared to only AD teams, Boston had lower amounts than the Nets and Knicks except for 2011 but more than the Sixers and not Raptors each year (table A4).

Relative to twenty-nine other clubs in the league during the five-year period, the Celtics finished as low as third in 2011 to a high of twenty-fourth in 2014. For economic and sport-specific reasons, the team's payroll was gradually reduced after the 2011–2013 seasons but then significantly increased in 2015. Despite a losing record in 2014, the club finished second in its division and qualified for the playoffs and then again in 2016 led by former Butler University coach Brad Stevens. For the Celtics to be consistently competitive and win a championship in future seasons, its payroll must increase into the league's top ten.

TD Garden

Owned by Delaware North and opened in September 1995 to replace the aging Boston Garden, the $160 million FleetCenter—renamed TD Garden in 2005—is a 755,000-square-foot sports and entertainment complex. It was constructed above a new five-story, 1,150-space MBTA parking garage and occupies a 3.2-acre development site with the arena floor extending east to west.[18]

Some miscellaneous facts about TD Garden were originally its two full-service dining areas; seven elevators, thirteen escalators, thirty-four restrooms, and thirty-six permanent concession stands; 104 executive suites, 135 ledge seats, 1,150 parking spaces, 2,442 club seats, 3,734 additional seats for games than in the old Garden; and an 18,854-seat capacity.

Besides the Celtics, the arena has long-term leases and contracts with such prominent organizations as the National Hockey League (NHL) Boston Bruins, Ringling Brothers Barnum & Bailey Circus, Walt Disney's World on Ice, and the World Wrestling Federation. Furthermore, it will continue to host the Beanpot college hockey tournament, Boston Shootout, Boston Blazers lacrosse program, and college and high school winter sports competitions.

Among venues of teams in the EC as of 2015, TD Garden ranked as the fifth oldest, twelfth in construction cost, and fourth in market value. In comparison to all NBA arenas, it tied for tenth in age with the Portland Trail Blazers' Moda Center, tied for nineteenth in cost with the Denver Nuggets' Pepsi Center, and tied for eighth in value with the Dallas Mavericks' American Airlines Center. Although relatively old, the TD Center is an above-average and sufficient facility for its tenants and also hosting local events (table A5).

For several years a Chicago-based company named Team Marketing Report (TMR) has prepared and published a Fan Cost Index (FCI) for the home games of teams in professional sports leagues. To attend a game for a typical family with two kids, an FCI includes the costs of four average-priced tickets, two cheapest-priced draft beers, four each cheapest-priced soft drinks and hot dogs, parking for one vehicle, and two each game programs and least-expensive, adult-size adjustable caps. Costs are determined by telephone calls with team representatives, venues, and concessionaires, and from questions asked during interviews.[19]

In the 2011–2015 NBA seasons, the FCIs for a family to attend a regular-season game at TD Garden ranged from a low of $392 in 2011 to a high of $444 in 2014. During this period among EC clubs, the Celtics arena's FCI at games ranked fourth each year. Compared to all NBA clubs, the Garden's FCI was fifth during the 2011–2014 seasons and then seventh in 2015 (table A6).

To reveal specific costs for a recent season in the NBA, the Celtics FCI in 2015–16 was approximately $419 and $25 or 6 percent less than in 2014–15. Listed from most to least in amount by item for one person, the team's tickets averaged between $66 and $67, parking one vehicle $45, a cap $20, single beer $8–$9, and a soft drink, hot dog, and program each about $5.

Among other teams in the conference's AD, they had rankings and FCIs from most to least as follows in the 2015–16 NBA season: Knicks first at $676; Nets eighth at $404; Raptors thirteenth at $323; and 76ers tied for twenty-first with the Jazz at $275. These results indicate, in part, that Boston's fans paid more money to attend a home game that season than those of the Nets in Brooklyn, Raptors in Toronto, and 76ers in Philadelphia, but less than the Knicks in New York.

The cheapest ticket cost, on average, was about $10 for a fan to see a Celtics home game at the TD Garden in 2015–16. This was almost $6 or 37 percent less than the league's average for a cheap seat. However, since the club's FCI was $80 above the amount of a typical NBA team, a family of four purchased tickets and enjoyed a basketball game in Boston at a significant premium relative to the majority of arenas within the league. These costs and prices, in turn, were set by the Celtics organization to earn revenue and maximize profits from its operations.

Business Highlights

Besides regular-season and postseason games, NBA franchises are involved in—and affected by—community events and business-related affairs, news, and projects. The following are a few of them for Boston's popular and financially successful professional basketball team.[20]

First, the Celtics ranked between sixth and twenty-fifth in the 2016 Brand Keys Sports Loyalty Index (SLI). Such things as pure entertainment, authenticity, history, and tradition affect a sports team's fan loyalty which, in turn, influences its broadcast viewership, merchandise purchases, and, to an extent, ticket revenues. Boston fans are loyal to the Celtics especially during seasons when the club competes for the playoffs and features star point guard Isiah Thomas and other players.

Second, as of mid-2016, the Celtics planned to establish a 70,000-square-foot, two-court practice facility at Boston Landing to join the NHL Boston Bruins in a high-profile sports hub on the edge of the Allston-Brighton area. The NB Development Group—a sister company to New Balance Athletics—proposed a six-story office, laboratory, and sports facility at 40 Guest Street to be anchored by the Celtics. According to plans, the facility will feature two state-of-the-art parquet floors, high-tech audio-visual systems, a large number of strength and conditioning equipment and a big media workroom, and a flexible hospitality area for hosting community relations activities.

Third, because of a slight decline in attendance at its home games, revolving-door roster of players, and a losing record for the second straight season, Boston's proud basketball franchise had a dilemma in 2015. Unable to sell fans on marquee names and championship dreams, Celtics officials were pressured to try new and perhaps unorthodox and non-traditional marketing strategies while feeling the weight of a distinguished legacy. After hiring a gymnast to play Lucky Leprechaun and perform acrobatic dunks during game breaks in 2003 and then being the last NBA organization to add a dance team three years later, the club decided to unveil new uniforms, offer discount tickets through Groupon to fill seats at its home games, and install a replica of the Garden's parquet floor at a downtown bus stop. Some longstanding fans, however, were upset and opposed these strategies when team officials adopted and implemented them.

Fourth, Massachusetts-based technology firm StratBridge Inc. signed a deal with the Celtics in October 2010 to implement dynamic ticket-pricing models in order to boost the company's profile in the quickly emerging space to about a dozen NBA teams. The club deployed dynamic pricing structures within its primary market—single-game tickets—to take fuller advantage of supply and demand factors by allowing prices to float on a daily or weekly basis. StratBridge, which had a longstanding agreement with the Celtics for ticketing analysis, discovered that for its prior dynamic pricing clients, some of them averaged six-figure boosts in incremental revenue with a few instances of 20 percent increases in price over face value.

Fifth, during 2011, the Celtics finalized a lucrative media rights package with Comcast SportsNet New England to extend their current deal by twenty years, which provided a big jump in annual rights fee and also gave the team a stake in the network. The Celtics and Comcast SportsNet have been partners since Comcast bought the regional sports network (RSN) from Cablevision in 2007. Celtics games have been part of the RSN's lineup since 1981, when it launched as Prism New England. The team provides the most valuable programming on the RSN, which competes in the Boston market with NESN—an RSN owned in part by the Major League Baseball (MLB) Red Sox and NHL Bruins organizations.

Brooklyn Nets

Born in Moscow in 1965, Mikhail Prokhorov's father worked for the Soviet State Sports Committee and his mother as a research scientist. After studying at the Moscow Finance Institute—now Finance University—he went to work in the banking sector. As chairman of Onexim Bank, he invested in Norilsk Nickel during the largely unregulated selloff of Russian industries in the 1990s. A decade later, he founded the Onexim Group, a private investment holding company. Besides metals, the group has businesses in the financial industry, and media and technology.

When Prokhorov acquired a controlling interest (80 percent) in the New Jersey Nets and Barclays Center (45 percent) in 2010, he became the first foreign owner of an NBA franchise. During late 2015, Prokhorov's Onexim bought out Chairman Bruce Ratner's Forest City Enterprises (FCE) and other investors, securing full ownership of the Nets and Barclays Center. According to a press release from the two companies, the valuation of the two entities was a combined \$1.7 billion: \$875 million for the team and \$825 million for the arena. The transaction concluded following the transfer of \$285 million in cash and notes from Onexim to Nets Sports and Entertainment, an FCE-dominated partnership. Only a quarter of the \$285 million involved cash.

Since 2010, the Nets have appeared in three playoffs but failed to win any division and conference titles and NBA championships. As an owner among those of other EC teams, Prokhorov's Nets respectively tied for ninth (division titles), for eighth (conference titles), and for fifth (championships). Compared to owners of twenty-nine different NBA clubs, his tied for twentieth in division titles, tied for sixteenth in conference titles, and tied for tenth in championships. Consequently, Prokhorov has been enthusiastic about and involved with improving the Nets' operations but not successful yet at winning titles and championships in the league (table A2).

Team Financials

Based on financial estimates by sports editors at *Forbes* magazine as of 2015, the Brooklyn Nets' estimated market value was $1.1 billion, revenue $220 million, operating loss of $5 million, gate receipts $63 million, debt-to-value ratio 15 percent, and players expenses $99 million. Among only EC clubs, the team tied for fifth with the Cleveland Cavaliers in value and also ranked third in revenue, fifteenth or last in operating income, fourth in gate receipts, ninth in debt-to-value, and first in players expenses. Except for operating income, the Nets had better financial results than the AD's 76ers and Raptors but not the Knicks or Celtics (table A3).

Compared to twenty-nine other NBA franchises as of their 2015–16 season, Brooklyn ranked from first (players expenses) to thirtieth (operating income). According to all amounts, the club is above-average financially although operating at a loss despite being located in a large, populated, and prosperous television and sports market. Thus, principal owner Mikhail Prokhorov needs to improve operations in order for the franchise to become profitable.

Besides market size, salary inflation, and other factors, an NBA team's annual payroll partly reflects its commitment to players and their current and potential contribution individually and as a group to winning games in regular seasons and postseasons. From the league's 2012 to 2014 seasons, for example, the Nets' payroll was the highest in the EC at respectively $83 million, $102.8 million, and $88.1 million, but then second to the Cavaliers in 2015 at $88.0 million. This data, in turn, contributed to two winning seasons and three playoff appearances but then only twenty-one victories and a fourth-place finish in its division in 2015–16 (table A4).

Compared to payrolls of all NBA franchises, the Nets ranked second in 2012, first in both 2013 and 2014, and sixth in 2015. These results suggest the club was very generous in payments to its players during the period and will likely demand and expect more productivity from them in the future, especially such players (salaries) as Brook Lopez ($21 million), Thaddeus

Young ($12.1 million), and Deron Williams ($5.5 million) in the 2016–17 season.

In short, the Nets are a very valuable team with relatively high amounts of revenue, gate receipts, and player expenses but average to below average debt. Furthermore, their franchise owner is a prosperous and wealthy business entrepreneur, who is willing to invest more money to improve his franchise in different ways, including additional compensation for coaches and perhaps acquiring more talented and experienced players.

Barclays Center

A multipurpose indoor arena located in the borough of Brooklyn of New York City and opened in 2012, the 17,750-seat Barclays Center sits partially on a platform over the Metropolitan Transportation Authority-owned Vanderbilt Yards at Atlantic Avenue for the Long Island Railroad. Originally, it was part of a $4.9 billion future business and residential complex known as Pacific Park.

Besides the NBA Nets, the Barclays Center is home to the NHL's New York Islanders. The arena, which also hosts concerts, conventions, and other sporting and entertainment events, competes with other facilities in the New York metropolitan area, including MSG in Manhattan, and the Prudential Center in Newark, New Jersey.

Compared to other teams' facilities in the league's EC as of 2015, the Barclays Center is the newest among them, second most expensive to construct, and third most valuable. Among all NBA arenas, it ranks thirtieth (age), second (cost), and third (value). Given its amenities, location, and size, this is an excellent venue for the Nets and Islanders to play their home games and entertain fans with different attractions (table A5).

According to an evaluation of the Barclays Center on the website rantsports.com, it reported in part:

> The [arena's] alternating light/dark wood paneling gives the floor a distinctive touch. Otherwise, the Barclays center is a beautiful, well-lit arena—something that doesn't translate well to TV—without the vile touch of over-advertisement. Try to divorce the pathetic Brooklyn Nets (and the debacle of their reinvention) from the new arena. It's impossible; the arena is inextricably linked to the rebranding. The food is overpriced, it's difficult to get to and the atmosphere is lethargic, much like the team.[21]

During the league's 2012 to 2015 seasons among venues of fourteen other EC teams, the FCI for a Nets home game at the Barclays Center ranked fifth each year and ranged in amounts from $365 in 2012 to $404 in both 2014 and 2015. Within only the AD, it was relatively more expensive for fans to attend

Knicks and Celtics home games but not those of the 76ers and Raptors. Compared to FCIs of all NBA arenas, the Barclays Center was seventh highest in expenses at games during 2012–2014 and also eighth in 2015 (table A6).

Listed from most to least in amount by item for one person at a Nets home game in their 2015–16 season, tickets averaged between $66 and $67, a cap $28 and parking one vehicle $17, one beer $8–$9, a hot dog $6, and a soft drink and program each $5. Thus, fans paid roughly the same for these products at games as in the team's 2014–15 season.

Among other clubs in the conference's AD, they had rankings and FCIs from most to least as follows in the 2015–16 NBA season: Knicks first at $676; Celtics seventh at $419; Raptors thirteenth at $323; and 76ers tied for twenty-first with the Utah Jazz at $275. These results indicate, in part, that Brooklyn's fans paid more at a home game that season than those of the Raptors in Toronto and 76ers in Philadelphia, but less than the Knicks in New York and Celtics in Boston.

The least expensive ticket cost, on average, $20 for a fan to attend a Nets home game at the Barclays Center in 2015–16. This was almost $6 or 26 percent more than the league's average for a cheap seat. Since the club's FCI was approximately $65 above the amount of a typical NBA team, a family of four purchased tickets and enjoyed a basketball game in Brooklyn at a significant premium relative to the majority of arenas within the league. These costs and prices, in turn, were set by the Nets organization to generate revenue and maximum profits from its operations.

Business Highlights

Similar to the other NBA teams, the Nets are involved in—and affected by—community events and business-related affairs, news, and projects. The following are a few of them for Brooklyn's moderately popular but also financially lucrative and relatively new professional basketball team.[22]

First, while playing preseason games during mid-October 2014 in Shanghai and Beijing, China, the Nets extended their "Hello Brooklyn" tag line to "Hello China" during the trip along with holding a series of events aimed at attracting more foreign fans and business partners. The public events ranged from co-hosting a breakfast with the American Chamber of Commerce in Shanghai to a spin class with executives from both teams. The Nets also hosted a hospitality event in a Beijing Adidas store that featured the team's brand as well as merchandise and digital signage along with player autograph sessions. "We believe in expanding our bandwidth globally," said Nets CEO (chief executive officer) Brett Yormark. "Our owner [Mikhail Prokhorov] is from Russia, our naming-rights partner [Barclays] is from the United Kingdom, and we want to establish ourselves as a team that speaks to a global audience."

Second, New York's Hospital for Special Surgery signed a ten-year deal with the Nets during mid-2014 to put its name on the team's training center, which is about three miles from the Barclays Center in Brooklyn. The 70,000-square-foot facility—opened before the 2015–16 NBA season—was built on the eighth floor and rooftop of a rehabbed warehouse in the city's Sunset Park neighborhood. Supposedly, the title sponsorship for the Hospital for Special Surgery Training Center, along with an accompanying package for Nets rights, totals in the low seven figures per year. The package includes branding inside and outside the practice facility, signage at the team's home games, logo placement on the Nets' practice jerseys, and hospitality at the practice facility and Barclays Center.

Third, during late 2015, the Nets extended their local cable television deal with the Fox-owned YES Network. The team used a contractual "reset" that occurs every five years to get YES to increase its rights fee to an annual average of around $40 million. The new pact kicks off with the league's 2017–18 season. A little more than one-half of one percent of the New York market's televisions tune to YES for Nets games. Those are the lowest television ratings for any NBA team, but do not mean the Nets have the smallest audience in the league. Because the New York area is a large and populated market, even a tiny percentage of it yields an audience larger than many of the smaller sports markets.

The YES deal is the second television rights boost for the team. In its 2016–17 season, the NBA's national television rights deal—negotiated with ESPN and the Turner Network Television (TNT)—nearly tripled what teams received in the past. From roughly $30 million a year, the national rights per team jumped to more than $80 million. Under terms of the proposed deal, the agreement between the two lets YES retain all broadcast television and digital rights to the Nets programming and shortens the time period. The current agreement goes through the team's 2031–32 season, with options beyond that year. Although the new deal is shorter, it still runs well into the next decade.

Fourth, with attendance flagging, the Nets planned to cut ticket prices by an average of 24 percent for its 2016–17 NBA season. The discounts applied to season tickets for some but not all of the best locations at the Barclays Center. Front-row seats were not scheduled to go on sale, nor were the $3,500-per-game Hollywood Seats between the bench and scorer's table. Floor seats on the baseline and seats in rows B through D—which cost as much as $1,450 per game—were reduced a blended 11 percent. The arena's more affordable seats will get even bigger discounts. Customers who already made multiyear commitments for tickets will also be given the one-year price reduction, which extended to July 1, 2016.

Fifth, Russia's main domestic security agency searched the offices of a company controlled by the Nets' owner, multibillionaire Mikhail Prokhorov. The country's Federal Security Service—which was the KGB's primary successor agency—reported that searching the Onexim group was part of a probe into alleged tax evasion. It added that the investigation is continuing. Some Russian media have speculated that the searches could have been aimed at pressuring Prokhorov into surrendering control over his media assets. In fact, organizations searched included RBC—an online newspaper that published reports critical of the Kremlin and also provided information about the so-called Panama Papers detailing offshore assets allegedly owned by top Russian businessmen and government officials.

The searches occurred just as Russian president Vladimir Putin held his annual call-in television show. Putin's spokesman, Dmitry Peskov, strongly denied any link between the searches and Prokhorov's media assets. The fifty-year-old Prokhorov, who is worth $8.2 billion according to *Forbes*, founded a liberal political party and challenged Putin in the 2012 presidential election by winning 8 percent of the popular vote. He, however, did not comment on the latest searches.

New York Knicks

Born in 1955 to Cablevision's founder Charles Dolan, James Dolan originally pursued a career in music. Eventually, he switched to a major in communications at State University of New York at New Paltz and then began working for Cablevision in various capacities including sales before being dispatched to Cleveland by his father to manage the launch of a sports radio station.

Four years after becoming CEO of Cablevision in 1995, James Dolan was given an increased role in managing Cablevision's sports properties including the NBA Knicks, NHL New York Rangers, Women's National Basketball Association (WNBA) New York Liberty, and the American Hockey League (AHL) Hartford Wolf Pack. As chairman of MSG, he is the primary manager of these assets and also supervises regional sports networks including the MSG network and MSG Plus. He also serves as a governor of the Knicks and Rangers to their respective leagues.

Since becoming the Knicks' principal owner in the late 1990s, his teams have won a division and conference title but not an NBA championship. Among other owners of franchises in the EC, Dolan's Knicks ranked eighth in winning the AD once, tied for sixth with the Pacers in conference titles, and tied for fifth with zero championships. Compared to owners of all NBA clubs as of the league's 2015–16 season, his was respectively tied for eighteenth (division titles), tied for thirteenth (conference titles), and tied for tenth (championships). Despite his teams' seven playoff appearances, Dolan has been an average to below-average owner and not successful at winning enough titles and any league championships during his tenure with the Knicks (table A2).

Team Financials

According to financial data published by *Forbes* magazine as of 2015, the Knicks' estimated market value was $3 billion, revenue $307 million, operating income $108 million, gate receipts $128 million, debt-to-value 0 percent, and players expenses $88 million. In comparison to other clubs in the EC, the team ranked first in these amounts except for being fourth in its players expenses and also fifteenth in the debt ratio. Within only the AD, the Knicks had the highest dollars but smallest debt and lower player expenses than the Nets (table A3).

Relative to all NBA teams, New York placed first (market value, revenue, and gate receipts), second (operating income) following the Lakers, seventh (players expenses), and tied for twenty-eighth with the Denver Nuggets and Los Angeles Clippers (debt percent). Based on these results, the Knicks are the biggest and most valuable business enterprise in the league and also profitable from operations at MSG and their local and regional television network.

As discussed for the Celtics and Nets, a team's payroll reflects its commitment to players and their current and potential contribution individually and as a group to winning games in regular seasons and postseasons. From the 2011 to 2015 NBA seasons, for example, the Knicks' payrolls among EC clubs ranged in rank from second ($88.1 million) in 2013 to tenth ($73.4 million) in 2015. Within only the AD, the Nets had the highest payrolls during four years while the Knicks' exceeded those of the 76ers and Raptors each season but not the Celtics in 2011 and 2015 (table A4).

Among twenty-nine other NBA teams, New York's payroll varied from second in 2013 to eighteenth in 2015. Interestingly, the amounts paid to players increased for two years as the club qualified for the playoffs but then declined during the Knicks' three consecutive losing seasons. In order to be competitive and win more titles and perhaps a championship, the franchise needs to be smarter about investing money and resources in its players in 2017 and thereafter.

Madison Square Garden

After opening in 1968 and renovated in 1991, MSG was extensively renovated again for $1 billion during 2011–2014. Its new features include a larger entrance with interactive kiosks; retail, climate-controlled space, and a broadcast studio; larger concourses; new lighting and LED video systems with HDTV; new seating; two new pedestrian walkways suspended from the ceiling to allow fans to look directly down onto the games being played below; more dining options; improved dressing, locker, and green rooms; and an upgraded roof and production offices.

The in-arena walkways were eliminated, and portals installed between sections. While the lower bowl concourse—called the Madison Concourse—remains on the sixth floor, the upper bowl concourse was relocated to the eighth floor and named the Garden Concourse. The seventh floor contains the Madison Suites and Madison Club. The upper bowl was built on top of these suites. Among arenas of all NBA teams as of 2015, MSG had the highest cost and most value (table A5).

According to a recent study of NBA venues, it ranked MSG first for the following reasons:

> With the court's theater lighting, the design on the court gets full exposure, which is why it's perfect that the Knicks chose to emphasize the blue and not overdo the designs. Like the Staples Center [in Los Angeles], there is an element of high drama with that theater lighting. MSG has one of the best assets at its disposal: New York City. The wide range of food choices, the professional and efficient staff and the non-stop entertainment (even in between the quarters of games) reflects the city in which it is located. MSG is a classic stadium, filled with enough rich history and entertainment that it's a better reason to go than the Knicks themselves.[23]

During the league's 2011–12 to 2015–16 seasons—among venues of all NBA teams—the Fan Cost Index (FCI) for a Knicks home game ranked first and ranged in amounts from $608 in 2011 to $676 in both 2014 and 2015. Among other clubs in the league's AD, they had rankings and FCIs from most to least as follows in the 2015 season: Celtics seventh at $419; Nets eighth at $404; Raptors thirteenth at $323; and 76ers tied for twenty-first with the Jazz at $275. These results indicate, in part, that New York's fans paid considerably more in total for tickets, beer, soft drinks, hot dogs, a cap, parking a vehicle, and a program at Knicks home games than those of the Celtics in Boston, Nets in Brooklyn, Raptors in Toronto, and 76ers in Philadelphia (table A6).

Business Highlights

Similar to the other NBA teams, the Knicks are involved in—and affected by—community events and business-related affairs, news, and projects. The following are a few of them for New York's mediocre-performing but also profitable, wealthy, and well-known professional basketball franchise.[24]

First, in an interview during late November 2015, *Business Insider* asked Blackstone CEO Steve Schwarzman which professional sports team he would buy as an investment project. After a lengthy pause, he picked the New York Knicks. He was also grim about the work that it would entail including completely transforming the team. Schwarzman's not saying anything that shocks Knicks fan since the last time they were NBA champions, Studio 54 was still a thing in New York City while Schwarzman barely started his Wall Street career.

Second, although the Knicks thought enough of former coach Derek Fisher to give him a four-year deal worth $17 million in 2014, they determined after 136 games that a horrible mistake had been made. So, Fisher was fired but not general manager Phil Jackson. The club's answer to terminating Fisher was to install Kurt Rambis as his replacement—who fashioned a 56–145 record in two other stints as an NBA coach.

Third, the Knicks introduced three new premium-seat products at the arena's highest level in August 2013. In addition to new lounge club seats—which sold in pairs for about $115–$120 a seat per game with no multiyear commitments required—group hospitality lounges (about $4,000 a game) and Chase Bridge seats (available for partial ticket plans, group packages, and single games) opened on the tenth floor as MSG officials put the finishing touches on a three-year, $1 billion makeover of the arena.

Fourth, during the NBA's 2010–11 season, Hugo Boss owned the third quarter of nearly half of the Knicks games with its "Best Dressed" fan activation. The promotion spotlighted fashionable fans on the team's scoreboard and based on crowd applause, awarded the winner a $500 Hugo Boss gift certificate. The promotion, while simple in presentation yet powerful in messaging, became one of the team's most popular sponsor activations and a cornerstone of the company's branding efforts at MSG.

Fifth, the Knicks had the league's third-biggest local television audience during their 2014–15 season despite a dismal 17–65 record. The team averaged 101,000 viewers on the MSG Network, down 37 percent from the previous season. Still, the only two clubs with more people watching on television were the Chicago Bulls with 163,000 and Cleveland Cavaliers 117,000. The split of the media and sports assets of the MSG Company precipitated a new media rights deal for the Knicks with the MSG regional sports network.

Philadelphia 76ers

Born into a Jewish family in 1965, Joshua Harris was raised in Chevy Chase, Maryland. He attended secondary school in Washington, DC, at the Field School and later graduated from the Wharton School at the University of Pennsylvania. Also, he received his MBA from the Harvard Business School.

Harris worked at private equity firm Drexel Burnham Lambert before co-founding Apollo Global Management in 1990 with fellow Drexel alumni Leon Black and Marc Rowan.

A basketball fan and long-distance runner, Harris is the managing partner of an investment group that, in 2011, won a $280 million-plus bid for the purchase of the Philadelphia 76ers from Comcast Spectacor. The acquisition did not include the Wells Fargo Center in Philadelphia or the Philadelphia Flyers, an NHL franchise owned by Comcast Spectacor.

During their 2011–12 to 2015–16 seasons, the 76ers appeared in one playoff but won zero titles and NBA championships. Among other principle owners of EC teams, Harris's tied for ninth in winning division titles, tied for eighth in conference titles, and tied for fifth in league championships. In comparison to performances of all clubs in the league, Philadelphia tied for last with ten others. Thus, Harris and his group have been unsuccessful as leaders of the 76ers franchise since 2011 (table A2).

Team Financials

According to financial data published in *Forbes* magazine as of 2015, the 76ers had an estimated market value of $700 million, revenue $124 million, operating income $13 million, gate receipts $21 million, debt-to-value 21 percent, and players expenses $60 million. Among fourteen other EC clubs, Philadelphia ranked fourteenth (market value and gate receipts), fifteenth (revenue and players expenses), tenth (operating income), and fourth (debt-to-value ratio). In comparison to only AD teams, the 76ers had the lowest amounts except for the Nets' operating income but also the highest debt percent (table A3).

Across the league, Philadelphia ranked twenty-eighth in market value and gate receipts, thirtieth in revenue and players expenses, twenty-second in operating income, and sixth from the top in debt-to-value. From a financial perspective, the 76ers are an inferior business that generates a below-average amount of revenue, gate receipts, and profit from its operations because of failing to control or manage other expenditures in the franchise's budget. These, in turn, were factors in the club's performances including its third, fourth, or fifth place finish in the AD since 2010.

A team's payroll reflects its commitment to players and their current and potential contribution individually and as a group to winning games in regular seasons and postseasons. From the 2011 to 2015 NBA seasons, for example, the 76ers' payroll in the EC ranked from a low of sixth in 2012 ($67.2 million) to a high of fifteenth in 2013 ($53.3 million) and 2014 ($53.5 million). Among only teams in its division, Philadelphia had the lowest payroll for three seasons but higher than the Knicks and Raptors in 2011 and also the Raptors in 2012 (table A4).

In comparison to twenty-nine other NBA clubs during the period, the 76ers' payroll ranged in rank between eleventh in 2012 and thirtieth in 2013 and 2014. Unless franchise owner Joshua Harris invests more money in contracts of players on the roster and boosts their salaries and benefits, the team will struggle to compete with the Celtics, Nets, Knicks, and Raptors in games of regular seasons and thus win a division and/or conference title.

Wells Fargo Center

Owned by Comcast Spectacor and built to replace Philadelphia's Spectrum, the $217 million, 21,000-seat Core States Center—renamed First Union Center and then Wachovia Center and finally Wells Fargo Center—opened in 1996 for the Sixers, NHL Flyers, and college's Villanova Wildcats basketball team. Besides a state-of-the-art, eight-sided video/matrix board on which live video, instant replays, and animated movie clips can be displayed and an ultra-modern sound system, the facility originally featured such amenities as: 2,000 more seats and 300,000 square feet than the Spectrum; thirty concession stands on two levels and twenty public restroom facilities; oval design for unobstructed-view seats; five concourses to alleviate crowd congestion; six each public escalators and elevators; twenty-three ticket windows for quick and convenient service; and eight brightly lit and patrolled parking lots for 6,100 cars.

In addition to these attractions, the Center contains several exhibit areas; two party suites with private seating for more than 140 people with each available for different types of business and social gatherings and furnished with private restrooms and service, television monitors, and coat closets; a banquet room for meetings and parties of up to 100 people; and a Victors Club that offers fine dining for members and a perfect setting for parties, business meetings, seminars, and banquets.

Among fourteen other venues of EC teams as of the league's 2015–16 season, the twenty-one-year-old Center was the sixth most expensive to build but also ranked fourteenth in value. In comparison to arenas of all NBA clubs, it was eleventh in cost and twenty-ninth in value. Consequently, the Sixers play in an aging facility that is less valuable than twenty-nine other arenas because of the team's relatively low market value, revenue, and gate receipts, and their dismal seasons in recent years (table A5).

In a recent study of twenty-nine NBA facilities, the Wells Fargo Center ranked twenty-seventh. Based on the arena's name and aesthetics, and fans' experiences at games in it, the study concluded that:

> Unlike the Bradley Center [in Milwaukee, Wisconsin], Wells Fargo is intimate rather than cramped, and that allows the energy of the game to be translated more easily. Red, white & blue is overdone, but for this team it is appropriate,

> and the court design emphasizes the blue and brings out tasteful, balanced shades. The Wells Fargo Center is truly a reflection of the city it inhabits: unwelcoming and self-conscious about its inferiority.[25]

Among venues of fourteen other EC teams during their 2011–2015 seasons, the Fan Cost Index (FCI) for a Sixers home game at the Wells Fargo Center ranged in rank from eighth to tenth and in amounts from a low of $260 in 2012 to $278 in 2014. Within only the AD, it was relatively more expensive for families to attend home games of the Celtics in Boston, Nets in Brooklyn, Knicks in New York, and Raptors in Toronto than any in Philadelphia. Compared to the FCIs of all NBA arenas, games at the Wells Fargo Center placed in cost from twentieth in 2014 to twenty-second in 2012 (table A6).

Listed from most to least in amount by item for an individual at a Sixers home game in their 2015–16 season, tickets averaged $38–$39, parking one vehicle $22, a cap approximately $18, one beer between $8 and $9, a hot dog $5 to $6, single program $5, and a soft drink $4. Thus, Philadelphia's basketball fans paid a few dollars less for tickets and some of these products than at games in the team's 2014–15 season.

Among other clubs in the league's AD, they had rankings and FCIs from most to least as follows in the 2015–16 NBA season: Knicks first at $676; Celtics seventh at $419; Nets eighth at $404; and Raptors thirteenth at $323. These results indicate, in part, that Sixers' fans paid less at a home game that season than those of the Knicks at MSG, Celtics at the TD Garden, Nets at the Barclays Center, and Raptors at the Air Canada Centre.

The least expensive ticket cost, on average, $10 for someone to attend a Sixers home game at the Wells Fargo Center in 2015–16. This was almost $6 or 37 percent less than the league's average for a cheap seat. Since the club's FCI was approximately $64 below the amount of a typical NBA team, a family of four purchased tickets and enjoyed a professional basketball game in Philadelphia at a significant discount compared to the majority of arenas within the league. These costs and prices, in turn, were set by the Sixers organization to generate revenue and maximize profit from their operations.

Business Highlights

Similar to the other NBA teams, the 76ers are involved in—and affected by—community events and business-related affairs, news, and projects besides its internal decisions and policies. The following are a few of them for Philadelphia's inferior-performing and also low-valued but profitable professional basketball franchise.[26]

First, the Sixers owners, who also own the NHL New Jersey Devils, recently acquired a stake in Crystal Palace, the once dismal English soccer (or British football) team that emerged as one of the better competitors in the English Premier League. In December 2015, a deal was forged in which Crystal Palace's chairman Steve Parish—along with Joshua Harris and David Blitzer—would take control of the club in a general partnership structure and then, along with the soccer team's limited shareholders, invest private capital to build a new stadium.

Second, the year 2016 is being defined by a series of market-shifting moves by individual sports franchises seeking to more closely manage all facets of their ticketing operations. The 76ers, for example, signed a multiyear partnership with StubHub and Spectra Ticketing & Fan Engagement to have the club's primary ticketing business within StubHub's website and mobile application—beginning with the 2016–17 NBA season—in a team-branded environment that blends primary and secondary inventory. Although the ticketing initiative is unique, it converges around the themes of teams having more direct involvement in all parts of the ticketing process and placing their own brands front and center.

Third, despite dismal performances in their season on the court and problems with attendance and local television ratings, the Sixers' business side began to improve as it rebuilt its roster by shedding cap space and trading for top future draft picks. Even with the past few seasons of futility, the Sixers entered their 2015–16 season with a 90 percent season ticket renewal rate and also added more than 2,000 new full-season tickets with a projection to reach a total of 7,500 full-season tickets—which would double the number from the prior eighteen months. Although this number is far below the league's 10,000 full-season benchmark, its progress given how bad the basketball team was during three years under principal owner Joshua Harris.

Fourth, since 2013, the Sixers have quadrupled the size of their sales staff and hired several veterans for their executive ranks as new CEO Scott O'Neil put his stamp on the franchise. After naming Chris Heck chief revenue officer, O'Neil increased the ticket sales staff from about fifteen to sixty employees with more sellers eventually to be added. The Sixers also hired Dan Hauser, formerly a senior executive with the Detroit Pistons, as senior vice president of sponsorship sales.

These changes came as Tom Ward, senior vice president of corporate partnerships and broadcasting, left the organization. A longtime senior-level industry executive, Ward was hired in July 2012 by former Sixers CEO Adam Aaron. Also joining the organization were Owen Morin, senior director of corporate partnerships and formerly of Excel Sports Management; Jake Reynolds, senior director of ticket sales and previously employed at Monumental Sports and Entertainment; Brian Norman, ticket sales manager and formerly of the Charlotte Bobcats; and Katie Grossman, director of partnership marketing who before worked at IMG College.

Fifth, the 76ers became the first NBA team to put a sponsorship logo on player uniforms by making a deal with StubHub for a spot on one of the hottest pieces of real estate available in professional sports. StubHub—a website that connects ticket buyers and sellers—will have its logo appear on the front-left of players' jerseys in 2017–18 for the start of a three-year trial period. The patches will appear opposite Nike's logo, and measure about 2.5-by-2.5 inches. StubHub's jersey patch will be included on all jerseys sold at Sixers' home games and appear in white lettering inside a blue rectangle for home jerseys, blue lettering inside a white rectangle for road jerseys, and red lettering inside a white rectangle for alternate jerseys.

To conclude this section of the chapter, Philadelphia's hoops fans would like more attention from the media given to the Sixers, who were in the midst of a multiyear tanking strategy that resulted in losses in 82 percent of its games from the NBA's 2012–13 to 2015–16 seasons. Meanwhile, ratings of Sixers games on CSN Philadelphia fell 25 percent in 2015 and to second lowest in the league. Attendance was a league-worst 13,940 per game. Also, the franchise was in the middle of an embarrassing spat with Wells Fargo, which still holds the naming rights to the team's home. After the banking giant refused to sponsor them, the Sixers stopped using the name in press releases and severely shrunk the logo on the court. In January 2016, the club signed a new banking sponsorship deal with First Trust Bank.

Toronto Raptors

After being born into a Jewish family in Toronto, Ontario, Canada, in 1945, Larry Tanenbaum earned a bachelor of science degree in economics twenty-three years later from Cornell University. Along with a successful career as an executive and then president of a large and multifaceted civil engineering construction company in Canada, he spearheaded an effort to bring an NBA franchise to Toronto during the early 1990s.

Two years after Tanenbaum bought an interest in the Toronto Maple Leafs ice hockey club and its arena in 1996, he was active in the acquisition of the Toronto Raptors franchise and Air Canada Centre, which—with the Toronto Maple Leafs—formed Maple Leaf Sports & Entertainment (MLSE). As of 2015, Tanenbaum owned 25 percent of MLSE through his holding company Kilmer Sports Inc. Besides being CEO of MLSE, he serves on the executive committee of the NBA Raptors, NHL Leafs, and Major League Soccer (MLS) Toronto FC.

Since becoming principal owner of the Raptors, his teams have appeared in eight playoffs and won four division titles but zero conference titles and NBA championships. Compared to the performances of other EC teams and their owners as of the league's 2015–16 season, Tanenbaum's Raptors tied for sixth with Dan Gilbert's Cavaliers in winning division titles but also tied for eighth in conference titles and for fifth in NBA championships. Based on these results, Tanenbaum has been above average among team owners in the AD and more successful than the Nets' Prokhorov, Knicks' Dolan, and 76ers' Harris, but not the Celtics' Grousbeck (table A2).

In a 2015 report, the Raptors' owner ranked eleventh best among others of NBA teams. According to a few comments about him in the report:

> Toronto isn't a free agent destination, but they've drafted well and traded well to build a team that has gone to the playoffs in two straight years. Larry Tanenbaum knows what he has north of the border and he's not letting go or allowing things to be screwed up like they are with the hockey team. Let's also not skate over the fan element to this. Tanenbaum has created and pandered to a fan base of truly passionate NBA fans—some of the most intense fans in the entire league. That takes talent and Tanenbaum deserves a lot of the credit for the atmosphere that the Raptors have in Toronto.[27]

Team Financials

In early 2016, *Forbes* magazine published some financial data of NBA franchises as of their 2015–16 season. Regarding the Raptors, their estimated market value was $980 million, revenue $163 million, operating income $23 million, gate receipts $48 million, debt-to-value 12 percent, and players expenses $87 million. Among fourteen other EC clubs, Toronto ranked seventh (market value, revenue, and gate receipts), sixth (operating income), eleventh (debt ratio), and tied for fifth with the Bulls and Cavaliers (players expenses). For most of their financials, the Raptors had lower amounts than the Celtics, Nets, and Knicks, but not the 76ers (table A3).

In comparison to twenty-nine other NBA clubs as of 2015–16, Toronto ranked from a tie for eighth in players expenses to eighteenth in its debt ratio. Given these results, the Raptors are an average franchise from a financial perspective and profitable as a business enterprise. Although players expenses seem too high given their actual performances, the team's other data is about right for a franchise located in city, region, and country of primarily ice hockey fans.

A team's payroll reflects its commitment to players and their current and potential contribution individually and as a group to winning games in regular seasons and postseasons. From the 2011 to 2015 NBA seasons, for example, the Raptors payroll in the EC ranked from fourth in 2014 ($79.9 million) to thirteenth in 2011 ($53.6 million) and 2015 ($71.3 million). Among only teams in its division, Toronto had the lowest payroll for two seasons but then higher than the 76ers in 2013, Celtics and 76ers in 2014, and 76ers in 2015 (table A4).

In comparison to those of twenty-nine other NBA clubs during the period, the Raptors payroll ranged in rank from fifth in 2014 to twenty-seventh in 2011. Despite an $8 million decrease in payroll from the 2014 to 2015 season, franchise owner Larry Tanenbaum will invest more in players' salaries and increase some contracts in the league's 2016–2017 seasons because of a significantly higher salary cap and additional money from television broadcasts. Otherwise, the team will struggle to win division titles while competing mostly against the Celtics, Nets, and Knicks, and sometimes the 76ers in games of regular seasons.

Air Canada Centre

To replace the obsolete SkyDome, the 19,800-seat Air Canada Centre opened in 1999 in downtown Toronto. Originally designed for sports fans, it focuses on intimacy and customer experience. Besides a club restaurant and bar, the building has the characteristics of a first-class, technology-advanced facility while maintaining the spirit and legend associated with that of Maple Leaf Gardens. There are televisions throughout the building, including all washrooms, and a fraction of the space is provided for the disabled by offering physically challenged individuals a choice of various ticket prices and seats.

Minutes from businesses in the metropolitan area and major highways, other special feature of the Air Canada Centre are: fully upholstered twenty-inch seats; at least forty unique courtside lounges within the 100-level plus sixty-five or more luxury suites located on the 200-level; a brew pub and themed food court and Galleria with a team store; and interactive "Raptofest" and computer areas.

Among arenas of fourteen other EC teams as of 2015, the Air Canada Centre had the tenth highest construction costs in a tie with the Chicago Bulls' United Center and ranked sixth in value. In comparison to venues of all NBA teams, it was tied for seventeenth with the Bulls' home in costs and also placed twelfth in value. Based on this information, the Raptors play their home games in a relatively attractive but aging facility within a large metropolitan area. It is, however, much less elaborate and valuable than the Knicks' MSG, Nets' Barclays Center, and Celtics' TD Garden (table A5).

In a recent study of NBA arenas, the Air Canada Centre was seventh best based on its name, aesthetics, and fans' game experience. The following are some comments from the study:

> It's a shame about the banners. Too bad they're all for the Maple Leafs, and too bad they're all from before Woodstock. The fact that the center court design is not the velociraptor dribbling a basketball is appalling, but otherwise the court design is sharp and the seats are good outside the nosebleeds. Food may be expensive, and the Leafs' banners might be depressing, but this is a well-organized arena that has comfortable seating and never feels too cramped. Even with this being said, the arena is always energetic, and it helps that the Raptors are heading towards their best season yet [in 2015–16]. Plus, Drake might be at the game. This is a great basketball arena that serves as an even better hockey arena. It helps that the Raptors are more relevant than ever.[28]

Among venues of fourteen other EC teams during the NBA's 2011–12 to 2015–16 seasons, the FCI for a Raptors home game at the Air Canada Centre ranged in rank from fifth to seventh and in amounts from a low of $289 in 2014 to $323 in 2015. Within the AD, it was relatively more expensive for families to attend home games of the Celtics in Boston, Nets in Brooklyn, and Knicks in New York than those in Toronto. Compared to the FCIs of all NBA arenas as of 2015, the Air Canada Centre was tied for eighth with the San Antonio Spurs' AT&T Center at $319 in 2011 but then ranked seventeenth in 2014 (table A6).

Listed from most to least in amount by item for one person at a Raptors home game in its 2015–16 season, tickets averaged $48–$49, a cap approximately $24, parking one vehicle $19, one beer between $7 and $8, a hot dog $5–$6, and a soft drink and single program each from $4 to $5. In comparison, fans paid $34 less for tickets and these products at games in the team's 2014–15 season at the Air Canada Centre.

Among other clubs in the league's AD, they had rankings and FCIs from most to least as follows in the 2015–16 NBA season: Knicks first at $676; Celtics seventh at $419; Nets eighth at $404; and 76ers tied for twenty-first with the Utah Jazz at $275. These results indicate, in part, that Toronto's sports fans paid less at a home game that season than those of the Knicks at MSG, Celtics at the TD Garden, and Nets at the Barclays Center, but more than those of the 76ers at the Wells Fargo Center.

The least expensive ticket cost, on average, was about $12 for a fan to attend a Raptors home game at the Air Canada Centre in the league's 2015 season. This was almost $4 or 25 percent less than the league's average for a cheap seat. Since the club's FCI was approximately $16 below the amount of a typical NBA team, a family of four purchased tickets and enjoyed a basketball game in Toronto at a moderate discount relative to twelve arenas within the league. These costs and prices, in turn, were set by the Raptors organization to maximize profit from their operations.

Business Highlights

Similar to other NBA teams, the Raptors are involved in—and affected by—community events and business-related affairs, news, and projects besides its internal decisions and policies. The following are a few of them regarding Toronto's relatively low-valued but profitable professional basketball franchise.[29]

First, MLSE hired advertising agency Sid Lee in early 2014 to rebrand the Raptors. The agency was responsible for a wide range of tasks including designing the new visual identity of the team—including a new logo—and also new uniforms. Because the NBA has a strict system of approvals in place for teams' visual identities and for any changes to team brands, it would be awhile before those were visible to Toronto fans. A new logo and other visual elements will also mean changes to the team's merchandise at the retail level. According to officials at Sid Lee, that will take a few years. In 2013, the Raptors appointed rapper Drake as global ambassador for the brand and directly involved in rebranding the team.

Second, Bell Media banked on the growing popularity of the Raptors with a twenty-eight-episode reality show on The Sports Network (TSN) plus extra content on mobile and on-demand exclusively for its customers, as the battle to retain viewers amid competition from over-the-top streaming services such as Netflix heated up. The reality show called Open Gym—available beginning in November 2014—was produced by MLSE in which Bell Media and Rogers Communications Inc. jointly own 75 percent. The series offered a glimpse into players' personal lives, the team's locker room, and road trips—an offering sweetened by the Raptors' standing at the top of the NBA's EC.

Third, during late 2010, Massachusetts-based technology firm StratBridge Inc. signed a deal with the Raptors to implement dynamic ticket pricing models, boosting the company's profile in the quickly emerging space to about a dozen NBA teams. The Raptors deployed dynamic pricing structures within their primary market—single-game tickets—to take fuller advantage of supply and demand factors by allowing prices to float on a daily or weekly basis. The club tested the system in three seating sections of the Air Canada Centre amounting to about 1,300 seats a game, with a potentially larger rollout to other MLSE properties.

Fourth, since hiring former MLSE president Tim Leiweke in 2013, the Raptors improved their business model by employing reliable management people—such as president/general manager Masai Ujiri—and instilling a culture that goes beyond the basketball court. The team went out of its way to gift Toronto International Film Festival tickets to player Patrick Patterson and/or help with charity drives for superstar Kyle Lowry. These types of things were just icing on the cake because of winning. You cannot have a successful sports franchise without wins. In fact, the basketball organization's goal is to create a strong and consistent model franchise where it will be in position to sign top free agents and compete in the playoffs but still remain flexible.

Fifth, over her sixteen-year career at MLSE, Shannon Hosford rose through the ranks, working on dozens of marketing campaigns for different franchises. As MLSE's vice president of marketing and communications, she manages a portfolio that includes the Raptors, Maple Leafs, and Toronto FC—and a staff of more than 100 that ensure each brand is maintained accordingly. Hosford oversees what was perhaps the largest rebranding effort in Canadian sports history. With one sixty-second ad, the #WeTheNorth campaign took the first step in bringing the Raptors to international prominence and a disenfranchised fan base back to the arena's bleachers. Hosford also faces a challenge of maintaining the brand—which she does from an office just five minutes away from the team's basketball court.

To conclude, the Raptors sold out their tickets in a recent season for the first time since home games in 2000–1. The team's strong start helped drive sales as it cruised to the AD title. As season ticket sales jumped 50 percent to 12,500, the team also added new sponsors such as Sun Life Insurance, Sentry Investments, Unilever, and Aeolus Tires.

NOTES

1. For historical information about professional basketball leagues and their teams and players, see Frank P. Jozsa Jr., *National Basketball Association Strategies: Business Expansions, Relocations, and Mergers* (New York: Springer, 2016), and also Connie Kirchberg, *Hoop Love: A History of the National Basketball Association* (Jefferson, NC: McFarland, 2007).
2. See such websites as www.basketball-reference.com, www.nba.com, and www.sportsencyclopedia.com for specific facts about the Boston Celtics and other NBA teams.
3. "Top 20 Greatest NBA Teams Ever," http://www.espn.go.com, cited June 1, 2016 and Jason Aisher, "The Ten Best NBA Teams of All Time," http://www.cheatsheet.com, cited June 3, 2016.
4. One article is "NBA Board of Governors Approves Sale of Nets to Prokhorov," http://www.nba.com, cited June 4, 2016.
5. Chad Ford and Kevin Pelton, "Future Power Rankings: Who Will Rise in the Next Three Years?" http://www.espn.go.com, cited June 5, 2016.
6. Besides the websites in note 2 above, another is "New York Knicks," http://www.nba.com, cited June 5, 2016.
7. Daniel Zillmer, "All 30 NBA Franchises Statistically Ranked by All-Time Greatness," http://www.fansided.com, cited June 6, 2016.

8. "Philadelphia 76ers Franchise Index," http://www.basketball-reference.com, cited June 6, 2016.

9. "All 30 NBA Franchises Statistically Ranked by All-Time Greatness."

10. See such readings as "Laying the Groundwork for the NBA in Toronto," http://www.nba.com, cited June 8, 2016.

11. For the historical performances of the Raptors, see "Toronto Raptors," http://www.nba.com, cited June 10, 2016.

12. "All 30 NBA Franchises Statistically Ranked by All-Time Greatness."

13. Ethan Bailey, "NBA Preseason Power Rankings: How Each Team is Looking in Preseason," http://www.bleacherreport.com, cited June 13, 2016.

14. Financial data on pro teams is also in Frank P. Jozsa Jr., *The National Basketball Association: Business, Organization and Strategy* (Hackensack, NJ: World Scientific, 2011).

15. Various online sources and different articles in references of the bibliography were used for information on NBA franchises owners.

16. See Josh Hill, "NBA Owners Power Ranking: Who is Best Owner in Basketball?" http://www.fansided.com, cited July 8, 2016.

17. The primary reading is Kurt Badenhausen, Mike Ozanian, and Christini Settimi, "The Business of Basketball," http://www.forbes.com, cited June 27, 2016.

18. "Present National Basketball Association Arenas," http://www.basketball.ballparks.com, cited June 27, 2016.

19. For NBA teams' costs and prices in seasons, this information is available online at "NBA FCIs," http://www.teammarketingreport.com, cited July 1, 2016.

20. Readings for the Celtics' business include Len Stein, "Thunder, Spurs and Heat NBA Fan Favorites in Brand Keys 2016 Sports Fan Loyalty Index," http://www.brandkeys.com, cited July 1, 2016; Catherine Carlock, "Celtics Join Bruins With New Facility at Boston Landing," http://www.bizjournals.com, cited July 9, 2016; Callum Borchers, "Celtics Bow to History to Draw Fans," http://www.bostonglobe.com, cited July 9, 2016; Eric Fisher, "Celtics, Raptors Offer Dynamic Pricing Through StratBridge," http://www.sportsbusinessdaily.com, cited July 9, 2016; John Ourand and John Lombardo, "New Deal to Give Celtics Stake in RSN," http://www.sportsbusinessdaily.com, cited July 9, 2016.

21. Luke Dahlgren, "Power Rankings: NBA Arenas," https://fansided.com, cited July 10, 2016.

22. The Nets' business highlights are discussed in John Lombardo, "Nets, Kings See Global Opportunity," http://www.sportsbusinessdaily.com, cited July 10, 2016; Terry Lefton, "Hospital Names Nets' New Practice Facility," http://www.sportsbusinessdaily.com, cited July 10, 2016; John Ourand and John Lombardo, "Settlement Puts Nets Games on YES Net Through 2031–32," http://www.sportsbusinessdaily.com, cited July 10, 2016; Scott Soshnick, "NBA's Brooklyn Nets to Cut Ticket Prices 24% Next Season," http://www.bloomberg.com, cited July 11, 2016; "Nets Owner Mikhail Prokhorov Has Company Searched in Russia," http://www.nbafeeds.com, cited July 11, 2016.

23. "Power Rankings: NBA Arenas."

24. For the Knicks' business highlights, read such articles as Don Muret, "MSG Rolling Out New Premium Areas," http://www.sportsbusinessdaily.com, cited July

12, 2016; John Lombardo, "Hugo Boss Likes the Look," http://www.sportsbusinessdaily.com, cited July 12, 2016; "Steve Schwartzman Likes the New York Knicks," http://www.thetrustedinsight.com, cited July 12, 2016; Brian Mahoney, "Knicks Fire Fisher, Name Rambis Interim Coach," http://www.nba.com, cited July 12, 2016; William Lee, "Pathetic Knicks Drawing Pathetic Ratings for MSG," http://www.dailyknicks.com, cited July 13, 2016.

25. Jacob Kornhauser, "Ranking Every NBA Arena From Worst to First," http://www.ranksports.com, cited July 13, 2016.

26. Recommended readings for the 76ers' business news include John Lombardo, "Sixers Quadruple Sales Staff, Add to Executive Ranks," http://www.sportsbusinessdaily.com, cited July 13, 2016; Adam Chandler, "NBA Lets in Advertising, 6.25 Square Inches at a Time," http://www.theatlantic.com, cited July 14, 2016; Erik Fisher, "Teams Continue to Shake up Ticketing Industry," http://www.sportsbusinessdaily.com, cited July 14, 2016; Dan Levy, "How in the World Will the Sixers Get to the NBA Salary Floor," http://www.billypenn.com, cited July 14, 2016; Aaron Carter, "Sixers Partners Invest in Crystal Palace," http://www.articles.philly.com, cited July 14, 2016.

27. "NBA Owners Power Ranking: Who is Best Owner in Basketball?"

28. "Power Rankings: NBA Arenas."

29. For the Raptors' business highlights, see Eric Fisher, "Celtics, Raptors Offer Dynamic Pricing Via StratBridge," http://www.sportsbusinessdaily.com, cited July 9, 2016; Armina Ligaya, "Bell Goes For Slam Dunk in Battle For Subscribers With Raptors Reality Show," http://www.business.financialpost.com, cited July 16, 2016; Sarah Niedoba, "Meet the Marketer Behind the Raptors' #WetheNorth Campaign," http://www.canadianbusiness.com, cited July 16, 2016; "New Logo for Toronto Raptors by Sid Lee," http://www.underconsideration.com, cited July 16, 2016; Satbir Singh, "Raptors in Good Hands With or Without Tim Leiweke," http://www.hoopshype.ca, cited July 18, 2016.

Chapter Two

Central Division

Organized in 1970 by the National Basketball Association (NBA), the Central Division (CD) of the league's Eastern Conference (EC) included the Atlanta Hawks, Baltimore Bullets, Cincinnati Royals, and Cleveland Cavaliers. The CD changed, however, when the Houston Rockets joined in 1972, New Orleans Jazz in 1974, San Antonio Spurs in 1976, Detroit Pistons in 1978, Indiana Pacers in 1979, Chicago Bulls and Milwaukee Bucks both in 1980, Orlando Magic in 1989, Charlotte Hornets in 1990, Toronto Raptors in 1995, and New Orleans Hornets in 2002; also when the Royals withdrew in 1972, Bullets in 1978, Jazz in 1979, Rockets and Spurs in 1980, Magic in 1990, Charlotte Hornets in 2002, and both the Raptors and New Orleans Hornets in 2004.

Given these changes in the conference's structure, this chapter discusses the historical development and highlights business news and financial data of CD teams based in Chicago, Illinois; Cleveland, Ohio; Detroit, Michigan; Indianapolis, Indiana; and Milwaukee, Wisconsin. Which of them, for example, had won the most division titles and NBA championships? What were their market values, operating incomes, and ticket prices in the league's 2015–16 or simply 2015 season? Who have been the least and most successful owners or ownership groups among the five clubs? How do their arenas rank in amenities and experiences among fans? The answers to these and other questions are covered in the chapter.[1]

TEAM PERFORMANCE

Chicago Bulls

After the NBA's Chicago Stags folded in 1950 and the Zephyrs' relocation from the city to Baltimore, Maryland, thirteen years later, there were doubts among NBA officials about Chicago being a viable home site for a professional basketball franchise. Nevertheless, during January 1966 the NBA granted Chicago an expansion franchise. Based on his two years playing for the National Basketball League (NBL) Chicago American Gears and a successful career distributing promotional materials to banks and other companies, businessman Dick Klein paid the NBA a fee of $1.25 million and became the new team's initial owner and then its president and general manager.[2]

Klein's first task was to assign a nickname to his team. He wanted one that evoked images of the Chicago stockyards, which were close to the stadium where the club expected to play its home games. When his son dismissed such names as Matadors or Toreadors as a bunch of bull, Klein decided to call the team "Bulls." He recruited a neighbor to design the Bulls' team logo and also chose the colors red and black from his former alma mater, Fort Madison High School.

Following the 1966 NBA expansion draft, the newly founded Chicago Bulls acquired players from previously established teams in the league for its upcoming 1966–67 season. As a result, the club posted the best record by an expansion team in NBA history, finished fourth in the Western Division (WD), and qualified for the playoffs but lost in the first round to the St. Louis Hawks in three games.

Historical Results

Since joining the NBA in 1966 and a member of the CD during the league's 1980–2015 seasons, the Bulls had victories in approximately 52 percent of their 4,022 games. That is, they won nine division and six conference titles and championships each in thirty-four playoff appearances. Among teams in the EC as of 2015–16, the club ranked second all-time in winning percentage, conference titles, and championships and also third in number of playoffs and tied for fourth with the Detroit Pistons in division titles. Within only the CD, Chicago has the best results except for the Milwaukee Bucks in winning division titles (table A1).

In comparison to twenty-nine other NBA teams as of their 2015 season, the Bulls ranked ninth (winning percentage), fifth (number of playoffs), tied for sixth (division titles) and also for third (conference titles) with the San Antonio Spurs, and third (league championships). According to its performances, Chicago has been an exceptional team for many of its fifty seasons following achievements of the Boston Celtics, Los Angeles Lakers, and most recently the Spurs.

Performance Highlights

During their history, the Bulls were in consecutive playoffs in seasons 1966–1967, 1969–1974, 1984–1997, 2004–2006, and 2008–2014. Led by such coaches as Dick Motta, Doug Collins, Phil Jackson, Scott Skiles, Vince Del Negro, and Tom Thibodeau, the club's superstars included Chet Walker in the 1970s, Artis Gilmore in the late 1970s/early 1980s, Michael Jordan from the mid-1980s to late 1990s, and Derrick Rose and Joakim Noah in the 2000s. While Red Kerr, Motta, Jackson, and Thibodeau were Coach of the Year, Jordan won five Most Valuable Player (MVP) awards and Rose one. Besides ten former Bulls' players and Coach Jackson, owner Jerry Reinsdorf is in the Naismith Memorial Basketball Hall of Fame.

The team, however, failed to qualify for conference playoffs consecutively in seasons 1977–1979, 1981–1983, and 1999–2003. Several factors including coaching problems, lack of talent and players' injuries, and superior performances in some years by the Cavaliers, Pistons, Pacers, and Bucks caused the Bulls to lose a majority of their games and finish relatively low in their division.

Because of consistently high scoring by Jordan, rebounding by Dennis Rodman, and defense and scoring by Scottie Pippen, the NBA's greatest all-time teams included the Bulls (ranked) in 1996 (first), 1991 (sixth), 1992 (tenth), 1998 (eleventh), and 1993 (twentieth). In 1996, for example, Chicago was 72–10 and won the CD by several games and a conference title, and then a championship in the playoffs led by Coach of the Year Jackson and MVP Jordan.

Among NBA franchises, the Bulls are the fourth-best all-time and also the beginning of the elite in league history. Although they won fewer total titles and championships than the Celtics, Lakers, and Spurs as of early 2016, their lack of high-end success before the Michael Jordan era is why they are not listed higher within the group. Even so, Bulls fans must be happy with the club's placement in a list that accounts for all-time success.

During July 2016, the Bulls signed two-time all-star and three-time NBA champion Dwayne Wade for two years and spent $47.5 million. While Wade's a future Hall of Famer, this move does not really add to the team's mix and its current pieces on the roster, or to its head coach's philosophy. Furthermore, signing Wade does not match general manager Gar Forman's initiative to make the team "younger and more athletic." Nevertheless, how

Coach Fred Hoiberg manages rotations will largely determine the effectiveness of the roster and its chances of winning games. The priority for Hoiberg and his staff is to find a balance between on-ball playmakers and shooting to ensure the Bulls create an offense that relies more on a logical blend of talent and fit than names and past accolades.[3]

Cleveland Cavaliers

Although amateur and semiprofessional baseball and football were popular team sports among fans in cities of northwestern Ohio during the 1930s–1940s, the Cleveland area also hosted for a few seasons three professional basketball teams that played in the NBL and one in the Basketball Association of America (BAA).[4]

In 1970, the NBA awarded new franchises to syndicates representing Buffalo, New York, and Portland, Oregon; and also to a group led primarily by author, entrepreneur, and lawyer Nick Mileti who paid the league an expansion fee of $3.7 million. Jerry Tomko—the father of future Major League Baseball (MLB) pitcher Brett Tomko—submitted the winning entry to name the team "Cavaliers" through a competition sponsored by *The Plain Dealer* while others preferred such names as "Jays" and "Presidents." According to folklore, Cavaliers referred to a group of daring men whose life pact was never to surrender no matter the odds.

Initially the club played its home games at 11,000-seat Cleveland Arena under the direction of head coach Bill Fitch. Before joining the Cavaliers, he coached basketball at such schools as Creighton University, Coe College, University of North Dakota, Bowling Green State University, and the University of Minnesota.

Historical Results

While a member of the CD from the league's 1970–71 to 2015–16 season, the team played 3,724 games and had victories in approximately 46 percent of them. More specifically, they won five division and three conference titles plus one NBA championship while appearing in twenty playoffs. Among other EC clubs, the Cavaliers tied for ninth with the Atlanta Hawks and Miami Heat in winning division titles, and tied for seventh with the Washington Wizards—former Capital/Washington Bullets—in conference titles and also with the Milwaukee Bucks and Wizards in championships (table A1).

Within its division as of 2015–16, Cleveland had the lowest winning percentage and least number of playoff appearances and division titles but also won more conference titles than the Indiana Pacers and Bucks and fewer championships than the Bulls and Pistons. In comparison to twenty-nine other NBA teams, Cleveland tied respectively for fourteenth (division titles), for tenth (conference titles), and for eleventh (league championships). Based on these results, the Cavaliers have been an average franchise while performing in their seasons since 1970.

Performance Highlights

The club's most success occurred in consecutive playoffs during seasons 1975–1977, 1987–1989, 1991–1995, 2005–2009, and 2014–2015. During these periods, they were led by such coaches as Bill Fitch, Lenny Wilkens, Mike Fratello, Mike Brown, David Blatt, and Tyronn Lue. Honored by sports writers, Fitch was Coach of the Year in 1976 and Brown in 2009. For personal and sport-specific reasons, however, the Cavaliers failed to qualify for consecutive playoffs during seasons 1970–1974, 1978–1983, 1985–1986, 1998–2004, and 2010–2013.[5]

While the Cavaliers' LeBron James was MVP in 2009 and 2010, the club has six members in the Hall of Fame led by longtime and well-respected coach Lenny Wilkens. It also retired uniform numbers of players including guards Austin Carr and Mark Price, forwards Bingo Smith and Larry Nance, and centers Brad Daugherty, Nate Thurmond, and Zydrunas Ligauskas along with announcer/broadcaster Joe Tait. As a group, these individual made significant contributions to the franchise's history and tradition in different ways.

Regarding their position among NBA franchises, the Cavaliers are somewhere in the bottom one-third despite winning a championship in the 2015–16 season. Besides its relatively low all-time winning percentage and number of playoffs, the club was not competitive and even pathetic in many years. If superstar James and former Rookie of the Year Kyrie Irving remain for a few more seasons, Cleveland will continue to be successful and perhaps compete for and win another championship and thus rank higher all-time.

Should the team trade power forward Kevin Love soon? Including their luxury tax, the Cavaliers have an unsustainable payroll. Because Love's contract does not have a no-trade clause and expires in about 2019—while James will get more expensive due to the league's exploding salary cap and J. R. Smith and Matthew Dellavedova will likely seek massive pay raises—it makes sense to trade Love as a way to improve the roster and shape it in order to continue challenging the Golden State Warriors and other rivals in both conferences.

Detroit Pistons

Established in Fort Wayne, Indiana in 1941, the Pistons played seven years in the NBL and one in the BAA under the guidance of their original owner, businessman Fred Zollner. Because he owned a large factory that made pistons for automobiles, he named his team Fort Wayne Zollner Pistons. After losing championship series in 1942 and 1943, they won NBL titles in 1944 and 1945.[6]

As players abandoned the NBL and joined the more popular and prosperous BAA, so did the Zollner Pistons and Minneapolis Lakers, Rochester Royals, and Indianapolis Kautskys following their 1947–48 season. Despite dropping Zollner from his team's nickname, Fred participated in the development of the BAA by providing transportation arrangements for the entire league.

In their first year the Pistons struggled to a 22–38 record, finished fifth in the Western Division, and missed the playoffs. When the BAA and NBL merged in 1948, the Fort Wayne Pistons joined the National Basketball Association (NBA) and put in its Western Division (WD) along with the Lakers, Royals, Chicago Stags, Indianapolis Jets, and St. Louis Bombers.

From the NBA's 1948–49 to 1956–57 seasons, the Pistons finished first twice, third five times, and fourth and fifth each once in their division. More specifically, they won the WD in 1955 and 1956 but were defeated in the final series by, respectively, the champion Syracuse Nationals and then Philadelphia Warriors.

During the mid-1950s, owner Fred Zollner felt that his team could not compete in a small market city. So in 1957, he moved the franchise from Fort Wayne, Indiana, to large-market Detroit, Michigan. Zollner decided to keep the Pistons name because they played home games at Olympia Stadium, which was also home of the NHL Detroit Red Wings in the Motor City.

Historical Results

While a member of the league's WD (1957–58 to 1966–67), Eastern Division (1967–68 to 1969–70), Midwest Division (1970–71 to 1977–78), and then the CD (1978–79 to 2015–16), the Pistons had victories in approximately 48 percent of their games and appeared in thirty-three playoffs. More specifically, they won nine division and five conference titles and also three NBA championships. Among teams in the EC as of 2015–16, Detroit tied for fourth in both number of playoffs and division titles but also tied for third in conference titles and championships. Within only the CD, the Pistons had, in part, the fourth highest winning percentage, second most playoff appearances, and less total titles than the Bulls (table A1).

In comparison to performances of twenty-nine other NBA clubs, the Pistons ranked nineteenth (winning percentage), tied for sixth (number of playoffs and division titles), and tied for fifth (conference titles and championships). According to these results, Detroit has been an above-average team since moving into the league in 1957 and especially while competing against the Bulls, Cavaliers, Pacers, and Bucks in its division.

Performance Highlights

The Pistons had the most success while appearing in consecutive playoffs during seasons 1957–1962, 1973–1976, 1983–1991, 1995–1996, 1998–1999, and 2001–2008. During these periods, a few outstanding coaches were Dick McGuire, Ray Scott, Chuck Daly, Doug Collins, Rick Carlisle, Larry Brown, and Flip Saunders. Daly won two championships and Brown one with Scott and Carlisle each being Coach of the Year once.

During various seasons, some great players of Pistons' teams included Bailey Howell, Bob Lanier, Bill Laimbeer, Grant Hill, and Chauncey Billups. Although the club had no MVPs, several of its players are in the Hall of Fame such as guards David Bing, Isiah Thomas, and Joe Dumars, forwards Bob McAdoo, Dennis Rodman, and Dave Debusschere, and centers Bob Houbregs, Bob Lanier, and Earl Lloyd. Also, the club retired a few of these players' uniform numbers.

Using their physical and defensive prowess, the 1989 Pistons rank in the league's top twenty of all-time. They had a 63–19 record, won their division and conference, and swept the Lakers in four games for the NBA championship. Simply put, that club had a great defense, excellent rebounders, and adequate scorers. Statistically, the club was first in the league.[7]

Alternatively the Pistons were least successful and failed to qualify for consecutive playoffs in seasons 1963–1966, 1968–1972, 1977–1982, 1992–1994, and 2009–2014. These occurred because of such things as coaching problems, lack of talented and/or injured players, and strong competition especially from such rivals as the Bulls, Cavaliers, Pacers, and Bucks.

According to a sports article published online, Detroit is the sixth greatest franchise of all-time in the league. In fact, it is underrated by many fans when it comes to the greatest teams. In fifty-nine years, they won nine division and five conference titles. The Pistons also won three NBA championships to go along with their other accomplishments. As graded in the article, they truly deserve their respectable rank following those of the Bulls, Heat, Spurs, Celtics, and Lakers.[8]

In one basketball expert's opinion, the Pistons are one of the few competitors to win championships with completely unique teams. The first two championships came during the "Bad Boys" era, led by Bill Laimbeer and Isiah Thomas. They were dubbed "Bad Boys" because of their aggressive and physical play. In their third championship, Detroit was one of the unique teams in the history of the game since there were no obvious Hall of Fame players on the roster.

Spurred by a young core in the NBA's 2015–16 season, the Pistons made the playoffs for the first time since 2009. Although swept by the Cavaliers in the first round, they showed promise for the future. But in a thirty-team league, they ranked twenty-first in the Entertainment Sports Programming Network (ESPN) future power rankings. Compiled by ESPN Insider analysts Chad Ford and Kevin Pelton, the rankings project the on-court success expected for each team in the league's 2016–17 through 2018–19 seasons. The Golden State Warriors topped the rankings, with the Cleveland Cavaliers second and Boston Celtics third. Following the Cavaliers in the CD, besides the Pistons, were the Pacers at fourteenth, Bulls at sixteenth, and Bucks at twenty-fifth.[9]

Indiana Pacers

While playing in the American Basketball Association (ABA) in the league's 1967 to 1975 seasons, the Indiana Pacers had a .573 winning percentage, appeared in the ED finals twice and WD finals three times, and won three championships in nine playoff appearances. Coached by former Indiana University All-American Bob Leonard, his teams were buoyed by the great play of such superstars such as Mel Daniels, George McGinnis, Bob Netolicky, Rick Mount, and Roger Brown. The Pacers were—and ended as—the most successful franchise in ABA history.

After the Pacers' 1975–76 season, they were one of four ABA teams admitted into the NBA following the ABA-NBA merger. Besides Indiana, the other clubs included the Denver Nuggets, New York Nets, and San Antonio Spurs. Subsequently, the NBA charged each of them an entry fee of $3.2 million. Also, since the NBA agreed to accept only four ABA teams when the league's merged, the Pacers, Nuggets, Nets, and Spurs each had to compensate the two remaining ABA franchises—St. Louis Spirits and Kentucky Colonels—$1.6 million each because they were not a part of the merger.

As a result of the merger, four former ABA teams incurred financial troubles. Additionally, the Pacers had other problems, which occurred during their waning days in the league. They, in fact, had to trade some of their star players and assets for cash in late 1976/early 1977. Interestingly these new NBA teams were also barred from sharing in national television revenues for four years.

Historical Results

As a member of the Midwest Division for three years and then CD during the league's 1979–80 to 2015–16 seasons, the Pacers played 3,231 games and had victories in approximately 49 percent of them. During the period, they won six divisions and also one conference title, but zero NBA championships in twenty-three playoffs. Among fourteen other EC teams as of 2015–16, Indiana ranked seventh in winning percentage, eighth in both number of playoffs and division titles, eleventh in conference titles, and tied for tenth with five other conference teams in championships. Within only the CD, the club had the fewest total titles including championships (table A1).

In comparison to twenty-nine other NBA teams as of early 2016, the Pacers were fifteenth (winning percentage and playoff appearances), tied for twelfth with the Phoenix Suns (number of division titles), tied for nineteenth with the Oklahoma City Thunder (conference titles), and tied for sixteenth with fourteen teams (each with zero championships). From a performance perspective, these results indicate that Indiana has been average to below average during its forty seasons in the league but for various reasons, it was superior while playing in the ABA for nine years.

Performance Highlights

Since joining the NBA in 1976, the Pacers had the most success while in consecutive playoffs during seasons 1989–1995, 1997–2005, and 2010–2013. During some of these periods, the club's best coaches included Bob Hill, Larry Brown, Larry Bird, Isiah Thomas, Rick Carlisle, and Frank Vogel. In 1998, Bird was the league's Coach of the Year because of his team's 58–24 record and finishing second in the CD, although losing in the conference finals to the Bulls. Furthermore, former coaches Brown, Bob Leonard, and Jack Ramsey are in basketball's Hall of Fame.

To be competitive in playoffs, the Pacers' most important players were Reggie Miller, Jermaine O'Neil, Danny Granger, Grant Hill, and Paul George. Besides Miller—whose uniform number was retired by the franchise—players Adrian Dantley, Alex English, and Chris Mullin are other Hall of Famers who played at least one year of their career for Indiana.

Other than 1997–98, Indiana's best season was 1999–2000. While finishing first in their division with a 56–26 record, the Pacers had scorers Reggie Miller and Jalen Rose plus rebounders Dale Davis and Austin Croshere to win division and conference titles but then losing to an outstanding Lakers team in the league's finals.

The Pacers were least successful and failed to qualify for consecutive playoffs in NBA seasons 1976–1979, 1981–1985, 1987–1988, and 2006–2009. Such factors as coaching problems, lack of talented and injured players, and too much competition from rivals like the Bulls, Cavaliers, Pistons, and Bucks negatively affected the team and its ability to win games.

In a recent report, the Pacers ranked twenty-first best of all-time. Although very successful in the ABA, that did not continue into the NBA. Sometimes history does not work out right for some teams. If things had turned out a bit differently, the Pacers could have signed Alex English and Michael Jordan to play together. Similarly, they tied for twentieth with the Brooklyn Nets in another study. It concluded:

> The Pacers were one of the top ABA teams, winning three league championships, but have yet to do the same in the NBA. That said, the team based in Indianapolis, has won its division six times along with one Eastern Conference title. [Historically], they have been competitive and could be a contender again soon. They have been in the NBA for a total of 39 years just like the Nets, Nuggets and Spurs.[10]

After finishing 45–37 and second in the CD during the 2015–16 season, and playing competitively but losing in divisional playoffs to the Toronto Raptors in seven games, the Pacers have a promising future. Excluding aging center Roy Hibbert—who was traded to the Charlotte Hornets—Coach Frank Vogel has players Paul George, Miles Turner, George Hill, and Monta Ellis, and key reserves Rodney Stuckey and C. J. Miles plus Thaddeus Young—acquired from the Philadelphia 76ers.

In ESPN's future power rankings for the 2016–2018 NBA seasons, the Pacers ranked fourteenth. The categories affecting the team's future power included *players*—worth 50 percent of the score and based on current players and their potential for the future, factoring in expected departures—at fourteenth; *management*—worth 16.7 percent and reflecting the quality and stability of the front office, ownership, and coaching—at seventeenth; *money*—worth 16.7 percent and based on the projected salary-cap situation and the ability and willingness to exceed the cap and pay luxury taxes—at tenth; *market*—worth 8.3 percent and determined by the appeal to future acquisitions and team quality, franchise reputation, city's desirability as a destination, market size, taxes, business, and entertainment opportunities, arena quality, and fans—at twenty-third; and *draft* —worth 8.3 percent and based on future draft picks and draft positioning—at fifteenth.[11]

The overall rankings of other CD teams were as follows: Cavaliers second, Bulls sixteenth, Pistons twenty-first, and Bucks twenty-fifth. If they assigned and distributed points objectively and considered the primary factors that affect each NBA franchise, ESPN insiders Chad Ford and Kevin Pelton are optimistic about Indiana's talent and the club being a good but not great team during these three seasons.

Milwaukee Bucks

From their 1951–52 to 1954–55 seasons, the Milwaukee Hawks played in the NBA's EC. In 281 games, they won approximately 32 percent of them and failed to qualify for the playoffs. As a result of the team's dismal record, small attendances at home games, and its financial problems, the club moved from Milwaukee, Wisconsin, to St. Louis, Missouri, in 1955 and renamed St. Louis Hawks.

Since the Chicago Bulls were the only NBA team based in the upper Midwest during the mid- to late 1960s, an organization named Milwaukee Professional Sports and Services Inc. (or Milwaukee Pro)—headed by businessmen Marvin Fishman and Wesley Pavalon—successfully bid for an expansion franchise and then paid $2 million to the league in 1968 to own and operate it. Given the popularity of hunting outdoors in Wisconsin, "Bucks" was selected in a local contest to be the club's nickname rather than "Skunks" or other entries representing animals.

With respect to financing the new franchise, an application from Milwaukee Pro was registered with the Wisconsin Department of Securities for the sale of 300,000 shares of common stock to Wisconsin residents at $5 per share. Because the stock issue attracted public attention, an additional 125,000 shares were offered when the stock opened on an over-the-counter market during late April 1968. As to the basketball side of the franchise, the team participated in both the college and expansion draft under the watchful eye of its first head coach, Larry Costello.

Historical Results

While a member of the league's Eastern Division (ED) from the 1968–69 to 1969–70 seasons, Midwest Division (MWD) for another ten years and then the CD from 1980–81 to 2015–16, the Bucks played 3,888 games and had victories in 51 percent of them. More specifically, they competed in twenty-eight playoffs and won thirteen division and two conference titles and also one NBA championship. Among EC teams as of 2015–16, Milwaukee ranked fourth in winning percentage, second in division titles, tied for ninth with the Orlando Magic in conference titles, and tied for seventh with the Cavaliers and Wizards in number of championships (table A1).

In comparison to twenty-nine other NBA teams, the forty-eight-year-old Bucks tied for eleventh (winning percentage and league championships), and also ranked twelfth (number of playoffs), fourth (division titles), and tied for fourteenth (conference titles). Based on these results, Milwaukee has been competitive and an above-average team in winning percentage and number of postseason appearances and total titles.

Performance Highlights

The Buck's most successful periods occurred among consecutive playoffs in seasons 1969–1973, 1979–1990, 1998–2000, and 2002–2003. During these periods, the club's most prominent head coaches were Larry Costello, Don Nelson, Del Harris, George Karl, and Terry Porter. Nelson, who led the team from 1976 to 1987, was NBA Coach of the Year in 1983 and 1985 while Costello and Harris also had exceptional careers with the franchise.

To win regular-season games and postseason titles, Milwaukee's most productive and popular players included Kareem Abdul-Jabbar, Marques Johnson, Sidney Moncrief, Jack Sikma, Ray Allen, and Michael Redd. Abdul-Jabbar was the league's MVP three times and Moncrief Defensive Player of the Year twice. Besides Abdul-Jabbar, nine other former Bucks' players are in the sport's Hall of Fame such as guards Guy Rodgers and Oscar Robertson, and center Bob Lanier.

In the Bucks' 1970–71 season, they had a 66–16 record and won their division, conference, and an NBA championship. Additionally, the club excelled from 1971–72 to 1973–74 by finishing first in the MWD but losing in the WC semifinals twice and championship game once. Led by Coach Nelson and players Johnson and Moncrief, Milwaukee also won its division during the league's 1979–80 to 1985–86 seasons.

Because of coaching problems, lack of talent and too many injured players, and competition from such division rivals as the Bulls and Pistons, Milwaukee failed to qualify for playoffs during consecutive seasons 1991–1997, 2006–2008, and 2010–2011. Thus, the Bucks have appeared in only nine playoffs since 1992 and lost eight series in the conference's first round. Following the departure of Coach Nelson and then Harris, and retirement of key players during the late 1980s/early 1990s, the team's performances declined within its division and conference compared to those of rivals.

Among thirty NBA franchises ranked statistically as of early 2016, the Bucks placed ninth of all-time. Although they won only one NBA championship in their history, the club deserves to be in the top ten based on its winning the fourth-most division crowns as well as two conference titles. They have been in the league for forty-eight years and despite an overall lack of championships, still boast an incredibly impressive history and a 51 percent winning percentage. If they become a great team again, Milwaukee could climb even higher on the all-time list.

As of August 2015, the Bucks were seventh in the NBA's future power rankings. Regarding its advantages as a basketball group, the report about Milwaukee's potential stated in part:

> The front office has done a great job building a team through the draft and adding free agents when needed. The Bucks currently retain their future firsts [in the draft] and could possibly have four additional second round selections. All players are on friendly deals with majority of their core locked up for at least the next three seasons. They may not be in the running for superstars, but will

> attract high level role players who can take them to the next level. This team is already great on defense and littered with versatile length at all positions and a matchup nightmare. Where Milwaukee needs to improve is when they have the ball. Their roster is filled with players who are young and can't really shoot. Under head coach Jason Kidd, who developed into a consistent jumper during his playing days, expect these young guns to improve on the offensive end.[12]

To conclude, the Bucks have not been relevant since Ray Allen left more than a decade ago, and even then, they were rarely in the NBA conversation. But something special is building where the cheese runs like beer. General manager John Hammond has compiled a lot of young talent, especially with twenty-one-year-old, 6'11" Giannis Antetokounmpo. Watch him go the length of the court in three dribbles and then dunk from the foul line. He can play point guard and had four triple-doubles in games within three weeks. The Bucks will be playoff contenders in the WC soon and could be in the mix for the NBA finals shortly thereafter.

FRANCHISE BUSINESS

Given the performances of them as teams, this section focuses on and examines the commercial aspects of NBA franchises including their principal owner or owners and also facts and other details in tables about each team's arena, various costs for families to attend home games, current and important financial data, and yearly trends in players' payrolls. In part, this information reveals why some franchises are more valuable and wealthy than others and therefore how successful or unsuccessful historically as business enterprises in the sports industry.[13]

Chicago Bulls

Born into a Jewish family in Brooklyn, New York in 1936, Jerry Reinsdorf attended Erasmus Hall High School in Brooklyn and then earned a bachelor's degree from George Washington University in Washington, DC. In 1957, he moved to Chicago, Illinois and after leveraging a full scholarship offer from the University of Chicago Law School into a scholarship from the Northwestern University School of Law, Reinsdorf became a certified public accountant and lawyer and also a registered mortgage underwriter and certified review appraiser.

In 1985, his syndicate bought 56 percent of the Chicago Bulls franchise for $9.2 million. Supposedly, about one-fourth of the team came from the estate of Arthur Wirtz and the remainder from minority owners Philip Klutznick,

Walter Shorenstein, and George Steinbrenner. The Bulls' chairman of the board Lester Crown, managing partner and vice president Jonathan Kovler, and sports entrepreneur Lamar Hunt continued as partners. After Reinsdorf acquired Kovler's 7 percent stake during January 1986, he ousted general manager Rod Thorn and replaced him with Jerry Krause. Reinsdorf controlled the business end of the organization and left its basketball decisions to Coach Kevin Loughery.[14]

Compared to owners of fourteen other EC teams as of the league's 2015–16 season, Reinsdorf's Bulls were second in division titles and first in both conference titles and championships. Among all NBA owners, his teams ranked respectively fourth (division titles), tied for second with the Phoenix Suns (conference titles), and second (championships) following the Lakers. Given these results, Reinsdorf has been outstanding and successful while leading the Bulls for thirty-one years (table A2).

In 2015, an ESPN panel rated every NBA team's owner or ownership group in terms of performances while guiding their franchise to overall on-the-court success, both short and long term. While the Bulls placed eleventh, others in the conference's CD were eighth (Pacers), fifteenth (Bucks), Cavaliers (seventeenth), and Pistons (nineteenth).[15]

At eighty years old, Jerry Reinsdorf is involved with the basketball side of the franchise but no longer active in the Bulls day-to-day business activities. That has been delegated to his son Michael, who in 2010 became the team's president and chief operating officer. But when asked about his future and how long he plans to oversee the team, Jerry's in no hurry to make a change.

Team Financials

Based on data published in *Forbes* about NBA franchises as of early 2016, the Bulls' estimated market value was $2.3 billion, revenue $228 million, operating income $67 million, gate receipts $72 million, debt-to-value 2 percent, and players expenses $87 million. Among fourteen other EC teams, Chicago's financials ranked second in market value, revenue, operating income, and gate receipts, fourteenth in the debt ratio, and tied for fifth with the Raptors and Cavaliers in players expenses. Within only the conference's CD, the Bulls had the highest amounts—although tied in players expenses—but also lowest debt-to-value percent (table A3).

In comparison to twenty-nine other NBA clubs as of their 2015–16 season, Chicago placed third in market value, fourth in both revenue and operating income, fifth in gate receipts, twenty-sixth in the debt ratio, and tied for eighth with the Raptors, Cavaliers, and Oklahoma City Thunder in players expenses. These results indicate, in part, that the Bulls are a very valuable and profitable club because of their stable ownership and historical performances, and also the franchise's location, wealth, and popularity among fans of the sport.

Besides market size, salary inflation, and other factors, an NBA team's annual payroll partly reflects its commitment to players and their current and potential contribution individually and as a group to winning games in regular seasons and postseasons. From 2011 to 2015, for example, the Bulls' payroll among fourteen EC teams ranged in rank from third in 2015 ($87.6 million) to eighth in 2014 ($66.8 million). More specifically, their amounts increased in 2012 ($74.2 million) and 2015 but fell in 2013 ($71.0 million) and 2014. Within only the CD, Chicago was either first, second, or third each year during the period (table A4).

Among twenty-nine other NBA teams, the Bulls' payroll ranked as low as fifth in 2012 to twentieth in 2014. While the team appeared in four playoffs during the league's 2011–2015 seasons, this data denotes how much and when their payroll changed based on such things as the front-office's commitment to win games, success in salary negotiations and renegotiations with players and their agents, and salary cap space.[16]

United Center

Opened in 1994 to replace an aging Chicago Stadium, the 21,500-seat, privately owned United Center was built during the heyday of Michael Jordan and the great Bulls' teams. In the lower concourse, for example, is Fandemonium—the main souvenir outlet for Bulls and NHL Chicago Blackhawks merchandise; private (Locker Room) and public (Windy City Grill) restaurants for season ticket holders; different types of concessions; and a Chicago Stadium Club—a Harbour style buffet restaurant with walls adorned with all kinds of prints and memorabilia from events that occurred at the Bulls and 'Hawks old stomping grounds. Besides the concourse, in the bowl area is an LED Daktronics display board, which circles the bowl between lower and club levels and between the club and upper levels.[17]

In comparison to other EC teams' venues as of early 2016, the United Center tied for third in age with the Cavaliers' Quicken Loans Arena, tied for tenth in construction costs with the Raptors' Air Canada Centre, and ranked second highest in value to the Knicks' Madison Square Garden. Relative to all NBA arenas, the Bulls' respectively tied for eighth in age, tied for seventeenth in cost, and placed second in value. Thus, the United Center is a relatively large and dated facility with plenty of amenities to entertain fans at Bulls and 'Hawks home games plus people there for concerts and other social events (table A5).

For several years a Chicago-based company named Team Marketing Report (TMR) has prepared and published a Fan Cost Index (FCI) for the home games of teams in professional sports leagues. To attend a game for a typical family with two kids, an FCI includes the costs of four average-priced tickets, two cheapest-priced draft beers, four each cheapest-priced soft drinks and hot dogs, parking for one car, and two each game programs and least-expensive, adult-size adjustable caps. Costs are determined by telephone calls with team representatives, venues and concessionaires, and from questions asked during interviews.[18]

In the 2011–2015 NBA seasons, the FCIs for a family to attend a regular-season game at the United Center ranged from a low of $393 in 2011 to a high of $477 in both 2014 and 2015. During this period among home games of fourteen other EC teams, the Bulls ranked in cost for fans from second in 2014 and 2015 to third during 2011–2013. Within only the CD, Chicago had the highest FCI each season (table A6).

To reveal specific costs for a recent season in the NBA, the Bulls' FCI in 2015–16 was approximately $477 and the same as in 2014–15. Listed from most to least in amount by item for one person, the team's tickets averaged between $82 and $83, a cap $25, parking one vehicle $24, a beer $8, soft drink and hot dog each $5 to $7, and a program $5.

Among other teams in the conference's CD, they had rankings and FCIs from most to least as follows: Bucks' eleventh at $325; Cavaliers' twenty-third at $274; Pistons' twenty-ninth at $215; and Pacers' twenty-fifth at $257. Consequently, Bulls' fans paid more at games in the United Center than those of twenty-eight other teams in their arenas.

The cheapest ticket cost $38 for a fan to watch a Bulls' home game at the United Center in 2015–16. This was $22 or about 250 percent more than the league's average for a cheap seat. Also, since the club's FCI was $138 above the amount of a typical NBA team, a family of four purchased tickets and enjoyed a professional basketball game in Chicago at a significant premium relative to the majority of arenas within the league. These costs and prices, in turn, were set by the Bulls organization to earn more revenue and maximize profit from their operations.

Business Highlights

Besides regular-season and postseason games, NBA franchises are involved in—and affected by—community events and business-related affairs, news, and projects. The following are a few of them for Chicago's popular and financially successful pro basketball team.[19]

First, former Iowa State University (ISU) basketball player and current Bulls head coach Fred Hoiberg realizes many points of view in the worlds of business and athletics. According to him, many fans would be surprised at the amount of people, time, and resources invested into the "final product" to prepare for and compete in games. Hoiberg's finance degree from ISU comes into play on a daily basis when you look at the business side of this profession. In general, sports teams and the NBA are corporations and when you factor in players, coaches and front-office contracts, ticket and merchandise revenue, television and radio contracts, and corporate sponsorships, there are numerous occasions where understanding the business side of athletics is a valuable tool.

Second, despite problems with fan involvement and failing to make the playoffs, the Bulls financially improved—except in television ratings—during the league's 2015–16 season. According to an article published in *Crain's Chicago Business Magazine* in April 2016, they led the NBA in paid attendance with an average of 21,820 tickets sold per game and online merchandise sales; sold naming rights for luxury suites to Vindanta Resorts; and increased their average ticket value by $6 or 5 percent.

Third, the Bulls recently signed their first internationally headquartered sponsor who does not have a presence in America. Polish foreign currency exchange firm Cinkciarz inked a seven-year deal with the club in hopes of reaching Chicago's large Polish community. The company hopes to make a name for itself among Chicago's large Polish population. From a business perspective, Cinkciarz became the Bulls' first-ever internationally headquartered sponsor with no major American presence—which could open up a new, lucrative sponsorship front for the franchise.

Fourth, according to a news report published by the *Sports Business Journal*, the Bulls' television ratings plummeted in the 2015–16 season. The team drew an average 3.52 rating on Comcast Sports Net, which was a decline of 29 percent from the previous season's results. The report also stated that the Bulls' decline was the fifth-worst in the NBA—which overall had its local television ratings increase by 6 percent.

Fifth, the Bulls occasionally lead the NBA in attendance, leaving bulls.com and the team's other digital assets to extend the franchise's brand outside the United Center. The top three traffic categories at website bulls.com have been team information—schedule, roster, and tickets—followed by content provided by online writer Sam Smith, and then multimedia content consisting of video, photos, and audio. In 2013, the club relied on seven full-time staff members and from three to six contracted workers to create their digital content. All video streamed on the team's television platform is edited in-house. Much of the digital content is player-related, with the organization enjoying a healthy relationship between the basketball and business operations departments, something not always true for professional sports teams.[20]

Cleveland Cavaliers

Born into a Jewish family in Detroit, Michigan in 1962, Dan Gilbert grew up in Southfield, Michigan. After graduating from high school, he earned a bachelor's degree from Michigan State University and then a Juris Doctor from Detroit's Wayne State University Law School. During college, he earned a real estate agent license and while in law school, worked part-time at his parents' Century 21 Real Estate agency.

Recognizing that the real potential was in originating mortgages and not in selling homes, Gilbert cofounded Rock Financial in 1985. Gradually, the company grew into one of the largest independent mortgage lenders in the nation. In 2000, software maker Intuit Inc. purchased Rock Financial and renamed its national web operation, Quicken Loans, which became the leading provider of direct-to-consumer home loans on the Internet. Two years later—while CEO of the company—Gilbert led a group of investors to purchase Quicken Loans and its affiliated national title company, Title Source Inc., from Intuit.

During January 2005, Gilbert purchased the Cavaliers and operational control of Gund Arena for $375 million from then-owner Gordon Gund, who along with his brother George, had acquired the team from Ted Stepien in 1983 for approximately $20 million. In buying the Cavaliers and its arena, Gilbert satisfied a craving that dated to his first job out of college as a television sports broadcaster.

Among owners of fourteen other EC teams as of their 2015–16 season, Gilbert's Cavaliers won four division and two conference titles, and also one NBA championship since 2005. Respectively, Cleveland tied for sixth in number of division titles, tied for eighth in conference titles, and tied for third in number of championships. In comparison to all NBA owners, Gilbert's club ranked respectively tied for tenth (division titles), tied for fifth (conference titles), and tied for sixth (league championships). Thus, Gilbert has been an above-average and productive owner and perhaps an outstanding leader of his franchise given these results (table A2).

One year before his team won a championship in 2016, Dan Gilbert ranked fourth best among NBA owners. Although he did not put together a winning franchise without superstar LeBron James, Gilbert learned from his past mistakes and invested more money in free agents and also veteran players on the roster. This, in turn, does not make him a great owner but truly someone with an applicable, smart, and rational strategy.[21]

Team Financials

Regarding all teams in the league as of their 2015–16 season, the Cavaliers' estimated market value was $1.1 billion, revenue $191 million, operating income $24 million, gate receipts $52 million, debt-to-value 18 percent, and players expenses $87 million. Relative to only clubs in the EC, Cleveland tied for fifth with the Brooklyn Nets in market value and also ranked fourth in revenue, fifth in operating income, sixth in gate receipts, tied for sixth with the Pacers in the debt ratio, and tied for fifth in players expenses. Except for players expenses, the Cavaliers' amounts were second to those of the Bulls in their division (table A3).

In comparison to twenty-nine other NBA teams, Cleveland tied for eleventh (market value and operating income) and placed seventh (revenue), eleventh (gate receipts), and tied for ninth (debt-to-value) and for eighth (players expenses). These results denote, in part, that the team is average to above-average as a business enterprise despite its historical performances and relatively small market size as a franchise in the sport.

The Cavaliers' payroll reflects the talents and accomplishments of its players in addition to their commitment to win games and compete for titles and championships. From the 2011 to 2015 seasons, for example, Cleveland's ranged from $50.9 million to $108.3 million. Among only EC teams, its amounts ranked as high as first in 2015 to fifteenth three seasons earlier. And within the CD, the Cavaliers' payroll increased each year and placed highest in both 2014 and 2015 (table A4).

Relative to all NBA teams during 2011–2015, the team's payroll was respectively twenty-eighth, tied for twenty-ninth, sixteenth, third, and first. These changes in rank occurred because of payments to superstar LeBron James and such key players as Kevin Love and Kyrie Irving. As a result, the Cavaliers finished first twice in their division, appeared in two consecutive playoffs and NBA finals, and won a championship in 2016.

If James takes another one-year contract from the Cavaliers in 2016, he would make at least $27.5 million for the season. This is because the team does not have salary-cap space and full Bird rights, which limits the size of his raise. Assuming he resigns with Cleveland, James could get $30.8 million if he took a two-year deal under league rules. In this case, he could sign for two years and approximately $64 million. An option is for him to take a one-year contract until the summer of 2017, when an even higher salary cap and potential new collective bargaining agreement rules would enable him to sign one of the largest deals in professional sports history.

Quicken Loans Arena

Opened in 1994 to replace the Richmond Coliseum, the 20,500-seat Quicken Loans Arena (QLA) is part of the Gateway Sports and Entertainment Complex. The Cavaliers' home originally included such special things as a four-sided, center-hung JT16 Sony Jumbotron video scoreboard that provides image magnification, instant replay, and crystal clear game action, and a full-service production facility which includes an on-line production suite, master control facility, and television and radio studios.[22]

In addition, the venue contains several multiscreen video walls; more than 500 television monitors; at least ninety suites with several of them located only fifteen rows from the arena floor; Gordon's Sports Bar; a regulation-sized practice basketball court; and a 2,500 square foot team shop. Besides Cavaliers home games, QLA is home to the Women's National Basketball Association (WNBA) Cleveland Rockers and International Hockey League (IHL) Cleveland Lumberjacks.

Among those of other EC teams as of early 2016, QLA tied for being the third oldest with the Bulls' United Center and also ranked thirteenth in construction cost and seventh in value. In comparison to all NBA arenas, it respectively tied for eighth in age and then twenty-first in cost and thirteenth in value. Based on this data, the Cavaliers play in relatively old but large facility and within five to ten years, it will likely to be renovated or perhaps replaced especially if the team generates more money for owner Gilbert and the city (table A5).

In the 2011–2015 NBA seasons, the FCIs for a family to attend a regular-season game at QLA ranged from a low of $271 in both 2013 and 2014 to a high of $287 in 2012. During this period among home games of fourteen other EC teams, the Cavaliers ranked in cost from seventh in 2011 ($275) to tenth in 2015 ($274). Within only the CD, Cleveland's FCI was neither the highest nor lowest each season and relative to all NBA clubs, placed between sixteenth and twenty-third (table A6).

To reveal specific costs for a recent season in the NBA, the Cavaliers' FCI in 2015–16 was approximately $247 or about 1 percent more than in 2014–15. Listed from most to least in amount by item for one person, the team's tickets averaged $48 to $49, a cap $20, parking one vehicle $10, a beer $4, and a soft drink and hot dog each $3.

Among other teams in the conference's CD, they had rankings and FCIs from most to least as follows: Bulls' third at $477; Bucks' eleventh at $325; Pacers' twenty-fifth at $257; and Pistons' twenty-ninth at $215. Consequently, Cavaliers' fans paid less at games in QLA than those of twenty-two other teams in their arenas.

The cheapest ticket available cost $11 for a fan to watch a Cavaliers' home game at QLA in 2015–16. That was almost $5 or about 30 percent less than the league's average for a cheap seat. Also, since the club's FCI was $65 below the amount of a typical NBA team, a family of four purchased tickets and enjoyed a basketball game in Cleveland at a significant discount relative to the majority of arenas within the league. These costs and prices, in turn, were set by the Cavaliers' organization to earn more revenue and maximize profit from their operations.

Business Highlights

Besides regular-season and postseason games, NBA franchises are also involved in—and affected by—community events and business-related affairs, news, and projects. The following are a few of them for Cleveland's basketball champions, who have become a financially improving and increasingly popular, professional team.[23]

First, the franchise's decision to fire Coach David Blatt during the 2015–16 season offered a critical lesson for business leaders. Sometimes high-profile sports managers or supervisors need to be terminated. This is necessary when their teams lose confidence in them. Irrespective of a manager's past accomplishments, they cannot lead a team to victory if their followers no longer have confidence in them. Consequently, the Cavaliers' staffing strategies provide business firms with a template for success: recruit top-notch employees, build teamwork and camaraderie, and fire anyone who threatens team cohesion.

Second, the Cavaliers were big winners at the NBA's annual sales and marketing meetings in January 2016. They were recognized for selling at least 10,000 full-season tickets and also won awards for new full-suite-equivalent sales, sponsorship account performance and growth, sponsorship retention, and game-experience satisfaction. The haul adds to the four awards Cleveland won at the 2015 meetings, which occurred during what was superstar LeBron James's first season back in Ohio.

Third, as reported in spring 2015 by business officials, the Cavaliers' marketing platform for beacon technology had charged sponsors by the message or as part of a larger integrated deal. To drive revenue, they work with partners to carve out messaging opportunities including out-of-venue with geofencing. The standard beacons are about the size of a deck of cards and powered by four AA batteries with no wiring. The total investment to place 100 beacons at an arena is between $15,000 and $25,000 and covers installation and software licensing costs depending on their use and number of users. The Cavaliers did not disclose their investment but six months later, they had a payoff through the more than 170,000 downloads of the new mobile app.

Fourth, during March 2015, Cleveland became the first NBA team to require all season ticket holders to agree to an automatic renewal policy, essentially eliminating the need for the club to pursue season ticket renewals annually. Although the Cavaliers began requiring all new season ticket buyers to agree to an auto-renew policy in 2012, this is the first time the team made all season ticket holders participate in the auto-renewal plan—including renewing customers along with new full- and partial-season buyers. One drawback to the new effort was allowing a fan to opt out of a season ticket package at any time during a year, instead of that separation coming only during the traditional NBA springtime renewal period.

Fifth, Cleveland planned to schedule an exhibition game in Cincinnati, Ohio. According to the school's athletic director, the 2016 NBA champions will return to Xavier University's Cintas Center in 2017. The Cavaliers expect to rotate exhibition stops each year between Columbus and Cincinnati for the foreseeable future. During 2014 and 2015, the Cintas Center also hosted Cavaliers' exhibition games.

For other business news about the franchise's recent history, LeBron James's return to the Cavaliers in 2014 was a boon for the club's bean counters. Although Cleveland did not raise ticket prices for their 2014–15 season, arena revenue surged more than 40 percent thanks to increased attendance and sponsorships and also a trip to the NBA finals. Attendance jumped 17 percent, second in the league behind the Bulls. Kia Motors and FanDuel signed on as top-dollar partners while ratings on Fox Sports Ohio surged 172 percent for Cavaliers' home games. During the league's 2015–16 season, the team went all in in their chase for a title with player costs exceeding $175 million, including a luxury tax of more than $60 million.[24]

Detroit Pistons

Tom Gores was born into a catholic family in Nazareth, Israel, in 1964. Four years later, they moved from Nazareth to Genesee, Michigan. While a student in high school, Tom played football, baseball, and basketball. He received a scholarship to Michigan State University and graduated from there in 1986 with a Bachelor of Science degree in construction management. Following school, Gores learned the buyout business with his older brother Alec.

During the mid-1990s, Tom founded Platinum Equity LLC as a way to acquire non-core divisions of Fortune 500 companies. Since then, Platinum Equity expanded and invested in public-to-private transactions and acquisitions from private sellers. Because of its success, Gores became a billionaire in the early 2000s.

In mid-2011, Platinum Equity bought Palace Sports and Entertainment—which was the parent company of the NBA Detroit Pistons and their debt-free arena, the Palace of Auburn Hills—for $325 million from Karen Davidson, the wife of the late Bill Davidson. As such, Platinum Equity became the third owner in the franchise's history.

In September 2015, Gores purchased Platinum Equity's share of the Pistons franchise, giving him 100 percent of the team. Since 2011, he had owned a 51 percent share of it. Nonetheless, it is unknown how much Gores paid for Platinum's 49 percent investment. From a leadership and control standpoint, however, nothing changed as a result of the deal.

Among owners of EC teams as of the league's 2015–16 season, Gores's Pistons had zero division and conference titles and NBA championships. Respectively, the club tied for ninth (division titles), eighth (conference titles), and fifth (championships) in its performances. Within only the CD, the Pistons had worse results than the Bulls, Cavaliers, and Pacers but not the Bucks. Because Detroit tied for twentieth, sixteenth, and tenth in titles and championships in comparison to twenty-nine other NBA teams, Gores has not been a successful owner from the league's 2011–12 to 2015–16 season (Table A2).

Based on his performance in guiding the franchise to any short- and long-term success, ESPN ranked Gores as the nineteenth best NBA owner in 2015. For others in the CD, the Pacers' Herb Stein rated eighth, Bulls' Reinsdorf eleventh, Bucks' Edens and Lasry fifteenth, and Cavaliers' Gilbert seventeenth. Since the Pistons finished 44–38, third in their division and in the playoffs in 2016, Gores moved higher up the list but so did Gilbert.[25]

Team Financials

In January 2016, *Forbes* magazine published financial data about each NBA team. Specifically, the Pistons had an estimated market value of $850 million, revenue $154 million, operating income $16 million, gate receipts $22 million, debt-to-value 22 percent, and players expenses $71 million. Among others in the EC, Detroit was tenth in market value, eighth in revenue, ninth in operating income, thirteenth in gate receipts, third in the debt ratio, and tied for tenth with the Bucks in players expenses (table A3).

While its amounts were lower than those of the CD's Bulls and Cavaliers, the Pistons ranked from a low of fourth in its debt-to-value ratio to a high of twenty-seventh in gate receipts, relative to all NBA clubs. According to these results, Detroit has been an average to below-average business enterprise with relatively high debt and not enough gate receipts and revenue to significantly improve its market value.

The Pistons' payroll reflects the talents and accomplishments of its players in addition to their commitment to win games and compete for titles and championships. From the 2011 to 2015 seasons, for example, the club's payroll ranged from $61.8 million in 2013 to $85.8 in 2015 million. Among only EC teams, Detroit's amounts ranked as high as third in 2011 ($70.6 million) to eleventh in both 2012 ($63.0 million) and 2013. And within the period, the team's payroll declined for two seasons and then increased in 2014 and 2015 (table A4).

With respect to all NBA teams during 2011–2015, the Piston's payroll consecutively tied for seventh in 2011 and then in the following four seasons to twentieth, twenty-fourth, twenty-second, and then ninth. Thus, the club's payroll did not improve comparatively until the league's 2015–16 season, which in turn, contributed to its winning record and playoff appearance.

In the league's 2016–17 season, Detroit's players' contracts equaled $110 million or third highest in the league primarily because of Andre Drummond's $22.1 million. As of mid- to late 2016, the former amount was considerably more than the Bulls' $94.4 million (thirteenth), Pacers' $83.4 million (nineteenth), Bucks' $78.9 million (twenty-first), and Cavaliers' $77.7 million (twenty-fourth without LeBron James's salary).[26]

Palace of Auburn Hills

Built in 1988 to replace the Pontiac Silverdome, Cobo Arena, and Joe Louis Arena, the $70 million, 22,000-seat Palace of Auburn Hills hosts the Pistons and WNBA Detroit Shock. The venue is split into two levels with some suites between the levels and in the midst of the lower level. Seats are a lavender color and a jumbotron hangs over midcourt. To perk things up, there is a live jazz band performing from a perch above the upper level, a unique touch in the style of Detroit's Motown musical tradition.

Encircling the arena, a single concourse is brightly lit and well decorated with many concession stands and exhibits. The centerpiece of it is a Hall of Fame and Museum displaying memorabilia from great events held there. Besides artifacts from the Pistons glory days, exhibits exist of other teams such as the IHL Vipers winning the Turner Cup in 1994 and also famous musicians and tributes to the greatest players who wore a Pistons jersey.

In comparison to arenas of other EC teams as of their 2015–16 season, the Palace of Auburn Hills tied for first with the Bucks' BMO Harris Bradley Center in age and ranked fifteenth in construction cost and twelfth in value. Among all those in the NBA, the Pistons' home respectively tied for second (age) and then placed twenty-ninth (construction cost) and twenty-fourth (value). Despite being outdated with not enough amenities, the Palace of Auburn Hills will be an NBA and WNBA arena for several years (table A5).

Ranked eighth best facility in a recent study, the Palace of Auburn Hills is energetic, compact, and great for rabid fans but not ideal for casual viewing. Although getting there from downtown Detroit is a hassle, it is one of the premier arenas in the league because of its beauty, grace, and memory of gyms in earlier years of the sport (table A5).[27]

In the 2011–2015 NBA seasons, the FCIs for a family to attend a regular-season game at the Palace of Auburn Hills ranged from $215 in 2015 to $262 in 2013. During this period among home games of fourteen other EC teams, the Pistons ranked in cost for fans from eleventh in 2011–2014 to fourteenth in 2015. Within only the CD, Detroit's FCI was third or fourth highest except for being lowest in 2015 (table A6).

To reveal specific costs for a recent season in the NBA, the Pistons' FCI in 2015–16 was approximately 17 percent less than in 2014–15. Listed from most to least in amount by item for one person, the team's tickets averaged between $31 and $32, parking one vehicle $15, a cap $10, a single beer $9–$10, and a soft drink and hot dog each about $5.

The cheapest ticket available cost about $8 for a fan to watch a Pistons' home game in 2015–16. This was almost 50 percent less than the league's average for a cheap seat. Also, since the club's FCI was $124 below the amount of a typical NBA team, a family of four purchased tickets and enjoyed a basketball game in Detroit at a significant discount relative to the majority of arenas within the league. These costs and prices, in turn, were set by the Pistons' organization to earn maximize profit from its operations.

Business Highlights

Besides regular-season and postseason games, NBA franchises are also involved in—and affected by—community events and business-related affairs, news, and projects. The following are a few of them for Detroit's competitive, longtime, and well-known professional basketball team.[28]

First, the club's attendance improved modestly to 16,515 per home game in the 2015–16 season. That number ranked twenty-fifth in the thirty-team NBA and an improvement of more than 1,200 per game over the previous season. When the Pistons win, they lead the league in attendance, something they did during 2003–2009—except for finishing second in 2006–7.

Second, Pistons owner Tom Gores and Huntington Bank CEO Steve Steninour jointly contributed $25 million to the battered businesses of Flint, Michigan. The program included $22 million in loans to small businesses, $2 million in mortgage financing, and another $1 million in grants to bolster businesses damaged by the water crisis. The economic development initiative also provided education programs for children and young adults to teach them about business, entrepreneurship, and money management.

Third, the Pistons kept their fans updated during home playoff games in 2016 thanks to real-time email, which provided them with live scores and statistics. The new email system for ticket holders was established through a partnership with Moveable Ink during late 2015/early 2016. Specifically, emails were forwarded to ticket holders two hours before tip-off at games and updated every time after being opened or reloaded. In addition to scores and statistics of all players on the court at that time, emails gave information on traffic after games and offered fans the best possible route to their home from the arena.

Fourth, the Ralph C. Wilson Jr. Foundation pumped $2 million into Grow Detroit's Young Talent—a public-private initiative to provide summer jobs in 2016. That money and $100,000 from the Pistons helped 8,000 youths, ages fourteen to twenty-four, enroll in a six-week summer employment program that combined work-readiness training and employer support. More than 150 employers volunteered to employ young workers—up from 144 in 2015. The goal was to secure commitments from about 225. Among organizations recruiting businesses to employ youths included the Detroit Regional Chamber, the Downtown Detroit Partnership, Michigan Black Chamber of Commerce, Detroit Employment Solutions Corporation, SER Metro, and City Connect Detroit.

Fifth, Pistons' owner Tom Gores and the Cavaliers' Dan Gilbert have partnered to form an investor group to bring a Major League Soccer (MLS) expansion club to the Detroit area. Their efforts are supported by MLS Commissioner Don Garber, who announced that the league planned to increase to twenty-eight teams and named Detroit as a city of interest. The investor group, which represents a cross-section of industries, said their plan includes construction of a stadium in downtown Detroit. The group also indicated that an MLS team would complement two lower division minor league soccer teams based in Detroit.

Indiana Pacers

Born in 1934 into a Jewish family in New York City, Herbert Simon grew up in the Bronx. After graduating from City College of New York with a Bachelor's in Business Administration, he became very successful in real estate. From 1993 to 1995, Herb served as CEO of the Simon Property Group Inc., as co-chairman of its Board during 1998–2007, and chairman emeritus since 2007.

In 1983, billionaire Herb and his brother Melvin purchased the struggling Pacers for approximately $11 million from co-owners Sam Nassi and Frank Mariani. More than two decades later, the brothers reorganized the Pacers ownership after Melvin no longer wanted to help fund the team, which had been suffering financial problems since 2004, and missing playoffs from the 2006–7 to 2009–10 seasons

Several years after Melvin died in 2009, Herb asked a court to declare that his late brother's estate and widow Bren had no financial stake in the team. Furthermore, he requested the court to keep documents on the matter under seal, arguing a public release would create "significant risk of substantial harm" to people who signed a confidential settlement in 2012 pertaining to Melvin Simon's estate.

Among owners of EC teams as of 2015–16, Simon's Pacers have won six division titles and also one conference title but zero NBA championships. Respectively in rank, Indiana tied for third with the Celtics (number of division titles), tied for sixth with the Knicks (conference titles), and tied for fifth with ten other teams (championships). In comparison to owners of twenty-nine other clubs, the Pacers tied for fifth in division titles, tied for twelfth in conference titles, and tied for tenth in league championships. Consequently, Herb and his late brother have been above-average owners based on their commitment to the franchise and the Pacers' twenty-two playoff appearances and winning seven titles since 1983 (table A2).

According to one report, Herb Simon ranked fourteenth best with respect to all NBA owners in 2015. To explain why, the reasons were:

> Last year [2015–16] was a bad year for the Pacers. They lost the conference finals to Miami and Paul George to an injury while Lance Stephenson lost his mind. From there, it's been a far fall for the Pacers, but they might be starting to figure things out. It's hard to root for ownership that allows the front office to treat players the way Roy Hibbert was treated on his way out, but they know how to right the ship—at least earned the benefit of the doubt. Still, moves like trading away Kawahi Leonard for George Hill and signing cancerous Andrew Bynum are blemishes on ownership, as they allowed these deals to happen on their dime. Larry Bird is the man who could be fired for all this, but ownership is just as guilty for letting it happen.[29]

In 2015, ESPN asked sports fans to rate each team's front-office management on its guidance and leadership in terms of how it affected overall on-court success, both in the short and long term. From there, the network calculated ratings to determine the NBA's best and worst front offices. While the Pacers ranked tenth in the survey, others in the CD were ninth (Bulls), fourteenth (Bucks), sixteenth (Cavaliers), and Pistons (nineteenth). Overall, the Spurs were first and Knicks thirtieth.[30]

Team Financials

In *Forbes* magazine's report on the financial data of NBA teams as of their 2015–16 season, the Pacers' estimated market value was $840 million, revenue $138 million, operating income $19 million, gate receipts $20 million, debt-to-value 18 percent, and players expenses $75 million. Among fourteen EC clubs, Indiana ranked eleventh in market value, thirteenth in revenue, eighth in operating income, fifteenth and last in gate receipts, tied for sixth with the Cavaliers in their debt ratio, and ninth in players expenses (table A2).

With most of their amounts less than those of the Bulls, Cavaliers, and Pistons in the CD, the Pacers' data among all NBA teams as of late 2015/ early 2016 was respectively twenty-third (market value), twenty-eighth (revenue), tied for eighteenth with the New Orleans Pelicans (operating income), twenty-ninth (gate receipts), tied for ninth with the Cavaliers and Phoenix Suns (debt-to-value), and twenty-second (players expenses). Given these results, Indiana is below-average financially—while operating as a franchise in the league—with a relatively high debt percent and very low revenue and gate receipts.

The Pacers' payroll, in part, reflects the talents and accomplishments of its players in addition to their commitment to win games and compete for titles and championships. From the 2011 to 2015 seasons, among only EC teams, their payroll ranged in rank from a low of sixth in 2014 ($74.4 million) to a high of fifteenth in 2011 ($43.9 million). Within the CD, the club's amounts were the lowest in 2011 ($43.9 million) and 2015 ($71.6 million) but not during 2012–2014 (table A4).

In comparison to all NBA teams from 2011 to 2015, the Pacers' payrolls consecutively placed thirtieth, fifteenth twice, and then ninth and twenty-third. For various reasons, they significantly increased salaries of players in 2012 and 2014 but not in other years. Because Indiana appeared in four playoffs and two conference finals in five seasons, these were good decisions based on its strategy regarding investments in players.

Bankers Life Fieldhouse

Opened in 1999 to replace Market Square Arena as the home of the Pacers and WNBA Indiana Fever, 18,200-seat Conseco Fieldhouse—renamed Bankers Life Fieldhouse (BLF) in 2011—is a short distance from the Lucas Oil Stadium (home of the NFL Indianapolis Colts) and also Circle Centre in the city's historic warehouse district. BLF has a distinct half-barrel type roof with a red brick and steel exterior. At the top of the building are huge skylights, which bathe the arena bowl in natural light during the day and provide a dramatic view of the skyline at night from inside the bowl.

In the main entry pavilion, there is an old fashioned box office with metal bars on the windows, and high above are retro advertising panels and also an old style message board similar to the type at a train station. Just off the pavilion is a coffee shop, team store, a bridge to the adjoining ramp, and the Pacers practice court.

All concourses in BLF are adorned with showcases and many displays of not only Pacers' ABA/NBA memorabilia, but also mementos of Indiana college and high school greats. Besides the team's history, other displays showcase the Indianapolis Motor Speedway and Indiana's health care. There are false storefronts of a 50s style Main Street, a shoeshine stand, barber shop with a face painter, and an old time television store that displays the old RCA Victor console sets.

Among those of fourteen other EC teams as of early 2016, BLF was tied for eighth with three of them in age and also ranked ninth in construction costs and eleventh in value. In comparison to all NBA arenas, the Pacers tied for nineteenth (age) and ranked sixteenth (construction costs) and twenty-third (value). Based on these criteria, BLF is an average facility while being the youngest but most expensive to build relative to arenas of other CD teams in the conference (table A5).

Based on its name, aesthetics, fan experiences and an overview, BLF ranked fourth among NBA arenas in 2015. After studying each of them, the following describes the Pacers' home site:

> The whole point of Indiana basketball is to romanticize amateurism, so calling it a "fieldhouse" like a high school track works in that direction. Every seat in the arena provides an excellent view of the game. The two-tone court is subtle, with the lighter tone along the sideline and baseline, a move that thankfully moves the Pacers away from too much use of their navy blue. The smaller feel of the stadium continues the "high school" motif. BLF is clean, comfortable and intimate, and the atmosphere the Pacers cultivate harkens to college basketball: intense, loud, and vibrant. Even so, the Pacers experience is welcoming and easy to access, with parking and close public transit. BLF provides the most underrated NBA experience out there, from the atmosphere to the convenience.[31]

In the 2011–2015 NBA seasons, the FCIs for a family to attend a regular-season game at the BLF ranged from $208 in 2011 to $257 in 2015. During this period among home games of fourteen other EC teams, the Pacers ranked in cost from twelfth in 2015 to fourteenth each year during 2011–2014. Within only the CD, Indiana's FCI was lowest of the group during the seasons except for the Pistons' games at $215 each in 2015 (table A6).

To reveal specific costs for a recent season in the NBA, the Pistons' FCI in 2015–16 was approximately 11 percent more than in 2014–15. Listed from most to least in amount by item for one person, the team's tickets averaged almost $39, a cap between $17 and $18, parking one vehicle $12, a single beer $7–$8, and a soft drink and hot dog each $4 to $5.

The cheapest ticket available cost $13 for a fan to watch a Pacers' home game in 2015–16. This was almost 22 percent less than the league's average for a cheap seat. Also, since the club's FCI was $82 below the amount of a typical NBA team, a family of four purchased tickets and enjoyed a basketball game in Indianapolis at a significant discount relative to the majority of arenas within the league. These costs and prices, in turn, were set by the Pacers' organization to earn maximize profit from its operations.

Business Highlights

Besides regular-season and postseason games, NBA franchises are also involved in—and affected by—community events and business-related affairs, news, and projects. The following are a few of them for Indiana's competitive, longtime, and well-known professional basketball team.[32]

First, a graduate of the 2011 Sports Marketing program and former president of Ferris State's chapter of the American Marketing Association, Eric Cole established his career with the Indiana Pacers after attending a Detroit Pistons job fair during his senior year at Ferris. He was hired as an Inside Sales Accounting Executive and promoted six months later to being a Group Events Specialist. Cole's main duty is bring different groups and organizations to a Pacers' basketball game. Whether the group and/or organization wants to be involved in a half time event, or just relax and enjoy the game, Cole creates a customized fan package based on their desires.

Second, Indianapolis's Capital Improvement Board approved a contract in late 2015 allowing the Pacers to build a $50 million practice facility. Board president Earl Goode said the five-story, 130,000-square-foot St. Vincent Center would be built in downtown Indianapolis across the street from Bankers Life Fieldhouse. Scheduled to open in 2017, the Pacers will pay for construction of the building on land owned by the Capital Improvement Board. The *Indianapolis Star* reports the practice facility will have two full basketball courts and offices for the Pacers and the team's parent company, Pacers Sports & Entertainment.

Third, the *Indianapolis Star* reported during June 2016 that the Pacers support having an advertisement emblazoned on the team's jerseys and also plan to have a corporate sponsorship deal in place by the league's 2017–18 season. While the 2.5-by-2.5 inch logo patch will take up only a small piece of real estate on the front of the team's jerseys, its addition has the potential to provide a large stream of revenue to a franchise that continues to rank in the bottom third of the league in attendance. Financial incentives aside, the decision to allow such brand placement will forever make any future corporate sponsor a third wheel in iconic moments. Regardless of the potential for negative consumer reaction to the further commercialization of athletes, the prospective cash flow will undoubtedly be too rich for teams to reject.

Fourth, the Pacers partnered with Umbel in early 2014 to collect and import over 300,000 fan profiles into the Umbel platform. By centralizing their fan data, Umbel helped the Pacers run far more sophisticated marketing campaigns for both new and existing fans. The team uses Umbel to segment fans based on ticket purchases, brand affinities, income, and other things. For example, the Pacers' marketing team ran a campaign where they offered $5 tickets to a targeted segment. Not only did this campaign outperform other marketing efforts, but fans also self-selected to purchase higher-priced tickets than the initial $5 offering.

Fifth, the Pacers' attendance for regular-season home games dipped slightly from 16,864 in 2014–15 to 16,847 in 2015–16. Despite that very minor change, the team's overall home ticket revenue increased thanks to dynamic pricing and ticket demand for marquee matchups. But the ticket revenue increase also shows the basketball market is solid and has room for growth. This is the second year the Pacers' home attendance had a small decrease. In fact, attendance for the 2013–14 season was 17,501. Despite these two small dips, the Pacers are far ahead of where they were when the team averaged an NBA-worst 13,538 during its 2010–11 season.

Milwaukee Bucks

During late 1985, businessman Herbert Kohl bought the Bucks franchise for $16.5 million from Jim Fitzgerald. Then in April 2014, a group led by billionaire hedge fund managers Wesley Edens and Marc Lasry agreed to purchase a majority interest in the team from Kohl. One month later, the sale was approved by other NBA team owners and the league's Board of Governors.

As of 2014, five prominent African-American business leaders and philanthropists, and two well-known Milwaukee business executives joined the franchise as co-owners. Their addition gave the Bucks' principal owners Edens and Lasry and new investor Jamie Dinan—whose ownership stake had not been widely known—enhanced credibility as they continue to work not only on rebuilding the franchise but also on setting the stage for what is expected to be a major downtown economic redevelopment project. While specifics of what the three have in mind beyond building a new arena had yet to be disclosed, the Bucks said that members of Partners for Community Impact (PCI) had previously been involved in urban economic development and renewal projects. This suggested that PCI may have a loftier goal in mind beyond rebuilding a franchise and building a new arena.

With respect to owners of other EC clubs and their performances as of the league's 2015–16 season, Edens's and Lasry's Bucks teams have not won any titles or championships. Ranked, their clubs tied for ninth in division titles, tied for eighth in conference titles, and tied for fifth with ten others in number of championships. In comparison to all NBA teams, the Bucks respectively tied for twentieth (division titles) and then fifteenth (conference titles) and tenth (NBA championship). Consequently, Milwaukee's owners and their basketball staff need to establish a roster of talented players who perform well enough for Coach Jason Kidd to have a winning record in regular seasons and qualify for the playoffs (table A2).

As of 2015, an online sports site rated Edens and Lasry thirteenth best among owners of NBA franchises. According to why they deserve to be in the top fifteen, the reasons given were as follows:

> The ownership group [led by Edens and Lasry] wants to not only keep the Bucks in Milwaukee, but aggressively try to build a winning team. The Bucks weren't supposed to do much of anything last year [2015–16], and losing Jabari Parker was a brutal blow. But the front office deals for Miles Plumlee and Michael Carter-Williams and signing Greg Monroe this summer [2016], all came after hiring Jason Kidd as the brilliant coach of the future. These were general manager moves but ownership signed off on them, which proves the group knows how to do good business in the NBA.[33]

Hired in 2008 as the Bucks' general manager, John Hammond was named the NBA's executive of the year for the 2009–10 season. Under his watch through 2015–16, Milwaukee appeared in the playoffs three times and had not won a playoff series since 2001 when it reached the EC finals. After receiving a one-year contract extension from team ownership in July 2016, Hammond will continue in his current position through the 2017–18 season. A league source confirmed Hammond's extension and said the transition of Justin Zanik to general manager is being planned for 2018 with Hammond remaining as a consultant with the team.

Team Financials

According to financial information published by *Forbes* magazine in early 2016 with respect to thirty NBA franchises, the Bucks' estimated market value was $675 million, revenue $126 million, operating income $11 million, gate receipts $24 million, debt-to-value 26 percent, and players expenses $71 million. Compared to the data of fourteen other EC teams, respectively, Milwaukee's placed fifteenth (market value) and then fourteenth (revenue), eleventh (operating income), tied for eleventh with the Charlotte Hornets (gate receipts), second (debt ratio), and tied for tenth (players expenses) with the Pistons (table A3).

Except for gate receipts, the Bucks' amounts were lowest, or tied for the lowest, in the CD. And among all NBA teams, Milwaukee ranked twenty-ninth in both market value and revenue, twenty-third in operating income, tied for twenty-fifth in gate receipts, second in debt percent, and tied for twenty-third in players expenses. Based on these results, the Bucks are relatively inferior financially in their operations and as a business enterprise with too much debt and not enough revenue and gate receipts.

The Bucks' payroll, in part, reflects the talents and accomplishments of its players in addition to their commitment to win games and compete for titles and championships. From the 2011 to 2015 seasons, among only EC teams, Milwaukee's payroll ranged in rank from a low of ninth in 2015 ($73.8 million) to a high of fourteenth in both 2013 ($55.3 million) and 2014 ($57.1 million). Within the CD, the club's amounts were lowest in seasons 2013–14 and third or fourth from the top in other years (table A4).

In comparison to all NBA teams from 2011 to 2015, the Bucks' payrolls placed consecutively eighteenth, twenty-second, twenty-eighth in both 2013 and 2014, and seventeenth. For various reasons, the amount paid to players significantly increased in 2015 but not in other years. Although Milwaukee appeared in two playoffs during the period, the club must further increase its payroll to effectively compete against the Cavaliers and other teams for a division title and advance in the conference's postseason.

BMO Harris Bradley Center

Opened in 1988 to replace across-the-street MECCA building, the 18,700-seat Bradley Center was a gift to the state of Wisconsin from Jane and Lloyd Pettit in memory of Jane's late father, Harry Lynde Bradley, and also the only major, public assembly facility in North America with construction underwritten through the philanthropy of a single family. Besides the Bucks, it is home to a few sports teams including Marquette University Golden Eagles basketball. As of 2009, the Bucks paid no rent for using the facility and received all signage and sponsorship income in addition to operational support in ticketing, building operations, event services, ushers, video services, and custodial services.

The $90 million structure originally featured glass-enclosed lobbies, three concourses, movable seats, and accommodations for both sports and non-sports events such as concerts, ice shows, and family entertainment. It has several entrances and exits with primary guest entryways located at each corner of the building. Inside each lobby, double rows of concrete columns with polished granite bases rise almost seventy feet to support a skylight system. The first level accommodates at least 8,000 spectators; second level includes private suites that encircle the arena and provide seating for nine to twelve people per suite; and the third level seats approximately 10,000 spectators in more than twenty rows of seats.

Among arenas of fourteen other EC teams as of early 2016, the BMO Harris Bradley Center tied for first with the Palace of Auburn Hills in age and also ranked fourteenth in construction cost and fifteenth in value. In comparison to all NBA venues, Milwaukee's tied for being the second oldest, tied for twenty-sixth in cost to build, and placed thirtieth or last in value. Thus, the Bucks play their home games in an outdated and low-valued facility that requires significant renovation or replacement in order to generate more revenue for the franchise in future seasons (table A5).

Based on its name, aesthetics, fan experiences, and an overview, the BMO Harris Bradley Center ranked twenty-ninth best among NBA arenas. After studying each of them, the author said this about the Bucks' home:

> The court sideline sports the slogan "Fear the Deer," and the wood paneling is in the pattern of an "M" on each half court side. Otherwise, the arena is a bit cramped and unpleasant to the eye. The Bucks are the team most in need of a renovation, and it should be alright transplanting the court design. This is the NBA stadium most likely to force you to have a hip replacement after you have visited it. The seats are so short, narrow, and cramped that watching the game is a notoriously painful experience. This is not assuaged by the food selection, which ends up being rather poor.[34]

In the 2011–2015 NBA seasons, the FCIs for a family to attend a regular-season game at the BMO Harris Bradley Center ranged from $289 in 2011 to $325 in both 2014 and 2015. During this period among home games of fourteen other EC teams, the Bucks ranked in cost for fans from sixth in 2011, 2014, and 2015 to seventh in 2012 ($313) and 2013 ($309). Within only the CD, Milwaukee's FCI was less than the Bulls' each season but more than those of the Cavaliers, Pistons, and Pacers (table A6).

To reveal specific costs for a recent season in the NBA, the Bucks' FCI in 2015–16 was the same as in 2014–15. Listed from most to least in amount by item for one person, the team's tickets averaged $50–$60, parking one vehicle $22–$23, a cap $20, a single beer $6–$7, and a soft drink and hot dog each about $5.

The cheapest ticket available cost $12 for a fan to watch a Bucks' home game in 2015–16. This was almost $4 or 32 percent less than the league's average for a cheap seat. Also, since the club's FCI was approximately $13 below the amount of a typical NBA team, a family of four purchased tickets and enjoyed a basketball game in Milwaukee at a discount relative to the majority of arenas within the league. These costs and prices, in turn, were set by the Bucks' organization to earn maximize profit from their operations.

Business Highlights

Besides regular-season and postseason games, NBA franchises are also involved in—and affected by—community events and business-related affairs, news, and projects. The following are a few of them for Milwaukee's struggling but longtime and well-known professional basketball team.[35]

First, Bucks' owners agreed to pay wages of at least $12 per hour—escalating to $15 by 2023—for service-sector jobs at the new arena and related facilities and also to hire union-represented employees and union-signatory subcontractors. The jobs agreement resulted, in part, from a deal with Democrat legislators in order to win their votes in summer 2015 for the state law that established $250 million in public funding for a new arena. Furthermore, the Bucks negotiated for months with Milwaukee-area labor union advocates on a wage floor that's higher than the national $7.25 hourly minimum wage.

Second, the team scrambled during May 2016 to limit the damage caused by an employee who fell for an email scam and provided W-2 income tax forms for the team's 2015 employees. Players' financial information was included in the release, which occurred after someone impersonated the team's president, Peter Feigin, and asked for the documents. After discovering the email spoofing attack, the club reported the incident to the Internal Revenue Service and Federal Bureau of Investigation and also notified impacted individuals to access three years of credit monitoring and non-expiring identity restoration services.

Third, the Bucks are consistently one of the lowest-drawing franchises in the NBA. They were in the bottom five in attendance during four consecutive years, drawing fewer than 15,000 fans per game each season. Although local television ratings on Fox Sports Wisconsin more than tripled in the 2014–15 season when the team made a surprise trip to the playoffs, the network only managed 19,000 viewers per game or fifth-lowest in the league.

Fourth, Bucks' owners hoped to finalize a naming rights deal for the new arena in downtown Milwaukee by late 2016. Marc Lasry and Jamie Dinan anticipate that BMO Harris Bank and Potawatomi Hotel & Casino will join the sponsor group—preferably a local organization. Naming rights will be an important revenue source because the club keeps all proceeds of a deal according to its lease with the Wisconsin Center District.

Fifth, for 2014–15, the Bucks' season ticket sales staff scored the highest mark among NBA clubs in a mystery shopper survey done by research firm IntelliShop. During every surveyed call, for example, the team's salesperson made an effort to engage in small talk outside the immediate discussion of the ticket sale. Additionally, 80 percent of the time, agents asked the caller to go to the team's website during the call in order to see the layout of the arena and also they touted the benefit of exclusive access to special areas for season ticket holders such as select food vendors or social areas. Ultimately, 90 percent of the Bucks' conversations were rated by the IntelliShop callers as above average or one of the best sales experiences ever.

NOTES

1. For more information about NBA seasons, teams, and their players see Connie Kirchberg, *Hoop Love: A History of the National Basketball Association* (Jefferson, NC: McFarland, 2007) and David G. Surdam, *The Rise of the National Basketball Association* (Urbana, IL: University of Illinois Press, 2012).

2. Data about the Chicago Bulls' and other teams' performances are available on such websites as http://www.sportsencyclopedia.com and http://www.basketball-reference.com.

3. See Mark Karantzoulis, "How the Bulls Should Use Wade," http://www.chicagonow.com, July 9, 2016.

4. These leagues, for the most part, are discussed in Frank P. Jozsa Jr., *The National Basketball Association: Business, Organization and Strategy* (Hackensack, NJ: World Scientific, 2011).

5. Performance highlights of teams and their coaches and players are contained in such sources as "NBA and ABA Team Index," http://www.basketball-reference.com, cited June 25, 2016 and "NBA Teams," http://www.basketball-reference.com, cited July 1, 2016.

6. Besides the websites in note 2, there are various details and other data in "Detroit Pistons," http://www.nba.com, cited July 2, 2016.

7. Chad Ford and Kevin Pelton, "Future Power Rankings: Who Will Rise in the Next Three Years?" http://www.espn.go.com, cited June 5, 2016.

8. See Daniel Zillmer, "All 30 NBA Franchises Statistically Ranked by All-Time Greatness," http://www.fansided.com, cited June 6, 2016.

9. "Future Power Rankings: Who Will Rise in the Next Three Years?"

10. "All 30 NBA Franchises Statistically Ranked by All-Time Greatness."

11. "Future Power Rankings: Who Will Rise in the Next Three Years?"

12. Another source is Adam Fromal, "Future Power Rankings For the 2016 NBA Lottery Teams," http://www.bleacherreport.com, cited July 15, 2016.

13. For a book about franchise business topics in professional sports, see Frank P. Jozsa Jr., *National Basketball Association Strategies: Business Expansions, Relocations, and Mergers* (New York: Springer, 2016).

14. The business details about this deal are in such articles as Bob Sakamoto, "Reinsdorf Buys Bulls," http://www.articles.chicagotribune.com, cited July 10, 2016.

15. "2015 Front-Office Rankings: Owners," http://www.espn.go.com, cited July 14, 2016.

16. Some payroll data of NBA teams and their players is in, for example, "Rod Fort's Sports Business Data," https://sites.google.com, cited July 1, 2016.

17. Besides teams online, websites about NBA arenas are http://www.basketball.ballparks.com and http://www.espn.go.com.

18. To research the cost to attend the Bulls' and other teams' home games, see "NBA FCIs," http://www.teammarketingreport.com, cited July 1, 2016.

19. See such readings as "Fred Hoiberg—Chicago Bulls," http://www.business.iastate.edu, cited July 15, 2016; Easy Eis, "The Bulls Are Still a Massive Success When it Comes to Making Money," http://www.blogabull.com, cited July 16, 2016;

James Naveau, "Bulls' TV Ratings Down Nearly 30 Percent in 2015–16 Season," http://www.nbcchicago.com, cited July 17, 2016; John Lombardo, "Chicago Bulls: Engaging the Fans," http://www.sportsdailybusiness.com, cited July 17, 2016; "We Are Bulls Prep," http://www.chicagobullscollegeprep.noblenetworks.org, cited July 18, 2016.

20. "Chicago Bulls: Engaging the Fans" and "We Are Bulls Prep."

21. Josh Hill, "NBA Owners Power Rankings: Who is Best Owner in Basketball?" http://www.fansided.com, cited July 8, 2016.

22. See sources in notes 15–16 for, respectively, information about Quicken Loans Arena and the FCIs of Cavaliers' home games.

23. Some Cavaliers' business highlights appear, for example, in Brett McIntyre, "What Business Leaders Can Learn From the Cleveland Cavaliers Championship," http://www.business.com, cited July 18, 2016; John Lombardo, "Cavs Clean Up at NBA Sales Awards," http://www.sportsbusinessdaily.com, cited July 19, 2016; Don Muret, "Getting the Signal," http://www.sportsbusinessdaily.com, cited July 20, 2016; "Cavaliers First in NBA to Require Automatic Renewal," http://www.sports-businessdaily.com, cited July 21, 2016; Mike Dyer, "Cleveland Cavaliers Announce Preseason Games in Cincinnati and Columbus," http://www.cincinnati.com, cited July 22, 2016.

24. Kurt Badenhausen, Mike Ozanian, and Christini Settimi, "The Business of Basketball," http://www.forbes.com, cited June 27, 2016.

25. See note 13 for what the Pistons' principal owner Tom Gores ranks among others within Detroit's division and conference, and the NBA.

26. "NBA Contract Index," http://www.basketball-reference.com, cited July 21, 2016.

27. An important reference about teams' home courts is Luke Dahlgren, "Power Rankings: NBA Arenas," https://fansided.com, cited July 10, 2016.

28. For some business highlights of the Pistons, read Bill Shea, "Detroit Pistons Business Scorecard Improves," http://www.crainsdetroit.com, cited July 22, 2016; Aaron Smith, "Flint Gets $25 Million From Detroit Pistons and a Local Bank," http://www.money.cnn.com, cited July 22, 2016; Stuart Goldman, "Detroit Pistons Keep Fans Updated With Real-Time Email," http://www.athleticbusiness.com, cited July 23, 2016; "Detroit Pistons Partner With Grow Detroit's Young Talent to Support Mayor Mike Duggan's Summer Youth Jobs Program," http://www.nba.com, cited July 23, 2016; Sam Stejskal, "NBA Owners Tom Gores, Dan Gilbert Partner to Bring MLS Team to Detroit," http://www.mlssoccer.com, cited July 24, 2016.

29. See note 18 for where Indiana Pacers' owner Herbert Simon ranks among his peers.

30. "NBA Front-Office Rankings: 2015," http://www.espn.go.com, cited July 23, 2016.

31. "Power Rankings: NBA Arenas."

32. Concerning the Indiana Pacers' business highlights, there is "Sports Marketing Alumnus Scores a Career With the Indiana Pacers," http://www.ferris.edu, cited July 23, 2016; Scott Davis, "Indiana Pacers Just Dumped Their Head Coach and Kicked Him on the Way Out," http://www.businessinsider.com, cited July 24, 2016; John

Lombardo, "Picking a Shamrock: Indiana Pacers Hire Marketing Firm to Help Them Bring in National Sponsors," http://www.sportsbusinessdaily.com, cited July 25, 2016; Mark Alesia, "CIB Signs Off on Pacers' $50 Million Practice Facility," http://www.indystar.com, cited July 24, 2016; "Indiana Pacers: Using Data to Grow Fan Loyalty," http://www.umbel.com, cited July 24, 2016.

33. "NBA Owners Power Ranking: Who is Best Owner in Basketball?"

34. See "Power Rankings: NBA Arenas" and also Jacob Kornhauser, "Ranking Every NBA Arena From Worst to First," http://www.ranksports.com, cited July 13, 2016.

35. Some of the Bucks' business topics are included, for example, in John Lombardo, "In Rebranding, the Bucks Aren't Stopping Here," http://www.sportsbusinessdaily.com, cited July 26, 2016; David Broughton, "Bucks Lead Way in NBA Phone Sales Survey," http://www.sportsbusinessdaily.com, cited July 27, 2016; Rich Kirchen, "Milwaukee Bucks' Owners Borrow $174 Million to Finance Their Share of Arena Costs," http://www.bizjournals.com, cited July 27, 2016; Des Bieler, "Milwaukee Bucks' Tax Information Released by Employee Who Fell for Email Scam," http://www.washingtonpost.com, cited July 27, 2016.

Chapter Three

Southeast Division

Organized in 2004 by the National Basketball Association (NBA), the Southeast Division (SED) of the league's Eastern Conference (EC) included the Atlanta Hawks, Charlotte Bobcats, Miami Heat, Orlando Magic, and Washington Wizards. The Hawks joined the SED from the league's Central Division (CD) and the Heat, Magic, and Wizards from the Atlantic Division (AD). Before their 2014–15 season, the Bobcats changed their name to Charlotte Hornets.

Given this change in the conference's structure, this chapter discusses the historical development and highlights business news and the financial facts of SED teams based respectively in Atlanta, Georgia; Charlotte, North Carolina; Miami, Florida; Orlando, Florida; and Washington, DC. During their history, which of them for example, had won the fewest division titles and largest number of NBA championships? What were their market values, gate receipts, and ticket prices in the league's 2015–16—or simply—2015 season? Who have been the least and most successful owners among the five clubs? How do their arenas rank in aesthetics, entertainment, and experience among fans? The answers to these and other questions are covered in the chapter.[1]

TEAM PERFORMANCE

Atlanta Hawks

Before the late 1960s, the Tri-Cities Blackhawks and then Milwaukee Hawks and St. Louis Hawks were in the NBA. The Blackhawks, who played in the league's 1949–50 and 1950–51 seasons, had a 54–78 record and lost in the 1950 Western Division (WD) semifinals. After relocating from the small-market Tri-Cities area to Milwaukee, Wisconsin, in 1951, the renamed Hawks finished fourth or fifth in their division during four seasons. Then, in 1955, the Hawks moved from Milwaukee to more-populous St. Louis, Missouri, where they appeared in twelve playoffs and won six division titles and in 1958, an NBA championship.[2]

Despite his club's success in St. Louis, Hawks' owner Ben Kerner became weary of the team's longtime home, Kiel Auditorium. The thirty-three-year-old arena seated only 10,000 people and its age showed. Although the Hawks occasionally played their home games against mostly popular opponents at the larger St. Louis Arena, Kerner was not willing to shift his team there because the venue had not been well-maintained since the 1940s.

Even though the St. Louis Arena was renovated to accommodate the arrival of the National Hockey League (NHL) Blues in 1967, Kerner wanted a new venue to attract more fans and increase his team's gate receipts, revenue, and profit. Unable to resolve the situation, Kerner sold the Hawks franchise in 1968 for $3.5 million to a syndicate headed by Atlanta real estate developer Tom Cousins and former Georgia governor Carl Sanders. As a result, the new owners moved their club that year from St. Louis to Atlanta, Georgia, and renamed it Atlanta Hawks.

Historical Results

From the league's 1968–69 to 2015–16 seasons, the Hawks played 3,888 games and had victories in approximately 50 percent of them. During the period, they won five division titles but zero conference titles and NBA championships in thirty-two playoffs. Among EC teams as of early 2016, Atlanta ranked fifth in winning percentage, sixth in playoff appearances, tied for ninth with the Cleveland Cavaliers and Orlando Magic in number of division titles, and tied for twelfth with three other teams in conference titles and also for tenth in NBA championships (table A1).

Within the SED as of their 2015–16 season, the forty-eight-year-old Hawks were second to the Heat in winning percentage, first in number of playoffs, and won more total titles and championships than the Charlotte Bobcats/Hornets but not the Heat, Magic, or Washington Wizards. In comparison to all NBA clubs, the Hawks' performances ranged from a tie for eighth in playoffs to a tie for twenty-first in conference titles. Based on these results, Atlanta has been an average to below-average competitor among other clubs in its conference and the league.

Performance Highlights

During their history, the Hawks were successful by qualifying for consecutive playoffs in NBA seasons 1968–1972, 1977–1979, 1981–1983,

1985–1988, 1992–1998, and 2007–2015. They had such memorable head coaches as Richie Guerin, Hubie Brown, Kevin Loughery, Mike Fratello, Lenny Wilkins, Mike Woodson, Larry Drew, and Mike Budenholzer. In their careers with the club, coaches Brown, Fratello, Wilkens, and Budenholzer each won a Coach of the Year award.

To win games in regular seasons and some postseasons, Atlanta had a group of talented players. These included such athletes as Lou Hudson, Walt Bellamy, Dan Roundfield, Dominique Wilkins, Mike Blaylock, Dikembe Mutombo, Al Horford, and Paul Millsap. Besides coaches Guerin, Brown, and Wilkins, players Bellamy Wilkins and Mutombo are in the Naismith Memorial Basketball Hall of Fame.

According to a recent poll, the Atlanta Hawks rank as the league's eighteenth best franchise of all-time. Based on its performances and the productivity of coaches and players, the team has been competitive during many seasons. In fact, it won sixty games once, at least fifty-nine times, and from forty to forty-nine in several years. Although Atlanta did not win its conference from 1968 to 2016, the club has performed better than most sports fans realize especially in qualifying for the playoffs.

Among teams in Entertainment Sports Programming Network (ESPN) 2016 future power rankings, Atlanta—by category (weight)—was seventeenth in *players* (50 percent); tenth in *management* (16.7 percent); ninth in *money* (16.7 percent); twentieth in *market* (8.3 percent); and twelfth in the *draft* (8.3 percent). For the NBA's 2016–17 to 2018–19 seasons, this data suggests that that the Hawks will be relatively strong in projecting their salary-cap situation and the ability and willingness to exceed the cap and pay a luxury tax but also comparatively weak in their appeal to future acquisitions based on team quality, franchise reputation, city's desirability as a destination, market size, taxes, business and entertainment opportunities, arena quality, and fans.[3]

Other than improving competitively, the franchise is following through on its pledge to "look at the world differently" after a racial scandal in late 2014. The organization has grown more conscious about creating an inclusive culture under its new ownership. That effort includes traditional philanthropy efforts like construction of basketball courts in poor Atlanta neighborhoods, programming halftime concerts featuring local hip-hop stars, and outreach to the lesbian, gay, bisexual, and transgender (LGBT) community with rainbow-colored team merchandise and prominent display of same-sex marriage proposals on the Philips Arena kiss cam.[4]

Charlotte Bobcats/Hornets

When the league planned to expand prior to its 1988–89 season, North Carolina author and sports entrepreneur George Shinn assembled a group of prominent, wealthy businessmen to bid for and head a prospective NBA franchise. A hotbed for college basketball and one of the fastest-growing cities in the United States, Charlotte was one of three in-state regional homes to the American Basketball Association (ABA) Carolina Cougars from 1969 to 1974.

Despite doubts from critics, Shinn's advantage was the Charlotte Coliseum—a state-of-the-art arena that held almost 24,000 spectators and the largest basketball-specific facility ever to serve as a full-time home for an NBA team. During April 1987, NBA Commissioner David Stern contacted Shinn and told him his syndicate was awarded the league's twenty-fourth franchise to begin play in 1988.

Named Charlotte Hornets, the team's first president and general manager Carl Sheer preferred a roster of veteran players in order to organize a competitive team as soon as possible. Former college coach and veteran NBA assistant Dick Harter was hired to be head coach. In the league's 1988 expansion draft, the Hornets stocked their inaugural roster with several experienced players who, as a group, formed a competitive lineup.

Because of ownership issues, defeat of a public referendum for a new arena, and other problems, the Hornets moved from Charlotte to New Orleans after their 2001–2 season and became the New Orleans Hornets. Two years later, an investment group from Charlotte led by Hall of Famer Michael Jordan applied to the league for a new franchise. As a result of their efforts, the NBA awarded them an expansion franchise to begin play in the league's 2004–5 season. Owned by Black Entertainment Television (BET) founder Robert Johnson, the club was nicknamed Bobcats.

Historical Results

While named the Bobcats for ten years and then renamed Hornets in the NBA's 2014–15 and 2015–16 seasons, the team played 968 games and had victories in approximately 38 percent of them. Among fourteen other clubs in the EC, it ranked fifteenth (last) in winning percentage, tied for fourteenth in number of playoffs and also division titles with the Brooklyn Nets, tied for twelfth in conference titles, and tied for tenth in championships. Within only the SED, the Bobcats/Hornets had the lowest winning percentage, appeared in the fewest playoffs, and won the least number of titles plus championships (table A1).

In comparison to twenty-nine other NBA teams as of early 2016, the Bobcats/Hornets were respectively thirtieth (winning percentage), tied for twenty-ninth (playoffs), tied for twenty-eighth (division titles), tied for twenty-first (conference titles), and tied for sixteenth (league championships). Thus far, this has been an inferior performing team within its division, conference, and across the league but also one that mostly played hard to win games despite only seven victories in 2011–12, eighteen in 2004–5, and twenty-one in 2012–13.

Performance Highlights

While named Bobcats, the team was able to qualify for the playoffs in NBA seasons 2009–10 and 2013–14, and then again when named Hornets in 2015–16. During one of more of these years, its successful head coaches included Larry Brown and Steve Clifford but not Bernie Bickerstaff, Sam Vincent, Paul Silas, and Mike Dunlap. Although Brown's and Clifford's teams lost series in the first round of the conference playoffs, they each won at least forty-three games in the regular season and finished third or fourth in their division.

The players most responsible for the team's success were small/power forward Gerald Wallace, center/power forward Al Jefferson, and point guard Kemba Walker. While some of them were all-stars and/or all-pro for one or more seasons, they did not win such major awards as NBA Most Valuable Player (MVP) or Player of the Year. However, for the previously named Charlotte Hornets franchise—which appeared in seven playoffs—local fans certainly remember talented Muggsy Bogues, Larry Johnson, Alonzo Mourning, and Glen Rice.

According to at least one report, the Charlotte Bobcats/Hornets rank as the worst or among the worst NBA franchises of all-time. The following is from one source as of 2013:

> Since the city of Charlotte got a pro team back after the Hornets left for New Orleans, it has been nothing but misery. Nine years have brought just one winning season and one playoff appearance. And to cap it off, the Bobcats achieved infamy in 2011–2012 when they set a league record for the worst regular-season winning percentage, winning just seven games in the lockout-shortened campaign for a .106 percentage. Charlotte's franchise win percentage of .344 is the worst of any franchise still in existence.[5]

In ESPN's 2016 future power rankings of thirty NBA teams, the Hornets—by category—ranked thirteenth in the *draft*, seventeenth in *money*, eighteenth in *management*, nineteenth in the *market*, and twenty-first in *players*. According to its position in each category, this Charlotte-based franchise is above average among teams in future draft picks and draft positioning but below average in its (a) projected salary-cap situation and ability and willingness to exceed the cap and pay a luxury tax; (b) quality and stability of the front office, ownership, and coaching; (c) appeal to future acquisitions given the team's quality, franchise reputation, city's desirability as a destination, market size, taxes, business and entertainment opportunities, arena quality, and fans; and (d) current players and their potential for the future while factoring in expected departures.[6]

For these and other reasons, the Hornets will not win an NBA championship in the next two or three seasons. While the club has enough talent to make the playoffs, it does not have time to develop young players and compete in the postseason or finals soon. A more realistic expectation is for the Hornets to make a finals appearance within the next decade.

Simply put, the club's lineup is not good enough to consistently defeat such teams as the Cleveland Cavaliers and Golden State Warriors in a five- or seven-game series. However, if players like Kemba Walker, Cody Zeller, Michael Kidd-Gilchrist, and Frank Kaminsky each continue to improve their skills, and if the talented Nicolas Batum becomes a star, the Hornets will win more regular-season games and eventually compete for a division and perhaps a conference title. In addition, owner Michael Jordan and his front-office staff must gradually increase the salaries for those on the roster to sustain Charlotte's success in the future.

Miami Heat

Because Florida had no NBA teams in the mid-1980s, groups from Orlando, Tampa/St. Petersburg, and Miami tried in different ways to attract an existing—or bid for a new—franchise. The Miami Sports and Exhibition Authority eventually endorsed a group led by three prominent individuals: NBA Hall of Famer and former head coach Billy Cunningham; the producer of stage extravaganzas Zev Buffman; and former sports agent Lewis Schaffel. The group, in turn, received financial support from Carnival Cruise Lines founder Ted Arison who would be majority owner of the franchise while minority shareholders Cunningham and Schaffel handled day-to-day administrative operations.

During April 1987, an NBA expansion committee endorsed bids—at \$32.5 million each—from groups representing Charlotte, North Carolina, and Minneapolis, Minnesota. However, the committee was split between awarding the third and final franchise to Miami or Orlando, causing representatives from both cities to complain and exchange negative comments about each other. Finally, the NBA decided to expand by four teams with clubs from Charlotte and Miami debuting in the league's 1988–89 season and others from Minneapolis and Orlando to begin play in 1989–90.

Following a contest that involved 20,000 entries, Miami Heat defeated Miami Vice—the famous detective show set among the palms of South Beach—and also beat out such nicknames as Flamingos and Waves to become the team's full name. Despite being located on the East Coast, the Heat was initially assigned to the Midwest Division (MWD) of the league's Western Conference (WC).[7]

Historical Results

As a member of the league's MWD in 1988–89, Atlantic Division (AD) from 1989–90 to 2003–4 and then the SED during its 2004–15 NBA seasons, the Heat played 2,248 games and had victories in approximately 52 percent of them. During the period, they won twelve division and five conference titles, and also three NBA championships in nineteen playoffs. Among EC teams, Miami ranked third in winning their division, tied for third with the 76ers and Pistons in conference titles, tied for third with the Pistons in league championships, and placed eleventh in playoff appearances (table A1).

While Miami had won the most championships of any in the SED as of 2016, in comparison to all NBA clubs it was fifth in winning division titles and also tied for fifth in both conference titles and championships. Based on these results, the Heat has been above average competitively in its division and conference and except for the Celtics, Bulls, Lakers, and Spurs, performed better than other teams throughout its twenty-eight years in the league.

Performance Highlights

During its history, the Heat had many memorable victories and qualified for the playoffs consecutively in seasons 1995–2000, 2003–2006, and 2008–2013. Besides Pat Riley, the club's most successful head coaches were Stan Van Gundy and Eric Spoelstra. Riley was Coach of the Year in 1997 because his team won its division with a 61–21 record but lost in the EC finals to the eventual NBA champion Chicago Bulls. In addition to him, Coach Van Gundy won one championship and Spoelstra two.

Miami's best players historically included Glen Rice, Alonzo Mourning, Tim Hardaway, Dwayne Wade, Chris Bosh, and LeBron James. While James had won the NBA MVP award twice and Mourning the league's Defensive Player of the Year in 1999 and 2000, Wade was unanimously voted by fans to perform in several all-star games. Most importantly, Coach Riley and center Mourning are in the Hall of Fame as of 2016.

The Heat failed to qualify for the playoffs in back-to-back seasons 1988–1990 and 2001–2002. Besides ownership problems, such coaches as Ron Rothstein and Kevin Loughery did not inspire their players to win enough games in regular seasons and consistently defeat others in their division. In fact, Miami had fewer than thirty-seven victories each year and only fifteen in 1989 and 2008.

Following the Celtics, Lakers, and Spurs, the Heat statistically ranked fourth all-time in greatness as of 2015. Actual reasons given for the club being fourth and ahead of a few other great teams are briefly:

> The Miami Heat have been one of the most consistent and successful franchises in NBA history. In just 26 years they've already won three NBA Championships, five conference titles and an incredible 11 [now 12] division crowns. That amount of success packed into just 26 [now 28] years is incredibly impressive and why they're ranked ahead of the Bulls in this list. They have been greater in terms of points (and success) per year than most franchises in NBA history.[8]

After rating each team in five (weighted percent) categories to determine their future power in the league, the Heat was thirteenth in *players* (50 percent), fourth in *management* (16.7 percent), tied for fourteenth with the Bucks and Kings in *money* (16.7 percent), second in the *market* (8.3 percent), and twenty-sixth in the *draft* (8.3 percent). Thus, Miami ranked highest on its appeal to future acquisitions based on team quality, franchise reputation, city's desirability as a destination, market size, taxes, business and entertainment opportunities, arena quality and fans, but then lowest on future draft picks including draft positioning.[9]

Orlando Magic

During the mid-1980s, Florida businessman Jim L. Hewitt approached Philadelphia 76ers general manager Pat Williams about bringing an NBA team to Orlando. Intrigued by the project, Williams became the front man of an investment group one year after leaving the 76ers franchise.

When Hewitt and Williams held a news conference to announce their intention of seeking an NBA team, they decided to hold a contest in the *Orlando Sentinel* to get names for it. Out of a more than 4,000 entries, "Magic" was picked after Williams brought his seven-year-old daughter, Karyn, to visit Orlando. The nickname, of course, alludes to the city's biggest tourist attraction and economic engine, Walt Disney World, along with its Magic Kingdom.

In 1986, Hewitt spoke with potential investors and also city officials in order for them to approve an arena project while Williams made presentations to NBA Commissioner David Stern and owners of other teams about Orlando being the best home site for a new team. As a result, the league awarded Hewitt's and Williams's group an expansion franchise for $32.5 million in 1987 and also to syndicates representing Charlotte, Miami, and Minneapolis-St. Paul.

Historical Results

As a member of the league's CD (1989–1990), MWD (1990–1991), AD (1991–1992), and then SED in the 2004–2015 seasons, the Magic played 2,166 games and had victories in approximately 49 percent of them. During the period, they won five division and two conference titles but zero NBA championships in fourteen playoffs. Among other EC teams as of 2016, Orlando tied for ninth with the Cavaliers and Hawks in division titles and also with the Bucks in winning their conference and five other clubs in number of league championships (table A1).

While the Magic had fewer titles plus championships than the Heat in the SED as of early 2016, the club won more of them than the Hawks or Bobcats/Hornets. In comparison to all NBA teams, Orlando tied for fourteenth in both division and conference titles, and also tied for sixteenth in not winning any championships. Based on these results, the Magic has been below average in its performances with respect to most teams in the league and thus not really successful from a competitive standpoint.

Performance Highlights

The Magic's most impressive seasons since 1989–90 occurred in consecutive playoffs during years 1993–1996, 2000–2002, and 2006–2011. During these periods, its head coaches were Byron Hill, Doc Rivers, and Stan Van Gundy. While Rivers was Coach of the Year in 1990, others such as Matt Guokas, Chuck Daly, Johnny Davis, and Jacque Vaughn struggled to win enough games in one or more regular seasons.

Orlando had some outstanding players in winning seasons including Shaquille O'Neal, Darrell Armstrong, Anfernee Hardaway, Tracy McGrady, and Dwight Howard. O'Neal was Rookie of the Year in 1993, on multiple all-star teams, and a current Hall of Famer while Howard won NBA Defensive Player of the Year awards in 2009–2011. Armstrong, Hardaway, and McGrady played competitively and frequently led their teams in scoring points and/or assists.

The Magic's best and worst seasons were, respectively, 1995–96 and 1989–90. In the former, it finished 60–22 in the regular season and first in the division but lost to the Bulls in the EC finals. However, because of dismal performances by players on the roster and coaching problems, the latter club won only eighteen games in its regular season and finished seventh in the CD.

With respect to NBA teams and their records and number of titles and championships in postseasons as of 2015, the Magic ranks twelfth among them. An expert who evaluated them wrote:

> The Orlando Magic is the highest ranked team on this list [NBA franchises statistically ranked] that hasn't won an NBA Championship. Now that isn't

> exactly what a franchise would like to be remembered by, but it does show that the franchise has been extremely competitive. They've been in the NBA for just 25 years, but have won an impressive five division titles and two Eastern Conference championships. If this team can win an NBA title in the coming years, it will jump much higher up this list.[10]

Regarding its potential based on ESPN's future power ratings, the Magic improved from twenty-third in the league's 2013–2015 seasons to thirteenth in 2016–2018. Projected to have the third-best cap position in the NBA for the next three years, Orlando has always been a popular destination for free agents because of the weather and lack of state income tax. With a number of interesting young players, the Magic have enough talent to perhaps lure a young star or two over the next few years. New head coach Frank Vogel was well-loved in Indiana, which could be attractive for an elite free agent—especially the Pacers' Paul George, who can opt out of his contract after the 2017–18 season.[11]

Washington Wizards

After two losing seasons, the NBA Chicago Packers—renamed Zephyrs—moved to west of the Chesapeake Bay. While there for ten years, the team won four division titles and appeared in seven playoffs led by Coach Gene Shue, but nevertheless, did not win an NBA championship.

In an inner city with severe neglect due to changing industry, white flight, and a budding drug trade, Bullets' owner Abe Pollin complained to city and local sports officials about the difficulty of drawing fans to the team's games at the downtown Baltimore Civic Center. Although they won three consecutive division titles, the Bullets' attendances at the city's Civic Center ranked eleventh among seventeen teams in the league's 1970 to 1972 seasons.

As a result, Pollin moved his franchise after the league's 1972–73 season from Baltimore to play its home games in a new facility to be built in Landover, Maryland, a short distance outside of Washington, DC. Thus, Baltimore's first major-league team in the modern era became the first to flee. Consequently, public officials and sports fans became concerned that the National Football League (NFL) Baltimore Colts and Major League Baseball (MLB) Baltimore Orioles would soon follow the Bullets' strategy and eventually leave the area. In fact, the Colts' and Orioles' franchise owners contributed to the jitters with frank and unfavorable assessments of their home site, Memorial Stadium.

Historical Results

In NBA (seasons) while named Capital Bullets (1973–74) and then Washington Bullets (1974–75 to 1996–97), and finally Washington Wizards (1997–98 to 2015–16), these teams played a total of 3,748 games and had victories in approximately 44 percent of them. Collectively, they won three division and also three conference titles, and one NBA championship. Ranked among EC teams as of early 2016, the Wizards were thirteenth in division titles, tied for seventh with the Cavaliers both in winning their conference and number of championships, and tied for ninth in playoff appearances (table A1).

Within the SED, the Wizards have played worse than the Hawks and Heat but not the Magic or Bobcats/Hornets. In comparison to all NBA clubs as of their 2015–16 season, Washington tied for twenty-second (number of division titles), tied for tenth (conference titles), tied for eleventh (championships), and tied for seventeenth (playoffs). Based on its winning percentage and other criteria, this has been a below-average franchise while performing in regular-season and some postseason games since 1973–74.

Performance Highlights

The club's most successful periods occurred during consecutive playoffs in seasons 1973–1979, 1983–1986, 2004–2007, and 2013–2014. During one or more of these years, its important head coaches included K. C. Jones, Dick Motta, Gene Shue, Kevin Loughery, Wes Unseld, Eddie Jordan, and Randy Wittman. Shue was Coach of the Year in 1982 because his team—despite lacking highly talented players—finished 43–39 and fourth in its division, but lost to the Celtics in the EC semifinals after sweeping the New Jersey Nets in the first round of the playoffs.

Throughout its history, the franchise had some outstanding players. Besides center Unseld, they were center/power forwards Elvin Hayes, Moses Malone, Chris Webber, and Marcin Gortat, point guard Gilbert Arenas, and small forward Greg Ballard. For being scorers, rebounders, and/or simply play-makers during their careers, Unseld, Hayes, Malone, and five other players are in pro basketball's Hall of Fame.

Washington's best and worst seasons were, respectively, 1974–75 and 2000–1. In the former, the club won sixty games and its division but lost in the NBA finals to the Golden State Warriors. But in the latter season, Washington had a 19–63 record and finished seventh in its division because of problems with players and also Coach Leonard Hamilton's failure to motivate them in regular-season games.

Based on such things as its winning percentage and the number of division and conference titles plus championships and playoff appearances, this NBA franchise is ranked nineteenth best of all-time. To summarize Washington's history of performances:

> It's hard to believe but there used to be a team in the world called the "Chicago Packers." It's not hard to understand why they changed it after a year. Eventually they became the Washington Wizards after a few name and location changes. Overall, the franchise at one time was a pretty successful one. From '65 to '88 they only missed the playoffs four times. They have only made it five times [seven as of 2016] since. Elvin Hayes and Wes Unseld fill up the record books and led the franchise to their only NBA championship.[12]

Regarding their power ranking in the NBA's 2016–17 to 2018–19 seasons, the Wizards were twelfth of thirty teams. In specific categories, they placed eighth in *players* and *money*, fourteenth in the *market*, nineteenth in the *draft*, and twenty-third in *management*. With respect to other SED clubs, the Heat ranked sixth, Magic thirteenth, Hawks fifteenth, and Hornets twenty-third.[13]

In other words, Washington scored relatively high regarding the potential of its current players and factoring in expected departures, and also about their projected salary-cap ability and willingness to exceed the cap and pay a luxury tax; approximately average in appealing to future acquisitions based on team quality, franchise reputation, city's desirability as a destination, market size, taxes, business and entertainment opportunities, arena quality, and fans; but below average based on future draft picks and draft positioning, and the quality and stability of front office, ownership, and coaching.

FRANCHISE BUSINESS

Given the performances of them as teams, this section focuses on and examines the commercial aspects of NBA franchises including their principal owner or owners and also facts and other details in tables about each team's arena, various costs for families to attend home games, current and important financial data, and yearly trends in players' payrolls. In part, this information reveals why some franchises are more valuable and wealthy than others and therefore how successful or unsuccessful historically as business enterprises in the sports industry.[14]

Atlanta Hawks

Born into a Jewish family in 1959, Anthony "Tony" Ressler was one of five children. During the 1980s and after graduating from Georgetown University's School of Foreign Service and earning a Master's of Business Administration (MBA) degree from Columbia University's Graduate School of Business, he worked at Wall Street investment banking firm Drexel Burnham Lambert. Eventually, Tony became a senior vice president in the company's High Yield Bond Department with responsibility for the New Issue/Syndicate Desk. However, because of security violations, the firm filed for bankruptcy in 1990.[15]

During mid- to late 1990, Ressler co-founded investment firm Apollo Management with his wealthy brother-in-law Leon Black. Seven years later, Ressler started Ares Management, which manages billions in investor assets and lends money to companies and occasionally buys them. In fact, Ares's private-equity branch has acquired all or large portions of different businesses for many years.

After the media revealed that the Atlanta Hawks' principal owner Bruce Levenson had forwarded one or more racist messages online in late 2014, the club was offered for sale. Leading a group of investors—that consisted of former NBA all-star Grant Hill, Clayton Dubilier & Rice partner Rich Schnall, and billionaire Spanx founder Sara Blakely and her husband Jesse Itzler—Ressler acquired the team in mid-2015. The deal, which included ownership of Philips Arena in Atlanta, was significantly less than Levenson's $1 billion price to sell the team. When purchasing the Hawks franchise, Ressler also had a minority interest in MLB's Milwaukee Brewers.

Among other owners of EC teams as of early 2016, Ressler's Hawks tied for ninth in number of division titles, tied for eighth in conference titles, and tied for fifth in league championships. In comparison to all current team owners in the league and their clubs' performances, Atlanta respectively tied for twentieth (division titles), tied for fifteenth (conference titles), and tied for tenth (NBA championships). Given his relatively recent purchase of the franchise, Ressler needs more time than the league's 2015–16 season to establish a record and compete for titles and championships (table A2).

In ESPN's ranking of NBA teams' front offices and specifically their owners as of March 2015, the Hawks were twentieth following the division's Miami Heat (second) and Wizards (sixteenth) but ahead of the Magic (twenty-third) and Hornets (twenty-sixth). For Atlanta to rank higher in the future, Ressler and his ownership group and front office must improve their team's roster of players and guide the franchise to overall on-court success, both in the short and long term.[16]

During his first year as principal owner, Ressler spent time observing the Hawks' entire operation. He admits that owning a professional sports franchise is much more complicated than he first imagined. It is correct, therefore, if you call him foolish or naive. Although a modest-sized business to a billionaire who co-founded two private equity firms, there are major concerns including negotiating player's contracts, upgrading basketball operations, vending good food and beverages, ensuring efficient parking, establishing sponsorships, implementing arena management policies, and scheduling attractive non-basketball events at Philips Arena.

Ressler has full trust in those in charge of different aspects of the organization. In fact, his group relies on the success of such people as president of basketball operations and head coach Mike Budenholzer, general manager Wes Wilcox, chief executive officer Steve Koonin, and executive vice presidents Thad Sheely, Andrew Saltzman, and Scott Wilkinson. But now, Ressler will become more involved and put together a roster of players capable of competing for a championship.[17]

Team Financials

According to financial data published in *Forbes* magazine about NBA teams as of their 2015–16 season, the Hawks' estimated market value was $825 million, revenue $142 million, operating income $7 million, gate receipts $30 million, debt-to-value 30 percent, and players expenses $67 million. Among only EC clubs, Atlanta had ranked twelfth in market value, tied for eleventh with the Hornets in revenue, twelfth in operating income, tenth in gate receipts, first in debt-to-value, and thirteenth in players expenses (table A3).

Within only the SED, the Hawks had lower amounts than the Heat but the highest debt-to-value of the group. In comparison to twenty-nine other NBA clubs, Atlanta ranked twenty-fourth (market value), tied for twenty-third (revenue), twenty-fifth (operating income), tied for twentieth (gate receipts), first (debt ratio), and tied for twenty-sixth (players expenses). Based on these results, this is a relatively low-valued franchise with below-average financial data because of its location, historical performances, and other demographic, economic, and sport-specific factors.

Besides market size, salary inflation, and other factors, an NBA team's annual payroll partly reflects its commitment to players and their current and potential contribution individually and as a group to winning games in regular seasons and postseasons. From 2011 to 2015, for example, the Hawks' payroll among fourteen EC teams ranged in rank from fourth in 2011 ($70.6 million) to thirteenth in 2014 ($58.4 million). Within the SED, the club had the second, third, or fourth highest payroll in the group during 2011–2013 and 2015 but also lowest amount in 2014 (table A4).

In comparison to all NBA teams, Atlanta was respectively tied for seventh with the Detroit Pistons in 2011, thirteenth in 2012 ($66.6 million), twenty-fifth in 2013 ($58.2 million), twenty-seventh in 2014, and twenty-second in 2015 ($71.6 million). Given these amounts, the Hawks decided to decrease and increase payroll each twice despite appearing in five consecutive playoffs during the period. To be consistently competitive in the future, however, the team needs to keep its payroll at least among the top fifteen in the league.

With Dwight Howard's salary being greater than $23 million each season from 2016–17 to 2018–19 and Paul Millsap's at least $20 million for two years and Kent Bazemore's $15–$19 million for four, there is a large difference between their amounts and those other players on the roster. Based on this distribution of salaries, the Hawks expect Howard, Millsap, and Bazemore to be outstanding by scoring most points and getting a majority of rebounds for the team to win enough games in regular seasons to qualify for and advance in the conference playoffs.[18]

Philips Arena

Opened in 1999 to replace the Omni, the 18,700-seat Philips Arena is situated on the east side of downtown, right next to or near the Georgia Dome, Georgia Convention Center, CNN Center, and Centennial Park. Inside the arena are concourses with plenty of merchandise and concession stands. The major merchandise store is located near the CNN Center entrance of the venue. In the lower concourse is the "HawkWalk," a prime area to find concessions, merchandise, and other things.[19]

While the arena bowl is a two-level seating area with suites, the building diverges in a major way from others when it comes to club seats and suite locations. Instead of the traditional suites and club seats between the upper and lower seating areas, Philips Arena has all club seats—consisting of the entire lower seating level—on one sideline with four levels of suites atop overlooking the club seats.

There is a four-sided Phillips videoboard in the center of the building along with dot matrix boards above the seating area at each end zone supplying statistics and out-of-town scores. The LED ribbon boards run around the circumference of the balcony and are complemented by companion boards at the base of the center scoreboard. The Hawks have three retired numbers including one for Bob Pettit, from the club's days in St. Louis, and others for Lou Hudson and Dominique Wilkins. They also have banners commemorating their division titles won while in Atlanta.

Among venues of fourteen other EC teams as of early 2016, the Hawks' Philips Arena tied for eighth in age with homes of the Raptors, Pacers, and Heat, tied for seventh in construction cost with the Heat's American Airlines Arena, and ranked eighth in value at $198 million. In comparison to all NBA teams' venues, Atlanta's tied for fourteenth (age), tied for twelfth (construction cost), and placed sixteenth (value). Consequently, the Hawks play their home games in a relatively middle-aged facility that needs more and better amenities for fans to generate additional revenue for the franchise (table A5).

For several years a Chicago-based company named Team Marketing Report (TMR) has prepared and published a Fan Cost Index (FCI) for the home games of teams in professional sports leagues. To attend a game for a typical family with two kids, an FCI includes the costs of four average-priced tickets, two cheapest-priced draft beers, four each cheapest-priced soft drinks and hot dogs, parking for one car, and two each game programs and least-expensive, adult-size adjustable caps. Costs are determined by telephone calls with team representatives, venues and concessionaires, and from questions asked during interviews.[20]

In the 2011–2015 NBA seasons, the FCIs for a family to attend a regular-season game at Philips Arena ranged from a low of $233 in 2012 to a high of $255 in 2015. With respect to amounts of all NBA teams, the Hawks ranked twenty-fourth in 2011 ($238) and twenty-sixth during 2012–2015 (table A6).

To reveal specific costs for a recent season in the NBA, the Hawks' FCI in 2015–16 was 4 percent more than in 2014–15. Listed from most to least in amount by item for one person, the team's tickets averaged $36–$37, a cap $18, parking one vehicle $12, a single beer $9 and hot dog $6, and a soft drink between $4 and $5.

Among other teams in the conference's SED, they had rankings and FCIs from most to least as follows: Heat fifth at $465; Wizards fourteenth at $322; Magic twenty-fourth at $263; and Hornets thirtieth at $212. Consequently, Hawks' fans paid less at games in Philips Arena than those of twenty-five other teams in their arenas.

The cheapest ticket cost $14 for a fan to watch a Hawks' home game in 2015–16. This was about $2 or about 12 percent less than the league's average for a cheap seat. Also, since the club's FCI was $84 below the amount of a typical NBA team, a family of four purchased tickets and enjoyed a basketball game in Atlanta at a significant discount relative to the majority of arenas within the league. These costs and prices, in turn, were set by the Hawks organization to earn more revenue and maximize profit from their operations.

Business Highlights

Besides regular-season and postseason games, NBA franchises are involved in—and affected by—community events and business-related affairs, news, and projects. The following are a few of them for Atlanta's popular, but from a financial perspective, below-average professional basketball team.[21]

First, although the NBA is male-dominated both on the court and in the boardroom, Hawks Chief Diversity and Inclusion Officer Nzinga Shaw is working to change that dynamic.

Serving as the league's first-ever diversity chief, Shaw stepped into her role with the Hawks in December 2014. In this role, the Spelman College alum is responsible for creating an inclusive culture across all business units for both the Hawks and Philips Arena as it relates to employee engagement, fan engagement, and strategic partnerships.

Second, announced in March 2016, the Hawks and Sentient Jet—a Directional Aviation Capital company—established a multiyear partnership agreement. As the official private jet partner of the team, Sentient Jet will launch an exclusive Atlanta Hawks-themed flight card and receive entitlement of the recently designated Sentient Jet owner's lounge inside Philips Arena, and also host on-site hospitality events with Hawks players and team management. The partnership marks the third NBA team sponsorship for the company.

Third, during late 2014, the Hawks organization disbanded its "board of ambassadors"—a one-year-old coalition of business and civic leaders aimed at generating community support for the city's professional basketball team. The group, which included about three dozen leaders from all walks of life, hoped to build stronger bridges between the business community and basketball franchise with the long-term goal of selling more season tickets and corporate sponsorships, and generating excitement in the team. However, its 2014–15 season became mired in controversy when problems went public after disclosing that Hawks general manager Danny Ferry made racially derogatory remarks in a telephone conversation with other NBA team owners.

Fourth, 2015 was a very good year according to Hawks CEO Steve Koonin and chief revenue officer Andrew Saltzman. That was because season ticket sales tripled, albeit from a very low level, to more than 9,000 and that eighteen new corporate sponsors came on board with deals generally in the mid- to high six figures. In a harbinger of upcoming priorities, the Hawks hired a new chief financial and real estate officer, Thad Sheely, who had previously worked on major stadium and arena projects as an executive with the NFL New York Jets and NBA Heat. His job description with the Hawks includes strategic leadership in construction of a practice facility and renovation of the arena.

Fifth, the Hawks were recognized as a top performer and sports industry leader in social media management. In 2015, for example, *Sports Illustrated* ranked them in their "Top 100 sports follow" list, as the number one follow in the NBA, and one of only three sports teams to make the Top 100 besides the NHL Los Angeles Kings and Team USA. Website Bleacher Report also ranked them the number one sports team follower in 2015 and the NBA league office provided a Digital Innovator award to the organization. For how to win in social media, the team first created a strategy and then defined its voice to followers, collaborated departmentally across the business, and worked fluidly and fast.

Charlotte Hornets

After his six-year tenure as majority owner of the NBA's thirtieth franchise, Black Entertainment Television (BET) founder Bob Johnson sold the Charlotte Bobcats for approximately $175 million in early 2010 to a syndicate led by basketball Hall of Famer Michael Jordan. Although the club had losing records during the league's 2004–5 to 2008–9 seasons, it finished fourth among SED teams in 2009–10 and qualified for the playoffs but lost in the conference's first round.

As an owner, Johnson was frequently criticized in the media for not attending enough Bobcats home games and spending too much time with his other business investments. In 2001, he sold BET to Viacom for $3 billion and then in 2010, decided to sell his NBA team after several years of financial losses. Jordan, who served as chief of basketball operations and a minority owner in the franchise, won championships while playing at the University of North Carolina and with the Chicago Bulls. Thus, he was familiar with the Bobcats—renamed Hornets in 2014—and their economic and sport-specific problems.

Among owners of fourteen other EC teams as of early 2016, Jordan's Hornets tied for ninth in winning division titles, tied for eighth in conference titles, and tied for fifth in number of championships. With respect to all NBA teams and their current owners, his respectively tied for twentieth (division titles), tied for fifteenth (conference titles), and tied for tenth (championships). Thus, Jordan has been a mediocre owner since 2010 although some of his teams improved their performances in regular-season games and became more popular while existing in a small market (table A2).

According to a recent report, Jordan rated as the league's twenty-sixth best owner. His relatively low ranking among twenty-nine others was justified as follows:

> *Everyone* is doubting his [Jordan's] competence as the owner of the Charlotte Hornets as things have been very bad basically ever since he took over the team. MJ has signed off on some terrible deals over the years, most notably the contract he gave to Lance Stephenson only to instantly regret it. Every time the Hornets have a high lottery pick, like in 2013, speculation immediately begins as to how Jordan and his front office will screw it up. There are other owners who are running their teams into the ground, but MJ has been doing it much longer and has created a special level of awful when it comes to being an owner. His ownership legacy isn't sealed, and the Hornets made some good moves this summer [2015], but MJ is far ways away from being considered a good professional sports owner.[22]

In early 2014, various sports bankers estimated the Hornets' worth to be between $600 million and $625 million. *Forbes* magazine, therefore, used $600 million to calculate Jordan's wealth. Because the team had $135 million of debt, this made Jordan's equity worth $416 million. After subtracting the cash Jordan invested in the team, *Forbes* estimated his net worth outside of the Hornets to be $600 million, giving him a total worth of at least $1 billion.[23]

Team Financials

Based on financial information published in early 2016 about NBA franchises, the Hornets' estimated market value was $750 million, revenue $142 million, operating income $3 million, gate receipts $24 million, debt-to-value 20 percent, and players expenses $82 million. Among only EC teams, Charlotte ranked thirteenth in both market value and operating income, tied for eleventh with the Hawks in revenue and the Bucks in gate receipts, fifth in debt-to-value, and eighth in players expenses (table A3).

Within the SED, the Hornets had smaller amounts than the Heat but not with other teams for some financial data. In comparison to twenty-nine other NBA clubs, Charlotte was respectively twenty-sixth (market value), tied for twenty-third (revenue), twenty-eighth (operating income), tied for twenty-fifth (gate receipts), seventh (debt ratio), and thirteenth (players expenses). Based on these results, the Hornets are below average financially in the league and an inferior business with too much debt and not enough income and revenue from gate receipts and other sources.

Besides market size, salary inflation, and other factors, an NBA team's annual payroll partly reflects its commitment to players and their current and potential contribution individually and as a group to winning games in regular seasons and postseasons. From 2011 to 2015, for example, the Hornets' payroll among fourteen EC teams ranged in rank from eighth in 2015 ($76.8 million) to fourteenth in 2012 ($57.4 million). Within the SED, the club had the smallest payroll in the group during 2012 but then third highest in 2013–2015 and fourth in 2011 (table A4).

In comparison to all NBA teams as of early 2016, Charlotte ranked as low as fifteenth in 2015 to a high of twenty-sixth in 2012. To be more competitive and challenge rivals, owner Michael Jordan increased the team's payroll for four seasons, which in turn contributed to its winning records and playoff appearances in 2014 and 2016.

With respect to salary commitments to a few well-paid Hornets players as of mid- to late 2016, veteran Nicholas Batum is guaranteed about $92.8

million, three others each from $36 million to $39 million, Jeremy Lamb $21 million, and Marco Belinelli $12.6 million. Consequently, the club will depend on these players for at least three seasons to produce enough wins to make the playoffs and perhaps compete for and win a conference title.[24]

Time Warner Cable Arena

Opened in 2005 to replace the obsolete Charlotte Coliseum, the 19,100-seat Time Warner Cable Arena (TWCA) became home to the NBA Hornets and WNBA Sting. Located near office buildings, restaurants, stores, and two city transit terminals, the venue plays host to a variety of events that range from college basketball games and tournaments to popular concerts and family shows.

The building was originally designed to represent the Charlotte area's diverse urban culture as well as the strength, stability, and foundation of the city's heritage. Contemporary elements highlight Charlotte's focus on—and anticipation of—excitement for the city, team, and arena. The architectural highlight of the building is a crescent "C" shape surrounding a large portion of the arena, beginning at the entry lobby on Trade Street and sweeping around the building toward Fifth Street. The "C" serves as a symbol of community unity and as a welcome icon for arena patrons.

Besides a number of founder and private suites, loge boxes, and club and courtside seats, the arena contains areas with special amenities. These include such things as a 6,000-square-foot sports bar on the main concourse; 3,400-square-foot team store at a main entry; 2,000-square-foot uptown terrace in the upper concourse over the lobby; general terraces with one each on the main concourse, loge level, and suite level; two additional terraces on the upper concourse; 5,000-square-foot fan interactive zone on the upper concourse; and a loge-level restaurant with premium seating and views into the seating bowl.

Among those of other teams in the EC as of early 2016, TWCA is the twelfth oldest, fourth highest in construction costs, and thirteenth most valuable. In comparison to twenty-nine NBA arenas, the Hornets' home is ranked twenty-seventh (age), seventh (cost), and twenty-sixth (value). According to these criteria, publicly owned TWCA is an attractive and relatively young and modern basketball facility with plenty of amenities for fans to generate revenue for teams and excitement in the community (table A5).

In the 2011–2015 NBA seasons, the FCIs for a family to attend a regular-season game at TWCA ranged from a low of $203 in 2011–2013 to a high of $212 in 2014 and 2015. With respect to those of all NBA teams, the Hornets' home games ranked twenty-ninth in 2011 to thirtieth during 2012–2015 (table A6).

To reveal specific costs for a recent season in the NBA, the Hornets' FCI in 2015–16 was the same as in 2014–15. Listed from most to least in amount by item for one person, the team's tickets averaged between $30 and $31, a cap $18, single beer $6–$7, parking one vehicle $5, and a hot dog and soft drink each between $4 and $5.

Among other teams in the conference's SED, they had rankings and FCIs from most to least as follows: Heat fifth at $465; Wizards fourteenth at $322; Magic twenty-fourth at $263; and Hawks twenty-sixth at $255. Consequently, Hornets' fans paid less at games in TWCA than those of twenty-nine other teams in their arenas.

The cheapest ticket cost $8 for a fan to watch a Hornets' home game in 2015–16. This was almost $8 or 50 percent less than the league's average for a cheap seat. Also, since the club's FCI was $127 below the amount of a typical NBA team, a family of four purchased tickets and enjoyed a basketball game in Atlanta at a significant discount relative to the majority of arenas within the league. These costs and prices, in turn, were set by the Hornets organization to earn additional revenue and maximize profit from their operations.

According to a recent survey of NBA teams' arenas, TWCA ranked nineteenth best among them. The comments about its aesthetics and fan experiences were as follows:

> This arena would not be nearly so high if it weren't for the boss court design. The honeycomb two-tone wood combined with a "Buzz City" logo combined one of the best color palettes in the league make the Hornets distinctive and generally likeable. If you have to pay $12 [now $6.50] for a beer, you better have an arena where the energy is palpable. Fortunately, the home of the Charlotte Hornets is that arena. The entrances/exits cause a good deal of chaos, so if you visit be prepared for a rush in and out. Much like Time Warner Cable, the arena pushes hard against the customer, with high prices and low convenience, but still provides a product just good enough not to quit.[25]

Business Highlights

Besides regular-season and postseason games, NBA franchises are involved in—and affected by—community events and business-related affairs, news, and projects. The following are a few of them for Charlotte's popular, but from a financial perspective, below-average professional basketball team.[26]

First, in a major economic blow to the city, the NBA moved the 2017 All-Star Weekend out of Charlotte over concerns about the state's House Bill 2 (HB2), as the latest and perhaps most high-profile fallout from the controversial law. While the league said the event is moving to a yet-to-be-determined alternate city (New Orleans), the NBA has assured the Hornets that the 2019 event will return to Charlotte if issues involving HB2 are resolved. Hornets president Fred Whitfield told the *Charlotte Observer* that the NBA has no plans to put 2019—the next available All-Star Weekend—out for general bid.

The NBA's decision raises questions about future sporting events in Charlotte. The National Collegiate Athletic Association (NCAA), which has men's basketball tournament games planned in North Carolina in 2017 and 2018, recently adopted an anti-discrimination requirement for sites bidding on NCAA events. Furthermore, the PGA Championship is scheduled to be at Charlotte's Quail Hollow Club in 2017.

Second, the Hornets announced in December 2015 that the team reached a multiyear agreement with Grant Thornton LLP to become the club's official accounting firm. The Hornets and Grant Thornton entered into a multiyear advertising arrangement that includes renaming of the Crown Club as the "Grant Thornton Crown Club." The agreement is the franchise's first in the accounting category. Grant Thornton provides accounting services for Hornets Sports & Entertainment. The firm will also enter into an entitlement agreement for the recently renovated and renamed Crown Club, which is an exclusive lounge area located on TWCA's event level for Hardwood Club, Courtside, and Inner Circle Club ticket holders.

Third, during June 2014, the Hornets joined the ranks of NBA franchises to have floor apron sponsorships, unveiling a multiyear agreement with Novant Health.Financial. North Carolina-based Novant is a founding sponsor of the franchise. Along with putting the company's name in front of both teams' benches, the new, enhanced deal includes suite-level branding inside TWCA. The sponsorship was unveiled as part of the team's debuting its rebranded court, reflecting the team's name change from Bobcats to Hornets.

Fourth, the Bobcats signed Blue Cross and Blue Shield (BCBS) of North Carolina as title sponsor for the team's training camp as of 2013. The multiyear sponsorship was part of a larger renewal signed by the company with the team. BCBS had branding at UNC-Asheville's Kimmel Arena, where the team trained on campus. The company used training camp for hospitality and community events. It also was the title sponsor for two Bobcats preseason games—one in Asheville and the other in Greensboro.

Fifth, in June 2010, video game maker 2K Sports signed its first NBA team sponsorship deal with the Bobcats, an agreement that came as the company featured owner Michael Jordan on the cover of its upcoming "NBA 2K11" game. The agreement gave 2K Sports signage inside TWCA, promotion during the team's home games, digital presence on website bobcats.com, and product placement inside the team store. In addition, 2K Sports held its "NBA 2K11" release during the club's home opener with the video game sampled at the arena and promoted on the team's LED boards and scoreboard.

Miami Heat

Born in 1949 to an Israeli-American businessman and chairman of the world's largest cruise operator, Micky Arison followed his education with a two-year stint in the Carnival Cruise Lines sales department. After becoming reservations manager in 1974, he took over the post of vice president of passenger traffic in 1976 and three years later became president of the corporation.

In 1987 the company went public, and generated $400 million for future expansion. As Carnival continued its growth through the traditional avenue of new ship construction, Arison also sought to expand the company's cruise operations by entering new market segments of the industry. In 1990, he was appointed chairman of the board of directors. As chairman, he oversaw diversified travel and tourism holdings including cruise ships serving virtually every market segment.

During February 1995, the Arison family bought out minority shareholders Billy Cunningham and Lewis Schaffel, which gave Ted Arison's wife Marilyn approximately 88 percent of the club. As a result, their son Micky was subsequently named managing general partner of the franchise. After his father Ted died in 1999, Micky continued his leadership role of the Miami Heat's operations.

Among fourteen other owners of EC teams as of early 2016, the Arison's Heat (1988–2016) ranked first in division titles and also second in both winning its conference and number of NBA championships. In comparison to owners of all NBA clubs, Miami tied for second with Peter Holt's Spurs (division titles) and also placed fourth (conference titles and championships). Because of his club's success in regular seasons and postseasons, Micky Arison has been a very productive owner of the franchise (table A2).

Among his peers in 2015, Micky Arison was third best as an NBA owner. According to one expert, the reasons for him being ranked so high are as follows:

> Say what you will about the Miami Heat and their stingy fans, they have one of the best owners in all of basketball. Mickey [Micky] Arison knows how to put a winning team together, and that extends far beyond just assembling winning pieces to put on the court on a given night. The man has learned how to let Pat Riley do his thing and that's been a major reason why the Heat has been dominant over the years. Sure, they landed LeBron James, which was huge, but Arison has been a part of a winning culture far beyond that. Riley gets the credit for putting the teams together but Arison needs to get credit for knowing how to not go full Dan Gilbert on things and get too involved. There's a balance between being James Dolan levels of involved in your team and being in the position Arison is in—and it looks like he's going to stay on the right side of that for a very long time.[27]

Team Financials

According to financial data published in *Forbes* magazine as of NBA teams' 2015–16 season, the Heat's market value was $1.3 billion, revenue $180 million, operating income $20 million, gate receipts $67 million, debt-to-value 7 percent, and players expenses $89 million. Among only EC franchises, Miami ranked respectively fourth in market value, sixth in revenue, seventh in operating income, third in gate receipts, thirteenth in its debt ratio, and tied for second with the Wizards in players expenses. Within only the SED, the club had the highest amounts except for operating income (table A3).

In comparison to the league's other twenty-nine clubs, the Heat was respectively ninth twice (market value and revenue) and also tied for fifteenth (operating income), sixth (gate receipts), tied for twenty-third (debt-to-value), and tied for fifth (players expenses). Based on these results, Miami is financially among the top third of NBA teams and a profitable business especially regarding its market value, revenue, and gate receipts.

With respect to another financial topic from 2011 to 2015, the Heats' payroll among fourteen EC teams ranged in rank from second in both 2011 ($76.2 million) and 2012 ($83.0 million) to fifth in 2014 ($75.6 million) and 2015 ($85.7 million). Within only the SED, the club had the highest payroll each year (table A4).

In comparison to all NBA teams' payrolls as of early 2016, Miami ranked as low as third in both 2012 and 2013 to a high of tenth in 2015. To be competitive and challenge rivals, owner Micky Arison significantly increased his team's payroll in 2012 and 2015. This strategy, in turn, contributed to the team's four division and three conference titles and its two championships.

American Airlines Arena

Opened in 1999 to replace the outdated Miami Arena, the 20,000-seat American Airlines Arena (AAA) has both interior and exterior features. Among the former is a view of the city skyline and bay from all concourses; public terraces/balconies from all concourses; private terraces with center court suites; restaurant/bar with interior view of the bowl; and a multiple purpose practice court with views of the bay.

Regarding exterior amenities, these include such things as direct access to parking from premium seating; bayside landscaped terrace with outdoor café, bar, and informal activity space; parking space concealed below arena; link with Bayside Market Place via a pedestrian bridge; artistic exterior lighting and graphics concept integral to the architectural design; transparency from city and bay into inner life of arena; and design emphasis on the unique opportunity of utilizing tropical outdoors.

Among arenas of fourteen conference teams as of early 2016, AAA tied for eighth with three other venues in age, tied for seventh with the Hawks' Philips Arena in construction cost, and ranked fifth in value at $308 million. Of all NBA arenas, Miami's was respectively tied for fourteenth (age), tied for twelfth (construction cost), and tenth (value). Thus, the Heat plays its games at home in an attractive but aging venue with plenty of interior and exterior amenities for fans to enjoy while rooting for their club to win more titles and championships (table A5).

In the 2011–2015 NBA seasons, the FCIs for a family to attend a regular-season game at AAA ranged from a low of $423 in 2011 to a high of $472 in 2013. With respect to those of all NBA teams, the Heat's home games ranked third most expensive during 2011–2013 to fifth at $465 in 2015 (table A6).

To reveal specific costs for a recent season in the NBA, the Heats' FCI in 2015–16 at AAA was about 1 percent lower than in 2014–15. Listed from most to least in amount by item for one person, the team's tickets averaged between $76 and $77, parking one vehicle $35, a cap $18 and program $10, single beer $8, and a hot dog $7 and soft drink $5.

The cheapest ticket cost $15 for a fan to watch a Heats' home game in 2015–16. This was almost $1 or 6 percent less than the league's average for a cheap seat. Yet, since the club's FCI was $126 above the amount of a typical NBA team, a family of four purchased regular tickets and enjoyed a basketball game at AAA in Miami at a significant premium relative to the majority of arenas within the league. These costs and prices, in turn, were set by the Heat's organization to earn more revenue and maximize profit from their operations.

Because of its location and various amenities, AAA ranks sixteenth best in the league. Based on a recent overview, it appeals to fans for the following reasons:

> The most impressive color combo in sports is red and black with the Heat among the best at using it. As a result, going to a game as an away fan at the Triple-A has the feeling of taking a journey with Dante and Virgil to the pit of hell. As a Heat fan, it's the same except you get to be the Devil. Going to a Miami Heat game means that you are set to have a good time, from the location right in downtown Miami to the fan base that is still electrifying in the post-LeBron era now that the fluff is gone. There's also easy access to parking, and perhaps the best food of any NBA arena. Overall, this is an ideal experience for the casual fan.[28]

Business Highlights

Besides regular-season and postseason games, NBA franchises are involved in—and affected by—community events and business-related affairs, news, and projects. The following are a few of them for Miami's popular, financially secure, and valuable but successful professional basketball team.[29]

First, five international business students with Professor Kenneth Cortsen published an article online during late 2013 about the Heat and role of brand positioning. More specifically, the group investigated and explained how supporters, including sports fans, mentally position their club in an imaginative map. The brand of the Heat, for example, has a specific place in supporters' perceptional world. To position themselves positively in the "map," sports organizations like the Heat must work and develop their brand awareness, image, equity, and loyalty.

Second, Entercom Communications announced on August 1, 2016 that 790 The Ticket renewed and extended its partnership with the Heat in a five-year agreement through 2021. The team's games and related programming, which have been on 790 The Ticket since the league's 2010–11 season, will remain on the station into the next decade and broadcast by Mike Inglis and John Crotty to the audience. While Tommy Tighe provides pre-game, half-time, and post-game reporting, Jonathan Zaslow—host of the popular Ticket morning show—serves as host of The Ticket pre-game and post-game shows.

Third, as of early 2015, the Heat was about to lose a discounted deal on public waterfront behind its county-owned arena. Miami-Dade officials realized the county had been significantly undercharging the team to rent a five-acre wedge of land next to AAA, which the Heat uses for valet parking, event staging, and even elephant habitat when the circus comes to town. A recent county study recommended nearly tripling the rent, which would generate an extra $150,000 annually for Miami-Dade. Because the Heat opposed the higher rent, the issue revived tensions over a vacant lot that has drawn controversy since the early days of the arena.

Fourth, AAA's Executive Vice President Kim Stone made her mark by playing a key role in growing the Heat's business. Bookings, for example, ranked among the top three years since the facility opened more than fifteen years ago, even though the team missed the NBA playoffs and cost the venue some dates. Stone is also involved in running the team's basketball business, where the Heat preserved its season ticket base after LeBron James left South Florida to return to Cleveland before the 2014–15 NBA season. Despite James's departure and the Heat's failure to make the postseason, Miami's season ticket renewal rate remained above 90 percent.

Fifth, NBA teams have started making the renewal of season tickets as easy as a couple of keystrokes on your phone. In 2016, the Heat began selling renewals through their mobile app. The team's new offering takes fans from the app to a proprietary customized payment center. As a result, fans in Miami are able to complete their renewals fully through their phones. But there is also something lost in the process, and that could in part explain why app-based season ticket renewals have been uncharted territory until now. Taking renewals through the app is convenient, but you miss a fan touch point. If a fan is positive on what they want, it is a no-brainer, but you are missing a chance to up-sell or to add on seats.

Orlando Magic

Born in Grand Rapids, Michigan, in 1926, Richard DeVos was educated at Calvin College and served in the United States Army Air Corps during World War II. Eight years after he and partner Jay Van Andel formed Ja-Ri Corporation to import wooden goods from South American companies, their organization had over 5,000 distributors. Subsequently, they started Amway Sales Corporation to procure and inventory products and handle the sales and marketing plan, and also launched Amway Services Corporation to handle insurance and other benefits for distributors.

After previously owning three International Hockey League (IHL) clubs and then failing to acquire a MLB team to play at home in Orlando, DeVos became interested in the Magic. When owners Bob Hewitt and Bill DuPont offered the Magic for sale, DeVos and his family—wife, three sons, and son-in-law—purchased the franchise for approximately $85 million in 1991.

Among owners of EC teams as of the league's 2015–16 season, DeVos's Magic won enough games to finish fifth in division titles, tied for third with the Celtics' Wycliffe Grousbeck and Cavaliers' Dan Gilbert in conference titles, and tied for fifth with ten others in NBA championships. In comparison to all clubs and their current owners, Orlando tied for eighth (division titles), tied for fifth (conference titles), and tied for tenth (championships). Since 1991, DeVos has been successful periodically in leading his franchise to victories in regular seasons and postseasons (table A2).

In 2015, ESPN asked a panel to rate each NBA team's owner or group of owners in terms of guiding their franchise to overall on-court success, both in the short and long term. The Magic's DeVos placed twenty-third and compared to others in the SED, he finished behind the Heat's Micky Arison (second), Wizards' Ted Leonsis (sixteenth), Hawks' Michael Gearon Jr. (twentieth), but ahead of the Hornets' Michael Jordan (twenty-sixth). Additionally, the Magic's front office also rated twenty-third according to the panel.[30]

Given his overall on- and off-the-court contributions to the team and organization, years of service, impact in the community, and general character, DeVos was inducted into the club's Hall of Fame during early 2016. As such, he became the fourth member honored following senior vice president

Pat Williams, community ambassador Nick Anderson, and former player Shaquille O'Neal.

Team Financials

Based on financial information published in *Forbes* magazine during early 2016, the Magic's estimated market was $900 million, revenue $143 million, operating income $35 million, gate receipts $34 million, debt-to-value 17 percent, and players expenses $66 million. Among only EC teams and their results, Orlando ranked ninth in market value, tenth in revenue, fourth in operating income, eighth in both gate receipts and the debt ratio, and fourteenth in players expenses. Within only the conference's SED, the Magic had the highest operating income but lowest players expenses (table A3).

With respect to twenty-nine other NBA teams as of their 2015–16 season, Orlando's data was nineteenth (market value), twenty-second (revenue), seventh (operating income), eighteenth (gate receipts), twelfth (debt-to-value), and twenty-eighth (players expenses). According to these results, the Magic is a below-average NBA franchise and business enterprise from a financial perspective but, for various reasons, above average in generating income from its operations.

Besides market size, salary inflation, and other factors, an NBA team's annual payroll partly reflects its commitment to players and their current and potential contribution individually and as a group to winning games in regular seasons and postseasons. From 2011 to 2015, for example, the Magic's payroll among fourteen EC teams ranged in rank from sixth in 2011 ($68.5 million) to fifteenth in 2015 ($62.3 million). Within the SED, the club had the third, fourth, or fifth highest payroll in the group during the period (table A4).

In comparison to all NBA teams, Orlando's amounts were respectively—from 2011 to 2015—eleventh, sixteenth, twenty-seventh, twenty-sixth, and twenty-ninth. After the club's payroll fell in 2012, it finished with a losing record and fifth four times in the SED. Unless DeVos increases the team's budget especially for players' salaries, the Magic will not be competitive enough to win many games in regular seasons and qualify for the conference's playoffs.

The Magic will likely exceed the NBA 2016–17 season's salary cap of $94.13 million by more than $10 million. Counting those players with free-agent agreements, it has contractual obligations with thirteen of them. While a team may carry a maximum of fifteen players on its roster during the regular season, Orlando will use cap space to sign point guard D. J. Augustin, center Bismack Biyombo, and forward Jeff Green. Also, the team will use its Bird rights for Evan Fournier to exceed the cap. Because the NBA set its luxury tax level at just over $113 million, the Magic is not in danger of paying it.

Amway Center

Opened in 2010 to replace the obsolete Amway Arena, the 18,500-seat Amway Center has fifteen stories and features a dramatic glass tower and an outdoor public balcony twice as big as its basketball court. The 800,000-square-foot building contains restaurants and bars in the interior along with restaurants and retail space accessible from the street when there are no games or events. Regarding the exterior, the new design incorporates a 20,000-square-foot, glass-front entryway facing Church Street and a 151-foot glass tower facing Interstate 4 (I-4).

A prominent element of the structure is balconies. One of them—the largest at 10,000 square feet—sits thirty-eight feet above the ground and several feet higher than the raised deck of I-4 as it passes by. The glass tower, meanwhile, features a second but smaller deck more than 100 feet above the ground with a sky bar. Instead of skyboxes along the roof line, between the three bowl levels are a row of luxury suites along with several other specialty suites.

While only 15 percent of the seats are premium, the Magic's premium-ticket holders have access to other events including concerts and college sports games. A public parking garage connected to the arena via a raised walkway has most spaces set aside for players and high-priced ticket holders. In contrast, the majority of fans must park in other nearby garages and lots or arrive via a nearby commuter rail station.

Among venues of other EC teams, the Amway Center is both the third youngest and most expensive and also tenth in value. In comparison to those of all clubs in the NBA, the arena ranks third (age), sixth (construction cost), and twenty-first (value). Based on these variables, the Magic play their home games in a modern facility with plenty of amenities to generate revenue for the franchise. For its first year in operation, city commissioners reported the Amway Center had a profit of almost $1 million. Even after some non-departmental expenses were included, the venue had a bottom line of more than $584,000 (table A5).

In the 2011–2015 NBA seasons, the FCIs for a family to attend a regular-season game at the Amway Center ranged from a low of $263 during 2013 through 2015 to a high of $275 in 2011. With respect to those of all NBA teams, the Magic's home games ranked between a tie for sixteenth in 2011 to twenty-fourth in 2015 (table A6).

To reveal specific costs for a recent season in the NBA, the Magic's FCI at the Amway Center in 2015–16 was $263 or approximately the same as in 2014–15. Listed from most to least in amount by item for one person, the team's tickets averaged between $39 and $40, a cap $20, parking one vehicle $10, single beer about $6, a program $5, and a hot dog and soft drink each $4–$5.

Among other teams in the conference's SED, they had rankings and FCIs from most to least as follows: Heat fifth at $465; Wizards fourteenth at $322; Hawks twenty-sixth at $255; and Hornets thirtieth at $212. Consequently, Magic's fans paid less at games in the Amway Center than those of twenty-three other teams in their arenas.

The cheapest ticket cost $12 for a fan to watch Magic's home game in 2015–16. This was about $4 or about 32 percent less than the league's average for a cheap seat. Also, since the club's FCI was $76 below the amount of a typical NBA team, a family of four purchased tickets and enjoyed a pro basketball game in Orlando at a significant discount relative to the majority of arenas within the league. These costs and prices, in turn, were set by the Magic's organization to earn additional revenue and maximize profit from their operations.

Business Highlights

Besides regular-season and postseason games, NBA franchises are involved in—and affected by—community events and business-related affairs, news, and projects. The following are a few of them for Orlando's popular but mediocre and financially below-average professional basketball team.[31]

First, the Magic uses computer software to study the resale ticket market in order to (a) price tickets better, (b) predict season ticket holders at risk of defection, (c) analyze concession and product merchandise sales to make sure the organization has what fans want every time they enter the arena, and (d) help coaches put together the best lineup. For example, when analytics showed the team that 80 percent of revenue was from season ticket holders, it decided to take a proactive approach to renewals and at-risk accounts. This allowed the club to better understand data mining tools and develop analytic models to predict season ticket holder renewals based on such things as tenure, ticket use, and secondary market activity.

Second, the franchise sold a ticket package called the Fall Fast Break Pass (FFBP) during the 2014–15 season. Fans could buy a ticket to eight games in October and November for a total of $49 or a ticket to eleven games for $70. They received their tickets on their mobile devices but did not learn the location of each game's ticket until arriving at the arena. If there was a high demand for tickets to a night game, an FFBP purchaser might be assigned a seat in the upper deck. If there was a minimal demand for tickets, an FFBP buyer might be assigned a seat in the lower bowl. Team officials sold 1,500 of these passes for the season, which equated to about 15,000 tickets overall. The program appealed to a group of fans, mostly Millennials, who never had previously bought seats from the team.

Third, in late 2013, the Magic and Fox Sports Florida (FSF) finalized a ten-year contract extension that made FSF the team's local television rights holder through the 2025–26 NBA season. Although officials did not release the financial details of the agreement, an industry source said the Magic ranks among the top quarter of NBA teams in local television revenue.

According to Nielsen, the Orlando-Daytona Beach-Melbourne market is the eighteenth largest television market in the United States.

Fourth, during the spring of 2016, the NBA's Board of Governors approved a three-year pilot program allowing teams to sell a corporate logo on their jerseys. Can you imagine a small Mickey Mouse on the corner of the Magic's jersey or the Amway logo—a company co-founded by Magic owner Richard DeVos? Or, assume the Walt Disney Company has a sponsorship agreement with the team. When you are at Disney World in the souvenir shop, you might see Magic merchandise available and maybe even themed Disney items. These opportunities exist, in part, because the Walt Disney Company is a corporate champion partner and sponsor of the team.

Fifth, VenueNext—the tech firm founded by the NFL San Francisco 49ers—signed a deal with the Magic during late 2015 to develop an all-inclusive mobile application at the Amway Center. Created by VenueNext, the new platform folds ticketing, food service, retail, parking, seat upgrades, gaming, and video content—all services typically isolated in separate systems—into one application. The single-source technology consolidates the data analytics piece, enabling the Magic to get a better handle on customizing the fan experience.

Washington Wizards

Born in 1957 into a family of working-class Greek immigrant parents in Brooklyn, New York, Ted Leonsis attended Brooklyn Technical High School before moving to Lowell, Massachusetts, and graduating from a high school there in 1973. Four years later, Leonsis graduated from Georgetown University at the top of his class while majoring in American studies.

After becoming a multimillionaire by publishing and selling magazines, Leonsis established the marketing communications company Redgate Communications Corporation. When the organization was acquired by America Online (AOL) in 1994, he began working with AOL as a senior executive and remained with the company for thirteen years.

Under his leadership, AOL increased its membership from under 800,000 members to over eight million while annual revenue expanded from $100 million to $1.5 billion. Leonsis held numerous positions at AOL, completing his tenure and retiring in 2006 as the audience group's president and vice chairman. Later, he served as vice chairman emeritus of AOL.

During mid-2010, the Pollin family sold its majority share of the Wizards and Verizon Center to a syndicate led by NHL Washington Capitals owner Ted Leonsis, giving the former AOL mogul control over two major professional sports franchises and their home arena. Leonsis and his group, Lincoln Holdings, would likely energize the culture at Washington Sports & Entertainment—the sports empire cobbled together by former owner Abe Pollin. Pollin, who suffered from a debilitating illness, died in November 2009 at eighty-five years old.

Among fourteen other EC teams and their owners as of the league's 2015–16 season, Leonsis's Wizards tied for ninth with zero division titles, for eighth in conference titles, and for fifth in number of championships. In comparison to all owners since 2010, Washington tied for twentieth (division titles), tied fifteenth (conference titles), and tied for tenth (NBA championships). Consequently, Pollin has been a mediocre owner whose teams had one winning season and appeared in two playoffs (table A2).

Published in 2015, an online report ranked Leonsis fifteenth best among NBA owners. For an overview of his impact on the franchise, consider the following statements:

> Like a good owner, he's [Leonsis] placed the right people in the right position to help the team succeed and it's worked wonders so far. Sure, the Wizards are still a few steps away from truly competing for a title but it's been a long climb back for the team and Leonsis has done a great job of not getting in the way of that. A lesser owner might have tried to get too hands on with things, but it takes a smart owner to know how to not be a stupid one. Leonsis has been anything but the latter, and it's making him really easy to root for with future success.[32]

Team Financials

In *Forbes* magazine's study of NBA teams' financial status as of early 2016, the Wizards' market value was $960 million, revenue $146 million, operating income $2 million, gate receipts $31 million, debt-to-value 14 percent, and players expenses $89 million. With respect to data of other EC teams, Washington ranked eighth (market value), ninth (revenue and gate receipts), fourteenth (operating income), tenth (debt ratio), and tied for second (players expenses). Within only the SED, the Wizards had the lowest profits but second highest market value and revenue of the group (table A3).

Among all NBA clubs, Washington's amounts ranged from a tie for fifth in players expenses to twenty-ninth in operating income. Based on these results, the Wizards are financially a below-average business operation and do not generate enough cash inflows from gate receipts, sponsorships, and television deals to be consistently competitive and challenge their rivals in regular seasons and any postseasons.

Besides market size, salary inflation, and other factors, an NBA team's annual payroll partly reflects its commitment to players and their current and potential contribution individually and as a group to winning games in regular-seasons and postseasons. From 2011 to 2015, for example, the Wizards' payroll among fourteen EC teams ranged in rank from sixth in both 2013 ($70.3 million) and 2015 ($83.0 million) to thirteenth in 2012 ($58.0 million). Within only the SED, the club had the lowest payroll for one year and then increased it for the next four during the period (table A4).

In comparison to all NBA teams, Washington's amounts were respectively—from the 2011 to 2015 seasons—ranked twenty-sixth, twenty-fifth, tenth, thirteenth, and twelfth. Although the club's payroll increased each season after 2011, it finished with a losing record initially and then improved to win more than forty games in three seasons and qualify for the playoffs in two of them. Apparently, owner Ted Leonsis has increased the team's budget for players' salaries, which in turn caused them to perform better in games of regular seasons.

As long as point guard John Wall is on the team, the Wizards are in a great place for the future. They have a well-respected head coach in Scott Brooks, their superstar Wall, and a young core of players such as Bradley Beal, Markieff Morris, and Otto Porter. Now Washington needs to focus on building a team around their all-star and give him the best options possible. With strong free agency classes and the Wizards' salary cap room, look for Washington to add a few new additions. Indeed, the club has a bright future with Wall leading the way.

Verizon Center

Opened in 1997 to replace the outdated US Airways Arena, the 20,300-seat Verizon Center—originally named MCI Center and currently owned by Monumental Sports and Entertainment—is located in the heart of downtown Washington and just blocks away from the Capitol, White House, and most national historic treasures as well as federal buildings. Besides the Wizards, the arena hosts the NHL Capitals, WNBA Mystics, and home basketball games of the Georgetown University Hoyas.

The venue contains more than 100 luxury suites and at least 3,000 club seats on different levels, 70,000 square feet of themed restaurants and retail stores, and a sports museum. Designed for use year-round, the entertainment center hosts concerts and special events when not in use by sports teams. In addition, the building is connected to a light rail station, which provides affordable transportation to and from events.

Among venues of fourteen other EC teams as of early 2016, the Verizon Center was the seventh oldest, fifth most expensive to construct, and ninth highest in value. In comparison to those of all NBA clubs, the arena ranked thirteenth (age), ninth (construction cost), and eighteenth (value). Based on these results, the Wizards play their home games in an average to above-average but relatively costly facility with enough amenities and other attractions to entertain fans and generate more cash for the team and its owner Ted Leonsis (table A5).

In the 2011–2015 NBA seasons, the FCIs for a family to attend a regular-season game at the Verizon Center ranged from a low of $212 in 2011 to a high of $322 in 2015. With respect to those of all NBA teams, the Wizard's ranked between eighth in 2015 to thirteenth in 2011 during the period (table A6).

To reveal specific costs for a recent season in the NBA, the Wizard's FCI in 2015–16 was approximately 24 percent higher than in 2014–15. Listed from most to least in amount by item for one person, the team's tickets averaged between $51 and $52, parking a vehicle and a cap each $20, one beer $8, a program $5, and a hot dog and soft drink each $4.

Among other teams in the conference's SED, they had rankings and FCIs from most to least as follows: Heat fifth at $465; Magic twenty-fourth at $263; Hawks twenty-sixth at $255; and Hornets thirtieth at $212. Consequently, Wizards fans paid less at games in the Verizon Center than those of thirteen other teams in their arenas.

The cheapest ticket cost $16 for a fan to watch a Wizards home game in 2015–16. This was slightly more than the league's average for a cheap seat. Also, since the club's FCI was $17 or 5 percent below that of a typical NBA team, a family of four purchased tickets and enjoyed a basketball game in Washington for a lower amount than in many arenas within the league. These costs and prices, in turn, were set by the Wizard's organization to earn additional revenue and maximize profit from its operations.

According to an online study, the Verizon Center ranked twenty-third best among all NBA teams' homes in early 2016. In terms of aesthetics and fan experiences, it rated in the league's bottom fourth because:

> Aesthetically, you gotta love the "dc" logo at center court, where the top of the "d" turns into a hand reaching for a basketball. Good choice to emphasize that over the wizard. Otherwise, this is a poorly lit arena with far too many advertisements. Not awful, but far below average as far as the eye test goes. As an experience, because jobs in DC are so very often government-related and temporary, the population of the city is always in flux, making most Wizards game attendees less than passionate about DC basketball. The Verizon Center is the friendliest place in the NBA for visiting fans, simply because attending a Wizards-Celtics game in DC as a resident of the city means that you are likely a Boston expatriate. The Verizon Center is an inessential visit, but fine if you happen to be in Washington DC.[33]

Business Highlights

Besides regular-season and postseason games, NBA franchises are involved in—and affected by—community events and business-related affairs, news, and projects. The following are a few of them for Washington's mediocre but financially average yet improving professional basketball team.[34]

First, during December 2013, the Wizards franchise held a Sports Career Day for thousands of students and their chaperones. The event included an educational sports business seminar hosted by members of the team's management, a college fair featuring as many as fifty schools from across the nation, and a Wizards basketball game. Students heard from executives representing several different departments within Monumental Sports & Entertainment. Speakers discussed the basic responsibilities of their department and offered insight and advice for students interested in becoming sports business professionals. Besides students, teachers, administrators, and chaperones, members of such important and well-respected organizations as DECA, FBLA, FCCLA, and Business Professionals of America were encouraged to participate in Sports Career Day.

Second, during mid-2016, the District's sports and convention arm—Events DC—proposed a series of upgrades to a planned Wizards practice facility and entertainment center that would likely reduce the number of seats but add $10 million to the original $55 million price tag. In the fall of 2015, DC Mayor Muriel E. Bowser announced plans to build the facility on the campus of the former St. Elizabeth's Hospital in the Congress Heights neighborhood, calling the project "bigger than basketball" and saying it would bring economic development to one of the poorest areas of the city. Wizards owner Ted Leonsis pledged to move the team's practices there and home games of the Washington Mystics and a future NBA D-League affiliate team. His company, Monumental Sports & Entertainment, agreed to pay $4.46 million or 8 percent of the original cost.

Third, when the Wizards unveiled their new, primary logo in April 2015, gone was the bearded, athletic wizard set against a basketball moon that served as the team's emblem since it changed its name from the Bullets to the Wizards in 1997. In the new logo, the ball design—that depicts the Washington monument in the middle of a basketball—is paired with the iconic striping from the team's uniforms, that is, three stars representing DC, Maryland, and Virginia, and the team's wordmarks. The Wizards will use the ball logo as well as the DC hands logo in team materials and on television while officially retiring the wizard.

Fourth, after two years of sometimes arduous negotiations, the NBC Sports Group reached a handshake agreement as of mid-2015 to extend its media rights deals with both the NBA Wizards' and NHL Capitals' franchises through their 2031–32 season. Although final contracts had been signed, the fifteen-year deals give the teams' owner, Monumental Sports & Entertainment, a 33 percent equity interest in the Comcast SportsNet Mid-Atlantic regional sports network that covers Washington, DC, and Baltimore.

The agreement represented a coup for owner Ted Leonsis, who still had several years remaining on both teams' contracts with the network. Leonsis inherited the Wizards' deal—which includes its 2020–21 season—and also the Capitals' through 2016–17. With the new agreement, both teams' local media rights will sync up, starting with their 2017–18 season.

Fifth, in early 2012, the Wizards initiated a season ticket renewal campaign laden with incentives as the team looked to boost business during a year of futility on the court. The team created a DC 12 Club marketing platform that gave new and renewing full-season ticket buyers access to some thirty events hosted by the team outside of Wizards games, all included in the price of the ticket. The "12" in the program's label is a nod to participants having access to events twelve months of the year.

NOTES

1. Two books about the NBA and its teams are Frank P. Jozsa Jr., *National Basketball Association Strategies: Business Expansions, Relocations, and Mergers* (New York: Springer, 2016) and Connie Kirchberg, *Hoop Love: A History of the National Basketball Association* (Jefferson, NC: McFarland, 2007).

2. Some websites for team performances include http://www.basketball-reference.com, http://www.nba.com, and http://www.sportsencyclopedia.com.

3. Chad Ford and Kevin Pelton, "Future NBA Power Rankings: Full Category Rankings," http://www.espn.go.com, cited August 3, 2016.

4. One source is Max Bleau, "Atlanta Hawks Work to Promote Diversity After Divisive Scandal," http://www.atlantamagazine.com, cited August 4, 2016.

5. There are references such as Chris Holmes, "The 10 Worst NBA Franchises, 2013 Edition," http://www.grayflannelsuit.net, cited August 6, 2016.

6. "Future NBA Power Rankings: Full Category Rankings."

7. Besides books in note 1, also see James Quirk and Rodney D. Fort, *Pay Dirt: The Business of Professional Team Sports* (Princeton, NJ: Princeton University Press, 1992), and David G. Surdam, *The Rise of the National Basketball Association* (Urbana, IL: University of Illinois Press, 2012).

8. Daniel Zillmer, "All 30 NBA Franchises Statistically Ranked by All-Time Greatness," https://www.fansided.com, cited June 6, 2016.

9. "Future NBA Power Rankings: Full Category Rankings."

10. For another reading about the best NBA franchises of all-time, see Josh Aisher, "The Ten Best NBA Teams of All Time," http://www.cheatsheet.com, cited June 3, 2016.

11. Philip Rossman-Reich, "Orlando Magic Rise 10 Spots in ESPN Future Power Rankings," http://www.orlandomagicdaily.com, cited August 9, 2016.

12. See, for example, Kelly Scaletta, "NBA Power Rankings: The Ultimate All-Time Ranking of Every NBA Franchise," http://www.bleacherreport.com, cited August 12, 2016.

13. "Future NBA Power Rankings: Full Category Rankings."

14. The business and economics of the league is covered in Frank P. Jozsa Jr., *The National Basketball Association: Business, Organization and Strategy* (Hackensack, NJ: World Scientific, 2011).

15. See the league and specific teams' websites for the history and success of principal owners and also their motivation and goal in financing and operating an NBA franchise.

16. Among readings about evaluating NBA team owners, there is "2015 Front-Office Rankings: Owners," http://www.espn.go.com, cited July 14, 2016.

17. Chris Vivlamore, "Hawks Owner Wants Great Franchise—and That Means a Championship," http://www.myjac.com, cited August 13, 2016.

18. A general source is "NBA Team Salaries," http://www.basketball-reference.com, cited August 14, 2016.

19. "Present National Basketball Association Arenas," http://www.basketball.ballparks.com, cited June 27, 2016.

20. For information, see "Fan Cost Index," http://www.teammarketingreport.com, cited August 1, 2016.

21. Read about some of the Hawks' business highlights in John Lombardo, "What a Difference a Year Makes for the Hawks," http://www.sportsbusinessdaily.com, cited August 16, 2016; Courtney Connelly, "Atlanta Hawks Chief Marketing Officer Talks the State of Diversity for Women in Sports Today," http://www.blackenterprise.com, cited August 17, 2016; "Sentient Jet Named Official Private Jet Partner of the Atlanta Hawks," http://www.businesswire.com, cited August 17, 2016; "The Secret to Social Media Success—From the Atlanta Hawks Playbook," http://www.sportsbusiness.solutions.com, cited August 10, 2016.

22. Josh Hill, "NBA Owners Power Rankings: Who is the Best Owner in Basketball?" http://www.fansided.com, cited July 8, 2016.

23. Scooby Axson, "Forbes: Hornets Owner Michael Jordan Now a Billionaire After Increasing Stake in Team," http://www.forbes.com, cited August 12, 2016.

24. "NBA Contract Index," http://www.basketball-reference.com, cited July 21, 2016.

25. Luke Dahlgren, "Power Rankings: NBA Arenas," https://fansided.com, cited July 10, 2016.

26. The Hornets' business highlights include such articles as Shawn Rice, "Charlotte Hornets and Michael Jordan Losing NBA All Star Game Due to Anti-Gay Legislation," http://www.business2community.com, cited August 11, 2016; Erik Spanberg, "How Team Paved Way for Beloved Brand's Return," http://www.sportsbusinessdaily.com, cited August 12, 2016; "Novant Lands Spot on Hornets' Floor," http://www.sportsbusinessdaily.com, cited August 12, 2016; "Hornets Announce Grant Thornton LLP to Become Team's Official Accounting Firm," https://www.nba.com, cited August 18, 2016.

27. "NBA's Power Rankings: Who is the Best Owner in Basketball?"

28. "Power Rankings: NBA Arenas."

29. For some of the Heat's business, see readings like "Kim Stone, Miami Heat/American Airlines Arena," http://www.sportsbusinessdaily.com, cited August 18, 2016; John Lombardo, "Control Supply to Heat Up Demand," http://www.sportsbusinessdaily.com, cited August 18, 2016; Kenneth Cortsen, "Guest Blog: Miami Heat and the Role of Brand Positioning," http://www.kennethcortsen.com, cited August 20, 2016; "790 The Ticket And Miami Heat Extend Broadcast Partnership," http://www.entercom.com, cited August 21, 2016.

30. "2015 Front-Office Rankings: Owners."

31. Some of the Orlando Magic's business highlights are discussed, for example, in Josh Robbins, "Losing Has Forced the Magic to Upgrade as a Business," http://www.orlandosentinel.com, cited August 21, 2016; "How The Orlando Magic Prosper With Analytics Despite Relatively Small Market," http://www.sporttechie.com, cited August 21, 2016; Don Muret, "Magic Selects VenueNext for App," http://www.sportsbusinessdaily.com, cited August 22, 2016; "NBA Honors Magic for Top Local Promotion," http://www.sportsbusinessdaily.com, cited August 23, 2016.

32. "NBA's Power Ranking: Who is the Best Owner in Basketball?"

33. "Power Rankings: NBA Arenas.

34. For the Wizards' business highlights, see such articles as Matthew Rocco, "Wizards Owner Ted Leonsis: Millennials Are Changing Sports on TV," http://www.foxbusiness.com, cited August 23, 2016; "WGL and Washington Gas Join Forces With Wizards," http://www.wglholdings.com, cited August 24, 2016; "SBA at the Washington Wizards," http://www.gwsba.org, cited August 25, 2016; Zachery Eanes, "Events D.C. Increases Price Tag for Wizards Practice Facility," http://www.bizjournals.com, cited August 25, 2016.

Part II

WESTERN CONFERENCE

Chapter Four

Northwest Division

Organized in 2004 by the National Basketball Association (NBA), the Northwest Division (NWD) of the league's Western Conference (WC) originally included the Denver Nuggets, Minnesota Timberwolves, Portland Trail Blazers, Seattle SuperSonics, and Utah Jazz. The Nuggets, Timberwolves, and Jazz joined the NWD from the Midwest Division (MWD) and the Trail Blazers and SuperSonics from the Pacific Division (PD). Before their 2008–9 season, the SuperSonics relocated from Seattle to Oklahoma City and were nicknamed the Thunder.

Given this change in the conference's structure, this chapter discusses the historical development and highlights business news and the financial facts of NWD teams based respectively in Denver, Colorado; Minneapolis, Minnesota; Oklahoma City, Oklahoma; Portland, Oregon; and Salt Lake City, Utah. During their history, which of them for example, had won the most division titles and fewest number of NBA championships? What were their market values, revenues, and ticket prices in the league's 2015–16—or simply—2015 season? Who have been the least and most successful owners among the five clubs? How do their arenas rank in aesthetics, entertainment, and experience among fans? The answers to these and other questions are covered in the chapter.[1]

TEAM PERFORMANCES

Denver Nuggets

An original member of the American Basketball Association (ABA), the Denver Nuggets existed for nine seasons in the league. Although they won approximately 53 percent of their 774 games and qualified for the playoffs each year, the club failed to win a championship despite a 65–19 record in the 1974–75 season and also finishing 60–24 the following year.[2]

By the end of basketball's 1975–76 season, the financial circumstances surrounding the ABA compelled the league's team owners to seek a merger with the NBA. Several ABA franchises had already disbanded or were in serious financial trouble, their home game attendances were poor, and the league failed to copyright its red, white, and blue basketball, secure a national television contract, or reach a mass audience. Consequently, prospects for another season appeared bleak. Because the ABA had rights to highly talented players, the NBA expressed interest in a merger with some of the stronger ABA franchises.

On August 5, 1976, seven ABA owners agreed to a merge with the NBA. Plans were made to dismantle three of the seven ABA franchises and incorporate their players into the NBA. Under the agreement, the Denver Nuggets and three other clubs joined the older league at a cost to them of $4 million to $5 million each. The merger agreement also provided that the four franchises compensate ABA team owners not accepted into the NBA. The Nuggets were required to pay an additional amount when, at the demand of the NBA, they had to un-sign three college stars before merger talks could proceed.

Historical Results

As a member of the league's MWD from 1976–77 to 2003–4 and then the NWD during the NBA's 2004–2015 seasons, the Nuggets played 3,232 games and had victories in approximately 48 percent of them. During the period, they won seven division titles but zero conference titles and NBA championships in twenty-four playoffs. Among WC teams as of early 2016, the club ranked tenth (winning percentage) and also fourth (division titles), tied for tenth (conference titles), and tied for seventh (championships). Within the NWD, Denver has outperformed the Timberwolves but not the Thunder, Trail Blazers, or Jazz (table A7).

With respect to all NBA teams as of their 2015–16 season, the Nuggets were twentieth in winning percentage, eleventh in number of division titles, tied for twenty-first in conference titles, and tied for sixteenth in championships. Based on this data, Denver has performed below average against most other teams in regular seasons because of such problems as its inferior coaches, lack of talented and committed players, and ownership issues.

Performance Highlights

The Nuggets' most successful periods were in qualifying for consecutive playoffs during NBA seasons 1976–1978, 1981–1989, 1993–1994, and

2003–2012. Its coaches included Larry Brown, Doug Moe, Dan Issel, Jeff Bzdelik, and George Karl. While Brown is in the Hall of fame, Moe and Karl were the league's Coach of the Year when their teams won more than 65 percent of regular-season games, finished first or second in the division, and competed but lost in conference playoffs.

During one or more of these periods, some Denver players had outstanding seasons. These were David Thompson, Dan Issel, Kiki Vandeweghe, Alex English, Fat Lever, Dikembe Mutombo, Andre Miller, and Nene Hilario. Besides Thompson, Issel, English, and Mutombo, a few other former Nuggets players are in the Naismith Memorial Basketball Hall of Fame.

The team, however, failed to be in the playoffs consecutively in seasons 1979–1980, 1990–1992, 1995–2002, and 2013–2015. Such things as players' injuries, wrong coaching decisions, poor drafts of college athletes, and simply low morale were responsible for the Nuggets underperforming during these years.

Among NBA franchises' performances, Denver ranks about eighteenth best of all-time. While the Nuggets have not won any league championships, they fielded some exciting teams to watch in games. During their 1997–98, 1984–85, and 2007–8 seasons, they played in the conference finals and set a scoring record in 1981–82 with 126.5 points per game. Headed by their Hall of Famers, the Nuggets were always good at entertaining fans.

Based on ESPN's future power rankings of NBA teams for their 2016–2018 seasons, the Nuggets were twentieth in the group. Listed by category from best to worst, they ranked third (*draft*), seventeenth (*market*), twentieth (*players*), twenty-first (*money*), and twenty-fourth (*management*). Primarily because of the club's young talent and high draft picks but not its front office, cap space or market, Denver may start a long-term move up in the standings. Interestingly, the rankings put the Nuggets tenth in the WC and ahead of the Mavericks, Lakers, Grizzlies, Suns, and Kings. However, Denver is last in the NWD with Oklahoma City fifth, Utah seventh, Portland eighth, and Minnesota ninth.[3]

Minnesota Timberwolves

Before the late 1980s, the Minneapolis Lakers had their home site in Minnesota while in seasons of the National Basketball League (1947–48), Basketball Association of America (1948–49), and NBA (1949–50 to 1959–60). Also, two ABA franchises existed there—Minnesota Muskies in 1967–68 and Minnesota Pipers in 1968–1969.

Twenty-nine years after the Lakers departed for sunny Los Angeles, the NBA returned to the Twin Cities. During April 1987, the league granted one of its four new expansion teams—the others being the Charlotte Hornets,

Miami Heat, and Orlando Magic—to original owners Harvey Ratner and Marv Wolfenson to begin play for the 1989–90 season. As a result, they paid the NBA $32.5 million for the franchise.

In a name-the-team contest, the franchise eventually selected two finalists, "Timberwolves" and "Polars," in December 1986. After the team asked more than eight hundred city councils in Minnesota to select the winner, "Timberwolves" prevailed by a wide margin. In January 1987, the team was officially named "Minnesota Timberwolves" in part because the state was home to the largest timber wolf population in the lower forty-eight states.

Historical Results

As a member of the league's MWD from its 1989–90 to 2003–4 season and then the NWD since 2004–5, the Timberwolves played 2,166 games and had victories in approximately 39 percent of them. During the period, they won one division title but zero conference titles and NBA championships in eight playoffs. Among WC teams as of early 2016, they tied for thirteenth with the Hornets/Pelicans (division titles), tied for tenth with five other teams (conference titles), and tied for seventh in number of championships (table A7).

Within only the conference's NWD, the Timberwolves have performed worse than the Nuggets, Thunder, Trail Blazers, and Jazz. In comparison to all NBA teams as of their 2015–16 season, Minnesota had the second-lowest winning percentage and also tied between sixteenth and twenty-sixth with several others in titles and championships. Based on these results, this franchise struggles to compete in most regular seasons against rivals because of weak leadership especially from coaches and players but also its owners.

Performance Highlights

The Timberwolves' most successful period was during consecutive playoffs in seasons 1996–1997 to 2003–2004. Although Coach Frank Saunders's teams lost seven times in the conference's first round, but then finished 58–24 and first in the division but lost in the 2004 conference finals to the Los Angeles Lakers. Other than Saunders, such head coaches as Bill Musselman, Jimmy Rodgers, Dwane Casey, Randy Whitman, Kent Rambis, and Rick Adelman had teams with losing seasons that ranked third to sixth in the division.

During one or more regular seasons, some of Minnesota's best players were Michael Williams, Kevin Garnett, and Kevin Love. Forward Garnett was an all-star and NBA Most Valuable Player (MVP), forward Love the Most Improved Player in the league, and forward Andrew Wiggins and center

Karl Anthony Towns each Rookie of the Year. After retiring from the sport in September 2016, Garnett will be inducted into the Hall of Fame.

Timberwolves' teams, however, did not appear in playoffs and had their worst performances in NBA seasons 1989–1996 and 2004–2015. During 1981–82, 2009–10, and 2014–15, for example, Minnesota won fewer than 20 percent of regular-season games and finished fifth or sixth in its division. These results occurred, in part, because of coaching and player problems and simply too much competition from such rivals as the Nuggets, Thunder, Trail Blazers, and Jazz.

With respect to other NBA franchises as of early 2016, the Timberwolves are one of the worst of all-time. They consistently draft quality players, yet unable to build enough around them in time to convince these players to stay when free agency looms. Part of that is because of Minnesota. The endorsement appeal—not to mention lifestyle differences between playing in Minneapolis versus Chicago, New York, or Los Angeles—means a club needs a superstar who enjoys living in a small town and his teammates. Basketball players like the bright lights and to win titles. If a franchise cannot consistently supply the latter, then players will chase the former.

In ESPN's future power rankings for NBA seasons 2016–2018, the Timberwolves were ninth following the NWD's Thunder (fifth), Jazz (seventh) and Trail Blazers (eighth), but ahead of the Nuggets (twentieth). Among five categories, Minnesota ranked highest in the draft and then players, money, management, and the market. Thus, the team will primarily improve because of its opportunities to draft quality players and also develop those on the roster such as Wiggins and Towns.[4]

Oklahoma City Thunder

From the 1967–68 to 2007–8 NBA seasons, the Seattle SuperSonics—or simply Sonics—had victories in approximately 52 percent of their games and won six division and three conference titles and also one league championship in twenty-two playoffs. But since their 1998–99 season, they won only one division title and appeared in three playoffs.

During October 2006, the NBA approved Howard Schultz's sale of the Sonics and WNBA Seattle Storm to an Oklahoma City group led by businessman Clayton Bennett for approximately $325 million. Four months later, Bennett requested at least $300 million in taxpayer money for a proposed $530 million arena in Renton, a city south of Seattle. After his request failed, Bennett filed papers to begin an arbitration process to get out of the final two years of the team's lease at Seattle's multipurpose KeyArena.

In February 2008, Bennett offered the city of Seattle $26.5 million if it let the Sonics out of the final two years of their lease, but the city declined his offer. Despite publicly insisting he wanted to keep the Sonics in the Pacific Northwest, Bennett's actions proved otherwise. After the club played its last game in Seattle in mid-April, NBA owners approved relocating the Sonics to Oklahoma City by a 28–2 vote with Dallas's Mark Cuban and Portland's Paul Allen—co-founder of Microsoft and owner of the NFL's Seattle Seahawks—opposing it.

During late April 2008, Schultz filed suit to rescind his sale of the franchise because Bennett was dishonest in his promise to keep the team in Seattle. Ultimately, Schultz dropped his suit. A few months later, an estimated 3,000 fans attended a raucous "Save Our Sonics" rally in Seattle where a judge presided over a trial to determine whether the team could leave immediately or must finish the two years of its lease.

In June 2008, Bennett predicted the Sonics would lose $60 million if forced to stay two more years. After the trial between the city and Sonics ended, Bennett and Seattle Mayor Greg Nickels held a news conference to announce a settlement. The team was allowed to move to Oklahoma City in exchange for a $45 million payment and no promise of a replacement.

Historical Results

As a member of the NWD in the league's 2008–9 to 2015–16 seasons, the Thunder had victories in approximately 61 percent of their regular-season games. During the period, they won their division five times and also conference once but had zero NBA championships in six playoff appearances. Among fourteen other WC teams, Oklahoma City ranked second in winning percentage, tied for sixth with the Trail Blazers and Rockets in number of division titles, ninth in conference titles, and tied for seventh with eight other teams in championships (table A7).

Within its division as of early 2016, the eight-year-old Thunder had already outperformed the Timberwolves in total titles and all teams in proportion of wins. In comparison to twenty-nine other NBA clubs, Oklahoma City was second (winning percentage), tied for twenty-eighth (playoffs), tied for fourteenth (division titles), tied for nineteenth (conference titles), and tied for sixteenth (league championships). Based on these results, the Thunder has been above average in performances thus far because of its excellent coaching staff and some great players.

Performance Highlights

The team's most successful period was in consecutive playoffs during seasons 2009–10 to 2013–14. During this period, the club won four division titles but lost in the NBA finals and first round each once, and in the conference finals twice. Scott Brooks was Coach of the Year in 2010 because his team had a .610 winning percentage despite finishing fourth in the NWD and losing in the first round of the playoffs.

A few players were outstanding while playing for the Thunder. Forward Kevin Durant was an all-star and league MVP each once, guard Russell Westbrook an all-star MVP twice, and guard James Harden was best sixth man in the league in 2012. During most games, Durant and Westbrook dominated their opponents by scoring many points on offense and out-rebounding other players at both ends of the court.

In contrast, Oklahoma City's worst seasons were 2008–9 and 2014–15. During the former one, the club won only twenty-three games and finished fifth in the NWD. In the latter season, the team had forty-five victories but failed to qualify for the playoffs. These performances occurred because of players' injuries, bad coaching decisions at least initially by P. J. Carlesimo and then by Scott Brooks, and also simply too much competition in regular-season games from such division rivals as the Trail Blazers and Jazz.

According to ESPN's future power rankings for NBA seasons 2016–17 to 2018–19, the Thunder was rated third best in the conference following the Cavaliers and Celtics but overall fifth in the league. For five categories, Oklahoma City's players rated fourth, management fifth, market twenty-first, draft twenty-fourth, and money situation twenty-fifth. Although the franchise ranked relatively low in three categories, it has a roster of players and front-office personnel to be successful in the future.

After his much-anticipated free agency announcement, the Thunder's Kevin Durant signed a two-year deal for $54 million with the conference's Golden State Warriors in the summer of 2016. According to Durant:

> The primary mandate I had for myself in making this decision was to have it based on the potential for my growth as a player—as that has always steered me in the right direction. But I am also at a point in my life where it is of equal importance to find an opportunity that encourages my evolution as a man—moving out of my comfort zone to a new city and community which offers the greatest potential for my contribution and personal growth.[5]

Portland Trail Blazers

During the mid-1950s, sports promoter Harry Glickman sought an NBA franchise for Portland, Oregon. In fact, he proposed two new expansion teams, the other to be located in Los Angeles, California. When Portland's Memorial Coliseum opened in 1960, Glickman realized its potential as a professional basketball venue. But it was not until early February 1970 that the NBA board of governors granted him the rights to a franchise in Portland.

To raise funds for the league's $3.7 million admission tax, Glickman became an associate to real estate magnates Bob Schmertz of New Jersey, Larry Weinberg of Los Angeles, and Herman Sarkowsky of Seattle. In late February, Glickman's management group held a contest to select the team's nickname and received more than ten thousand entries.

The most popular choice, "Pioneers," was excluded from consideration for being used by sports teams at Portland's Lewis and Clark College. Because the nickname "Trail Blazers" received almost two hundred entries, it was ultimately selected by a judging panel and then revealed in mid-March during the halftime of a basketball game at Memorial Coliseum.

Derived from trail blazing activity by explorers making paths through forests, Glickman considered it a nickname that reflected both the ruggedness of the Pacific Northwest and the start of a major league sports era in the state. Despite initial mixed responses to the Trail Blazers as a nickname—often shortened to "Blazers"—it eventually became popular among people and especially sports fans in Oregon.

Historical Results

As a member of the PD from the 1970–71 to 2003–4 seasons and then the league's NWD through 2015–16, the Trail Blazers had victories in approximately 53 percent of their games. During the period, they won five division and three conference titles and also one NBA championship in thirty-two playoffs. Among WC teams as of early 2016, Portland was sixth in winning percentage, tied for sixth with the Thunder and Rockets in division titles, tied for fourth with the Warriors in conference titles, and tied for fifth with the Mavericks in number of championships (table A7).

In comparison to twenty-nine other NBA clubs as of their 2015–16 season, the Trail Blazers ranked seventh (winning percentage), tied for fourteenth (division titles), tied for tenth (conference titles), and tied for eleventh (league championships). Based on this data, Portland has performed above average against its opponents in regular-season games and also while competing in conference playoffs.

Performance Highlights

The Trail Blazers' most successful periods were in consecutive playoffs during seasons 1976–1980, 1982–2002, 2008–2010, and 2013–2015. Such head coaches as Jack Ramsay, Mike Schuler, Rick Adelman, P. J. Carlesimo, Mike Dunleavy, Nate McMillan, and Terry Stotts led their clubs to win games in various ways. While Ramsay became a Hall of Famer, Schuler and Dunleavy each won Coach of the Year awards.

To win games in regular seasons and postseasons, the team's most impressive players included Bill Walton, Kiki Vandeweghe, Clyde Drexler, Rasheed Wallace, Arvydas Sabonis, Brandon Roy, and Damian Lillard. Walton was both MVP in the league and finals series, and Roy and Lillard each Rookie of the Year along with players Geoff Petrie and Sidney Wicks. Besides Walton, Drexler, and Sabonis, five other players are in the Hall of Fame.

Two of the team's best seasons were in 1976–77 and 1990–91. In the former, they won an NBA championship despite finishing second in the division, while in the latter season, the Trail Blazers had victories in sixty-three games and claimed the division title but lost in the conference finals. Alternatively, the club's worst season was 1971–72 when it had only eighteen wins and ended in fifth place of its division.

As of 2015, the Trail Blazers were sixteenth best among NBA franchises of all-time. According to the website fansided.com, here is the reason for their success across seasons:

> The Trail Blazers come in ranked a bit higher than many people realize in terms of all-time success. This franchise has been in the NBA for more than 40 years and won one league championship. But they've also won four division championships [five as of 2016] and three conference championships. This varied amount of success is what has them ranked ahead of many other NBA franchises.[6]

Based on ESPN's power ranking projections of NBA teams for the 2016–2018 seasons, Portland was in eighth place. The Blazers have star players, a smart front office, and enough money to make a splash in free agency. However, they are a midmarket team that has not historically drawn interest, and their future cap/draft pick situation is not inspiring. Given the level of success they achieved in rebuilding their roster, a gradual climb to a high rung is feasible. Yet, the Blazers are ranked between number seven Jazz and number nine Timberwolves, two other strong upstarts—so the battle to become the next young success story will be a competitive one.[7]

In sum, the Trail Blazers have a promising future because of a good coach, fantastic management, and a very solid roster. Although they still cannot compete with the Golden State Warriors or San Antonio Spurs on paper, the club has a legitimate shot at a third or fourth seed in the 2016–17 season. It would be no surprise if Damian Lillard—a potential MVP candidate—led them to fifty or more wins.

Utah Jazz

An NBA expansion team, the New Orleans Jazz played five seasons (1974–75 to 1978–79) and won only 39 percent of their 410 regular-season games. Although superstar Pete Maravich was considered one of the most entertaining players in the league and won the scoring championship in 1977 with 31.1 points per game, the Jazz' best record while in New Orleans was 39–43 in their 1977–78 season.

While based in New Orleans, venue issues were a continual problem for the team. In the Jazz's first season, they played games in the Municipal Auditorium and Loyola Field House, where the basketball court was raised so high that the NBA Players Association made the team put a net around the court so players would not fall off of the court and into the stands. Later, the Jazz played its home games in the Louisiana Superdome, but things were no better there due to onerous lease terms. They also faced the prospect of spending a whole month on the road each year due to Mardi Gras festivities.

Despite being barely competitive, the Jazz had good attendance during its first five years. By 1979, however, the franchise was sinking financially. One factor was paying an 11 percent amusement tax, highest in the United States at the time. The team also could not attract much local corporate support—an important factor even in those days—or local investors. Thus, owner Sam Battistone concluded that the franchise was no longer viable in New Orleans and decided to move it elsewhere. After scouting several new sites, he decided to move his team to Salt Lake City, a smaller market than New Orleans.

Historical Results

As a member of the MWD in the league's 1979–80 to 2003–4 season and then the NWD through 2015–16, the Jazz had victories in approximately 55 percent of its games. During the period, the club won eight division and two conference titles but zero championships in twenty-five playoffs. Among fourteen other WC teams, Utah ranked fourth in winning percentage, third in number of division titles, tied for sixth with the Suns and Mavericks in conference titles, and tied for seventh with eight different clubs in championships (table A7).

In comparison to twenty-nine other NBA teams as of their 2015–16 season, the Jazz was fifth (winning percentage), tied for eighth (division titles), tied for fourteenth (conference titles), and tied for sixteenth (championships). Based on these results, Utah has been an above-average team and competitive within its division and in the conference throughout its thirty-seven years in the league.

Performance Highlights

The Jazz's most successful periods were during consecutive playoffs in seasons 1983–2002 and 2006–2009. Head coaches Frank Layden and Jerry

Sloan led their teams to victories in home and away games and in several postseasons. Because his team won forty-five games and finished first in the division, Layden was NBA Coach of the Year in 1984. Furthermore, Sloan joined the Hall of Fame based on his great career with the Jazz.

Some players had memorable seasons for the franchise. Besides forward Karl Malone and guard John Stockton, these included forward Adrian Dantley, guard Darrell Griffith, and center Mark Eaton. Malone was a two-time MVP in the league; Stockton a leader in assists during multiple seasons; Griffith Rookie of the Year; and Eaton Defensive Player of the Year twice. Dantley, Malone, and Stockton are in the basketball Hall of Fame.

The club's best and worst seasons were, respectively, 1996–97 and 1979–80. In the former, the Jazz won 78 percent of its regular-season games and the division title but lost in the finals. Regarding the latter season, Utah had a 24–58 record and ended fifth in the division with Tom Nissalke as head coach. The differences in these teams' seasons occurred because of such things as their coaches' decisions, players' injuries and lack of talent, too much competition from rivals, and retirement of superstars like Malone and Stockton.

According to a study, the Jazz ranked twentieth best all-time among NBA teams as of mid-2016. It has the fourth-highest winning percentage of active franchises and fortunate enough to have some of the game's most talented power forwards, point guards, and coaches, but likely to trade that for just one NBA championship. The team made the playoffs every season from 1983–84 through 2002–3, making the NBA finals in 1997 and 1998. Indeed, the club won enough games during the mid-1990s before running into Michael Jordan and his Chicago Bulls' teams.[8]

In ESPN's future power rankings for the league's 2016–2018 seasons, the Jazz was seventh overall and behind its division rival Thunder (fifth) but ahead of the Trail Blazers (eighth), Timberwolves (ninth), and Nuggets (twentieth). Among five categories, Utah rated sixth in the draft, seventh in both players and money, eighth in management, and twenty-ninth in market.

Regarding its high positon in the draft, the following comments summarize the Jazz's strengths and weaknesses:

> The Utah Jazz may have finished in the lottery, but they weren't really a lottery team. Plagued by significant injuries to key pieces throughout the 2015–16 season, they underperformed relative to their overall talent and still produced some underlying metrics indicative of a playoff finish. According to basketball-reference.com, which looks only at strength of schedule and margin of victory, they were the No. 10 team in the Association, slightly ahead of the Indiana Pacers, Miami Heat and Portland Trail Blazers. They also outscored the opposition by two points per 100 possessions—notably better than some organizations that

> played postseason basketball. Now, the Jazz get to keep their core together and add to it. If Utah misses out on the postseason again, it will be inexcusable. Its floor is higher than that of any other lottery squad in this countdown, even if its ceiling still falls a bit short of the No. 1 team.[9]

Based on the historical performances of these five NWD teams, the most successful has been the Thunder and then the Trail Blazers, Jazz, Nuggets, and Timberwolves. Such things as their winning percentages and number of playoffs, titles, and league championships were important factors in listing the clubs from most to least successful. Without superstar Kevin Durant, however, the Thunder's future is uncertain. This, in turn, will affect its performances particularly in scoring enough points to win games.

FRANCHISE BUSINESS

Given the performances of them as teams, this section focuses on and examines the commercial aspects of NBA franchises including their principal owner or owners and also facts and other details in tables about each team's arena, various costs for families to attend home games, current and important financial data, and yearly trends in players' payrolls. In part, this information reveals why some franchises are more valuable and wealthy than others and therefore how successful or unsuccessful historically as business enterprises in the sports industry.

Denver Nuggets

Born in the small, unincorporated community of Mora, Missouri, where his father owned a lumber company, Stanley Kroenke attended Cole Camp High School and played basketball and baseball and also ran on the track team. He graduated from the University of Missouri with undergraduate degrees in arts and science and a Master's of Business Administration.

About ten years after marrying Walmart heiress Ann Walton in 1974, he founded the Kroenke Group—a real estate development firm that built numerous shopping centers and apartment buildings, and many plazas near Walmart stores. Based in St. Louis, he is also chairman of independent real estate development company, The Realty, which specializes in suburban development.

Because of financial problems, Comsat sold Ascent Entertainment to AT&T's Liberty Media Group in 1997 for $755 million. Liberty immediately put Ascent's sports assets—NBA Nuggets, National Hockey League (NHL) Colorado Avalanche, and the Pepsi Center—for sale while retaining control of the video movie component. Three years later following considerable intrigue, false bidders, and failed negotiations by other bidders, Kroenke purchased the three sports assets in a $450 million deal.

The agreement, while complex, included $268 million in cash to buy 93.5 percent of the teams and arena plus $136 million for the assumption of debt on the Pepsi Center. Additionally, Kroenke paid $27.3 million in advance ticket sales that had been earmarked for the next season's operations while Liberty retained a 6.5 percent stake worth $18.7 million. Kroenke's bid for the teams and arena came after failed talks with Denver billionaire Donald Strum, who offered $461 million for the sports assets but could not reach agreement with the city over whether the teams must remain in Denver for twenty-five years if he died before that term expired.

Among fourteen other WC teams as of their 2015–16 season, Kroenke's Nuggets have won three NWD titles but zero conference titles and league championships in ten playoffs. Specifically, they tied for sixth in both division titles and championships and also tied for eighth in conference titles. In comparison to all NBA teams, Denver tied for thirteenth (division titles), for fifteenth (conference titles), and for tenth (league championships). Based on these results, Kroenke has been an average owner whose teams lost in the first round of nine playoffs and once in the conference finals (table A8).

In ESPN's ranking of NBA teams' front offices and specifically their owners as of March 2015, the Nuggets were twenty-fifth following the division's Trail Blazers (sixth), Jazz (ninth), and Thunder (fourteenth) but ahead of the Timberwolves (twenty-seventh). For Denver to rank higher in the future, Kroenke and his front office and coaches must improve their team's performances and guide the franchise to overall on-court success, both in the short and long term.[10]

Since becoming president and governor of the Nuggets in 2000, Stan's son Josh must solve the team's problems. The club failed, for example, to qualify for the playoffs in three consecutive seasons (2013–2015) after looking like the next big contender in the WC along with the Warriors and Grizzlies. In fact, Denver quit on itself and became unsure whether previous head coach Brian Shaw needed to be fired. Supposedly, Shaw was hired to take what George Karl built and make it into something golden. But Karl was already turning his team to gold and his departure ruined what allure the Nuggets had among fans and in the league.

Team Financials

According to financial information published by *Forbes* magazine about NBA teams as of early 2016, the Nuggets had a market value of $855 million, revenue $140 million, operating income and gate receipts each $26 million, debt-to-value zero percent, and players expenses $64 million. Among fourteen other WC teams, Denver ranked from sixth in operating income to fifteenth in both revenue and players expenses. Within only the NWD, the team had the lowest debt ratio of the group but not the highest of any amounts (table A9).

With respect to all NBA teams, the Nuggets' financials were twenty-first (market value), twenty-seventh (revenue), tenth (operating income), twenty-fourth (gate receipts), tied for twenty-eighth (debt ratio), and twenty-ninth (players expenses). Based on these results, this is a relatively low-valued franchise with below-average financial data because of its location, historical performances, and other economic and sport-specific factors.

Besides market size, salary inflation, and other factors, an NBA team's annual payroll partly reflects its commitment to players and their current and potential contribution individually and as a group to winning games in regular seasons and postseasons. From 2011 to 2015, for example, the Nuggets' payroll among WC teams ranged in rank from seventh in 2012 ($64.0 million) to fifteenth in 2014 ($56.7 million). Within the NWD, the club had the second, third, or fourth highest payroll in the group during 2011–2013 and 2015 but lowest amount in 2014 (table A10).

In comparison to all NBA teams, Denver was respectively twenty-first in 2011 ($58.5 million), seventeenth in 2012, eighteenth in 2013 ($65.6 million), twenty-ninth in 2014, and nineteenth in 2015 ($72.5 million). Given these amounts, the Nuggets decided to increase their payroll three times yet failed to make the playoffs in the NBA's 2013–2015 seasons. To be consistently competitive in the future, however, the team needs to keep its payroll among the top fifteen in the league.

Although the Nuggets' financial status improved from the 2014–15 to 2015–16 season, there are several financial figures that present a less than optimistic picture of the team coupled with the knowledge that future numbers will be generated on its NBA-worst attendance and continuously declining viewership on television. While operating at a profit, the club's market value is stagnating, ticket prices must become more reasonable, and overall financial performance needs to rebound.

For Kroenke Sports Enterprises, the company appears to be fiscally healthy and it seems unlikely their ownership will change hands soon. However, in order for the Nuggets to appreciate in value closer to the rest of the league, they need to find a way to start regaining fan interest—and by extension revenue—that has been sharply declining over recent years.[11]

Pepsi Center

Opened in 1999 to replace the obsolete McNichols Sports Arena, the 19,300-seat privately financed Pepsi Center has several features. When built for the NBA Nuggets and NHL Colorado Avalanche, these included such things as (a) two six-story atrium entranceways and views of the Central Platte Valley, Rocky Mountains, and downtown Denver; (b) a 236-seat club level restaurant; (c) ninety-five fully furnished luxury suites located on two levels; (d) a full-sized NBA practice facility; (d) 4,200 parking spaces on site and 2,200 shared spaces with the Elitch Gardens amusement park; and (e) a fully equipped and integrated production studio.

Besides those amenities, other original attractions were a center-hung video scoreboard; seventeen permanent concession stands which included 150 points of sale plus numerous concession stands; forty-one restrooms; separate locker rooms for the Nuggets and Avalanche and four each auxiliary locker and entertainer dressing rooms; 20,000 square feet of administrative office space at the service level and mezzanine and 2,400 square feet in the ticket lobby; and a 3,000-square-foot novelty store at the grand atrium and five novelty stores on the concourses.

The Pepsi Center's exterior color scheme has a red brick tone, which is intended to reflect the historical nature of the old railroad yard and the neighboring brick buildings remaining in the area. A dramatic canopy at the north entrance accents the elevation with a downtown exposure. Land adjacent to the arena was developed with a mix of specialty retail, restaurant, and office buildings, and other types of businesses.

Among venues of fourteen other WC teams as of early 2016, the Pepsi Center tied for seventh in age and also ranked eighth highest in construction cost and twelfth in value. In comparison to arenas of all NBA teams, the Nuggets' respectively tied for fourteenth (age), tied for nineteenth (construction cost), and also ranked twenty-second (value). Thus, three Denver professional teams—including the National Lacrosse League (NLL) Colorado Mammoth—play their home games in a low-valued but relatively expensive facility with plenty of amenities to generate revenue and additional profit for the franchises (table A11).

For several years a Chicago-based company named Team Marketing Report (TMR) has prepared and published a Fan Cost Index (FCI) for the home games of teams in professional sports leagues. To attend a game for a typical family with two kids, an FCI includes the costs of four average-priced tickets, two cheapest-priced draft beers, four each cheapest-priced soft drinks and hot dogs, parking for one car, and two each game programs and least-expensive, adult-size adjustable caps. Costs are determined by telephone calls with team representatives, venues, and concessionaires, and from questions asked during interviews.[12]

In the 2011–2015 NBA seasons, the FCIs for a family to attend a regular-season game at the Pepsi Center ranged from a low of $295 in 2011 to a high of $326 in 2012. With respect to those of all NBA teams, the Nuggets' games ranked between tenth highest in 2012 to sixteenth in 2015 ($316) and also the twelfth most costly in 2011, thirteenth at $322 in 2014, and fourteenth at $319 in 2013 (table A12).

To reveal specific costs for a recent season in the NBA, the Nuggets' FCI in 2015–16 was 2 percent less than in 2014–15. Listed from most to least in amount by item for one person, the team's tickets averaged $52–$53, a cap $18, parking one vehicle $10, a beer almost $7, and a hot dog and soft drink each between $4 and $5.

Among other teams in the conference's NWD, they had rankings and FCIs from most to least as follows: Trail Blazers fifteenth at $319; Thunder seventeenth at $296; Timberwolves nineteenth at $281.06; and the Jazz tied for twenty-first at $275. Consequently, Nuggets fans paid less at games in the Pepsi Center than those of fifteen other teams in their arenas.

The cheapest ticket cost $15 for a fan to watch a Nuggets home game in 2015–16. This was about $1 or approximately 5 percent less than the league's average for a cheap seat. Also, since the club's FCI was $23 below the amount of a typical NBA team, a family of four purchased tickets and enjoyed a basketball game in Denver at a small discount relative to the majority of arenas within the league. These costs and prices, in turn, were set by the Nuggets organization to earn more revenue and maximize profit from their operations.

Business Highlights

Besides regular-season and postseason games, NBA franchises are involved in—and affected by—community events and business-related affairs, news, and projects. The following are a few of them for Denver's relatively low-performing, and from a financial perspective, below-average professional basketball team.[13]

First, the Nuggets partnered with the National Basketball Academy to present the Youth Hoops Program (YHP). The YHP consists of Nuggets camps, clinics, leagues, and individualized training, all designed to teach the fundamentals of basketball in a fun and positive atmosphere. Each clinic contains Nuggets teachings by the National Basketball Academy, strict fundamentals, drills, games, and contests. Players will be at select camps and visit the NBA website to see updates. Each YHP participant receives a basketball, tee-shirt, and a ticket to a future Nuggets game.

Second, the Nuggets and Pacers will face off at London's O2 Arena during January 2017. London has hosted regular season match-ups in each of the last four NBA seasons though no team from the league's WC played a competitive match in Britain, largely due to the increased travel burden in a season where every team must play eighty-two games. Fans in the United Kingdom can watch the game live on BT Sport while fans in Europe will be able to view it through the NBA's official local broadcast partners.

Third, the 5th Annual giveSPORTS Equipment Drive was held at the Pepsi Center during August 2016. Event co-founders—Kroenke Sports Charities and A Precious Child—invited the public to support underprivileged children to participate in sports by donating new and gently used sports equipment and monetary donations to benefit A Precious Child's giveSPORTS program.

Fourth, the Nuggets' Community Ambassadors (NCAs) are past NBA players, coaches, and referees who make free, special appearances in school classrooms and at a variety of community events and organizations across the seven-county Denver metropolitan area. From kindergarten to high school, the NCAs reach out to students by encouraging them to embrace learning, respect others, value good sportsmanship, and practice to achieve excellence. They are available for basketball clinics, school assemblies, and community events.

Fifth, the NBA's 2014–15 season was especially bad for the Nuggets since being acquired by Stan Kroenke in 2000. After making the playoffs every season from 2003–4 to 2012–13, the Nuggets posted a losing record and missed the playoffs for the second straight season. The team also had the sharpest year-over-year decline (50 percent) in average local television ratings, and the fourth-smallest average audience size on Altitude (13,000) in the NBA. The club's average attendance (14,700) ranked third worst in the NBA and last (14,095) in its 2015–16 season.

Minnesota Timberwolves

Born in Springfield, Minnesota, Glen Taylor grew up on a farm in Comfrey, Minnesota. After graduating from Comfrey High School in 1959, three years later he received a Bachelor's of Science in mathematics, physics, and social studies from Minnesota State University–Mankato and then in 1978, earned an executive MBA from Harvard Business School.

During and after college, Taylor worked at Carlson Wedding Service, a Mankato print shop specializing in formal invitations. In 1975, company owner Bill Carlson wanted to retire, and Taylor offered to pay him $2 million over ten years for the company. The purchase formed the basis for the Taylor Corporation, a privately held multinational printing and electronics company with more than 15,000 employees and based in North Mankato. Taylor serves as its chairman and CEO.

When the cost to build a new arena for the Timberwolves exceeded estimates by 50 percent to about $100 million, co-owners Marv Wolfenson and Harvey Ratner decided to sell the team. In 1994, they reached an agreement with a group that planned to relocate it to New Orleans. But David Stern—NBA commissioner and a friend of Wolfenson and Ratner—stopped the move. Even so, they sold the team in 1995 for $89 million to Taylor who promised to keep the Timberwolves in Minneapolis. Furthermore, the city of Minneapolis bought the Target Center.

During mid-2016, Taylor sold 5 percent of the Timberwolves and also the WNBA Minnesota Lynx to Shanghai-based businessman Lizhang Jiang. Jiang, who founded Chinese marketing company Double-Edge Sports, previously worked with the NBA in China. In addition, Taylor sold a share of the Timberwolves to New York-based real estate magnate Meyer Orbach. Chairman of the Orbach Group, he owns retail and residential buildings in New York, New Jersey, Pennsylvania, and California.

Among WC teams and their owners as of early 2016, Taylor's Timberwolves have won one division crown but zero conference titles and championships since the mid-1990s. Respectively, the club ranked eleventh (division titles), tied for eighth (conference titles), and tied for sixth (championships). In comparison to owners of all NBA teams, Taylor's respectively tied for eighteenth, tied for fifteenth, and tied for tenth. Thus, he has not been successful as a leader of his NBA franchise (table A8).

According to a study in 2015, Taylor was the league's twenty-fourth best owner. The reasons for him being ranked relatively low were as follows:

> Taylor seems like a guy who has his heart in the right place but he just doesn't care enough to do anything about it. It has been since 2004 that the Timberwolves were in the postseason and they've pushed away two superstars—Kevin Garnett and Kevin Love—in the process. As an owner the most winning that Taylor has done is with the Minnesota Lynx, the team he has barely any influence over but still happens to win with. He has literally lucked his way into a basketball dynasty he doesn't deserve and it should be only a matter of time before he runs the Lynx into the ground and drives Mya Moore off to another franchise.[14]

Team Financials

Based on financial information published in *Forbes* magazine about NBA teams as of early 2016, the Timberwolves had a market value of $720 million, revenue $146 million, operating income $15 million, gate receipts $19 million, debt-to-value 14 percent, and players expenses $76 million. In comparison to others in the WC, the club ranked fourteenth (market value), tied for eleventh with the Jazz (revenue), and twelfth (operating income), fifteenth (gate receipts), sixth (debt-to-value), and tied for tenth (players expenses). Within the NWD, Minnesota's amounts were mostly fourth or fifth highest (table A9).

With respect to all NBA clubs, the Timberwolves' financials ranged from a tie for fifteenth (debt-to-value) to thirtieth (gate receipts). Based on these results, Minnesota is a relatively low-valued and financially inferior franchise because of its history of performances, market size, and too much competition from division rivals in regular-season games.

Besides market size, salary inflation, and other factors, an NBA team's annual payroll partly reflects its commitment to players and their current and potential contribution individually and as a group to winning games in regular seasons and postseasons. From 2011 to 2015, for example, the Timberwolves' payroll among WC teams ranged in rank from sixth in 2013 ($67.5 million) to fourteenth in 2011 ($56.8 million).Within the NWD, the club usually had either the third, fourth, or fifth highest payroll in the group during the period (table A10).

In comparison to payrolls of all NBA teams, Minnesota was respectively twenty-fifth in 2011, nineteenth in both 2012 ($63.1 million) and 2014 ($69.2 million), thirteenth in 2013, and twentieth in 2015 ($72.2 million). Given these amounts, the Timberwolves decided to increase their payroll each year yet failed to make the playoffs during the league's 2011–2015 seasons. To be consistently competitive in the future and win more regular-season games, the team needs to change its strategy of compensating players and be at least in the top fifteen of the league.

As of 2016, the Timberwolves guaranteed players $141 million in salaries. The top three amounts (seasons) include Ricky Rubio's $42 million (2016–2018), Nikola Petrovic's $23 million (2016–2017), and Cole Aldrich's $17 million (2016–2018). Each of them being less than thirty-one years old, they will develop and mature as teammates and contribute to Minnesota's victories in future seasons.[15]

Target Center

Opened in 1990, the 20,500-seat Target Center—home of the NBA Timberwolves and WNBA Lynx—is a clean, bright, and spacious arena within an exciting and alive downtown setting with plenty of things for people to do in the area. Financed with city bonds and private debt, the Target Corporation acquired the original and current naming rights to the facility.

Being the nation's first NBA arena with "No Smoking," some facts and amenities about it initially included: movable arena floor with ice-making capabilities; 20,000 theater-style cushioned seats and over 100 wheelchair seat locations on two levels; ten dressing rooms of various sizes; over 11,000 parking spaces within three blocks; eighteen escalators and nine elevators; and abundant restroom accommodations, averaging one for every forty-five customers.

In addition, the venue features a video, audio, and MATV lines; full-service marketing department including advertising, promotions, public relations, and group sales; complete box office and ticketing services; ticket lobby with one of the largest neon sculptures in America; more than ten ticket windows in the main lobby; a TDD line to the box office for the hearing impaired; and a complete tele-production studio and professional catering service.

Among arenas of fourteen other WC teams as of early 2016, the Timberwolves' home was the third oldest and also eleventh most expensive and fourteenth highest in value. In comparison to all NBA clubs, the Target Center ranked fifth (age), twenty-fourth (construction cost), and twenty-seventh (value). Based on this data, Minnesota plays in a relatively old facility with not enough amenities to generate a large amount of revenue for the franchise (table A11).

In the 2011–2015 NBA seasons, the FCIs for a family to attend a regular-season game at the Target Center ranged from a low of $225 in 2011 to a high of $281 in 2014 and 2015. With respect to those of all NBA teams, the Timberwolves ranked between eighteenth highest in 2014 to twenty-fifth in 2011, and also twenty-first most in fan cost at $261 in 2012, nineteenth at $273 in 2013, and tied for nineteenth with the Mavericks in 2015 (table A12).

To reveal specific costs for a recent season in the NBA, the Timberwolves' FCI in 2015–16 was the same as in 2014–15. Listed from most to least in amount by item for one person, the team's tickets averaged between $37 and $38, a cap $24, parking one vehicle $15, a beer $9–$10, and a program, hot dog, and soft drink each $5.

Among other teams in the conference's NWD, they had rankings and FCIs from most to least as follows: Trail Blazers fifteenth at $319; Nuggets sixteenth at $316; Thunder seventeenth at $296; and Jazz tied for twenty-first at $275. Consequently, Timberwolves fans paid less at games in the Target Center than those of eighteen other teams in their arenas.

The cheapest ticket cost $12 for anyone to watch a Timberwolves home game in 2015–16. This was about $4 or approximately 32 percent less than the league's average for a cheap seat. Also, since the club's FCI was $58 below the amount of a typical NBA team, a family of four purchased tickets and enjoyed a basketball game in Minnesota at a significant discount relative to the majority of arenas within the league. These costs and prices, in turn, were set by the Timberwolves organization to earn revenue and maximize profit from their operations.

According to a sports expert, the Target Center needs to be demolished. For the following reasons, it was inferior as of 2015:

> There's nothing to love about the Target Center. It's simply old without any vintage charms that other older stadiums across sports have. It doesn't help that the most significant event in the stadium's history involved Jesse Ventura winning the gubernatorial race back in 1999. Nothing about the Target Center is fun. The team is awful, the seats are gross and the stadium just stinks of boredom and mediocrity. That's not even getting to the food and how atrocious that is. Hot dogs at gas stations are higher quality cuisine that what is offered at the Target Center. It's a disgusting stadium that needs to be either completely torn down or totally renovated. It doesn't help that it sits next to the gorgeous and majestic Target Field, which makes the Target Center look like even more of a dump than it already is.[16]

As reported in *Forbes* magazine, the Timberwolves began a $129 million renovation of the Target Center in 2015. Three upgrades, for example, are new suites, locker rooms, and a scoreboard. According to trade publication Pollstar, the arena ranked number six in the United States based on the number of event tickets sold in 2014. In fact, it hosted eleven sold-out Garth Brooks concerts, breaking the artist's record for the most tickets sold (203,000) for a single city in North America.[17]

Business Highlights

Besides regular-season and postseason games, NBA franchises are involved in—and affected by—community events and business-related affairs, news, and projects. The following are a few of them for Minnesota's low home attendance, and from a financial perspective, below-average professional basketball team.[18]

First, longtime executive Rob Moor resigned in the summer of 2016 to assist owner Glen Taylor with other business interests. Moor served as CEO for both the NBA Timberwolves and WNBA Lynx since 2004 and also helped Taylor execute the purchase of the Timberwolves in 1995. Moor worked primarily with the business side of the franchises and joined assistant general manager Rob Babcock and coaches Sam Mitchell and Sidney Lowe on the list of those who had good relationships with Taylor but departed anyway

Second, during early 2014, the Mayo Clinic, Timberwolves, and Lynx established a partnership extending the Mayo Model of Care for patients in sports medicine to the Twin Cities. The collaboration included opening a Mayo Clinic Sports Medicine Center, designating Mayo as the preferred medical provider for the teams, and utilizing the teams' international reach to educate the public about numerous health and wellness topics. As the designated medical provider for these sports franchises, Mayo specialists diagnose, treat, and rehabilitate musculoskeletal injuries, as well as implement programs for optimal performance and injury prevention. In addition, Mayo utilizes the teams' marketing platforms to provide public education about numerous wellness topics including nutrition and physical fitness.

Third, during March 2014, the Timberwolves initiated a marketing campaign for a game they never had on their original regular-season home schedule. The game on April 8, against the San Antonio Spurs, was originally scheduled in December 2013 in Mexico City but cancelled because of smoke from a generator fire at the city's arena. The campaign poked fun at the rescheduling. A television spot, for example, recalled the canceled game and asks fans to come out and watch the Timberwolves "smoke" the Spurs in Minneapolis.

Fourth, the Timberwolves offered season ticket packages in March 2013 with year-round benefits. The plan carried a pricing-related twist that made it unique among other NBA teams' programs to entice Minnesota's fan base after an unexpectedly disappointing season. It also came as the club prepared to increase the average cost of season tickets for the next season by 10 percent.

Fifth, the Timberwolves consolidated all their social media channels into a new site with an eye toward driving more revenue through its digital efforts. In mid-2012, it launched WolvesNation.com, a website that aggregated the team's social media activity into a single site. To drive fan traffic on the site, the 'Wolves offered prizes, merchandise and concession discounts, and memorabilia while also allowing fans on the site to help dictate in-game entertainment including selecting songs and video packages for games.

Oklahoma City Thunder

Born in 1959 and chairman of a diversified private investment group named Dorchester Capital Corporation, Clayton Bennett organized a syndicate to purchase the Seattle Supersonics from owner Howard Schultz in 2006 for approximately $325 million. One condition of the deal was that Bennett gave a good-faith effort to keep the team in Seattle. However, according to emails between various business officials, Bennett's group never intended to keep the team in Seattle and planned to transfer the team elsewhere.

After failing to get $500 million in public funding from local taxes to build a new suburban arena, Bennett notified the NBA during November 2007 of the ownership group's intent to move his team to Oklahoma City. Four months later, Bennett revealed his plan to relocate the basketball franchise without his group retaining rights to the original team's name, logo, colors, and history.

In April 2008, NBA owners approved of shifting the franchise from Seattle for the league's 2008–9 season pending the outcome of the city's case to uphold the lease and the former ownership group's lawsuit to rescind the purchase. On July 2, 2008, Bennett's syndicate reached a settlement agreement in the lawsuit filed by the city of Seattle, which in turn allowed his franchise to move from Seattle to Oklahoma City and nickname it Thunder.

Among other owners of WC teams as of their 2015–16 season, Bennett's Thunder ranked fourth in winning division titles, seventh in conference titles, and tied for sixth in number of NBA championships. In comparison to owners of all NBA clubs, Oklahoma City tied for eighth (division titles), tied for twelfth (conference titles), and tied for tenth (league championships). These results indicate the Thunder, while owned by Bennett, has been successful in part for appearing in six playoffs since the 2006–7 season (table A8).

In 2015, ESPN ranked Bennett fourteenth best of all NBA owners. Among others in the NWD, Portland's Paul Allen placed sixth, Utah's Greg Miller ninth, Denver's Josh Kroenke twenty-fifth, and Minnesota's Glen Taylor twenty-seventh. And in a study of teams' front offices, the Thunder was fourth. Following are reasons for the organization's relatively high rank:

> In eight short years, the team in the smallest market in the NBA—Oklahoma City Thunder—has emerged as one of the league's top flight organizations. Yes, losing superstar Kevin Durant to rival Golden State in 2016 NBA free agency stinks, but the Thunder are about as well run of a small market basketball organization as anybody in the NBA, outside of one team in Texas [Dallas Mavericks or Houston Rockets].Though majority owner Clay Bennett and coaches Scott Brooks and Billy Donovan have been key to the Thunder's overall success since leaving Seattle after the 2007–08 NBA season, without outstanding general manager Sam Presti, what are the Thunder? Presti has done remarkable work in NBA Drafts. Given that Oklahoma City shouldn't normally be a marquee free agent destination because of market size, the Thunder has to win every NBA Draft, instill a culture of player development to second-tier free agents, and orchestrate the occasional lopsided trade.[19]

Team Financials

With respect to financial information published in *Forbes* magazine for NBA teams as of their 2015–16 season, the Thunder's market value was $950 million, revenue $157 million, operating income $20 million, gate receipts $48 million, debt-to-value 15 percent, and players expenses $87 million. Among only WC clubs, Oklahoma City ranked ninth (market value), tied for seventh with the Trail Blazers (revenue), tied for ninth with the Clippers (operating income), sixth (gate receipts), fifth (debt ratio), and fourth (players expenses). Within the NWD, the Thunder's amounts were first, second, or third (table A9).

In comparison to twenty-nine other teams in the league as of early 2016, Oklahoma City's data ranged in rank from being tied for eighth in players expenses to seventeenth in market value. As a business enterprise, the Thunder is average to above-average financially including its revenue and profit. Nevertheless, the team's debt percent is relatively high especially when compared to others in the WC.

Besides market size, salary inflation, and other factors, an NBA team's annual payroll partly reflects its commitment to players and their current and potential contribution individually and as a group to winning games in regular seasons and postseasons. From 2011 to 2015, for example, the Thunder's payroll among WC teams ranged in rank from second in both 2014 ($79.7 million) and 2015 ($96.5 million) to ninth in 2011 ($59.9 million).Within only the NWD, the club had the highest payroll in the group except in 2011 (table A10).

In comparison to payrolls of all NBA teams, Oklahoma City was respectively nineteenth in 2011, tenth in 2012 ($67.4 million), eleventh in 2013 ($70.1 million), sixth in 2014, and third in 2015. Given these amounts, the Thunder decided to increase its payroll each year and qualified for the playoffs during four of the five seasons. To be consistently competitive in the future and continue winning most of its regular-season games, the team needs to keep players' payroll at least in the top ten of the league.

As of 2016, the Thunder guaranteed its players $154 million in salaries. The top three amounts—for the NBA's 2016–2018 seasons—included Russell Westbrook's $42 million, Enes Kanter's $35 million, and Alex Abrines's $17 million. Each of them not yet twenty-eight years old, they will develop and mature as teammates and contribute to Oklahoma City's victories in future years.

Passed by the state legislature in 1993, Oklahoma's Quality Jobs Act was meant to attract manufacturing and service jobs. But the list of companies receiving subsidies—such as Continental, Devon, and Chesapeake—has ballooned in recent years to include the Thunder. In fact, $4 million of tax money goes to the NBA franchise and its 168 jobs. Most of the companies can stay on the "quality jobs" list for ten years. State leaders, however, made an exception for the Thunder, who will get more than $4 million for fifteen years.[20]

Chesapeake Energy Arena

Opened in 2002, the Chesapeake Energy Arena (CEA)—previously named Ford Center and Oklahoma City Arena—is a 586,000-square-foot facility that originally featured four seating levels and a press level with a maximum seating capacity of 20,817 for a concert set in-the-round. Located between the 6,300-seat Oklahoman Level (lower level) and the 7,700-seat Oklahoman Bedlam Level (upper level) is the Cox Communications Club and Suite Level that includes 3,380 club seats, at least seven Oklahoma State Park Suites, and approximately forty-eight private suites.

The exterior of the arena is a yellow brick façade with two major entrances. A statue sits near the west entry celebrating the 1989 Olympic Festival that took place in Oklahoma City. Once inside, people either head straight forward up the stairs/escalators to the club/upper deck or swing a left/right—depending on entry—to the arena's main concourse. The signature feature of both upper and lower concourses is a series of murals depicting many of the things that made Oklahoma famous such as pioneer wagons and cowboy hats. These murals, which dot the floor of the lower concourse and emblazon the ceiling of the upper level, greatly enhance the look of what are otherwise somewhat dark and bland concourses.

Since opening its doors, CEA has hosted numerous events with attendance in the millions. Besides the Thunder, it is home to the Central Hockey League's Oklahoma City Blazers and Arena Football2's Oklahoma City Yard Dawgz. From the 2005–6 to 2006–7 NBA seasons, the venue also served as the temporary home of the New Orleans Hornets and played host to major concerts, family events, ice shows, sporting events, and the latest in showstopping entertainment.

Among facilities of fourteen other WC teams as of early 2016, CEA is tied for twelfth in age with the Spurs' AT&T Center, fourteenth most expensive to build, and ninth highest in value. In comparison to those of all NBA clubs, CEA is tied for twenty-third (age) and also ranks twenty-eighth (construction cost) and seventeenth (value). Based on this data, the Thunder plays its home games in a relatively large, modern, and busy arena with amenities to generate more revenue for the franchise (table A11).

In the 2011–2015 NBA seasons, the FCIs for a family to attend a regular-season game at CEA ranged from a low of $278 in 2012 to a high of $296 in 2015. With respect to those of all NBA teams, the Thunders ranked between fourteenth highest in 2011 ($280) to seventeenth most in 2012, 2013 ($295), and 2015 and also sixteenth at $295 in 2014 (table A12).[21]

To reveal specific costs for a recent season in the NBA, the Thunder's FCI in 2015–16 was less than 1 percent higher than in 2014–15. Listed from most to least in amount by item for one person, the team's tickets averaged between $55 and $56, a cap $15, parking one vehicle $10, a beer $5, hot dog $3–$4, and a soft drink $3.

Among other teams in the conference's NWD, they had rankings and FCIs from most to least as follows: Trail Blazers fifteenth at $319; Nuggets sixteenth at $316; Timberwolves nineteenth at $281; and Jazz tied for twenty-first at $275. Consequently, Thunder's fans paid less at games in CEA than did those of sixteen other teams in their hometown arenas.

The cheapest ticket cost $15 for a fan to watch a Thunder home game in 2015–16. This was about $1 or approximately 5 percent less than the league's average for a cheap seat. Also, since the club's FCI was $43 below the amount of a typical NBA team, a family of four purchased tickets and enjoyed a basketball game in Oklahoma City at a small discount relative to the majority of arenas within the league. These costs and prices, in turn, were set by the Thunder organization to earn revenue and maximize profit from their operations.

Based on such things as number of concessions, overall atmosphere, location, fans, access including traffic, parking, and ability to move around inside, overall return on investment and one category for any extras or unusual amenities, the *Stadium Journal* ranked CEA twelfth in 2015. A reviewer of the venue wrote:

> The Chesapeake Energy Arena has one of the best NBA atmospheres in the country. The arena promotes the entire upper seating as Loud City with signage around the arena. There is a food concession stand called Loud City Grill, along with a sign showing the population of the upper deck seating of 7,631 at one portal. This is a great preview of how the atmosphere inside the arena will be during the game. The decibel level of noise is high throughout the game. The pregame ceremony on the top notch hi-definition scoreboard over the court shows tribute to the state of Oklahoma. Once the lights go off for the Thunder introductions, a loud tornado siren with artificial lighting goes off inside the arena.[22]

Business Highlights

Besides regular-season and postseason games, NBA franchises are involved in—and affected by—community events and business-related affairs, news, and projects. The following are a few of them for Oklahoma City's popular, and from a financial perspective, average to above-average professional basketball team.[23]

First, after indebted Oklahoma City energy magnate Aubrey McClendon died in a car crash during March 2016, some of his creditors wanted input as to how his 20 percent interest in the Thunder franchise will be disposed of by his estate, viewing the basketball team as one of McClendon's few assets of value. The lenders requested the stake be sold for top dollar but feared it would be sold for less than that to McClendon's wife, Kathleen, because she is family, said a lawyer representing a syndicate of banks led by Wilmington Trust that loaned $465 million to a company McClendon founded in 2013, American Energy Partners LP.

Second, during the spring 2016, the National Rifle Association supported bills in Oklahoma that would let people carry guns in public even if they had no training or background checks. This is known as a "constitutional carry" measure. As a result, Moms Demand Action teamed with the Thunder, law enforcement agencies, universities, chambers of commerce, and other businesses to oppose the proposals. Although a bill sailed through Oklahoma's two chambers, it died in committee in May 2016. Several months earlier, the NBA launched a campaign against gun violence with testimonials from several basketball stars including Golden State Warriors guard Steph Curry.

Third, on the official Thunder website, an overwhelming amount of information fills the screen. Schedules, videos, statistics, and promotions are squeezed into most of the available space on the homepage. The goal of the team's digital marketing strategy is to use this information to its advantage by disseminating the right content through the right platform. Once published, its dedicated fan base will take care of the rest—through engagement and sharing. Nurturing a global fan base is no easy task, but the Thunder's digital marketing team does it exceptionally well with such things as a multimedia library with specific video channels—recaps, highlights, and post-game interviews, streaming social media integration, custom website for commercial merchandise, and data entry subscription forms like text, email, and newsletter notifications

Fourth, six weeks into its 2012–13 season-ticket renewal campaign, the Thunder sold out the club's full-season ticket allotment for 2013–14. The team had a self-imposed limit of 14,000 season tickets and wrapped it up with renewals at 98 percent. With virtually every season ticket holder having an active deposit, it was a record sellout timewise.

Fifth, the Thunder went 45–37 during the league's 2014–15 season but missed the playoffs and ended its five-year consecutive postseason run. The team, which slipped from first to third place in local television ratings, averaged a 7.04 rating on FS Oklahoma or 20 percent lower than the previous season. But the Thunder once again played in front of a packed house during the entire 2014–15 season as fans continued to fill Chesapeake Energy Arena. After registering sellouts during forty-one home games in each of the four previous seasons, the Thunder recorded sellouts in 187 consecutive regular season home outings and 222 games overall, including the postseason.

Portland Trail Blazers

Born in 1953 in Seattle, Washington, Paul Allen is an American businessman, philanthropist, investor, musician, innovator, and best known as the cofounder of Microsoft Corporation alongside Bill Gates. He is the founder and CEO of Vulcan Inc., which manages his various business and philanthropic efforts, and also has a multi-billion-dollar investment portfolio including technology and media companies, real estate holdings, and stakes in other companies.

Allen, who purchased the NBA Trail Blazers in 1988 from California real estate developer Larry Weinberg for $70 million, was instrumental in the development and funding of the Moda Center—previously known as the Rose Garden—where the Blazers play their home games. He purchased the arena in April 2007, stating that this was a major milestone and a positive step for the franchise. Besides the Trail Blazers, Allen also owns the NFL Seattle Seahawks and MLS Seattle Sounders FC.

Among owners of WC teams as of early 2016, Allen's Trail Blazers ranked fifth in winning four division titles, tied for fourth with three other teams in number of conference titles, and tied for sixth in NBA championships. In comparison to those of all NBA clubs, his Trail Blazers tied for tenth (division titles and league championships) and tied for fifth (conference titles). Given these results, Allen has been an average to above-average owner whose teams competed in twenty-one playoffs since the 1987–88 season but failed to win an NBA championship (table A8).

After ESPN asked some voters to rate each NBA team's ownership performance-wise in guiding their franchise to overall on-court success both in the short and long term as of 2015, Allen ranked sixth of the group. Within the conference's NWD, he placed higher than the Jazz's Gail Miller (ninth), Thunder's Clayton Bennett (fourteenth), Nuggets' Josh Kroenke (twenty-fifth), and Timberwolves' Glen Taylor (twenty-seventh). Apparently, Allen does not get in the way of his front office and manages to make sure things are running smoothly. He is one of the well-regarded owners in all of sports, and one of the reasons many people root for the Blazers to finally get over the hump.[24]

After hiring former longtime SuperSonics play-by-play man Kevin Calabro as the Trail Blazers' new voice in the summer of 2016, a columnist in *The Oregonian* wrote that owner Paul Allen might try to sneak the team out of Portland and bring it back to Seattle. In fact, he once hired "Mr. Sonic" Nate McMillan to coach his team and drafted Seattle prep star Martell Webster over Chris Paul. Allen's Blazers grabbed University of Washington star Brandon Roy on draft day in 2006 and even put another beloved Seattleite, Jamal Crawford, in black and red for a stretch.[25]

Team Financials

According to financial data published in *Forbes* magazine about NBA teams as of early 2016, the Trail Blazers' market value was $975 million, revenue $157 million, operating income $4 million, gate receipts $42 million, debt-to-value 11 percent, and players expenses $94 million. With respect to competitors in the WC, Portland ranked eighth in market value, gate receipts and the debt ratio, tied for seventh with the Thunder in revenue, tied for fourteenth with the Kings in operating income, and placed first in players expenses (table A9).

Within only the conference's NWD, the Blazers were the most valuable team and among twenty-nine other clubs in the league ranged in rank from second (players expenses) to a tie for twenty-sixth (operating income). Based on these amounts, Portland is average from a financial perspective despite its relatively low income from operations and high players expenses.

Besides market size, salary inflation, and other factors, an NBA team's annual payroll partly reflects its commitment to players and their current and potential contribution individually and as a group to winning games in regular seasons and postseasons. From 2011 to 2015, for example, the Trail Blazer's payroll among WC teams ranged in rank from eighth in 2011 ($64.3 million) to fifteenth in 2015 ($61.6 million). Within the NWD, the club had the highest payroll in the group in 2011 but not in other years (table A10).

In comparison to payrolls of all NBA teams, Portland was respectively fifteenth in 2011, twenty-fourth in 2012 ($58.4 million), twenty-second in 2013 ($62.5 million), sixteenth in 2014 ($71.6 million), and thirtieth in 2015. Given these amounts, the Trail Blazers decided to reduce their payroll in two of these years yet qualified for the playoffs during three consecutive seasons. To be consistently competitive in the future and continue winning most of its regular-season games, the team needs to significantly increase its payroll in 2017 and thereafter.

Portland has committed $101.2 million to players on the roster in 2017 and $101.6 in 2018. In other words, the club went from being a small-market team with low total player salaries to a freewheeling spending machine. But the problem now is too much expensive talent and no place for all its high-priced players to fit into the lineup. Given the league's salary cap, there is little to no room to spend more without a luxury tax or to continue rebuilding during the next few seasons.[26]

Moda Center

Opened in 1995 to replace the undersized and outdated Memorial Coliseum, the 21,300-seat Moda Center—former Rose Garden—is a flexible, multipurpose facility hosting a variety of events including NBA and college basketball, professional hockey, indoor soccer, indoor track and field, gymnastics, major concerts, and other types of activities such as professional wrestling, and convention and trade shows. Originally, the arena had approximately seventy luxury suites and more than 2,300 club seats.

Like other basketball arenas built during the mid-1990s, the Moda Center has wide concourses for anyone to navigate through with their special Blazers souvenir and also plenty of concession outlets for food and different types of beverages. Despite the building's size, the arena's bowl retains a sense of intimacy, unlike other places which are huge and barnlike. Between two levels is the suite level, while the club level is at the upper half of the lower sideline seats. There are also a few super suites atop the seating area in one corner of the building which provides a nice, if distant view of the action.

In 1995, the Moda Center introduced a new trend in advertising in which there would be simultaneous scrolling advertising panels around the entire circumference of the bowl. This design has been copied by many other arenas and although made obsolete with new technology, it still added a nice touch for fans.

For information fanatics who need to know every statistic possible about an event on the floor, high above the seating area are several boards that keep track of data for fans. One at each end keeps track of individual players and each team. Another board displays both teams' intangible statistics such as blocks, steals, and rebounds. Still another one tracks positive and negative data like missed free throws and turnovers. In general, the information is concise, non-confusing, and well organized.

With respect to arenas of fourteen other WC teams as of early 2016, the Trail Blazers' home was the sixth oldest, fourth most expensive to build, and seventh in value. In comparison to all NBA teams' venues, the Moda Center tied for tenth with the Celtics' TD Garden (age), and ranked eighth (construction cost) and fourteenth (value). Thus, Portland plays its home games in a relatively old but privately financed facility with plenty of amenities to earn addition revenue for the team (table A11).

In the 2011–2015 NBA seasons, the FCIs for a family to attend a regular-season game at the Moda Center ranged from a low of $296 in both 2011 and 2012 to a high of $319 in 2015. With respect to those of all NBA teams, the Trail Blazers' home games ranked between the eleventh highest in 2011 to sixteenth in 2013 ($308) but also fourteenth in 2014 ($317) and fifteenth in 2012 and 2015 (table A12).

To reveal specific costs for a recent season in the NBA, the Thunder's FCI in 2015–16 was less than 1 percent higher than in 2014–15. Listed from most to least in amount by item for one person, the team's tickets averaged between $53 and $54, a cap $16 and parking one vehicle $15, single beer $7, hot dog $6, and a soft drink $5.

Among other teams in the conference's NWD, they had rankings and FCIs from most to least as follows: Nuggets sixteenth at $316; Thunder seventeenth at $296; Timberwolves nineteenth at $281; and Jazz tied for twenty-first at $275. Consequently, Trail Blazers fans paid less at games in their hometown arena than those of fourteen other teams in their arenas.

The cheapest ticket cost $10 for a fan to watch a Trail Blazers' home game in 2015–16. This was about $6 or approximately 6 percent less than the league's average for a cheap seat. Also, since the club's FCI was $20 below the amount of a typical NBA team, a family of four purchased tickets and enjoyed a basketball game in Portland at a discount relative to the majority of arenas within the league. These costs and prices, in turn, were set by the Trail Blazers organization to earn revenue and maximize profit from their operations.

In a study of all NBA arenas as of 2015, the Moda Center was third best in the league based on its concessions, overall atmosphere, local neighborhood, accessibility, overall return on investment, and one category for any extras or unusual amenities. Following the Spurs' AT&T Center and Lakers' Staple Center, the Moda Center placed relatively high, in part, because:

> When you get to your seat, you will see banners of division and conference titles, along with the lone NBA championship on one side, and retired jerseys hanging from the other side. The organization takes great pride in their history, and is bold about telling visitors just where they've been. Being the only major league team in town for many years, the Blazers are THE game in town. A Blazers game is a great excuse to see one of the most unique American cities.[27]

Regarding the arena's naming rights company as of early 2016, Moda Health was in trouble after two states clamped down on the floundering health insurer. More specifically, Alaska and Oregon mandated that Moda stop selling health plans in their states, where the company had a big presence in the employer and individual markets. As a result, insurance ratings agency A.M. Best downgraded Moda's credit rating to "under regulatory supervision," a designation reserved for companies that are impaired and could be nearing insolvency. The sanctions coincided with the end of the Affordable Care Act's third open-enrollment period, and raised red flags about health insurers that struggled to incorporate the new individual and small-group exchanges into their business models.

Business Highlights

Besides regular-season and postseason games, NBA franchises are involved in—and affected by—community events and business-related affairs, news, and projects. The following are a few of them for Portland's popular, and from a financial perspective, average professional basketball team.[28]

First, since 2012, the Trail Blazers organization has become about basketball again. Win or lose, basketball leads and business follows. The Blazers have leaders—general manager Neil Olshey and president Chris McGowan—who work very closely together promoting vision, talking strategy, and organization messaging. While Olshey focuses primarily on basketball operations, McGowan has improved the fan experience, stopped the organization from posturing and started genuinely soliciting feedback from fans, and ended the franchise's perpetrating the long-running sellout streak myth.

Second, the Trail Blazers and parent company Vulcan Inc. have spent $20 million in capital improvements of the Moda Center since 2013. From upgrading private suites to adding an on-site bar and restaurant and also welcoming more local food purveyors to operate concessions, franchise owner Paul Allen has opted to invest in an extended life of the twenty-two-year-old facility (as of 2016). While the enormous new fountain and torch that welcome fans may be splashy, it is arguably the technology behind the scenes at the arena that sets the team up best for the future.

Third, during early 2016, the Trail Blazers became the first NBA team to begin selling renewals through their mobile app. According to senior vice president of brand strategy and digital Dewayne Hankins, the team's biggest fans and ticket holders are comfortable with the app, and thus sensible to make it about renewals.

Fourth, the Trail Blazers won an NBA award in 2013 for best local team promotion held during the recently completed regular season. Tied to a locally based restaurant group named Burgerville, the promotion included naming a hamburger after the team. The food company was in the third year of a three-year sponsorship with the club.

Fifth, the Trail Blazers lost 80 percent of their starting lineup from the 2014–15, fifty-one-win squad. Even so, fans felt strongly about the team. Season ticket renewals for the 2015–16 season were 97 percent and ranked fifth in the NBA. New additions to the Moda Center in 2015 included a refurbished courtside lounge and a kid-friendly activity area. Later, the Trail Blazers are in line for a new television deal because their pact with Comcast SportsNet Northwest expires after the league's 2016–17 season.

Utah Jazz

Businessman Larry Miller became co-owner of the Utah Jazz when he purchased a 50 percent interest in the team for $9.5 million during April 1985. Fourteen months later, he acquired the remaining 50 percent of it from Sam Battistone for $17.3 million. This, in turn, averted a bid by a Minneapolis group to move the Jazz from Salt Lake City to Minnesota. Miller also owned the WNBA Utah Starzz franchise but sold it in 2002 to San Antonio Spurs owner Peter Holt.

After her husband Larry Miller died in 2009 from complications of Type II diabetes, his wife Gail assumed 100 percent ownership of their businesses. These consisted of approximately fifty-four automobile dealerships, a movie theater chain, and the Jazz. Besides these investments, she also became chairwoman of the Larry H. Miller Group of Companies and Salt Lake Community College.

As of early 2016, Gail Miller's Jazz had won zero division and conference titles and NBA championships from the league's 2009–10 season. Among owners of only WC teams, her club tied for eleventh (division titles), tied for eighth (conference titles), and tied for sixth (championships). In comparison to the performances of twenty-nine others in the league, Miller's performance as an owner, respectively, tied for nineteenth, tied for fifteenth, and tied for tenth. Consequently, she has been mediocre in leading Jazz teams to victories during seven regular seasons and two postseasons following the death of her husband Larry (table A8).

In 2015, ESPN asked some voters to rate each NBA team's ownership while guiding their franchise to overall on-court success, both in the short and long term. The Jazz's Gail Miller ranked ninth and among others in the NWD, she trailed the Trail Blazers' Paul Allen (sixth) but ahead of the Thunder's Clayton Bennett (fourteenth), Nuggets' Josh Kroenke (twenty-fifth), and Timberwolves' Glen Taylor (twenty-seventh). For their accomplishments, her franchise's front office, general manager, and president received similar ratings as Miller.

Based on another report, Gail Miller's son Greg—the team's CEO who resigned in late 2015—was also ninth. The reasons given for his relatively high rank were as follows:

> There isn't a whole lot that the Jazz do wrong, but they're far from a perfect franchise. They have an owner [CEO] in Greg Miller who has survived the post-Jerry Sloan era better than most, and he's done it all without the help of a star point guard. He's managed to keep attendance up despite the winning being down in a small market like Salt Lake City. That's often times an overlooked aspect of being an owner, as it's easy to sell seats when you're winning but doing so when your team isn't at the top is a lot harder. Miller knowns the passionate fan base he has, and isn't going to push them away to make an extra buck. That's something not all NBA owners can say.[29]

Team Financials

Regarding financial information contained in *Forbes* magazine about NBA teams as of early 2016, the Jazz had a market value of $875 million, revenue $146 million, operating income $27 million, gate receipts $36 million, debt-to-value 9 percent, and players expenses $67 million. Within only the WC,

Utah's amounts placed eleventh in market value, tied for eleventh with the Timberwolves in revenue, fifth in operating income, ninth in gate both receipts and the debt ratio, and fourteen in players expenses (table A9).

Other than operating income, the Jazz's results were worse than the NWD's Thunder and Trail Blazers. Among all NBA teams, however, the Utah ranked between ninth in operating income to being tied for twenty-sixth in players expenses. From a financial perspective, Utah is a below-average franchise rather than a prosperous business enterprise, in part because of its fan base, historical performances, location, and other demographic and sport-specific factors.

Besides market size, salary inflation, and other factors, an NBA team's annual payroll partly reflects its commitment to players and their current and potential contribution individually and as a group to winning games in regular seasons and postseasons. From 2011 to 2015, for example, the Jazz's payroll among WC teams ranged in rank from sixth in 2012 ($66.9 million) to fourteenth in 2013 ($56.9 million), 2014 ($60.2 million), and 2015 ($63.0 million).Within the NWD, the club had the lowest payroll in the group in 2013 but second to fourth in other years (table A10).

In comparison to payrolls of all NBA teams, Utah was respectively twentieth in 2011, twelfth in 2012, twenty-six in 2013, twenty-fifth in 2014, and twenty-eighth in 2015. Given these rankings, the Jazz decided to reduce their payroll in one year but then increased it in 2012, 2014, and 2015 while qualifying for only one playoff during the period. To be consistently competitive in the future and win the majority of its regular-season games, the team needs to significantly increase its payroll in 2017 and if necessary in 2018 and 2019.

Utah has committed $83.7 million to players on the roster in the league's 2016–17 season and $71.4 million in 2017–18, and $14.9 million in 2018–19. Additionally, four players are guaranteed between $16 million and $32 million and another nine from $900,000 to $8 million. Of the group, only Joe Johnson, George Hill, and Boris Diaw are each more than thirty years old. Thus, the Jazz are a relatively young but talented team that needs to guarantee more money to at least four of its first-round draft picks to be potentially more successful in the future.[30]

Virint Smart Home Arena

Opened in 1991 to replace the obsolete Salt Palace, the 19,900-seat Virint Smart Home Arena (VSHA)—previously named Delta Center (1991–2005) and then EnergySolutions Arena (2006–2015)—is a large concrete-and-silver, cube-like structure with plenty of windows. From the front, it looks more like an imposing office building than the home of an NBA team.

This is a two-concourse facility serving the two main seating areas in the building. As in many venues, it is the lower concourse that provides most of the points of interest. There is not much trouble walking out and about, especially in the four corners of the building where the design of the seating bowl makes these areas larger than at the baseline/sideline portions of the concourse.

Mostly light green seats exist in the seating bowl, which is split into two levels. Sandwiched between the two is a ring of suites for those who would rather watch games on television but be there at the same time. The advertising and dot matrix message boards are on the suite level balcony.

In the summer of 2010, the arena was remodeled. This included the installation of Bear's Backyard and a playground for kids, a new dining area for adults, and over 500 television screens. After being announced in June 2013, the venue received a new scoreboard and ribbon display technology, with display screens in each of its corners. These were installed in the league's 2013–14 offseason. On October 26, 2015, naming rights to the building were acquired as part of a ten-year contract with home security and automation provider Vivint of Salt Lake City.

Among facilities of fourteen other WC teams as of early 2016, the Jazz's is the fourth oldest, twelfth most expensive, and tenth in value. In comparison to all NBA arenas, Utah's ranks sixth (age), twenty-fifth (construction cost), and nineteenth (value). Based on these results, the Jazz play their home games in a relatively outdated building with several amenities to earn more revenue for the franchise.

In the 2011–2015 NBA seasons, the FCIs for a family to attend a regular-season game at VSHA ranged from a low of $271 in 2011 to a high of $280 in 2013. With respect to those of all NBA teams, the Jazz's home was tied for nineteenth highest in 2011, eighteenth in 2012 ($276) and 2013, twenty-first in 2014 ($275), and tied for twenty-first at $275 in 2015 (table A12).

To reveal specific costs for a recent season in the NBA, the Jazz's FCI in 2015–2016 at games in VSHA was the same as in 2014–15. Listed from most to least in amount by item for one person, the team's tickets averaged between $43 and $44, a cap $20 and parking one vehicle $10, single beer $7–$8, program $5, and a hot dog and soft drink each $3–$4.

Among other teams in the conference's NWD, they had rankings and FCIs from most to least as follows: Trail Blazers fifteenth at $319; Nuggets sixteenth at $316; Thunder seventeenth at $296; and Timberwolves nineteenth at $281. Consequently, the Jazz fans paid less at games in its arena than those of twenty other teams in their arenas.

The cheapest ticket cost about $10 for a fan to watch a Jazz home game in 2015–16. This was about $6 or approximately 6 percent less than the league's average for a cheap seat. Also, since the club's FCI was $64 below the amount of a typical NBA team, a family of four purchased tickets and enjoyed a basketball game in Salt Lake City at a significant discount relative to the majority of arenas within the league. These costs and prices, in turn, were set by the Jazz organization to earn revenue and maximize profit from their operations.

In its annual ranking of all thirty NBA game-day experiences as of 2016, the *Stadium Journey* rated the VSHA sixteenth. Indeed:

> The defining characteristic of Vivint Smart Home Arena is the volume. Jazz fans consistently rank among the loudest in the NBA, even during "down" years. If you have sensitive hearing (or want to prevent having it), earplugs are always available at guest services. Otherwise, be prepared to soak in (or bring) the noise.[31]

Business Highlights

Besides regular-season and postseason games, NBA franchises are involved in—and affected by—community events and business-related affairs, news, and projects. The following are a few of them for Salt Lake City's popular, but from a financial perspective, below-average professional basketball team.[32]

First, Utah became the first NBA franchise to unveil a bold new product that allowed season ticket holders to sell their "seat location rights" to buyers, creating potential new revenue for season ticket holders and the team. Although personal seat license transfers had been common in the NFL, no NBA team offered them until 2010. In a partnership with STR Marketplace, the Jazz allowed fans to sell rights to their season tickets at a premium set by the market. While the transfer of season ticket location from seller to buyer is permanent, the team's ticket office bills the buyer for the season tickets.

Second, the Larry H. Miller Group's hopes for tax breaks to help cover the cost of $110 million in planned arena renovations ran into opposition from at least one political advocacy group. As of mid-2016, the Utah chapter of Americans for Prosperity launched a campaign to stop Salt Lake City's Redevelopment Agency (RDA) from giving out a tax break potentially worth up to $22.7 million. The Group's leaders planned to present their proposal for funding to the city and request that the Miller family cover the cost of the project upfront, then, through an RDA tax increment reimbursement program, recoup up to $22.7 million over the next twenty-five years.

Third, after doing different things and thinking about a new career, former Jazz executive Greg Miller bought an underperforming Toyota car dealership during mid-2016 from Bob Baker in San Diego, California. Greg planned to spend the foreseeable future flying back and forth from Salt Lake City to San Diego while juggling duties with LHM, church, and spending time with his family.

Fourth, when Dennis Lindsey became general manager of the Jazz in 2015, he was assigned one job: rebuild a once proud organization into a perennial championship contender. To build a championship team, there are several traditional paths that found success in recent history. While yet to fully take shape—and a deep run through the playoffs is surely needed to judge its success—a new model emerged in the process. Understanding that he cannot lure the NBA's best free agents to Salt Lake City, Lindsey decided to borrow elements from previous successful rebuilding efforts, consolidate them, and then expect great results.

Fifth, as announced in early 2016, Western Governors University (WGU) and the Jazz teamed up to provide four Utah students with a full year of tuition. Awarded during halftime of a Jazz-Clippers game, the scholarships allow four students to attend WGU—an online, nonprofit university—tuition-free for one year. All winners are new enrollees at WGU and had submitted an official entry form earlier in the Jazz season. Proud to join WGU to give these students free tuition for one year, the Jazz organization places great value on education and was thus thrilled to help provide academic assistance to members of the community.

NOTES

1. The league's success and each of its teams' history, in part, appears in Frank P. Jozsa Jr., *National Basketball Association Strategies: Business Expansions, Relocations, and Mergers* (New York: Springer, 2016), and James Quirk and Rodney D. Fort, *Pay Dirt: The Business of Professional Team Sports* (Princeton, NJ: Princeton University Press, 1992).
2. Three websites to research for different NBA regular seasons and postseasons and team performances are http://www.basketball-reference.com, http://www.nba.com, and http://www.sportsalmanac.com.
3. Daniel C. Lewis, "Nuggets Climb to 20th Overall in ESPN Future Power Rankings," http://www.denverstiffs.com, cited August 5, 2016.
4. Chad Ford and Kevin Pelton, "Future NBA Power Rankings: Full Category Rankings," http://www.espn.go.com, cited August 3, 2016.
5. "Kevin Durant to Sign With Warriors," http://www.espn.com, cited August 5, 2016.
6. See Daniel Zillmer, "All 30 NBA Franchises Statistically Ranked by All-Time Greatness," http://www.fansided.com, cited June 6, 2016.
7. The primary source is David Mackay, "Trail Blazers Climb High in ESPN Future Power Rankings," http://www.blazersedge.com, cited August 7, 2016.

8. William Case, "Ranking the Greatest Franchises in NBA History," http://www.listlicled.com, cited August 8, 2016.

9. Adam Fromal, "Future Power Rankings for the 2016 NBA Lottery Teams," http://www.bleacherreport.com, cited July 15, 2016.

10. "2015 Front-Office Rankings: Owners," http://www.espn.go.com, cited July 14, 2016.

11. Zach Mikash, "Forbes Paints a Murky Financial Picture for the Denver Nuggets," http://www.denverstiffs.com, cited August 15, 2016.

12. "NBA FCIs," http://www.teammarketingreport.com, cited July 1, 2016

13. Some Nuggets business and social highlights are reported in Daniel Kaplan, "Kroenke to Offer Plan to Comply With NFL Rules," http://www.sportsbusinessdaily.com, cited July 26, 2016; George Flood, "Indiana Pacers Will Meet Denver Nuggets at NBA Global Games London in 2017," http://www.ibtimes.co.uk, cited August 1, 2016; "The National Basketball Academy: Denver Nuggets," http://www.nba.com, cited August 5, 2016; "Denver Nuggets Community Ambassadors," http://www.nba.com, cited August 7, 2016.

14. Josh Hill, "NBA Owners Power Ranking: Who is the Best Owner in Basketball?" http://www.fansided.com, cited July 8, 2016.

15. "NBA Team Salaries," http://www.basketball-reference.com, cited August 14, 2016.

16. See Josh Hill, "NBA: Five Arenas That Need to be Torn Down Now," http://www.fansided.com, cited July 15, 2016.

17. Eric Roper, "Target Center Renovation Clears Final Hurdle From Minneapolis City Council," http://www.startribune.com, cited August 20, 2016.

18. Minnesota's business highlights include such articles in publications as John Lombardo, "Wolves Get Creative in Efforts to Sell Late Addition to Home Schedule," http://www.sportsbusinessdaily.com, cited August 10, 2016; "New Seats, Signs for Wolves," http://www.sportsbusinessdaily.com, cited August 15, 2016; "Wolves, Lynx Announce New Practice Facility, Partnership With Mayo Clinic," http://www.nba.com, cited August 20, 2016; "Longtime Timberwolves, Lynx CEO Rob Moor Steps Down," http://www.espn.com, cited August 18, 2016.

19. John Buhler, "10 Best NBA Front Offices," http://www.fansided.com, cited August 21, 2016.

20. Abby Broyles, "'We Shouldn't be Subsidizing Their Payroll,' State Program Funds OKC Thunder, Other Big Companies' Payroll, Amid Budget Crisis," http://www.kfor.com, cited July 28, 2016.

21. "Fan Cost Index," http://www.teammarketingreport.com, cited August 1, 2016.

22. To review facts and more details about NBA facilities as of early 2016, see Paul Swaney, "2015 NBA Arena Experience Rankings," http://www.scout.com, cited August 15, 2016.

23. The Thunder's business highlights appear in such readings as "Thunder Sells Out '12–13 Season Tickets, Starts Wait List," http://www.sportsbusinessdaily.com, cited August 11, 2016; Bill Sutton, "How Inclusiveness Allows OKC to Think Big in a Small Market," http://www.sportsbusinessdaily.com, cited August 25, 2016; Jes-

sica DiNapoli, "The Case of a Dead Oil and Gas Mogul Takes an Unexpected Turn, and It Involves the Oklahoma City Thunder," http://www.businessinsider.com, cited August 20, 2016; Mitchell Schnurman, "What Texas Businesses Can Learn From the Oklahoma City Thunder's Gun Activism," http://www.dallasnews.com, cited August 21, 2016.

24. "2015 Front Office Rankings: Owners."

25. Sam Fortier, "Portland Columnist Suspicious Paul Allen Will Move Trail Blazers to Seattle," http://www.seattlepi.com, cited July 25, 2016.

26. "On the Portland Trail Blazers, the Looming Salary Cap and the Curious Case of Moe Harkless," http://www.blazersedge.com, cited August 3, 2016.

27. "2015 NBA Arena Experience Rankings."

28. For the Trail Blazers' business highlights, three readings are "Blazers, Heat Renew Season Tickets Via App," http://www.sportsbusinessdaily.com, cited August 15, 2016; John Lombardo, "Blazers Win NBA Promo Award," http://www.sportsbusinessdaily.com, cited August 27, 2016; John Canzano, "Canzano: Portland Trail Blazers All About the Business of Basketball," http://www.oregonlive.com, cited August 28, 2016.

29. "NBA Owners Power Ranking: Who is the Best Owner in Basketball?"

30. "Utah Jazz Team Payroll," http://www.basketball-reference.com, cited August 27, 2016.

31. Paul Baker, "2016 NBA Arena Experience Rankings," http://www.scout.com, cited August 1, 2016.

32. Sample references include Aaron Falk, "Utah Jazz: Advocacy Group Opposes LHM Proposal for Arena Tax Breaks," http://www.sltrib.com, cited August 5, 2016; "Jazz Offers Fans Chance to Sell Rights to Tickets," http://www.sportsbusinessdaily.com, cited August 6, 2016; Lee Benson, "About Utah: Former Utah Jazz CEO Greg Miller is Back in the Briar Patch," http://www.desertnews.com, cited August 8, 2016.

Chapter Five

Pacific Division

Organized in 1970 by the National Basketball Association (NBA), the Pacific Division (PD) of the league's Western Conference (WC) originally included the Los Angeles Lakers, Portland Trail Blazers, San Diego Rockets, San Francisco Warriors, and Seattle Supersonics. Since 1970, however, the Trail Blazers shifted from the league's PD to Northwest Division (NWD) in 2004, and the Rockets moved from San Diego to Houston—and Warriors from San Francisco to Oakland—both in 1971, and the Supersonics relocated from Seattle to Oklahoma City in 2008. In 1972, the Phoenix Suns transferred from the Midwest Division (MWD)—and sixteen years later the Sacramento Kings—each to the PD.

Given this change in the conference's structure, this chapter discusses the historical development and highlights business news and the financial facts of PD teams based respectively in Oakland, California; Los Angeles, California; Phoenix, Arizona; and Sacramento, California. During their history, which of them, for example, had won the fewest division titles and largest number of NBA championships? What were their market values, gate receipts, and ticket prices in the league's 2015–16—or simply—2015 season? Who have been the least and most successful owners among the five clubs? How do their arenas rank in aesthetics, entertainment, and experience among fans? The answers to these and other questions are covered in the chapter.[1]

TEAM PERFORMANCES

Golden State Warriors

From their 1946–47 to 1961–62 season, the Philadelphia Warriors played 1,103 games and won three division titles and two NBA championships in twelve playoffs. After moving from Philadelphia to San Francisco in 1962, the Warriors won two more division titles but zero championships in five playoff appearances.[2]

Because of superstar Rick Barry's absence and other factors during the mid- to late 1960s, the San Francisco Warriors were no longer title contenders although the team's leaders included all-stars Nate Thurmond, Jeff Mullin, and Rudy LaRusso. As a result of poor attendance at its games, the club began scheduling more of them in Oakland after the Oakland Coliseum Arena opened in 1966. Although the Warriors played in but lost in the NBA finals in 1967 and despite three more playoff appearances, the 1970–71 season was their last in San Francisco.

In mid- to late 1971, the franchise moved from San Francisco to Oakland and adopted Golden State Warriors as its brand name prior to the league's 1971–72 season. This change, in turn, meant that the team represented the state of California and not only a city within it. In addition, almost all Warriors home games that season were played in Oakland while six others took place in San Diego but none in San Francisco or Daly City, California. Thus, the Oakland Coliseum Arena became the team's exclusive home court in 1972.

Historical Results

As a member of the WC during the NBA's 1971–72 to 2015–16 seasons, Golden State had victories in approximately 46 percent of its games. In the period, the team won four division and three conference titles, and also championships in 1975 and 2015. Among fourteen other clubs in their conference, the Warriors were eleventh in winning percentage, ninth in both number of playoffs and division titles, tied for fourth with the Trail Blazers in conference titles, and tied for third with the Rockets in league championships (table A7).

Within the PD as of early 2016, the Warriors had the third lowest winning percentage but more total titles and championships than the Clippers, Suns, or Kings. In comparison to all NBA teams, Golden State ranked twenty-first (winning percentage), tied for twentieth (division titles), tied for tenth (conference titles), and tied for seventh (championships). Based on these results, the forty-five-year-old Warriors have been an average to below-average team against opponents in its conference and the league.

Performance Highlights

The club had its most success when appearing in consecutive playoffs during NBA seasons 1971–1972, 1974–1976, 1990–1991, and 2012–2015. This occurred, in part, because of such head coaches as Al Attles, Don Nelson, Mark

Jackson, and Steve Kerr. For their leadership, Nelson and Kerr each won Coach of the Year awards while Attles finished runner-up after a few seasons.

During these periods of success, the club had some outstanding players. Besides Barry, Mullin, and LaRusso, a few of these included Jerry Lucas, Tim Hardaway, and Stephen Curry. While Barry was an NBA Finals Most Valuable Player (MVP), Curry won NBA MVP twice. In addition to them, Gilbert Arenas and Monta Ellis became the league's Most Improved Players, and Keith Wilkes, Mitch Richmond, and Chris Webber each Rookie of the Year.

In contrast, Golden State did not appear in playoffs consecutively in their 1977–1985, 1994–2005, and 2007–2011 seasons. During these periods, the team had more losses than wins because of such things as subpar coaching from Johnny Bach, Ron Adelman, Pete Carlesimo, Dave Cowens, and Eric Musselman, lack of dedicated, talented, and experienced players, and simply too much competition from the Lakers, Suns, and others in its division.

The Warriors best performance was in the league's 2014–15 season. They won 81 percent of their regular-season games and defeated the Cleveland Cavaliers in the championship series primarily because of Curry's scoring and his teammates' pressure on defense. Alternatively, Golden State had only seventeen victories in their 2000–2001 season due to coaching issues, players' injuries, morale problems, and simply failing to play together as a team.

Based on the Entertainment Sports and Programming Network (ESPN) future power rankings for the NBA's 2016–2018 seasons, Golden State ranked first overall. In specific categories, the team placed second in both players and management, seventh in the market category, twenty-seventh in money, and twenty-eighth in the draft. Thus, the Warriors rated behind the Cleveland Cavaliers with respect to current players and their potential for the future and following the San Antonio Spurs in the quality and stability of their front office, ownership, and coaching, but lowest regarding future draft picks and draft positioning.[3]

Among other all-time NBA franchises as of early 2016, Golden State has been mediocre (sixteenth). Except for its 2014–15 season, the club won its division only four times and finished second in six years. Within only the conference's PD, other teams' rankings included the Lakers (first), Suns (fifteenth), and such below-average performers as the Kings (twenty-second) and Clippers (twenty-ninth). According to these results, the Warriors have not been consistent in regular seasons and frequently not competitive especially from 1994 to 2013.[4]

Los Angeles Clippers

An expansion team, the Buffalo Braves played eight seasons (1970–1978) in the NBA but failed to win its division and advance in three playoffs. Because of small home-game attendances, financial problems, and the club's poor performances, franchise co-owners Irv Levin and Harold Lipton moved the Braves from Buffalo to San Diego in 1978 and changed their nickname to Clippers.

While in San Diego for six seasons, the club had a 37 percent winning percentage and played its home games before tiny crowds at the city's Sports Arena. The league's 1981–82 season, however, brought changes to the franchise when Southern California businessman Levin sold the team to Los Angeles-area real estate developer/attorney Donald Sterling for approximately $13.5 million. However, the Clippers' inferior play in their final years in San Diego resulted in only 4,500 fans per game. As a result, Sterling lobbied the NBA to shift his team to Los Angeles.

In 1984, the Clippers moved north to Los Angeles and played their home games at the city's Memorial Sports Arena. Even so the move was not approved by the NBA, which fined Sterling about $25 million for invading territory of the Los Angeles Lakers. Sterling, however, sued the league for $100 million but then dropped the suit when it agreed to reduce his penalty to $6 million.

Historical Results

A member of the WC from the league's 1984–85 to 2015–16 seasons, the Clippers had victories in approximately 39 percent of their total games. During the period, they won two division titles but zero conference or NBA championships while appearing in nine playoffs. Among teams in their conference as of early 2016, the Clippers ranked fourteenth in winning percentage, tied for eleventh with the Kings in division titles, tied for tenth with five other clubs in not winning a conference title, and tied for seventh in number of league championships (table A7).

Within only the PD, the Clippers won fewer crowns than the Warriors, Lakers, and Suns. Furthermore, in comparison to twenty-nine other NBA teams as of early 2016, Los Angeles was twenty-eighth (winning percentage), tied for twenty-fourth (division titles), tied for twenty-first (conference titles), and tied for sixteenth (championships). According to these results, the thirty-two-year-old Clippers have been below average in regular-season and postseason performances and not consistent or very competitive since moving from San Diego in 1984.

Performance Highlights

The Clippers' most successful years occurred when they competed in playoffs consecutively in NBA seasons 1991–92, 1996–97, 2005–6, and

2011–15. Led by such head coaches as Larry Brown, Bill Fitch, Mike Dunleavy, Vinny Del Negro, and Doc Rivers, the team lost five times in the conference's first round and four in semifinals of the playoffs. While Brown is in the Hall of Fame, Rivers's teams have been in three consecutive postseasons as of 2016.

To win games in regular seasons, the team's outstanding players included Danny Manning, Loy Vaught, Elton Brand, Chris Paul, and Blake Griffin. Beside Griffin being Rookie of the Year in 2011 and Paul the all-star game MVP in 2013, forward Bobby Simmons was the NBA's most improved player in 2005 and forward Jamal Crawford being the league's Sixth Man of the Year in 2014 and 2016. With teammates Griffin and Paul, the Clippers are a threat to win another division title.

Because of failing to qualify for the playoffs, the team's least productive seasons consecutively were 1984–1990, 1993–1995, 1997–2004, and 2006–2010. Such head coaches as Jim Lynam, Don Chaney, Gene Shue, Chris Ford, and Alvin Gentry did not consistently motivate their players who, in turn, had problems scoring points, rebounding, and playing as a unit on defense.

The Clippers' worst and best seasons were, respectively, 1986–87 and 2013–14. In the former, they had a hideous 12–70 record and finished last in their division but in the latter season, the club won 69 percent of its games and ended first in the PD but then lost in six games to the Thunder in the conference semifinals.

Before Game 5 in Los Angeles, there was talk that Los Angeles's players would boycott the series unless the NBA punished owner Donald Sterling for making racial comments. Acting swiftly in April 2014, the league issued a lifetime ban to Sterling, fined him $2.5 million—the highest allowable by the NBA—and barred him from attending games or practices involving any NBA team; from being present in any Clippers office or facility; and from participating in any team business, player personnel decisions, or league activity. New NBA Commissioner Adam Silver also stated that he would try to force Sterling to sell the Clippers, which he did that year.

Based on several all-time statistics of NBA teams as of early 2016, the Clippers are in the bottom one-third of the league. Without a higher winning percentage, more division titles in regular seasons and at least one championship, and despite five consecutive playoffs since 2010–11, the club has not performed to expectations historically and simply been outplayed, for example, in many years by the conference's Mavericks, Lakers, Spurs, and Warriors.

For ESPN's 2016 future power rankings, which include five categories for the league's 2016–2018 seasons, the Clippers placed tenth overall. In weighted proportions, they were fifth in players (50 percent), fourteenth in management (16.7 percent), twenty-seventh in money (16.7 percent), fourth in the market (8.3 percent), and twenty-third in the draft (8.3 percent). While some of the team's current players are very good athletically with great potential and since Los Angeles exists as a large sports market, the club's management—front office, ownership, and coaching—is average in quality and stability. Near the bottom in two categories, however, are (a) the franchise's money category including its projected salary-cap situation, ability and willingness to exceed cap and pay a luxury tax, and (b) its future draft picks and draft positioning.[5]

According to one expert's opinion, the combination of Chris Paul, Blake Griffin, and DeAndre Jordan—that the Clippers have built around—has not worked for them. As good as each of these players are individually, and no matter how good they work together, they will never find success as a combined unit. The answer to the team's problems are simple but hard to swallow: they have to give up at least one or two of their "big three" players and attempt to replace them with someone else.[6]

Los Angeles Lakers

While located in Minneapolis, Minnesota, during the NBA's 1949–50 to 1959–60 seasons, the Lakers appeared in eleven playoffs and won four Western Division titles and five NBA championships. The team was led by head coach John Kundla and propelled by such players as the league's first superstar, center George Mikan, and also guard Slater Martin, forwards Elgin Baylor, Jim Pollard, and Vern Mikkelsen, and center Clyde Lovellette.

In their last season in Minneapolis, the Lakers finished 25–50 and third in their division following the St. Louis Hawks and Detroit Pistons but ahead of the Cincinnati Royals. On January 18, 1960, the team was coming off a loss and traveling to St. Louis when their plane crash-landed. Snowstorms had caused the pilot to drift 150 miles off course, thus forcing his airplane to land in a cornfield near Carroll, Iowa. Fortunately, nobody was hurt.

Because of dwindling attendance at its home games in the Minneapolis Armory and being placed on financial probation by the NBA in the late 1950s, the franchise's problems continued to worsen during and after their 1959–60 season. As a result, the Lakers became the NBA's first West Coast team when owner Bob Short decided to move them to Los Angeles, California in early 1960. Despite no lakes anywhere in the area, the team retained its old nickname. To help the Lakers compete against others in their conference, they selected West Virginia guard Jerry West as a number one pick in the NBA draft.

Historical Results

As a member of the Western Division (WD) in the NBA's 1960–1969 seasons and then the PD during 1970–71 to 2015–16, the Los Angeles Lakers had victories in approximately 61 percent of their games. During the period, they won twenty-eight division and eighteen conference titles and also eleven league championships in forty-nine playoffs. Among others in the WC, the team was third in winning percentage and first in playoffs and number of titles and championships (table A7).

In comparison to all NBA clubs as of their 2015–16 season, the Lakers ranked third (winning percentage), second (number of playoffs, division titles, and championships), and first (conference titles). Based on these results, the franchise has been productive for fifty-six years and also competitive and very successful on the court against opponents within its division and conference and thus important to the league in different ways.

Performance Highlights

The Lakers' most successful periods were during consecutive playoffs in seasons 1960–1973, 1976–1992, 1994–2003, and 2005–2012. Such head coaches as Fred Schaus, Butch Van Breda Kolff, Bill Sharman, Paul Westhead, Pat Riley, Del Harris, and Phil Jackson led their teams in regular season and postseasons. Sharman, Riley, and Harris won Coach of the Year awards and except for Harris, joined Jackson in the Hall of Fame.

Several players had memorable and productive careers with the franchise. A few of them were Jerry West, Wilt Chamberlain, Kareem Abdul-Jabbar, Erving "Magic" Johnson, Shaquille O'Neal, Kobe Bryant, and Pau Gasol. These players received many awards and honors including being all-stars while some chosen NBA MVP—Abdul-Jabbar, Johnson, O'Neal, and Bryant. Besides them, others such as Gail Goodrich, James Worthy, and Jamaal Wilkes are in the Hall of Fame.

In contrast to its successful years, the club failed to qualify for the playoffs in seasons 1974–75, 1993–94, 2004–5, and 2013–2015. Such head coaches as Randy Pfund, Bill Bertka, Rudy Tomjanovich, Frank Hamblen, Mike Brown, Mike D'Antoni, and Byron Scott did not inspire their players enough to compete and win more games than lose them.

The Lakers' best and worst seasons were, respectively, 1971–72 and 2015–16. In the former season, they had victories in sixty-nine regular-season games, finished first in the PD, and won the league championship. But in the latter, the Lakers won only seventeen games and ended fifth in the PD. For sure, guard Kobe Bryant was frequently injured and decided to retire from the sport after a great twenty-year career with the team in Los Angeles.

According to several sources, the Los Angeles Lakers are the greatest NBA franchise of all-time. One expert explained it this way:

> Those numbers [records and performance statistics] cannot be ignored or disputed; the Lakers truly are the greatest franchise in NBA history. Remember, I didn't choose the Lakers to be atop this list, the numbers did. No team has been more consistently dominant than the Lakers and they've won the most championships of the "modern era" too. But this list is about all-time history and in that category the Lakers come out on top as well. From the beginning of league history until today, Los Angeles has dominated the NBA more thoroughly than anyone else. Their consistency of dominance year-in and year-out is what vaults them atop this list. Enjoy this title Lakers fans, you deserve it.[7]

In ESPN's 2016 future power rankings, the Lakers placed twenty-fourth overall and third in the PD following the Warriors (first) and Clippers (tenth). For the five categories listed in the rankings, Los Angeles was first in both money and market, fifth in the draft, twenty-seventh in management, and twenty-ninth in players. Power rankings have not been kind to the Lakers as of late, and for good reason. In the past three NBA seasons (2013–2015), the team has combined for just sixty-five wins, the same amount of losses they had in just the 2015–16 season.

Despite racking up three top ten draft picks in a row, the team failed to reel in any free agents of significant value in the same time span. It has been the hope of the entire Lakers' fan base for the past few seasons that the team would defy the odds and prove these power rankings wrong, but sadly the purple and gold failed to do so time and time again.

Phoenix Suns

After continual prodding by businessman Richard Bloch, the NBA Board of Governors awarded an expansion team to him and his syndicate in early 1968 for a fee of $2 million. Based in Phoenix, Arizona, it was the first major professional sports franchise in the state of Arizona, and the only one until the NFL Cardinals relocated there in 1988 from St. Louis. Formed by an ownership group, the franchise consisted of principal owner and president Bloch, publicity executive Karl Eller, major investors Don Pitt, Don Diamond, Bhavik Darji, and Marvin Meyer, and also such entertainers as Andy Williams, Bobbie Gentry, and Ed Ames.

Many critics, including then-NBA commissioner J. Walter Kennedy, believed that Phoenix was too hot, small, and far away to be a successful NBA market. Nevertheless, the Phoenix metropolitan area's population was growing rapidly and the team had built-in geographical foes in places like Los Angeles, San Diego, San Francisco, and Seattle.

The team's nickname, "Suns," was among 28,000 entries formally chosen in a "Name the Team" contest sponsored by the *Arizona Republic*—an American daily newspaper published in Phoenix. Player-scout Jerry Colangelo, from the Chicago Bulls, became the Suns' first general manager when twenty-eight years old, and also from the Bulls, former head coach Johnny Kerr. In the 1968 NBA expansion draft, notable Suns selected were future Hall of Famer Gail Goodrich and Dick Van Arsdale.

Historical Results

A member of the WD in seasons 1968–1969, Midwest Division in 1970–1971 and PD in 1972–2015, the Suns had victories in approximately 54 percent of their games. During the period, they won six division and two conference titles but zero NBA championships. Among only WC teams, Phoenix was fifth (winning percentage and division titles), tied for sixth with the Jazz and Mavericks (conference titles), and tied for seventh (championships). Within only the PD, the Suns had a better record than the Clippers and Kings but worse than the Lakers (table A7).

In comparison to all-time records of twenty-nine other NBA teams as of their 2015–16 season, Phoenix ranked sixth in winning percentage and in a tie for tenth to sixteenth in number of playoffs, titles, and championships. Based on this data, the forty-eight-year-old Suns have been an average club in their performances against competitors in their division and conference but not when playing the superior Lakers, Spurs, or Thunder.

Performance Highlights

The Suns' most productive periods historically occurred during consecutive playoffs in NBA seasons 1977–1984, 1988–2000, and 2004–2007. Such head coaches as John MacLeod, Cotton Fitzsimmons, Paul Westphal, Danny Ainge, and Mike D'Antoni led their teams to many wins. For their knowledge, leadership, and vision, Fitzsimmons and D'Antoni were each an NBA Coach of the Year. Besides them, MacLeod and the other coaches had prominent years in the sport.

Several Suns players performed above expectations and excelled as teammates and at their position on the court. Some of them included Paul Westphal, Larry Nance, Kevin Johnson, Charles Barkley, Shawn Marion, and Steve Nash. Barkley (once) and Nash (twice) were each NBA MVPs while players Alvan Adams, Walter Davis, and Amare Stoudemire won an NBA Rookie of the Year award. Also, Barkley and former executive Jerry Colangelo and forward Connie Hawkins are members of the Hall of Fame.

The club's worst periods occurred when it failed to qualify for consecutive playoffs in seasons 1970–1975, 1985–1987, and 2010–2015. In part, head coaches Fitzsimmons, MacLeod, and also Scott Skiles, Frank Johnson, Alvin Gentry, and Jeff Hornacek did not excite or motivate players enough to win a majority of their games in various seasons especially against such conference opponents as the Lakers, Mavericks, and Spurs.

Phoenix had its worst and two best seasons in, respectively, 1968–69 and then 1992–93 and 2004–5. In the former season, the club won only sixteen games and finished seventh in the WD. But in the latter two, the Suns had a 75 percent winning percentage in regular seasons, won their division, and in the playoffs, respectively, lost in the league finals and then in 2004–5 the WC finals. Despite ending in third place during its regular season, the team was also defeated in the conference's 1976 finals.

The Suns have been an NBA franchise for forty-eight years and seen some success during that time. They have won a division title six times and twice their conference but no league championship. In other words, the team's age and lack of high-end success ranks it nineteenth all-time among clubs in the league as of early 2016.

In ESPNs future power rankings of the league's 2016–2018 seasons, the Suns are twenty-seventh from the bottom after finishing twenty-second as of 2015. Ranked by category were *players* at twenty-seventh—the Suns roster is not loaded with talent but have three proven but young starters but no star, which is a fair critique; *management* at twenty-eighth—an indictment of owner Robert Sarver much more so than general manager Ryan McDonough; *money* at sixth—seems surprisingly high given the team has three contracts worth approximately $40 million a year although website basketball-reference.com shows the club with twelfth most money in 2016–17, fifteenth most in 2017–18, and fifth most in 2018–2019; *market* at ninth—which denotes that players are likely to come play there; and *draft* at fourth—the Suns have all their own picks plus others in 2016–2018.[8]

Sacramento Kings

The oldest franchise in the NBA and one of the oldest continuously operating professional basketball franchises in the nation, the Kings originated in western New York as a semiprofessional basketball team named the "Rochester Seagrams" in 1923. Twenty-two years later, they joined the National Basketball League (NBL) as the "Rochester Royals" and then in 1948 shifted to the Basketball Association of America (BAA).

Although often successful and winning an NBA championship in 1951, the Royals found it increasingly difficult to be profitable in the comparatively small market of Rochester. Thus, the club relocated to Cincinnati in 1957 and became the Cincinnati Royals. Unable to continue operating while based in southeast Ohio, the team then relocated to Kansas City, Missouri, in 1972 and was renamed Kansas City-Omaha Kings because it initially split home games between Kansas City and Omaha, Nebraska. In 1975, the club ceased playing home games in Omaha and simply became the Kansas City Kings.

In 1979, the roof collapsed at Kansas City's Kemper Arena because of a severe storm, forcing the Kings to play most of their 1979–80 season at the much smaller Municipal Auditorium. This, in part, caused the team's ownership group to sell the franchise in 1982 to a Sacramento, California, syndicate for $11 million. The Kings also had to compete with indoor soccer's Kansas City Comets for the winter sports dollar.

The Kings' final season in Kansas City—1984–85—resulted in a 31–51 record and a sixth place finish in the MWD. That caused most fans to stay away from games at Kemper Arena with the team's average attendance only about 6,400. Consequently, the franchise moved from Kansas City to Sacramento in 1985 and was renamed Sacramento Kings.

Historical Results

A member of the conference's MWD in the league's 1985–86 to 1987–88 seasons and then in the PD from 1988–89 to 2015–16, the Kings had victories in approximately 42 percent of their games. During the period, they won two division titles but zero conference titles and NBA championships in ten playoffs. Among only WC teams, Sacramento was thirteenth (winning percentage), tenth (number of playoffs), tied for eleventh with the Clippers (division titles), tied for tenth (conference titles), and tied for seventh (league championships). Within the PD, the Kings have actually outperformed the Clippers but not the Warriors, Lakers, or Suns (table A7).

In comparison to all NBA teams as of early 2016, Sacramento ranked twenty-seventh in winning percentage and also tied for twenty-fourth in division titles, for twenty-first in conference titles, and for sixteenth with zero league championships. Based on this data, the thirty-one-year-old Kings have been an inferior NBA team and not very competitive or consistently performed up to expectations against clubs in their division and conference.

Performance Highlights

The Kings' success occurred when they qualified for playoffs in seasons 1985–1986, 1995–96, and then during 1998–99 to 2005–6. One or more of these teams were led by head coaches Phil Johnson, Garry St. Jean, and Rick Adelman. While coaching during the league's 1998–2005 seasons, Adelman's teams each played above .500 and won two division titles but lost in the first round of the playoffs four times and then in three semifinals and one finals. Both Johnson and St. Jean's clubs lost in the first round.

Several players had excellent performances with the club, particularly in playoff seasons. These included Reggie Theus, Mitch Richmond, Vlade Divac, Chris Webber, Peja Stojakovic, and Brad Miller. While Richmond was the all-star game MVP in 1985, guards Bobby Jackson won the NBA sixth man award in 2003 and Tyreke Evans Rookie of the Year in 2010. For being outstanding on the court for the Kings in various years, players Richmond, Divac, Webber, and Stojakovic had their numbers retired but only Richmond became a Hall of Famer specifically for the franchise.

The club's best and worst seasons chronologically were 2001–2 and 2008–9. In the former, the Kings won their division with a 61–21 record and played competitively yet lost in the conference finals to the Lakers in overtime by six points. But in the latter season, Sacramento performed poorly and finished with only seventeen wins and placing fifth in the division. As a result, head coach Reggie Theus was replaced by Kenny Natt.

Based on their winning percentage and number of titles and championships, the Kings are in the bottom five of NBA franchises of all-time as of early 2016. Except for their ten seasons in the playoffs since relocating from Kansas City to Sacramento in 1985, they simply have underperformed because of being inconsistent and experiencing problems with their owners, coaches, and players.

In ESPN's future power rankings of thirty NBA teams as of 2016, the Kings were twenty-ninth overall. Among five categories, the club was sixteenth in *money*, seventeenth in the *draft*, twenty-sixth in *players*, and thirtieth in both *management* and the *market*. Because of constant issues with the front office and coaching staff, and also for playing its home games in an inferior sports market with a small fan base, Sacramento also ranked twenty-ninth in ESPN's 2014 and 2015 list.

In short, it is difficult to look at the Kings roster with any sort of optimism. Therein lies the rub: Sacramento is not a "sexy" market and the team has not made wise decisions in free agency or the draft. This means fans see a perpetually mediocre roster from which more-than-capable coach George Karl is tasked with coaxing basketball games wins. Much of this can be traced to the ownership, which seems too "hands-on" without a clear idea of a mission. Unfortunately, the end result has been an inferior product on the court each season since 2007.

FRANCHISE BUSINESS

Given the performances of them as teams, this section focuses on and examines the commercial aspects of NBA franchises including their principal owner or owners and also facts and other details in tables about each team's arena, various costs for families to attend home games, current and important financial data, and yearly trends in players' payrolls. In part, this information reveals why some franchises are more valuable and wealthy than others and therefore how successful or unsuccessful historically as business enterprises in the sports industry.

Golden State Warriors

Born in 1956, Joe Lacob grew up in a Jewish family in New Bedford, Massachusetts. After his family relocated to Anaheim, California, he earned a bachelor's degree in biological sciences and a master's in public health from the University of California and then a Master's of Business Administration (MBA) from the Stanford Graduate School of Business.[9]

During his career in business, Lacob held executive positions with Cetus Corporation (now Chiron), health maintenance organization FHP International, and management-consulting's Booz, Allen & Hamilton. Since the late 1980s, he has been a partner at Kleiner Perkins, a venture capital investing firm. While there, he invested in companies involved in life sciences, medical technology, Internet, and energy, and such enterprises as AutoTrading.com, Invisalign, and NuVasive.

After investing in the defunct women's American Basketball League (ABL) and NBA's Boston Celtics, Lacob outbid several other groups and headed a syndicate that purchased the Golden State Warriors in 2010 from Chris Cohan for $450 million. This, in turn, required him to sell his minority interest in the Celtics. Previously, Lacob had been a Warriors season ticket holder for several years and had extensive experience operating an NBA team as co-owner of the Celtics. Currently, Lacob manages the franchise's daily operations in the Bay Area.

Among owners of fourteen other WC teams and their performances as of early 2016, Lacob's Warriors tied for ninth in winning division titles and tied for fourth in both number of conference titles and NBA championships. In comparison to all NBA teams and their current owners, Golden State tied for fourteenth (division titles), for fifth (conference titles), and for sixth (league championships). Because his clubs qualified for four playoffs and two finals—and then won one in 2015—Joe Lacob has been a successful owner since acquiring the franchise in 2010 (table A8).

Based on his team's results, Lacob is the sixth best owner in the league. The following comments are why he ranks so high:

> There are few things that the Golden State Warriors ownership has done wrong over the years as they've built what could end up being the next great NBA

> dynasty. A lot of luck was involved in crafting this team, like Steph Curry falling to them in 2009 but there has been a lot of smart moves made by ownership along the way as well. Staying dug in on not trading Klay Thompson was the right move, not overspending to sign free agents was the right move and find talent like Draymond Green was the right move. They're NBA champs, and ownership is a big reason why they're going to stay at the top for years to come.[10]

Team Financials

With respect to financial data published in *Forbes* magazine about NBA franchises as of early 2016, the Warriors' market value was $1.9 billion, revenue $201 million, operating income $57 million, gate receipts $77 million, debt-to-value 13 percent, and players expenses $80 million. Among WC teams in the league, Golden State ranked third (market value, revenue, and operating income), second (gate receipts), seventh (debt ratio), and tied for eighth (players expenses). Within only the PD, the Warriors' amounts were generally much higher than those of the Suns and Kings except for players expenses, but also lower than the Lakers (table A9).

In comparison to data of twenty-nine other NBA teams as of their 2015–16 season, Golden State was sixth in both market value and revenue, tied for fifth with the Celtics in operating income, third in gate receipts, seventeenth in debt-to-value, and tied for sixteenth with the Pelicans in player expenses. Given these results, the Warriors are above-average financially as a sports enterprise and operate at a profit with plenty of cash flow to invest in assets and also to spend on acquiring free agents and veterans.

Besides market size, salary inflation, and other factors, an NBA team's annual payroll partly reflects its commitment to players and their current and potential contribution individually and as a group to winning games in regular seasons and postseasons. From 2011 to 2015, for example, the Warriors' payroll among WC teams ranged in rank from third in 2012 ($69.6 million) and 2015 ($93.6 million) to twelfth in 2011 ($57.1 million). Within only the PD, the club had the second, third, or fourth highest payroll in the group during the period (table A10).

In comparison to payrolls of all NBA teams, Golden State's was chronologically twenty-third in 2011, eighth in 2012, seventh in 2013, fourteenth in 2014, and fourth in 2015. Based on this data, the Warriors increased their payroll each season to become more competitive and advance in postseasons. This was a smart strategy because it resulted in four playoffs and a championship for the team in 2015.

Because the Warriors had to use so much cap space to sign superstar Kevin Durant in 2016, bringing him back at his full maximum salary will not be easy. The expectation was that he would exercise a player option and opt out of his new contract following the coming season, allowing him to resign with Golden State for more money ahead of the league's 2017–18 season. But now with a lower projected cap, he may need to accept something short of the maximum money or perhaps take a pay cut. Resigning players Andre Iguodala and Shaun Livingston next may require Durant to endure such a cut and at a minimum will stretch Golden State's cap space thin to keep together the group Durant grew enamored with after signing his contract.[11]

Oracle Arena

Opened in November 1966, the 19,756-seat Oakland-Alameda County Coliseum Arena has hosted teams in various sports including the NBA Warriors. After a major renovation in 1997, the building was renamed The Arena in Oakland until 2005 and then Oakland Arena from 2005 to 2006.[12]

During October 2006, the Warriors and Oracle Corporation announced a ten-year agreement in which the Oakland Arena became known as the Oracle Arena. It is managed by the Oakland-Alameda County Authority, who approved the deal. With the Warriors' resurgence since 2012, the Oracle Arena has been one of the loudest arenas in the NBA. It is often called "Roaracle" because of the painfully high decibel levels generated at Warriors games.

Over time, the Warriors' home became increasingly outdated and lacked the luxuries of newer ones. Rather than construct a new arena in Oakland—or in San Francisco or San Jose—the decision was made to proceed with a $121 million renovation that involved tearing down much of the old arena's interior and building a new seating bowl within the existing structure. The original arena's external walls, roof, and foundation remained intact, similar to what was done to Seattle's KeyArena. During the renovation, which began in mid-1996 and was completed in the fall of 1997, the Warriors played their home games in the National Hockey League (NHL) Sharks' San Jose Arena.

Among facilities of fourteen other WC teams as of early 2016, the Warriors' is the oldest, ninth most expensive (including renovations), and second highest in value. In comparison to all NBA arenas, Golden State's ranks first (age), twenty-second (cost), and fifth (value). Based on these results, the Warriors play their home games in a relatively outdated building with enough amenities to earn an adequate amount of revenues for the franchise (table A11).

For several years a Chicago-based company named Team Marketing Report (TMR) has prepared and published a Fan Cost Index (FCI) for the home games of teams in professional sports leagues. To attend a game for a typical family with two kids, an FCI includes the costs of four average-priced tickets, two cheapest-priced draft beers, four each cheapest-priced soft drinks and hot dogs, parking for one car, and two each game programs and least-expensive, adult-size adjustable caps. Costs are determined by telephone calls with team representatives, venues, and concessionaires, and from questions asked during interviews.[13]

In the 2011–2015 NBA seasons, the Fan Cost Index (FCI) for a family to attend a regular-season game at Oracle Arena ranged from a low of $252 in 2011 to a high of $471 in 2015. With respect to those of all NBA teams, the Warriors' Index was twenty-third in 2011, tied for twenty-second in 2012, eleventh in 2013 and 2014, and fourth in 2015 (table A12).

To reveal specific costs for a recent season in the NBA, the Warriors' FCI in 2015–16 was more than 40 percent higher than in 2014–15. Listed from most to least in amount by item for one person, the team's tickets averaged between $79 and $80, parking one vehicle $30, a cap $25, single beer $7, hot dog and soft drink each $6, and a program $5.

Among other teams in the conference's PD, they had rankings and FCIs from most to least as follows: Lakers second at $545; Clippers sixth at $437; Suns tenth at $341; and Kings eighteenth at $286. Consequently, Warriors fans paid less at games in Oracle Arena than those of three other NBA teams in their arenas.

The cheapest ticket cost about $35 for a fan to watch a Warriors' home game in 2015–16. This was about $20 or approximately 220 percent more than the league's average for a cheap seat. Also, since the club's FCI was $132 above the amount of a typical NBA team, a family of four purchased tickets and enjoyed a basketball game in Oakland at a significant premium relative to the majority of arenas within the league. These costs and prices, in turn, were set by the Warriors organization to earn revenue and maximize profit from their operations.

In its annual ranking of all thirty NBA game-day experiences as of 2016, the *Stadium Journey* rated Oracle Arena twenty-fifth. The relatively low rank was explained as follows:

> Oracle Arena has long been considered one of the better atmospheres in all of basketball. This was put on display when they FINALLY reached the playoffs in 2007, and upset the Dallas Mavericks in the first round. This put the national spotlight on the great atmosphere at Oracle. Even though the arena is over 45 [50] years old the exterior façade and the interior aesthetics don't show their age as you might think. The x pattern around the building is actually a modern look and the renovated concourses are quite nice, albeit narrow. The neighborhood is one of the worst in the NBA, but in your seat it's a pleasure to watch this Warriors team.[14]

During early 2013, the Warriors announced their intention to build a new arena in the San Francisco area and move back to that city. Originally the new arena was to be built on sites near the foot of the Bay Bridge, but the plan met opposition because of potential traffic congestion, environmental impacts, and obstructed views. In April 2014, the Warriors purchased twelve acres in Mission Bay as the site for a new 18,000-seat arena to open for their 2018–19 season. However, due to litigation filed by opponents, the new arena—named the Chase Center—is planned for completion by the club's 2019–20 season.

Business Highlights

Besides regular-season and postseason games, NBA franchises are involved in—and affected by—community events and business-related affairs, news, and projects. The following are a few of them for Golden State's popular, successful, and from a financial perspective, above-average professional basketball team.[15]

First, sometimes basketball team-building can be incredibly complex, like projecting the health of a player or trying to exploit the intricacies of the salary cap. Yet, other times it is not complex. The Warriors' decisions in 2012 to tank (not trying to exactly win) in the second half of the season to keep their draft pick and remembering that long-term thinking demands organizational support were straightforward but special and challenging in their own way. At that moment, the Warriors began developing their business philosophy. The entire organization of a team permeates through every part of whether you win or lose. With the 2012 decisions serving as a beacon of why organizations matter, the Warriors advantages derived from the franchise as a whole.

Second, 2014–15 was a breakout season for guard Stephen Curry, who won the NBA MVP award and led the Warriors to their first NBA title in forty years. Curry had the NBA's best-selling jersey and was the leading vote-getter for the all-star game. In-arena merchandise sales doubled for the Warriors and the team sold out every game for the second season in a row. The team's proposed new arena took another step forward in December 2015 when the San Francisco Board of Supervisors approved the environmental report for the multiuse arena planned for San Francisco's Mission Bay neighborhood. The project's cost expects to exceed $1 billion.

Third, Houston-area ticket broker Patrick Ryan, through his companies, ranks among the biggest resellers of Warriors tickets anywhere in the country, holding a large collection of season tickets at Oracle Arena. Ryan's brokerage, The Ticket Experience, and secondary ticket analytics outfit Eventellect generate plenty of fan interest for the NBA's 2015 defending champion—the current best team and by far the hottest basketball ticket on the resale markets. But the club announced a new price structure in which brokers will be charged ticket prices for the 2016–17 regular season in some cases more than double the rates for individual fans.

Fourth, there is a chef carving turkey at the Bridge Club, just steps from the court inside Oracle Arena, and servers pour all the Dehlinger chardonnay and Radio-Coteau pinot noir to drink. When the Warriors leave their locker room, you can watch through one-way glass as they run down the corridor. Mark Stevens owns less than 10 percent of the team, but like every other investor, the former partner at Sequoia Capital is invited to the party. Before a game, he greets the other owners and their guests. Rather than local car dealers and plastic surgeons sipping the Dehlinger in the Bridge Club, Stevens hobnobs with many of Silicon Valley's bold-faced names.

Fifth, the Warriors emerged as the big winners at the NBA's annual sales and marketing meetings in January 2015. They had the most full-season suite equivalents sold league-wide and for having a 90 percent full-season ticket renewal rate. Golden State also won an account growth award in corporate sponsorships and a digital innovator award, and the team was recognized for selling more than 10,000 full-season tickets.

Los Angeles Clippers

Born in 1956 in Detroit, Michigan, Steve Ballmer grew up in the affluent community of Farmington Hills, Michigan. In 1973, he attended college prep and engineering classes at Lawrence Technological University but then graduated from Detroit Country Day School, a private college preparatory school in Beverly Hills, Michigan

In 1977, Ballmer graduated from Harvard University with bachelor's degrees in mathematics and economics. After working two years at Procter & Gamble as a product manager, he attended the Stanford University Graduate School of Business. In 1980, Ballmer left school to become a business manager for Bill Gates, a friend from Harvard who had dropped out of school and co-founded Microsoft Inc. Over the next two decades, Ballmer held various executive positions as Microsoft became one of the most powerful and profitable companies in American history.

After outbidding Los Angeles–based investors Tony Ressler and Bruce Karsh and also a group that included David Geffen and executives from the Guggenheim Group—which owns the Los Angeles Dodgers—Ballmer acquired the Los Angeles Clippers in 2014 from Donald Sterling for $2 billion. As an owner, Ballmer pledged to use his analytical and managerial skills as a leader and turn the team into a consistent NBA powerhouse and win a championship. As of the league's 2013–14 season, the Clippers have improved in their conference and appeared in three consecutive playoffs.

Among owners of WC teams as of early 2016, Ballmer's Clippers tied for eleventh in division titles, for eighth in conference titles, and for sixth in league championships. In comparison to all NBA teams and their current owners, Los Angeles tied for nineteenth (division titles), for fifteenth (conference titles), and tied for tenth (championships). Thus far, Ballmer's clubs have performed above average as competitors but not quite good enough to win a conference title or NBA championship (Table A8).

Based on his team's performances as of early 2016, Ballmer is sixth among owners of NBA franchises. Although relatively new to the sport, he ranked high, in part because:

> Steve Ballmer is already a hundred times the owner we were hoping for to replace Sterling. Not only is he in a position to change the face of the franchise—literally and figuratively—but Ballmer is on Mark Cuban levels of passionate. The way Cuban gets loud in Dallas is being equated in the way Ballmer's face turns beat red on nightly basis. He's the type of owner who is so over-the-top that he's starting to put people who abhor Cuban in his camp for the sole purpose of just not being in Ballmer's circus. Ballmer seems like the type of owner who will lose his mind over a free throw the same way he will if the Clippers ever win the NBA Finals—and God Bless him for that level of insane passion.[16]

With an estimated net worth of $23.5 billion, Ballmer was the world's richest sports team owner as of mid-2016. His winning bid for the Clippers at $2 billion was viewed as a massive overpay until the NBA signed a nine-year, $24 billion television contract extension later in 2014 that exceeded almost everyone's expectations at three times the value of the previous deal.

Team Financials

According to financial data published by *Forbes* magazine for NBA teams as of early 2016, the Clippers' market value was $2 billion, revenue $176 million, operating income $20 million, gate receipts $59 million, debt-to-value zero percent, and players expenses $92 million. With respect to fourteen other WC clubs, Los Angeles ranked second (market value), fifth (revenue), tied for ninth with the Thunder (operating income), tied for fourth with the Spurs (gate receipts), tied for fourteenth with the Nuggets (debt ratio), and second (players expenses). But within the PD, the Clippers in part had the lowest debt percent but highest players expenses (table A9).

In comparison to all NBA franchises, the Clippers ranged in rank from third in players expenses to a tie for twenty-eighth in debt-to-value. Based on the club's total financial data, this is a profitable and prosperous business organization with plenty of cash flows to invest in players and other assets of the franchise. If the team wins a championship, these amounts will soar because of its location, merchandise sales, new ownership, and television deals.

Besides market size, salary inflation, and other factors, an NBA team's annual payroll partly reflects its commitment to players and their current and potential contribution individually and as a group to winning games in regular seasons and postseasons. From 2011 to 2015, for example, the Clippers' payroll among WC teams ranged in rank from first in 2014 ($84.2 million) and 2015 ($97.0 million) to sixth in 2011 ($66.7 million). Within the PD, the club had the third highest payroll in its 2011–12 seasons but then second in 2013 and first during 2014 and 2015 (table A10).

In comparison to payrolls of all NBA teams, Los Angeles's was chronologically twelfth in 2011, ninth in 2012, fifth in 2013, and second in 2014 and 2015. Based on these amounts, the Clippers increased their payroll each season to become more competitive and win enough regular-season games to qualify for the playoffs. This strategy may or may not succeed in the future if such clubs as the Warriors and Spurs spend more money and significantly improve their rosters.

Based on their commitment and future payments to players as of March 2016, the Clippers had a starting cap space of $27.3 million and a maximum cap space of $8.1 million, and also six guaranteed contracts, one partial/non-guaranteed contract, and seven potential free agents. Overall, the team had the league's second least starting cap space following the Cleveland Cavaliers and thirtieth least maximum cap space. This, in turn, means the Clippers will not be active in the free agent and trade markets for new and veteran players.[17]

Staples Center

Opened in 1999 to replace the Great Western Forum, the $400 million Staples Center is a 900,000 square foot multipurpose building in downtown Los Angeles—owned and operated by the Anschutz Entertainment Group—that seats approximately 20,000 for basketball and 19,000 for hockey. Initially, it had more than twenty concession stands over five concourses, an eight-sided video scoreboard, and a 20,000 square foot plaza entrance with a large, digital screen to greet visitors. Suites were arranged in three levels in the center of the bowl.[18]

A private restaurant is available for its members. The club takes about 200, who pay more than $10,500 annually for the privilege, and have access to a private wine cellar and humidors. Another upscale restaurant seats several hundred people and features menus and prices to match the city's top restaurants with food prepared by a renowned chef. Only suite holders and club seat holders can make reservations. A separate sports bar and restaurant is open to the public. The suite concessionaire provides themed menus and grilled specialties along with Asian and Italian offerings in its service to club seat and suite customers.

Outside the arena at the Star Plaza are statues of former players Wayne Gretzky and Magic Johnson, although both played at the Los Angeles Forum. In addition to them, there are statues of the late long time Lakers broadcaster Chick Hearn, legend Jerry West dribbling a basketball, former player Kareem Abdul-Jabbar, and retired National Hockey League Kings Hall of Fame left wing Luc Robitaille. The Lakers will honor Shaquille O'Neal with a statue at the Staples Center during their 2016–17 season.

Among arenas of other WC teams as of early 2016, the Clippers' Staples Center tied for seventh in age, for second following the Mavericks' American Airlines Center in construction cost, and ranked fourth in value. With respect to all NBA teams' venues, the Staples Center tied for fourteenth (age) and fourth (construction cost), and placed seventh (value). Based on this data, the Clippers play their home games in a relatively modern facility within a large, popular, and prosperous sports market (table A11).

In the 2011–2015 NBA seasons, the FCI for a family to attend a Clippers' regular-season game at the Staples Center ranged from a low of $322 in 2011 to a high of $437 in 2015. With respect to those of all NBA teams, the Clippers' were seventh in 2011 and then sixth from 2012 to 2015 (table A12).

To reveal specific costs for a recent season in the NBA, the Clippers' FCI in 2015–16 at home games was about 1 percent higher than in 2014–15. Listed from most to least in amount by item for one person, the team's tickets averaged between $79 and $80, parking one vehicle $18, a cap $15, single beer $8–$9, hot dog $6, and a soft drink and program each $5.

Among other teams in the conference's PD, they had rankings and FCIs from most to least as follows: Lakers second at $545; Warriors fourth at $471; Suns tenth at $341; and Kings eighteenth at $286. Consequently, Clippers fans paid less at games in the Staples Center than those of five other NBA clubs in their arenas.

The cheapest ticket cost $18 for a fan to watch a Clippers' home game in 2015–16. This was about $4 or approximately 13 percent more than the league's average for a cheap seat. Also, since the club's FCI was $98 above the amount of a typical NBA team, a family of four purchased tickets and enjoyed a basketball game in Los Angeles at a premium relative to the majority of arenas within the league. These costs and prices, in turn, were set by the Clippers organization to earn revenue and maximize profit from their operations.

In its annual ranking of all thirty NBA game-day experiences as of 2016, the *Stadium Journey* rated the Staples Center ninth. Its relatively high rank was explained as follows:

> Even with their rise in popularity, there is no mistaking that the Clippers are not the top tenant. Statues and banners paying tribute to the other 3 Staples Center

teams still dwarf any history the Clippers are doing their best to create. Things continue to look up for Clipper Nation. Their loyal following has endured through the long-standing rough times. Fervent support continues to rise for the Clippers with expectations at an all-time high. The days of accepting failure are long gone now. All that awaits for Clipper Nation is that big prize awarded to the last one standing come June.[19]

Business Highlights

Besides regular-season and postseason games, NBA franchises are involved in—and affected by—community events and business-related affairs, news, and projects. The following are a few of them for the Clippers, a popular, successful, and from a financial perspective, above-average professional basketball team.[20]

First, in a move that upended the traditional cable rights package, tech-savvy owner Steve Ballmer held back most of the traditional digital rights in his next media deal as of 2016 so that the team could launch a second-screen over-the-top (OTT) service to supplement its games. Although these rights did not include live games, they allowed for other in-game programming such as player-specific cameras, in-game highlights, and real-time statistics. This was the first time an NBA team carved out a significant portion of digital rights from a regional sports network deal to develop a team-run OTT service. It also was a maverick decision by former Microsoft chief executive officer Ballmer and a hard-charging business style to bring a new approach to team ownership.

Second, the Clippers could move out of the Staples Center once their current lease expires in June 2024. Team owner Steve Ballmer is actively seeking potential sites for a new arena—with the Westside in particular catching Ballmer's attention. As third tenants, the Clippers are entitled to a smaller share of proceeds generated from suites and club seats than the arena's two other tenants. A new facility would provide in-house revenue-generating opportunities for Ballmer and the Clippers while also opening up the possibility for Ballmer to develop the surrounding area with upscale restaurants, hotels, and residents deriving the most economic benefit from the project.

Third, during late 2014, team owner Steve Ballmer hired forty-five-year-old Gillian Zucker to be the new president of business operations. Zucker spent the last nine years as president of Auto Club Speedway (ACS) in Fontana, the West Coast's largest racetrack. At ACS, she oversaw operations, ticketing, finance, communications, and marketing for nine years. She previously was Daytona International Speedway's vice president of business and development and once worked in minor league baseball as the assistant general manager of the Durham Bulls in North Carolina. Ballmer described

Zucker as someone with enough intensity, enthusiasm, and wisdom to really do the job well.

Fourth, the Brand Keys Sports Fan Loyalty Index (SLI) was designed to help professional sports team marketers identify the key drivers of fan loyalty in their home and national markets by identifying emotional aspects surrounding the team that require strategic brand coaching. Fan loyalty correlates very highly with broadcast viewership, merchandise purchases, and, to a certain degree, ticket revenues. In the 2016 SLI, the Clippers tied for fifth with the Chicago Bulls after finishing second to the Bulls in 2015 and third in 2014 following the Oklahoma City Thunder and San Antonio Spurs.

Fifth, Terminal 4 at Los Angeles International had two reasons to be decked out in red, white, and blue during early 2015 as the Clippers announced their corporate sponsorship with American Airlines. The club's president of basketball operations and head coach Doc Rivers, president of business operations Gillian Zucker, American Airlines vice president of global marketing Fernand Fernandez, and player J. J. Redick took part in announcing the major, multiyear agreement between American Airlines and the Clippers in front of an audience inside the terminal. In front of Rivers, Zucker, and Fernandez stood a model of where the "American Airlines" name is placed on the court. The logo will be impossible to miss, appearing on the court in the space that covers the out-of-bounds area on the sideline between the baselines and coaches' box.

Los Angeles Lakers

Born in 1933 in Salt Lake City, Utah, Jerry Buss was nine years old when he moved with his mother to Los Angeles and then to Kemmerer, Wyoming. He earned a scholarship to the University of Wyoming and graduated from there with a Bachelor's of Science degree in in 1953. He then returned to Los Angeles where he earned master's and doctorate degrees in physical chemistry from the University of Southern California (USC).

After starting as a chemist for the Bureau of Mines, he then worked in the aerospace industry and was a faculty member in USC's chemistry department. Buss originally invested in real estate to provide an income to continue teaching. Finding great success in the real estate business, he pursued real estate investing and became very rich.

In 1979, Buss purchased the NBA Lakers and NHL Kings franchises, the Forum arena, and some Nevada real estate from Jack Kent Cooke for approximately $67 million. Under his leadership, the Lakers became Southern California's most beloved sports franchise and a worldwide extension of Hollywood glamour. He acquired, nurtured, and befriended a staggering array of talented players and basketball minds during his Hall of Fame tenure.

After battling cancer for several months, Buss died of kidney failure in February 2013. As a result, his 66 percent controlling ownership of the Lakers passed to his six children via a trust, with each child receiving an equal vote. In Buss's succession plan, his daughter Jeanie became the Lakers' governor as well as its team representative at NBA Board of Governors meetings while son Jim controlled the team's basketball operations.[21]

Since purchasing the Lakers franchise in 1979, the Buss's teams have won the most titles and championships when compared to those of owners of other NBA teams. More specifically, the club won eighteen division and sixteen conference titles, and ten league championships. As an ownership group, Jerry (now deceased) and his family is undoubtedly the most successful leaders in the sport and historically within the PD, WC, and league (table A8).

Team Financials

As reported in *Forbes* magazine during early 2016, the Lakers' worth was $2.7 billion, revenue $304 million, operating income $133 million, gate receipts $98 million, debt-to-value 1 percent, and players expenses $76 million. Among fourteen other WC teams, the club ranked first (market value, revenue, operating income, and gate receipts), thirteenth (debt ratio), and tied for tenth with the Timberwolves, Suns, and Spurs (players expenses). Within only the PD, the Lakers had the highest amounts in four financials but also tied the Suns with the lowest players expenses and had the second smallest debt percent following the Clippers (table A9).

In comparison to twenty-nine other NBA teams, Los Angeles was first in operating income, second in market value, revenue, and gate receipts, twenty-seventh in debt-to-value, and tied for eighteenth in players expenses. Based on these results, the Lakers are a commercially powerful and rich business franchise with plenty of cash flow and revenue to invest in its operations including the Staples Center and other assets. Because of its large sports market and successful history in the sport, the club has been—and likely will continue to be—a competitive, popular, and prominent commercial enterprise despite the death of former owner Jerry Buss in 2013.

Besides market size, salary inflation, and other factors, an NBA team's annual payroll partly reflects its commitment to players and their current and potential contribution individually and as a group to winning games in regular seasons and postseasons. From 2011 to 2015, for example, the Lakers' payroll among WC teams ranged in rank from first in 2011 ($87.9 million), 2012 ($99.9 million), and 2013 ($77.0 million) to tenth in 2014 ($70.1 million) and eleventh in 2015 ($72.1 million). Within the PD, the club had the third highest payroll in its 2011–2013 seasons but then fell to fourth in 2014 and third in 2015 (table A10).

In comparison to payrolls of all NBA teams, Los Angeles's was chronologically first in 2011 and 2012, fourth in 2013, seventeenth in 2014, and twenty-first in 2015. Based on these amounts, the Lakers increased their payroll for one season, decreased it for the next two, and then marginally increased it from 2014 to 2015. To become more competitive and win enough regular-season games to qualify again for the playoffs, the club must improve its roster and inflate payroll to amounts that exceed $85–$90 million within a few years.

As of 2016, the Lakers had about $76 million in active contracts with salary-cap maximum space of $25.3 million. That number could change in the team's favor if the front office makes more roster movements. Nick Young ($5.6 million in 2017–18) and seldom-used Anthony Brown ($1.01 million in 2017–18) do not figure into the Lakers' long-term plans. Meanwhile, Louis Williams will be in the final year of his contract, which pays him $7 million a year, and expiring contracts are often easy to trade.

Oklahoma City Thunder's star Russell Westbrook, who earns approximately $17.7 million, will be joined by the Warriors' Stephen Curry and Clippers' Blake Griffin on the free-agent market in 2017. The Lakers will likely pursue Westbrook more than any other player, even though the team currently lacks star power in the frontcourt. From a salary cap standpoint, the Lakers are one of the few teams who can slap together a reasonable bunch of young cheap players for a sign-and-trade deal, as well as veterans with reasonable contracts, and the requisite cap space to accommodate Westbrook's current and future salaries in future seasons.[22]

Staples Center

As described earlier in this chapter for the Los Angeles Clippers, the Staples Center is a relatively modern but urban arena with plenty of amenities for its tenants including the Lakers. Among venues of other WC teams, it tied for seventh with the Nuggets' Pepsi Center and Pelicans' Smoothie Kings Arena in age, second most expensive in construction plus renovation costs following the Mavericks' American Airlines Center, and placed fifth in value. With respect to all NBA arenas, the Staples Center tied for fourteenth (age) and fourth (costs), and ranked fourth (value). Thus, the Lakers play their home games in a glamorous facility that generates large amounts of revenue from various activities, events, and other business sources (table A11).

In the 2011–2015 NBA seasons, the FCI for a family to attend a Lakers regular-season game at the Staples Center ranged from a low of $514 in 2011 to a high of $545 in 2015. With respect to those of all NBA teams, the Lakers were second after the New York Knicks' at Madison Square Garden (table A12).

To reveal specific costs for a recent season in the NBA, the Lakers' FCI in 2015–16 was approximately 1 percent higher than in 2014–15. Listed from most to least in amount by item for one person, the team's tickets averaged between $103 and $104, parking one vehicle $25, a cap $18, single beer $8–$9, soft drink and hot dog each $5–$6, and a program $5.

Among other teams in the conference's PD, they had rankings and FCIs from most to least as follows: Warriors fourth at $471; Clippers sixth at $437; Suns tenth at $341; and Kings eighteenth at $286. Consequently, Lakers fans paid more at games in the Staples Center than twenty-eight other NBA clubs in their arenas.

The cheapest ticket cost $36 for a fan to watch a Lakers home game in 2015–16. This was about $20 or 230 percent more than the league's average for a cheap seat. Also, since the club's FCI was $206 above the amount of a typical NBA team, a family of four purchased tickets and enjoyed a basketball game in Los Angeles at a significant premium relative to the majority of arenas within the league. These costs and prices, in turn, were set by the Lakers organization to earn revenue and maximize profit from their operations.

In its annual ranking of all thirty NBA game-day experiences as of mid-2016, the *Stadium Journey* rated the Staples Center second best among the group when the Lakers played their home games. The arena's relatively high rank was explained as follows: "In recent years, the Staples Center has seemingly become the basketball capital of the world. With its futuristic look and cascading lights atop the arena, the venue has become one of the most identifiable in all of sports. If the vibe of downtown LA prior to a Laker game fails to get you excited, stepping inside and spotting the championship banners will."[23]

Business Highlights

Besides regular-season and postseason games, NBA franchises are involved in—and affected by—community events and business-related affairs, news, and projects. The following are a few of them for the Lakers, a historically successful, and from a financial perspective, above-average professional basketball team.[24]

First, Delta Air Lines (DAL) signed a multiyear deal during early 2011 to become an official sponsor and exclusive airline partner of the Lakers, in a deal that DAL made at least in part to showcase its high-end services to the team's glamorous high-end ticket holders at the Staples Center. The airline received center-court rotational sign space, rotating sign space between the second and third level of suites, branding on the center-hung video board and rotating scrolling message space on the LED boards, as well as other in-arena branding opportunities. The deal was between the team and DAL, and not

Staples Center owner Anschutz Entertainment Group. In addition, the airline replaced Virgin America as the Lakers' official sponsor.

Second, to preserve the past and protect the future, a company named Iron Mountain collected all of the Lakers' content—including media preserved in a vault—and also tapes being stored by previous broadcast partners. For the latter, Iron Mountain securely transported the content between locations and cleaned and quality-checked all media. Then, it converted the media to a common format and preserved it in its Digital Content Repository (DCR), a leading-edge digital asset management tool, which created a complete, secure, and accessible catalog of the organization's content. This archived footage—which includes over 5,000 hours of highlight reels, full games, and related media—can be accessed from the DCR by the Lakers, its television partners, and potentially even fans or other media outlets via an easy-to-use, Web-based interface.

Third, the Lakers signed Chinese Olympian and power forward Yi Jianlian following his performance at the 2016 Olympics in Rio de Janeiro. In five games, he averaged 20.4 points and 6.6 rebounds. The twenty-eight year old last played in the NBA in 2012 with the Dallas Mavericks, spent the past four seasons playing in the Chinese Basketball Association, and considered the second most popular player on the mainland after former NBA center Yao Ming. The Lakers did not disclose Yi's contract details although reports indicate he signed for one year with a veterans' minimum of $1.1 million that could reach $8 million with bonuses.

Fourth, entering her first season as president after fourteen seasons as executive vice president of business operations, Jeanie Buss is responsible for running all aspects of the Lakers organization. Buss, who continues to lead all business operations—which include managing team marketing and sponsorships as well as relationships with broadcast partners—will also oversee the team's basketball operations. She works closely with executive vice president of basketball operations Jim Buss and general manager Mitch Kupchak.

Fifth, NBA teams are allowed to sell to any company so long as it does not deal in gambling, alcohol, or politics. The league has given protected status—meaning the companies' competitors cannot show up on a team jersey—to a number of its national partners: media partners ESPN, ABC, and Turner; apparel partner Nike starting in 2017–18; and on-court partners Tissot and Spaulding. No other league partners, including Ticketmaster, a StubHub competitor, are protected. What does this mean for the Lakers? There are an abundance of companies that would spend plenty of money to appear on any of the jerseys that the Lakers sport from season to season. Potential sponsor ideas include Snapchat, Warner Brothers, and possibly Staples.

Phoenix Suns

Born into a Jewish family in Tucson, Arizona in 1961, Robert "Bob" Sarver worked for his father's company—American Savings and Loan—when sixteen years old. In 1979, he graduated from Sabino High School in Tucson and three years later from the University of Arizona with a bachelor's degree in business administration, and then became a certified public accountant.

In 1984, Sarver founded the National Bank of Tucson and during the 1990s, co-founded the real estate company Southwest Value Partners; sold his bank—then the largest independent one in the state—to Zions Bancorporation; purchased the Emerald Plaza in San Diego; and acquired Grossmont Bank. In 2004, Southwest Value Partners sold the Emerald Plaza and two other San Diego office buildings to a Santa Ana real estate firm for $274.5 million.

A lifelong sports fan, Sarver's quest to purchase an NBA team began with a conversation with University of Arizona basketball coach Lute Olson. Olson referred Sarver to Steve Kerr—a former player at Arizona and a fifteen-year NBA veteran—to assist him in buying an NBA franchise. During the spring of 2004, he acquired the Phoenix Suns franchise from Jerry Colangelo for approximately $404 million.

With respect to fourteen other owners of WC teams, Sarver's Suns tied for fifth with the Nuggets' Stanley Kroenke in winning three division titles, for eighth with zero conference titles, and for sixth in number of NBA championships. Among all teams and their respective owners, Phoenix tied for twelfth (division titles), for fifteenth (conference titles), and for tenth (league championships). Despite his teams competing in five playoffs since the 2003–4 season, Sarver's failed to win their conference (table A8).

According to sports columnist Mark Heisler, Robert Sarver is the NBA's fifth worst owner as of 2016. In his view, Heisler said this about Sarver's abilities as an owner:

> Despite his vow to keep everyone upon arrival in their heyday in 2004, everyone from paterfamilias Jerry Colangelo down found themselves on the way out. The revolving door hasn't stopped spinning yet. Just blew up the young team that won 48 two seasons ago, putting Isaiah Thomas alongside Eric Bledsoe and Goran Dragic upsetting everyone so badly, they had to deal Thomas and Dragic. [The club] just lost Bledsoe for the season so they're starting over, again.[25]

After scoring only twenty-two points in the first half versus the league's worst defense in the woeful Lakers, and getting blown out without ever really challenging, Suns owner Robert Sarver blamed, in part, Millennials. He said the Millennial culture has a tough time dealing with setbacks, and player

Markieff Morris is the perfect example. Morris had a setback with his brother in the offseason and apparently did not recover from it. Not a fan of social media, Sarver is unsure of technology or instant gratification of being online. In fact, he tells his kids the only thing people put online are good things that happen to them, or things they make up, and this creates unrealistic expectations. His solution to the Suns' problems is for the entire organization to simply step up their game.[26]

Team Financials

Based on financial data published in *Forbes* magazine as of early 2016 about NBA teams, the Suns' market value was an estimated $1 billion and their revenue $154 million, operating income $21 million, gate receipts $35 million, debt-to-value 18 percent, and players expenses $76 million. Among fourteen other clubs in the WC, Phoenix placed seventh (market value), ninth (revenue), eighth (operating income), tenth (gate receipts), fourth (debt ratio), and tied for tenth with the Timberwolves, Lakers, and Spurs (players expenses). Within only the PD, the Suns generally had lower amounts than the Warriors, Clippers, and Lakers but not the Kings (table A9).

With respect to twenty-nine NBA teams, Phoenix ranged in rank from a tie for ninth in its debt-to-value to a tie for eighteenth in players expenses. According to these results, the Suns are an average franchise financially and as a business organization when compared to others in their conference. The club's cash flows from gate receipts and other sources are enough to pay its debts, compensate players, and invest in assets to improve operations.

Besides market size, salary inflation, and other factors, an NBA team's annual payroll partly reflects its commitment to players and their current and potential contribution individually and as a group to winning games in regular seasons and postseasons. From 2011 to 2015, for example, the Suns' payroll among WC teams ranged in rank from second in 2011 ($79.9 million) to fifteenth in 2012 ($53.3 million) and 2013 ($55.0 million). Within only the PD, the club had the second highest payroll in its 2011 season following the Lakers but then fell to fifth from 2012 to 2015 (table A10).

In comparison to payrolls of all NBA teams during the league's 2011–2015 seasons, Phoenix's was chronologically second and then tied for twenty-ninth, twenty-ninth, twenty-third, and twenty-sixth. These changes in payrolls, in part, caused the team to finish third three times and fourth and fifth each once in the PD. For the Suns to be competitive in the 2016–17 season and thereafter, they must gradually increase payments to players and also make good short- and long-term decisions about keeping or trading them.

From their 2016–17 to 2018–19 seasons, Phoenix had committed respectively $80.9 million, $70.2 million, and $64.9 million in salaries. In addition, four players were guaranteed between $30 million and $56 million through 2021–22 including Eric Bledsoe, Brandon Knight, Tyson Chandler, and Jared Dudley. Thus, the club will depend on them to perform and as a group, win at least fifty games in regular seasons to qualify for the playoffs.

The Suns have kept the capability to sign a maximum-salary free agent in 2017 while maintaining their core players. That payroll positioning took a slight hit when the NBA announced that the projected salary cap for the 2017–18 season is $102 million or $5 million less than initially anticipated. Even so, general manager Ryan McDonough believes the team can easily maneuver to get maximum-salary contract space.[27]

Talking Stick Resort Arena

Opened in 1992 to replace Memorial Coliseum, the 19,000-seat America West Arena—former US Airways Center and then renamed Talking Stick Resort Arena in 2016—is the home site of the Suns, Arena Football League's Arizona Rattlers, and Women National Basketball Association's Phoenix Mercury. During the early 1990s, the Suns hired former player Alvan Adams to tour the nation's finest basketball facilities. As a result, the best of their features were incorporated into the arena's design. Originally, everything was state-of-the-art, built for not only fans but also players.

Unlike most NBA teams, the Suns practice where they play, in a gym built next to the locker rooms at the arena. All seats, even the less expensive ones, have great sight lines. The arena is attractive with the Suns' team colors—purple, orange, and copper—displayed everywhere. While the downtown location is ideal with low crime, plenty of police and security officers help with traffic and directions into and out of the arena's eleven acres.

The arena's concourses underwent a facelift. With terrazzo tile flooring, walls are backlit in a soft blue with futuristic looking silver panels on the ceiling and silver wall accents. There is an escalator tower to the upper concourse, and inside the main northwest entrance is a team store and lobby that provide ample entrance space.

Renovations were completed in March 2003. They featured a 16,000-square-foot air conditioned, glass-enclosed atrium built on the northwest side of the arena to keep patrons cool while waiting in line for tickets or spending time inside the building before events. The arena's upgrading was done as part of the Suns' plan to keep itself economically competitive.

Among those of other WC teams as of early 2016, the Suns' arena was fifth in age, thirteenth most in dollars to build, and eighth in economic value. Compared to venues of all NBA clubs, Phoenix's ranked seventh (age), tied for twenty-sixth (construction costs), and fifteenth (value). Consequently, the Suns play their home games in a relatively old but not ultra-expensive building that generates an average amount of income from advertisements, gate receipts, and other sources for the franchise mostly during NBA seasons (table A11).

In the league's 2011–2015 seasons, the FCIs for a family to attend a Suns regular-season home game ranged from a low of $333 in 2012 to a high of $346 in 2011. With respect to those of twenty-nine teams, Phoenix's ranged in rank from sixth in 2011 to tenth at $341 in 2015 (table A12).

To reveal specific costs for a recent season in the NBA, the Suns' FCI in 2015–16 was the same as in 2014–15. Listed from most to least in amount by item for one person, the team's tickets averaged between $50 and $60, a cap $23 and parking one vehicle $12, single beer between $10 and $11, soft drink $6–$7, and a hot dog $3–$4.

Among other teams in the conference's PD, they had rankings and FCIs from most to least as follows: Lakers second at $545; Warriors fourth at $471; Clippers sixth at $437; and Kings eighteenth at $286. Consequently, Suns fans paid less at games in the recently named Talking Stick Resort Arena than nine other NBA clubs in their arenas.

The cheapest ticket cost almost $16 for a fan to watch a Suns home game in 2015–16. This was about the same as the league's average for a cheap seat. Also, since the club's FCI was only $2 above the amount of a typical NBA team, a family of four purchased tickets and enjoyed a basketball game in Phoenix at a tiny premium relative to the majority of arenas within the league. These costs and prices, in turn, were set by the Suns organization to earn revenue and maximize profit from their operations.

In its annual ranking of all thirty NBA game-day experiences as of mid-2016, the *Stadium Journey* rated the Talking Stick Resort Arena twentieth best among the group when the Suns played their home games. The arena's relatively low rank was explained as follows: "Everything is clean and nice and the venue certainly doesn't feel like one of the oldest in the NBA. However, Talking Stick Resort Arena conveys the feeling of going to a movie theater. Perhaps it was because of the concession stand layout. Perhaps it was because of the colors—all purples and oranges. The venue doesn't necessarily scream basketball."[28]

Business Highlights

Besides regular-season and postseason games, NBA franchises are involved in—and affected by—community events and business-related affairs, news, and projects. The following are a few of them for the Suns, a low-performing, and from a financial perspective, average professional basketball team.[29]

First, the Suns signed a multiyear sponsorship deal in mid-2013 with hamburger chain Carl's Jr. that included the opening of a restaurant in the team's arena that operates during non-game-day hours. The deal also provided a separate, Carl's Jr. mini-store on the arena's concourse, open during arena events. The sponsorship filled the quick-service restaurant (QSR) category for the team. According to one source, the sponsorship is a five-year deal valued at more than $4 million. It replaced the Suns' previous agreements with Jack in the Box and McDonald's, who shared the QSR category.

Second, when it involves social media, the Suns are one of the most progressive teams in the NBA. Consider that the team launched a new website in 2011 called fans.suns.com that incorporated all of its social media channels while allowing fans to post their videos, blogs, and other digital content into a single site. The site, which replaced the team's planetorange.com, was sponsored by Southwest Airlines and represented the latest effort among teams to build a digital community to drive interest in the Phoenix-based franchise and create new revenue streams.

Third, the Suns became the first NBA team to sign the UNITY Pledge in support of full inclusion and equality in the workplace, housing, and public accommodations for all Arizonians, including gay and transgender people. The team joined more than 1,500 businesses and organizations including the Arizona Diamondbacks, San Francisco Giants, Frys Food & Drug Stores, GoDaddy, professional firefighters of Arizona, PetSmart, Yelp, and Coca-Cola in supporting a fully inclusive Arizona. "We are dedicated to the principle of treating everyone as equals," said Suns president Jason Rowley. "With the signing of the UNITY Pledge, we aim to publicly show support of our diverse community," concluded Rowley.

Fourth, the Suns created more meaningful experiences for its employees using Ultimate Software's comprehensive cloud solution beginning in 2016. The Phoenix, Arizona-based organization established a key human resources objective of enhancing its employees' work experiences by delivering more useful tools and better information to its people. With UltiPro as their solution of record, the Suns will impact the entire employee experience—from onboarding to talent management—regardless of whether the person is in the office or on the road. This accelerated onboarding process also aides the Suns in achieving their goal to ensure the safety of employees and customers by automating employee credentialing.

Fifth, the Suns were one of five NBA teams that tested a new ticketing tool to reach young fans in 2014–15. Atlanta technology firm Experience helped the Suns create "College Pass" to offer inexpensive, last-minute tickets to some of the 100,000-plus college students in the Phoenix area. Most of the seats were in the upper deck and the Suns sold 500 tickets on some nights.

Sacramento Kings

Born in the Juhu area of Bombay (now Mumbai) in 1957, Vivek Ranadivé was accepted to Massachusetts Institute of Technology (MIT) when he was sixteen years old. After earning both a bachelor's and master's degree in electrical engineering from MIT, he obtained his Master's of Business Administration (MBA) degree from Harvard University in 1983. Ranadivé started his first company, a UNIX consulting company, and also held management and engineering positions with Ford Motor Company, M/A-Com Linkabit, and Fortune Systems soon after college.

In 1997, Ranadivé founded Tibco Software Inc. with funding from Cisco and Reuters. He began to apply real-time software that he developed in Tibco's first year and teamed with CBS Sportsline to enable real-time news of all major sporting events including the NFL, NBA, and PGA. By 2011, Ranadivé had grown Tibco's annual revenues to $920 million and its customer base to 4,000. During September 2014, Ranadivé sold Tibco Software to Vista Equity Partners for $4.3 billion.

After rejecting a bid for the NBA Kings franchise by Microsoft executive Steve Ballmer, the league approved Ranadivé's offer in 2013. An investor in and vice chairman of the Golden State Warriors and also a former coach of his daughter's basketball team, Ranadivé won the support of Sacramento Mayor Kevin Johnson and other NBA owners to be a successful leader of the franchise. Johnson said Ranadivé understood technology and startups, and would not move the Kings to another city.[30]

Through the team's 2015–16 season, Ranadivé's Kings had not won a division title or qualified for the playoffs. According to an online website in 2015, he was the twenty-fifth best among thirty NBA owners. This, in part, was the reason for him being ranked so low (table A8):

> But he's [Ranadivé's] only owned the team for two years now and things are looking no better than they were when he took over. He fired Mike Malone, allowed a grass fire of DeMarcus Cousins trade rumors to spread throughout the locker room and he has seemingly lost control of his franchise. This all comes a year after the Kings won a Summer League title and Ranadivé said it was the first step on the road to the NBA Finals. That's a road that is still unpaved, undiscovered and unrealistic.[31]

Team Financials

Based on financial data reported in *Forbes* magazine during early 2016 for WC teams, the Kings ranked tenth in market value ($925 million) and also fourteenth in revenue ($141 million), tied for fourteenth with the Trail Blazers in operating income ($4 million), twelfth in gate receipts ($29 million), first in debt-to-value (25 percent), and tied for sixth with the Grizzlies in players expenses ($81 million). Within the PD, Sacramento had the lowest amounts—except for players expenses—but the highest debt ratio (table A9).

Among all teams in the league, the Kings ranged in rank from a tie for fourteenth in players expenses to twenty-sixth in revenue. Thus, this franchise has been and is below average from a financial perspective because of such factors as its coaches' decisions, lack of enough talented players, location, historically poor performances in the PD, and various ownership problems.

From 2011 to 2015, the Kings' payroll among WC teams ranged in rank from sixth in 2014 ($73.8 million) to fifteenth in 2011 ($48.9 million). Within the PD, the club had the lowest payroll in its 2011 season, fourth in three other years, but also second after the Clippers in 2014 (table A10).

In comparison to payrolls of all NBA teams during the league's 2011–2015 seasons, Sacramento's was chronologically twenty-ninth and then twenty-eighth, twenty-third, twelfth, and twenty-fifth. These changes in payrolls, in part, caused the team to finish third and fifth each once and fourth three times in the PD. For the Kings to be competitive in the 2016–17 season and thereafter, they must gradually increase payments to their players and also make good short- and long-term decisions about keeping or trading them.

Sleep Train Arena

Opened in 1988, the 17,300-seat ARCO Arena—renamed Power Balance Pavilion in 2011 and then Sleep Train Arena in 2012—was the fifth oldest, thirteenth most expensive to build, and eighth in economic value among those of other WC teams as of early 2016. Compared to venues of all NBA clubs, it ranked seventh (age), tied for twenty-sixth (construction cost), and fifteenth (value). Based on this data, the Kings play their home games in an outdated and inferior facility that required renovation and more amenities to generate sufficient revenue for the franchise from gate receipts and other sources (table A11).

In the league's 2011–2015 seasons, the FCIs for a family to attend a Kings regular-season home game ranged from a low of $268 in 2012 and 2013 to a high of $286 in 2015. With respect to those of twenty-nine other NBA teams, Phoenix's fluctuated in rank from fifteenth in 2011 ($277) to twenty-first in 2013 (table A12).

To open their 2016–17 season, the Kings moved into a new $507 million downtown arena. Before the season started, sales at the Golden 1 Center were brisk with all thirty-four luxury suites reserved plus forty-eight lofts. More than 12,000 fans put their names on a waiting list for season tickets. Sacramento-based Golden 1—one of the nation's largest credit unions—acquired naming rights to the arena in a deal worth $6 million annually. Fans can only hope the new building can turn around the team's fortunes on the hardwood where they established ten consecutive losing seasons or from 2006–7 to 2015–16.

Business Highlights

Besides regular-season and postseason games, NBA franchises are involved in—and affected by—community events and business-related affairs, news, and projects. The following are a few of them for the Kings, a low-performing, and from a financial perspective, below-average professional basketball team.[32]

First, to showcase premium seats at their new arena, the Kings' 8,000-square-foot Experience Center has both augmented and virtual reality in its marketing pitch. Instead of a physical model produced by an architect, the club uses a tablet containing 3-D images of the arena seating bowl that pops up on the tablet screen when waved over a tabletop equipped with augmented reality. In the Experience Center, season ticket holders and new buyers, for example, can put on a pair of Oculus Rift goggles that vividly take them through a midcourt experience with player DeMarcus Cousins.

Second, while traveling to China in October 2012 as part of the league's annual Global Games, the Kings extended their brand overseas just as much as preseason games against the New York Nets in Shanghai and Beijing. Though neither team had a Chinese player on its roster, both of them used the trip to increase their international profile and land global sponsors. The Kings last played internationally in 2004—with a trip to China against the Yao Ming-led Houston Rockets.

Third, the Kings signed a four-year deal during mid-2014 to acquire control over two sponsorship packages for the U.S. Ski and Snowboard Association's Grand Prix series. Each sponsorship and hospitality package included three Grand Prix events, which featured snowboarding and free-skiing competition. Those events were held in Lake Tahoe, California; Copper Mountain, Colorado; and Park City, Utah. Although financial terms of the deal were not disclosed, Grand Prix sponsorships typically are priced in the mid-six figures.

Fourth, the Kings lead the NBA in game-day marketing. They were the first team to have a direct integration with Uber. The Uber interface changes when there's a game, and one of the options is "Kings Game" and includes the Kings logo. When the partnership launched, all season ticket holders received Uber credits. The Kings' RV is one of the special cars that pick up Kings fans sometimes along with a former player or an executive involved with the Kings. The goal of the organization is to create a great atmosphere across the city on game days.

Fifth, during a home game in April 2016, the Kings broke new ground with Capitalize, a contest it organized with Velocity Venture Capital. The club had a few startups pitch their ideas to fans who voted for their favorite company through Twitter. Startups within seventy-five miles of Sacramento applied for the contest and more than thirty picked to pitch to a panel of judges consisting of local investors and technology executives at Velocity Venture Capital's Sacramento office. This was the first time an NBA team hosted a "crowd-sourced local technology startup competition."

NOTES

1. Two books about NBA franchises and their history are Frank P. Jozsa Jr., *The National Basketball Association: Business, Organization and Strategy* (Hackensack, NJ: World Scientific, 2011) and James Quirk and Rodney D. Fort, *Pay Dirt: The Business of Professional Team Sports* (Princeton, NJ: Princeton University Press, 1992).

2. For data and other information regarding team performances, see such websites as http://www.basketball-reference.com, http://www.nba.com, and also http://www.sportsencyclopedia.com.

3. Chad Ford and Kevin Pelton, "Future Power Rankings: Who Will Rise in the Next Three Years?" http://www.espn.go.com, cited June 5, 2016.

4. One important reference is Chris Holmes, "All-Time NBA Franchise Rankings, 2015–16 Edition," http://www.greyflannelsuit.net, cited August 15, 2016.

5. See, for example, Chad Ford and Kevin Pelton, "Future NBA Power Rankings: Full Category Rankings," http://www.espn.go.com, cited August 3, 2016.

6. Jared White, "What is Next for the Los Angeles Clippers?" http://www.nba-lead.com, cited August 20, 2016.

7. This quote was taken from Daniel Zillmer, "All 30 NBA Franchises Statistically Ranked by All-Time Greatness," http://www.fansided.com, cited June 6, 2016.

8. Scott Hanna-Riggs, "ESPN Insider's Future Power Rankings: Phoenix Suns 4th Worst in NBA," http://www.valleyofthesuns.com, cited June 28, 2016.

9. For two readings about NBA owners and their careers in business and sports, including the Warriors' Joe Lacob, see John Buhler, "10 Best NBA Front Offices," http://www.fansided.com, cited August 21, 2016 and Josh Hill, "NBA Owners Power Ranking: Who is Best Owner in Basketball?" http://www.fansided.com, cited July 8, 2016.

10. "NBA Owners Power Rankings: Who is the Best Owner in Basketball?"

11. Tim Bontemps, "Kevin Durant and the Warriors Dream Team May Become a Salary Nightmare Next July," http://www.washingtonpost.com, cited August 28, 2016.

12. This topic, in part, is covered in Jacob Kornhauser, "Ranking Every NBA Arena From Worst to First," http://www.ranksports.com, cited July 13, 2016.

13. See "Fan Cost Index," http://www.teammarketingreport.com, cited August 1, 2016 and "NBA FCIs," http://www.teammarketingreport.com, cited July 1, 2016.

14. See Paul Swaney, "2015 NBA Arena Experience Rankings," http://www.scout.com, cited August 15, 2016.

15. For some Warriors business news and events, there is Ed Frauenheim, "What Business Can Learn From the Golden State Warriors," http://www.fortune.com, cited September 1, 2016; J. K. Dineen, "Warriors Win Judgement in Fight Over SF Mission Bay Arena," http://www.sfgate.com, cited September 1, 2016; Eric Fisher, "Teams Put Pressure on Ticket Brokers," http://www.sportsbusinessdaily.com, cited September 2, 2016; Bruce Shoenfeld, "Limited Owners, Unlimited Expectations," http://www.sportsbusinessdaily.com, cited September 2, 2016; "Warriors Honored for Sales/Marketing," http://www.sportsbusinessdaily.com, cited September 3, 2016.

16. "NBA Owners Power Ranking: Who is the Best Owner in Basketball?"

17. Keith Smith, "The Maximum Available 2016 Cap Space for ALL 30 NBA Teams, Version 2.0," http://www.basketball.realgm.com, cited September 4, 2016.

18. "Ranking Every NBA Arena From Worst to First."

19. Besides notes 12, 14, and 18, see "NBA Arenas," http://www.nbaarenas.com, cited September 4, 2016.

20. The Clippers' business news includes such readings as "Steve Ballmer's for Local TV," http://www.sportsbusinessdaily.com, cited September 5, 2016; Jonathan Ponciano, "Los Angeles Clippers May Leave Staples Center for Westside," http://www.labusinessjournal.com, cited September 5, 2016; "Gillian Zucker Replaces Andy Roeser," http://www.espn.com, cited September 5, 2016; "Thunder, Spurs and Heat NBA Fan Favorites in Brand Keys 2016 Sports Fan Loyalty Index," http://www.brandkeys.com, cited September 1, 2016; "Clippers Announce Partnership With American Airlines," http://www.nba.com, cited September 2, 2016.

21. Kevin Ding, "A Family Divided: Unrest Growing in Buss Family as Lakers Struggle to Rebuild," http://www.bleacherreport.com, cited September 7, 2016.

22. Greg Price, "Lakers Rumors: Is there Cap Space to Sign Russell Westbrook in 2017?" http://www.ibtimes.com, cited September 5, 2016.

23. Paul Baker, "2016 NBA Arena Experience Rankings," http://www.scout.com, cited August 1, 2016.

24. The Lakers' business news is covered, for example, in Liz Mullen, "Delta Air Lines Signs Multiyear Deal With Lakers," http://wwwsportsbusinessdaily.com, cited September 3, 2016; "Los Angeles Lakers: A Secure, Future-Proof, Fan-Friendly Video Archive," http://www.ironmountain.com, cited September 4, 2016; "Los Angeles Lakers Sign Chinese Olympian Yi Jianlain," http://www.bbc.com, cited September 6, 2016; "Jeanie Buss: Los Angeles Lakers," http://www.concordia.net, cited September 6, 2016; Keith Rivas, "Lakers Jersey Ads: Which Companies Should Sponsor Los Angeles in the Future?" http://www.lasportshub.com, cited September 7, 2016.

25. Mark Heisler, "Heisler: From Bad to Worse to Vivek: Top 10 Worst Owners in NBA," http://www.dailynews.com, cited September 8, 2016.

26. See Matt Moore, "It's Robert Sarver vs. Millennials as the Phoenix Suns Hit Rock Bottom," http://www.cbssports.com, cited September 6, 2016.

27. Paul Coro, “Phoenix Suns Likely to Hold $13 Million Cap Space for Later,” http://www.azcentral.com, cited September 8, 2016.

28. “2016 NBA Arena Experience Rankings.”

29. John Lombardo, “Suns, Verizon Team for a Tech ‘Wonderland,’” http://www.sportsbusinessdaily.com, cited September 1, 2016; “Social Experiment,” http://www.sportsbusinessdaily.com, cited September 2, 2016; Angela Hughey, “Phoenix Suns Become First NBA Team to Sign the UNITY Pledge,” http://www.openaz.com, cited September 3, 2016; “The Phoenix Suns Create ‘People First’ Employee Experiences With UltiPro,” http://www.tucson.com, cited September 5, 2016.

30. For more about this transaction, see Peter Delevett, “How Vivek Ranadive Beat Out Steve Ballmer to Buy Sacramento Kings,” http://www.mercurynews.com, cited September 6, 2016.

31. “NBA Owners Power Ranking: Who is Best Owner in Basketball?”

32. Don Muret, “Teams Pour More Money, Tech Into Preview Centers,” http://www.sportsbusinessdaily.com, cited September 6, 2016; “Nets, Kings See Global Opportunity,” http://www.sportsbusinessdaily.com, cited September 6, 2016; “NBA Kings to Package USSA Sponsorship Deals With Its Own,” http://www.sportsbusinessdaily.com, cited September 7, 2016; Jonathan Lacoste, “How the CMO of the Sacramento Kings Makes Game Day an Interactive Experience,” http://www.inc.com, cited September 7, 2016; Taylor Soper, “Sacramento Kings Will Host a Startup Pitch Contest During an NBA Game,” http://www.geekwire.com, cited September 8, 2016.

Chapter Six

Southwest Division

Established in 2004 by the National Basketball Association (NBA), the Southwest Division (SWD) of the league's Western Conference (WC) originally included the Dallas Mavericks, Houston Rockets, Memphis Grizzlies, and New Orleans Hornets—who moved from Charlotte, North Carolina, in 2002—and the San Antonio Spurs. After completing their 2003–4 season, the Mavericks, Rockets, Grizzlies, and Spurs joined the SWD from the league's defunct Midwest Division (MWD) and the Hornets—renamed Pelicans in 2013—from the Central Division (CD).

Given these change in the conference's structure, this chapter discusses the historical developments and highlights business news and the financial facts of SWD teams based respectively in Dallas, Texas; Houston, Texas; Memphis, Tennessee; New Orleans, Louisiana; and San Antonio, Texas. During their history, which of them, for example, had won the most division titles and fewest number of NBA championships? What were their market values, revenues, and ticket prices in the league's 2015–16—or simply—2015 season? Who have been the least and most successful owners among the five clubs? How do their arenas rank in aesthetics, entertainment, and experience among fans? The answers to these and other questions are covered in the chapter.[1]

TEAM PERFORMANCES

Dallas Mavericks

In 1978, Californian businessman Garn Eckardt and Texas lawyer Doug Adkins discussed the relocation of an existing NBA team to Dallas. As a partner,

Adkins recommended one of his clients, Home Interiors and Gifts owner Don Carter. Although negotiations with Eckardt stopped, Carter remained interested in the sports business as a gift to his wife Linda. Meanwhile, the league's Buffalo Braves president and general manager Norman Sonjus was also interested in bringing the NBA to Dallas while studying potential sites for the Braves franchise.[2]

When the Braves transferred to California in 1978 and became the San Diego Clippers, Sonju returned to Texas. While there, he was introduced to Carter by Dallas mayor Robert Folsom, who co-owned the American Basketball Association (ABA) Dallas Chaparrals—which moved to San Antonio in 1973 and was nicknamed Spurs.

Sonju and Carter tried purchasing both the NBA Milwaukee Bucks and Kansas City Kings, but disagreed on relocation, which led them to seek an expansion team. Initially, the league was reluctant to expand into Dallas since Texas had both the Spurs and Rockets and because its 1978 season was unprofitable and also unpopular on television. Even so, during the 1979 all-star game weekend, Commissioner Larry O'Brien announced the addition of new teams in Dallas and Minneapolis (who later withdrew its bid).

The Dallas team's nickname "Mavericks" came from a television show and chosen by fans over "Wranglers" and "Express." In fact, the show's namesake character James Garner was a member of the original ownership group along with Carter, Sonjus, and Adkins. Dick Motta, who had guided the Washington Bullets to the NBA championship in the 1977–78 season, became the Mavericks' first head coach in 1980.

Historical Results

As a member of the WC during the 1980 to 2015 NBA seasons, the Mavericks had victories in approximately 51 percent of their games. In the period, the team won three division and two conference titles, and one championship in twenty-one playoffs. Among teams in the conference, Dallas ranked eighth (winning percentage) and also tenth (division titles), tied for sixth with the Jazz and Suns (conference titles), and tied for fifth with the Trail Blazers (championships). Within only the SWD, the Mavericks have been less successful than the Rockets and Spurs but not the Grizzlies or Hornets/Pelicans (table A7).

In comparison to records of twenty-nine other NBA teams as of early 2016, Dallas tied for eleventh in both winning percentage and number of championships, for twenty-second in division titles, and for fourteenth in conference titles. Based on these results and other information, this has been an average performing team during its thirty-six years in the league.

Performance Highlights

The club was most competitive when appearing in consecutive playoffs during NBA seasons 1983–1987, 2001–2011, and 2013–2015. These teams were led by such head coaches as Dick Motta, John MacLeod, Don Nelson, Avery Johnson, and Rick Carlisle. Nelson is in the sport's Hall of Fame and Johnson a former NBA Coach of the Year.

To win games in regular seasons and postseasons, the Mavericks had some outstanding players. The group included Brad Davis, Rolando Blackman, Sam Perkins, Derek Harper, Dirk Nowitzki, and Tyson Chandler. While Davis, Blackman, and Harper had their uniform numbers retired by the team, Nowitzki was the NBA Most Valuable Player (MVP) in 2007. Besides them, Jason Kidd won a Rookie of the Year award in 1995.

In contrast, Dallas failed to qualify for the playoffs in seasons 1988–89, 1990–99, and 2012–13. This occurred, in part, because coaches MacLeod, Richie Adubato, Quinn Buckner, Jim Cleamons, Nelson, and Carlisle did not motivate their players enough to compete in games and also due to other reasons such as injuries and outstanding performances by the Rockets, Spurs, and several other clubs in the WC.

The Mavericks' worst and then two best seasons were respectively 1992–93, and 2006–7 and 2010–11. In the former season, the club had only eleven victories and finished sixth in its division but then won sixty-seven games and a division title in the 2006–7 campaign and an NBA championship in 2011. The differences in Dallas's performances happened because of such things as coaching problems, lack of motivated and talented players, and better teams in its division and conference.

In the Entertainment Sports Programming Network (ESPN) future power rankings regarding the league's 2016–2018 seasons, the Mavericks ranked twenty-second. Every category except market dropped, and only five teams rated worse in terms of players. Management continues to be the Mavericks' top-ranked category, but at a certain point you wonder why when management is responsible for the lack of talent on the roster and poor draft results. At some point, superstar Dirk Nowitzki will retire, and then rebuilding the roster will be necessary. Also, is owner Mark Cuban truly committed to building through the draft? Will coach Rick Carlisle bolt for another team and Mark for politics? For now, the Mavericks' future is uncertain and not bright.[3]

Among other NBA franchises as of mid-2016, the Mavericks were twenty-second all-time in one study. The reason for their relatively low ranking was explained as follows:

> The Mavs franchise has been remarkably consistent over the last 16 seasons, with no losing seasons and just one year where they missed the playoffs. A large

part of that was due to a savvy draft-day trade in which they sent Robert Traylor to the Bucks in exchange for Pat Garrity and Dirk Nowitzki. Of course, that was on the heels of zero winning seasons in the 1990s, but I digress. They won their only championship in 2011, upsetting the Big Three-era Miami Heat behind a veteran-laden squad led by Dirk, Jason Kidd, Jason Terry, and Shawn Marion.[4]

Houston Rockets

An expansion team founded in 1967, the San Diego Rockets played four seasons in the NBA while at home in the San Diego Sports Arena. During the period, they won approximately 36 percent of their total regular-season games and in 1969, finished fourth in the Western Division but lost in the divisional semifinal playoffs to the Atlanta Hawks.

Despite adding such players as Calvin Murphy and Rudy Tomjanovich and the management skill and experience of Hall of Fame coach Alex Hannum, the Rockets tallied a 67–97 record in their 1969–70 plus 1970–71 seasons and thus did not make the playoffs. Because of an outdated arena, inferior performances by their players, small attendances at home games, and a tiny fan base, the Rockets' principal owner Robert Breitbard offered to sell the team to investors and also various syndicates.

In 1971, Texas Sports Investment—headed by businessmen Billy Goldberg and Wayne Puddlestein—bought the franchise for $5.6 million from Breitbard, and moved it from San Diego to Houston, Texas. Interestingly, the franchise was the first NBA team in Texas, and its nickname "Rockets" became more relevant after the move because of Houston's historical connection to the space industry.

Historical Results

As a member of the PD during the league's 1971–72 season, CD from 1972–73 to 1979–80, and then the MWD to 2003–4 followed by the SWD from 2004–5 to 2015–16, the Rockets had a 53 percent winning percentage. During the period, they won five division plus four conference titles, and also two NBA championship in twenty-nine playoff appearances. Among only WC teams, Houston ranked seventh (winning percentage), tied for fourth with the Suns (number of playoffs), tied for sixth with the Thunder and Trail Blazers (division titles), third (conference titles), and tied for third in championships with the Warriors (table A7).

Against teams only in the SWD as of early 2016, the Rockets placed second to the Spurs in all-time performances. However, in comparison to all NBA clubs, Houston ranked from eighth highest in winning percentage to being tied for fourteenth in division titles. Based on these results and other historical information, this has been an above-average competitor relative to those in its and other divisions of the conference. Simply put, the Rockets have been good to very good in games but not superior throughout forty-five seasons in the league.

Performance Highlights

While based in Houston, the Rockets had the most success in consecutive playoffs during NBA seasons 1978–1981, 1984–1990, 1992–1998, 2003–2004, 2006–2008, and 2012–2015. These teams included such prominent head coaches as Tom Nissalke, Del Harris, Bill Fitch, Don Chaney, Rudy Tomjanovich, Jeff Van Gundy, Rick Adelman, and Kevin McHale. For their knowledge, leadership, and record in various seasons, Nissalke and Chaney were each an NBA Coach of the Year.

To win games in regular seasons and postseasons, Houston had several outstanding players. They were, for example, center/power forward Moses Malone, centers Hakeem Olajuwon, Ralph Sampson and Yao Ming, power/small forward Charles Barkley, and shooting guard James Harden. Because of their talent, Malone was NBA MVP in 1979 and 1982, Olajuwon Defensive Player of the Year in 1993 and 1994, and Sampson Rookie of the Year in 1984 and all-star game MVP in 1985. Besides them, such Rockets players as Calvin Murphy, Rick Barry, and Clyde Drexler are in the sport's Hall of Fame.

The Rockets, however, did not qualify for consecutive playoffs during seasons 1971–1973, 1999–2002, and 2009–2011. While head coaches Tex Winter, Johnny Egan, Rudy Tomjanovich, and Rick Adelman each failed to motivate their players enough in regular seasons, there were other problems with the teams and also too much competition especially from division rivals like the Mavericks and Spurs.

Houston's worst and two most impressive seasons were respectively 1982–83, and then 1993–94 and 1994–95. In the former season, the club won only fourteen games and finished sixth in its division. But in 1994 and 1995, the Rockets won their only NBA championships primarily because of Tomjanovich's coaching decisions, rebounding and scoring of Olajuwon and Otis Thorpe, and the offensive and defensive skills of shooting guard Clyde Drexler.

According to ESPN's 2016 future power rankings of NBA teams regarding their 2016 to 2018 seasons, the Rockets were eleventh following the SWD's Spurs (fourth) but ahead of the Pelicans (eighteenth), Mavericks (twenty-second), and Grizzlies (twenty-sixth). By category, Houston ranked eighth in the market, twelfth in both management and players, twentieth in money, and twenty-second in the draft. Because they exist in a big and prosperous sports market and have talented and veteran players in addition to experienced front office personnel, the Rockets should be eligible for the playoffs each year and perhaps win another division and/or conference title.[5]

Given their average winning percentage, number of titles and championships, careers of their former but outstanding coaches and players, and other historical performances in regular seasons and postseasons as of 2016, the Rockets are in the top ten among NBA franchises of all-time. In a recent article on a sports website, for example, they ranked tenth because of their on-the-court success particularly in the 1980s and 1990s. More specifically, the article's author wrote:

> The Houston Rockets just barely cracked the top 10 NBA franchises of all-time and should be proud of its placement on this list. They've been in the NBA for 47 years [actually 45 in Houston] and have seen some great success in that time. The franchise has won four [five] division titles and four conference championships. But the real reason they made the top 10 is because they've won two NBA championships in the modern era of professional basketball.[6]

Except for the Spurs and their head coach Gregg Popovich, the NBA is controlled by players. The growth in contract amounts, ability to force trades, and shorter contracts have transferred power to such superstars as Houston's James Harden. While not being publicly communicated, Harden has an opinion of what specialties the team's head coach needs to succeed. In some ways, J. B. Bickerstaff fits much of what Harden wants in a coach. Because of differences between Harden, owner Les Alexander, and general manager Daryl Morey, this may be a problem for the Rockets franchise and its future in the league.[7]

Memphis Grizzlies

An expansion team in 1995, the Vancouver Grizzlies played six seasons in the NBA. During the period, they won approximately 21 percent of their total games and finished sixth once and seventh five times in their division. In the league's 1998–99 season, the club had only eight victories and a 16 percent winning percentage but then marginally improved to twenty-two and then twenty-three wins in their next two seasons.

In their first four seasons, the Grizzlies' average attendance was in the middle-third of all teams. However, because of its history of poor performances, the 1998–99 owners' lockout and weak Canadian dollar, lack of local ownership and an unwillingness of some U.S. and foreign basketball players to live in Canada, the club's home attendance dwindled to among the lowest in the NBA.

The Grizzlies' president of basketball operations Dick Versace stated in 2000 that franchise owner Orca Bay Sports and Entertainment had losses of $40 million per season despite the team's $48 million salary cap. Versace also believed the team did not get sufficient support from the business community. Indeed, it was difficult for the Grizzlies to attract corporate sponsors because of losing too many games, lack of good draft picks, and failing to ask for help regarding their management issues.

In 1999, National Hockey League (NHL) St. Louis Blues owner Bill Laurie attempted to buy the Grizzlies with the intent of moving them from Vancouver to St. Louis. After NBA officials interfered in Laurie's proposal, the Grizzlies were sold to American businessman Michael Heisley—who immediately started the process of relocating the team to another city. After evaluating such metropolitan areas as Anaheim, Buffalo, Louisville, Las Vegas, New Orleans, and San Diego, Heisley chose Memphis as the team's new home as of its 2001–2 season.

Historical Results

A member of the WC's MWD for three seasons and then the SWD from 2004–5 to 2015–16, the Grizzlies had victories in approximately 48 percent of their games. During the period, they failed to win any titles or championships in nine playoffs. Among fourteen different conference teams, Memphis ranked ninth (winning percentage), tied for eleventh (number of playoffs), and also fifteenth (division titles), tied for tenth with five other clubs (conference titles), and tied in championships for seventh (table A7).

Within only the SWD, the Grizzlies have been outperformed by the Mavericks, Rockies, and Spurs but not the Hornets/Pelicans—who had a lower winning percentage and fewer playoff appearances. Furthermore, in comparison to all NBA teams as of early 2016, Memphis ranged in rank from a tie for sixteenth with zero championships to being tied for twenty-eighth with only six playoffs. Based on these results and other sport-specific information, the Grizzlies have been below average during their performances against the majority of other clubs in their conference since moving from Vancouver in 2001.

Performance Highlights

The Grizzlies had the most success while in consecutive playoffs in NBA seasons 2003–5 and 2010–15. As a group, head coaches Hubie Brown, Mike Fratello, Lionel Hollins, and Dave Joerger led their teams to finishing second, third, or fourth in the SWD and into the playoffs but losing six times in the conference's first round, twice in the semifinals, and once in the finals.

Brown was NBA Coach of the Year in 2004 and lately inducted into the sport's Hall of Fame.

To win enough games and qualify for postseasons, the Grizzlies had some talented players. Among them were James Posey, Shane Battier, Pau Gasol and his brother Marc, Zach Randolph, and Mike Conley. Besides being selected to several all-star teams, Pau was Rookie of the Year in 2002 and Marc Defensive Player of the Year in 2013. In addition to them, guard Mike Miller won the league's Sixth Man award in 2008.

The Grizzlies two worst seasons and also their best were respectively 2006–7 and 2007–8, 2012–13. During the first two, they won twenty-two games and finished fifth in their division each season because, in part, Pau Gasol broke his foot and was then traded to the Lakers, coach Fratello was fired and replaced by player personnel director Tony Barone Sr., and general manager Jerry West resigned ending his disappointing tenure in Memphis. However, in 2012–13, the club won 68 percent of its games, finished second in the SWD, but lost in the conference finals to the Spurs.

In ESPN's future power rankings for the league's 2016–2018 seasons, the Grizzlies were twenty-sixth while other SWD teams placed fourth (Spurs), eleventh (Rockets), eighteenth (Pelicans), and twenty-second (Mavericks). Among five categories, Memphis rated highest in money and then management, players, market, and the draft. Worth 16.7 percent of the score, the category money included the club's projected salary-cap situation and its ability and willingness to exceed the salary cap and pay a luxury tax. In their weakest category, the Grizzles have a dim future regarding draft picks and draft positioning.[8]

According to website grayflannelsuit.net, the Grizzlies are the twenty-eighth best franchise all-time as of the league's 2015–16 season. Based on such things as teams' performances in regular seasons and postseasons, and also rewarding consistently good play and not giving older franchises too much of an advantage by virtue of being around many years, Memphis placed higher than only the Clippers (twenty-ninth) and Timberwolves (thirtieth). Given their nine playoff appearances in fifteen years and six consecutive appearances since 2010–11, the Memphis Grizzlies deserve to be much higher in rank. Obviously, the website included the franchise's dismal record while located in Vancouver from the 1995–96 to 2000–2001 season. In the list, other SWD franchises were third (Spurs), eleventh (Rockets), thirteenth (Mavericks), and twenty-fifth (Pelicans).[9]

New Orleans Hornets/Pelicans

Three years after a referendum to finance a new arena was defeated, Charlotte Hornets' owners George Shinn and Ray Woolridge said they needed to relocate their team to avoid millions of dollars in annual losses, in part from drastically declining attendance. An offer from New Orleans was described in league circles as extremely generous, and a seven-owner NBA relocation committee recommended approval of it.

The club's move from North Carolina to Louisiana in 2002 came after an unprecedented effort by city and state officials, members of Congress, and civic leaders to convince NBA officials that the poverty-riddled state's economic future was bright and that the financially struggling city could support a second pro-sports franchise in addition to the National Football League (NFL) Saints. Furthermore, New Orleans business leaders had spearheaded an effort to sell season tickets and suites, eventually exceeding the league's goals.

In addition to those actions, Louisiana governor Mike Foster promised and delivered legislative approval of millions of dollars in incentive expenditures for the team including $10 million to upgrade the state-owned New Orleans Arena plus several million more to be generated each year from the New Orleans area hotel tax. Previously, the city had tried but failed to attract an NBA team since the Jazz left for Utah in 1979.

After missing out on the Timberwolves in 1994 and Grizzlies in 2001, the city and state went all out to get the Hornets. The Hornets' ownership in New Orleans, however, would not be involved in the operation of the Women's National Basketball Association (WNBA) Sting, which remained in Charlotte.

Historical Results

A member of the CD for two years and then the league's SWD from the 2004–5 to 2015–16 season, the Hornets/Pelicans had victories in approximately 46 percent of their games. During the period, they won one division title and appeared in six playoffs. Among fourteen other WC teams, New Orleans ranked twelfth (winning percentage), tied for fourteenth with the Thunder (number of playoffs), tied for thirteenth with the Timberwolves (division titles), tied for tenth with five other clubs (conference titles), and tied for seventh (championships). Within the SWD, the Hornets/Pelicans had the worst or among the worst results except in winning division titles.

In comparison to the performances of all NBA teams as of early 2016, New Orleans ranked from a tie for sixteenth in championships to a tie for twenty-eighth in number of playoff appearances. Based on these results, the club has been below average overall and especially while competing against its rivals in the conference and for various reasons, not consistent or very successful at winning games in regular seasons and qualifying for postseasons.

Performance Highlights

The Hornets/Pelicans had played best when they qualified for the playoffs during consecutive seasons 2002–3 and 2007–8, and also in 2010–11 and 2014–15. Head coaches Paul Silas, Tim Floyd, Byron Scott, and Monty Williams were effective at motivating their players to win enough games in regular seasons to appear and compete in the conference's postseasons. Scott was NBA Coach of the Year in 2008 while the others received votes for the award in different years.

New Orleans had several outstanding players at their positions on the court. Among the group were center/power forwards P. J. Brown and Anthony Davis, power/small forward David West, and point guard Chris Paul. Besides Paul—who was Rookie of the Year in 2006—these players were all-stars and led their Hornets/Pelicans teams in such things as points scored, rebounds, assists, and/or other statistics offensively.

The club's worst and best seasons were respectively 2004–5 and 2007–8. In the former season, the Hornets won eighteen games and finished fifth in the SWD while in the latter, they had a 56–26 regular-season record, placed first in the division, but lost in the conference semifinals to the Spurs in a seven-game series. In other playoffs, New Orleans lost five times in the WC's first round.

In 2013, a website analyzed the all-time performances of NBA franchises and provided an overview of the Hornets/Pelicans history. To paraphrase it: The New Orleans Pelicans are a perfect example of how the NBA over-expanded and the danger of having owners who use teams as toys with no sense of loyalty to the communities in which they reside. The Pelicans used to be the Charlotte Hornets, who arguably had the best home court advantage in the NBA—its intensely loyal fan base. Then fans realized that owner George Shinn was not interested in winning but primarily with making a profit.

After being accused of rape and being cranky that the stadium did not have enough luxury boxes, Shinn did what some mega-rich people do: he behaved petulantly. After Katrina, the league took over the franchise, which became the Pelicans. In other words, the organization started out with promise, had a few good years, went absolutely insane, settled down, and maybe become something. Being led by New Orleans Saints owner Tom Benson is a huge plus.[10]

In ESPN's 2016 future power rankings for the league's 2016–2018 seasons, the Pelicans rated eighteenth following the SWD's Spurs at fourth and Rockets at eleventh but ahead of the Mavericks at twenty-second and Grizzlies at twenty-sixth. By category, New Orleans ranked higher in players and the draft than in management, money, and the market. As such, the Pelicans are a power primarily because of current players and their potential for the future and factoring in expected departures in addition to future draft picks and draft positioning.[11]

Regarding the Pelican's current and future draft status, there is nothing wrong with building for the present especially as it hemorrhages support from a largely ambivalent local fan base. The team transmuted into darlings during its 2014–15 playoff push, and with a clean bill of health, the fun will continue in an Alvin Gentry offense that finished just outside the top ten during the 2015–16 season. But until the Pelicans prioritize the future, it is hard to see any step toward winning a title not being followed soon by two steps backward.[12]

San Antonio Spurs

Founded in 1967 and a member of the American Basketball Association (ABA), the Dallas/Texas/Dallas Chaparrals—renamed San Antonio Spurs in 1973—won approximately 51 percent of their games and in eight playoffs, they lost six times in the West Division semifinals and once in the finals, and also once in the league semifinals. The Chaparrals/Spurs, however, suffered from poor attendance at their home games and also general disinterest for professional basketball among people in the Dallas area.

In an attempt to expand regionally, the team played its home games in Fort Worth, Texas, at the Tarrant County Convention Center and in Lubbock, Texas, at the Lubbock Municipal Coliseum. After this strategy failed, the team returned full-time to Dallas for the 1971–72 season, and split their games between the Moody Coliseum and Dallas Convention Center Arena.

During June 1976, the ABA and NBA merged to unify and form one league. As a result, the ABA's Spurs, Nuggets, Pacers, and Nets joined the NBA for a fee of \$3.2 million each and also agreed to pay owners of the former ABA Kentucky Colonels and St. Louis Spirits \$1.6 million each as compensation for not becoming an NBA team. This agreement, in turn, put financial pressure on the Spurs and the other three teams. Interestingly, the Spirits' owners reached an agreement with the NBA in 2014 to end perpetual payments and instead received a lump sum of \$500 million.

Historical Results

While in the NBA's CD from the 1976–77 to 1979–80 seasons, MWD during the 1980–2003 seasons, and finally SWD since 2004–5, the Spurs had victories in approximately 62 percent of their games. During the period, they won twenty-one division and six conference titles, and five championships in thirty-six playoffs. Among fourteen other WC teams as of early 2016, San Antonio ranked first (winning percentage) and second (number of playoffs, titles, and championships). Within only the conference's SWD, Spurs teams had better performances all-time than those of the Mavericks, Rockets, Grizzlies, and Hornets/Pelicans (table A7).

In comparison to the performances of twenty-nine other NBA clubs as of early 2016, San Antonio placed first in winning percentage, third in division titles, tied for third with the Bulls in conference titles, and fourth in both number of championships and playoffs. Based on these results, the forty-year-old Spurs have been a superior team and top-notch organization in the league for decades in part because of their competitiveness, commitment to excellence, and simply great relationships between coaches, players, and the franchise's owners.

Performance Highlights

The Spurs were most successful during consecutive playoffs in NBA seasons 1976–1982, 1984–1985, 1989–1995, and 1997–2015. Such head coaches as Doug Moe, Stan Albeck, Cotton Fitzsimmons, Larry Brown, Bob Hill, and Gregg Popovich motivated their players enough to win the majority of games in regular seasons and vigorously compete in the playoffs. As of early 2016, Popovich was Coach of the Year three times and Brown a Hall of Famer.

Several San Antonio players had memorable careers with the franchise. Some of them were George Gervin, Artis Gilmore, David Robinson, Tim Duncan, Manu Ginobili, and Tony Parker. Besides Rookie of the Year in 1998, Duncan was a two-time NBA MVP and five-time finals MVP. Gervin, Robinson, Ginobili, and Parker also won awards for their accomplishments in various seasons and so did Most Improved Player/Defensive Player of the Year Alvin Robertson. Along with Coach Brown, players Gervin, Gilmore, and Robinson are in the sport's Hall of Fame.

The Spurs two worst and five best seasons were respectively 1988–89 and 1996–97, and 1998–99, 2002–3, 2004–5, 2006–7, 2013–14. During each of the former years, their winning percentage was about 25 percent. Meanwhile in the latter seasons, they won at least 70 percent of all games and also an NBA championship. In 2015–16, San Antonio finished first in its division with a 67–15 all-time-high record but nevertheless lost in the WC's semifinals to the Los Angeles Clippers in a seven-game series.

In mid-2016, online website listicled.com rated the Spurs as the third greatest NBA franchise in history following the Los Angeles Lakers and Boston Celtics. For a summary of San Antonio's success, the analysis stated:

> The Spurs are largely looked at as the gold standard of how to run an organization in the modern era. They used a little bit of luck (winning the lottery for Tim Duncan), and brought in a terrific coach in Gregg Popovich and used tre-

> mendous drafting (Tony Parker 28th, Manu Ginobili 57th) in combination with savvy trades (Kawhi Leonard for George Hill) to create a dynasty. They've won five NBA Championships since 1999, and have won no less than 61 percent of their games in any season since 1997–98. It's hard to pick a favorite, but I enjoyed their first win in 1999, with David Robinson, Sean Elliot and Avery Johnson—they'd go 15–2 in the playoffs.[13]

According to ESPN's future power rankings for the NBA's 2016–2018 seasons, the Spurs—by category—were second in *management*, third in *players*, thirteenth in the *market*, twenty-third in the *draft*, and twenty-ninth in *money*. As such, there is very high quality and stability regarding the club's front office, ownership, and coaching, but not with respect to its three-year projected salary-cap situation, ability and willingness to exceed the salary cap, and pay a luxury tax.[14]

Despite their great success since the early 1990s, the Spurs have potential problems. First, the end of an era may be near given Duncan and Ginobili's ages and their ability to continue playing at a high level in 2016 and thereafter; second, changes are needed regarding players and their competitiveness; third, adapting a playing style with a new or revised roster; and fourth, effects and consequences of the draft. These issues, in part, will determine the future of the franchise in the WC and particularly among rivals in the SWD.

FRANCHISE BUSINESS

Dallas Mavericks

Born in 1958 in Pittsburgh, Pennsylvania, Mark Cuban displayed tenacity for making a deal and carving out a better life for himself. When he was twelve years old, he sold garbage bags and in high school earned money mainly by becoming a stamp and coin salesman. After graduating from Indiana University in 1981, Cuban moved back to Pittsburgh and took a job with Mellon Bank. One year later, he left Pittsburgh for Dallas and formed a consulting business and named it MicroSolutions.

An expert in computers and computer networking and having a knack for building a smart, profitable company, Cuban sold his firm in 1990 to CompuServe for $6 million. Sensing that a new world awaited with the development of the Internet, Cuban and his business partner, Todd Wagner, started AudioNet in 1995. Its formation was rooted in a desire to be able to listen to Indiana Hoosiers basketball games online. The company, despite its early critics, proved to be a success. Renamed Brodcast.com, the firm went public in 1998 and its stock reached $200 a share. A year later, Wagner and Cuban sold their firm to Yahoo! for nearly $6 billion.

In 2000, Mark Cuban introduced himself to the NBA community when he purchased the Dallas Mavericks for $280 million from Ross Perot Jr. For Cuban, a longtime season ticket holder, the chance to be a part of the professional sports world was a dream. The Mavericks, however, were far from a dream franchise. Plagued by poor personnel decisions and mediocre players and coaches, the club experienced more than a decade of non-playoff basketball games.

With his trademark enthusiasm and doggedness, he revamped the culture of the team and its roster, erected a new stadium, and pampered his players.[15]

Among owners of WC teams and their performances as of early 2016, Cuban's Mavericks were tied for seventh in winning division titles (two) and also tied for fourth in both number of conference titles (two) and NBA championships (one). In comparison to all the league's teams and their respective owners, Dallas tied for fourteenth in number of division titles, tied for fifth in conference titles, and tied for sixth in championships. Based on these results and the club's fifteen playoff appearances since the 2000–1 season, Cuban has been a successful owner and leader of his franchise (table A8).

According to website fansided.com, Mark Cuban is the second best team owner in the league. The reasons for his success were given as follows:

> You can fault him for being insane and over-the-top in his passion for his team, but it's a unique brand of passion that is exclusive to Cuban. Sure, he's not always the cuddliest of owners, but the man knows what he wants and is willing to pay for it and support it. His relationship with [player] Dirk Nowtizki is a prime example of how Cuban takes care of his own and promotes the same out of his players. Dirk has taken less money to stay with the Mavericks when he could go elsewhere and get paid to win. The reason is Cuban, who takes credit for the good decisions and owns the bad ones that he makes. That's what an owner should do and like him or not, Cuban is one of the best.[16]

Team Financials

Based on financial data published in *Forbes* magazine about NBA franchises as of early 2016, the Mavericks' market value was $1.4 billion, revenue $177 million, operating income $24 million, gate receipts $45 million, debt-to-value 8 percent, and players expenses $90 million. With respect to other WC teams, it ranked fifth (market value), fourth (revenue), seventh (operating income and gate receipts), tenth (debt ratio), and third (player expenses). Within the SWD, Dallas had higher amounts than the Grizzlies and Hornets/Pelicans and also in some financial categories, more than the Rockets and Spurs (table A9).

In comparison to twenty-nine other NBA clubs, the Mavericks were eighth in market value, tenth in revenue, tied for eleventh with the Cavaliers in operating income, fourteenth in gate receipts, tied for twenty-first with Celtics in debt-to-value, and fourth in players expenses. From a financial perspective, Dallas is an above-average business operation and enterprise based on estimates reported in *Forbes*.

Besides market size, salary inflation, and other factors, an NBA team's annual payroll partly reflects its commitment to players and their current and potential contribution individually and as a group to winning games in regular seasons and postseasons. From 2011 to 2015, for example, the Mavericks' payroll among WC teams ranged in rank from third in 2011 ($76.3 million) and 2014 ($74.9 million) to eleventh in 2012 ($61.5 million). Within only the SWD, the club had chronologically the first and then fourth, second, first, and fifth highest payroll in the group during the five-season period (table A10).

With respect to the payrolls of all NBA teams, Dallas was fourth in 2011, twenty-third in 2012, fourteenth in 2013, eighth in 2014, and sixteenth in 2015. Based on these amounts, the Mavericks decreased their payroll once but then increased it three times to become more competitive and qualify for postseasons. This was a successful strategy because it resulted in three consecutive playoff appearances and first-round losses in the conference, but also a championship in 2011.

Shortly after free agency opened on July 1, 2016, thirteen-time all-star Dirk Nowitzki signed a two-year deal for $50 million with $30 million in guaranteed money to remain with the Mavericks. He became the highest-paid player on the team, surpassing newcomer Harrison Barnes, who inked a four-year, $94 million deal on July 1.

Nowitzki, who averaged 18.3 points and 6.5 rebounds in the 2015–16 season, has been with the club for eighteen years. During his tenure, he guided the Mavericks to many of the franchise's greatest achievements. He led Dallas to its first-ever sixty-win season in 2002–3, first NBA Finals appearance in 2006, a franchise-high sixty-seven wins in 2006–7, and the organization's first championship after defeating the Miami Heat in the 2011 NBA Finals. He is currently the longest-tenured player in the league with one team.

American Airlines Center

Opened in 2001, the 21,100-seat American Airlines Center (AAC) is part of a multiple acre north end redevelopment site, which includes housing, office, and retail businesses to create an entire neighborhood for the arena. Despite the openness of surrounding lands, the grounds around the building are beautiful, especially on the south side with a huge public plaza/walkway, complete with fountains, benches, and mood lighting. The arena has a light brick facade, dramatic arches, and entryways on all four sides, plenty of glass, and a castle-like appearance.

Some of the building's special features are octagon-shaped concourses with colors in soft whites and beiges with grey and white mosaic tile flooring; a seating bowl area divided into lower and upper levels, and in between, mini-levels of combined club seats and more than 100 suites; and premium seating with amenities similar to other facilities.

Among venues of fourteen other WC teams as of early 2016, the Mavericks' is the eleventh oldest, most expensive (including renovations), and fifth highest in value. In comparison to all NBA arenas, Dallas's ranks twenty-second (age), third (construction cost plus renovations), and tied for eighth with the Celtics' TD Garden (value). Based on these results, the Mavericks play their home games in a relatively mature but impressive building with enough amenities to earn an adequate amount of revenue for the franchise (table A11).

For several years a Chicago-based company named Team Marketing Report (TMR) has prepared and published a Fan Cost Index (FCI) for the home games of teams in professional sports leagues. To attend a game for a typical family with two kids, an FCI includes the costs of four average-priced tickets, two cheapest-priced draft beers, four each cheapest-priced soft drinks and hot dogs, parking for one car, and two each game programs and least-expensive, adult-size adjustable caps. Costs are determined by telephone calls with team representatives, venues, and concessionaires, and from questions asked during interviews.[17]

In the 2011–2015 NBA seasons, the Fan Cost Index (FCI) for a family to attend a regular-season game at the AAC ranged from a low of $281 in 2015 to a high of $321 in both 2012 and 2013. With respect to home games of all NBA teams, the Mavericks' was tenth in 2011, eleventh in 2012, tied for twelfth with the Raptors in 2013, fifteenth in 2014, and tied for nineteenth with the Timberwolves in 2015 (table A12).

To reveal specific costs for a recent season in the NBA, the Mavericks' FCI in 2015–16 was 10 percent less than in 2014–15. Listed from most to least in amount by item for one person, the team's tickets averaged between $49 and $50, a cap $13 and parking one vehicle $10, single beer and program each $5, a hot dog $3–$4, and a soft drink $3.

Among other teams in the conference's SWD, they had rankings and FCIs from most to least as follows: Rockets eighth at $376; Spurs twelfth at $325; Grizzlies twenty-seventh at $223; and Pelicans twenty-eighth at $221. Consequently, Mavericks fans paid less at games in the AAC than those of nineteen other NBA teams in their arenas.

The cheapest ticket cost $10 for a fan to watch a Mavericks home game in 2015–16. This was about $6 or approximately 63 percent less than the league's average for a cheap seat. Also, since the club's FCI was $58 below the amount of a typical NBA team, a family of four purchased tickets and enjoyed a basketball game in Dallas at a significant discount relative to the majority of arenas within the league. These costs and prices, in turn, were set by the Mavericks organization to earn revenue and maximize profit from their operations.

In its annual ranking of all thirty NBA game-day experiences as of 2016, the *Stadium Journey* rated the AAC twelfth. This ranking was explained as follows:

> The Dallas Mavericks are continually in the top five of the NBA when it comes to attendance. Fans are engaged, energetic, and at times can make the AAC one of the loudest arenas in the NBA. Having an owner such as Mark Cuban, who started his journey as a fan and sits on the sidelines cheering on the Mavs and often arguing over a bad referee call, really keeps the fans engaged. They are such a solid and proud fan base that the title of MFFL—Mavs Fan for Life—is not just a saying but a reality.[18]

Business Highlights

Besides regular-season and postseason games, NBA franchises are involved in—and affected by—community events and business-related affairs, news, and projects. The following are a few of them for Dallas's popular, successful, and from a financial perspective, above-average professional basketball team.[19]

First, franchise owner Mark Cuban closed on a land deal for a new practice facility and headquarters in June 2016. The ten-acre site, worth an estimated $43 million, includes an IBM-affiliated Softlayer data center and a Community Beer brewery. The two building tenants have a few years left on leases for the property. According to Cuban, the existing leases have no impact on his plans to immediately begin retrofitting the building for the team's practice facility, which could help him attract free agent players. The building has about 90,000 square feet of vacant space the Mavericks can immediately use. Cuban acquired the property from longtime owners Grossman & Frank, which is an investment group in Dallas.

Second, Cuban believes Kevin Durant's decision to join the Golden State Warriors will benefit the NBA from a business perspective, despite commissioner Adam Silver's concerns about the forming of a super team. Cuban, who had never shied away from going against the grain, is confident that adding a former MVP to a recent championship team that already features two-time MVP Stephen Curry and all-stars Klay Thompson and Draymond Green will drive interest in the league. Silver indicated that changes in the collective bargaining agreement are needed to prevent similar situations from developing in the future. "Just like when LeBron James went to Miami, I loved that there was a villain. They become the villain. I'm fine with that. Everybody's going to root for them to lose."

Third, Mavericks star forward Dirk Nowitzki starred in a hilarious spoof campaign ad in 2015 where he donned a wig that resembled Donald Trump's hair and mentioned the idea of building a wall. But Nowitzki just wanted to build a "wall of noise" to excite Mavericks fans. In the video, Nowitzki mocked the 2016 presidential candidate's outlandish rhetoric and mannerisms. "I'll make literally billions and billions of baskets," the forward says in the video. "I'mma score so many points it'll make your head spin."

Fourth, the Mavericks launched a fan contest to help design a new court for their 2016–17 season. Fans visited the team's website for official logos and colors, plus ideas for court design. They were able to upload their designs to Facebook, Twitter, or Instagram. A panel of judges chose the top three designs on March 18, 2016. Teams like the Lakers and Celtics boasted classic designs to match their history. Younger teams such as the Timberwolves have tweaked their tone a bunch over the years. You have bold and loud designs, as well as quaint and muted ones. But in the end, all that matters is execution. In April 2016, website aol.com sports editors ranked each team's hardwood based on how easy they were on the eyes.

Fifth, Cuban was laughed at when he paid $280 million for the Mavericks and a 50 percent stake in the American Airlines Center in 2000. It was a record amount for an NBA team and the club had not been to the playoffs in a decade. Subsequently, Cuban built one of the most stable, well-supported franchises. The Mavericks made the playoffs in all but one of the last fifteen years and Rick Carlisle is tied for the second-longest tenured coach in the NBA. The club had the longest active sellout streak in American sports at 620 games, including playoffs, at the end of the league's 2014–15 season.

Houston Rockets

Born into a Jewish family in 1944, Leslie "Les" Alexander graduated from New York University in 1965 with a bachelor's degree in economics and later earned his juris doctor from the Thomas Jefferson School of Law. Alexander began his career as an attorney, and from 1978 to 2009, he was a member of the California State Bar. His first job was trading options and bonds for the Wall Street firm Lawrence Kotkin Associates. In 1980, he left to form his own investment company, The Alexander Group. Alexander also owns a stake in First Marblehead, a private student loan company.

Like any good businessman, Leslie spent several years researching sports franchises and waiting for the right purchase opportunity before he bought the Houston Rockets from Charlie Thomas during July 1993 for $85 million. His research and dedication to the Rockets franchise paid off when they won back-to-back NBA championships in 1994–1995, becoming only the fifth team in NBA history to do it. The Rockets made history in 2002, drafting the first international player, Yao Ming from China, to be a number one overall pick.

Building a sports empire in Houston, Alexander acquired the WNBA's Houston Comets and then the Thunderbears, an Arena Football team, in 1995. The Comets won the league's first four championships from 1997 to 2000. Later, Alexander sold the team to Hilton Koch before it folded in 2001. Besides founding the Rockets Clutch City Foundation, Alexander also raised over $5 million for the local charity in Houston.

With respect to other NBA teams and their owners as of early 2016, Alexander's Rockets won two each division and conference titles in addition to NBA championships in 1994 and 1995. Among those in the WC, the club tied for seventh (division titles) and for fourth (conference titles), and then ranked third (league championships) following the Lakers and Spurs. In comparison to all clubs in the league, the Rockets tied for fourteenth in division titles and for fifth in winning their conference, and then placed fifth in number of championships. Consequently, Alexander has been a very productive owner because of several factors including his decisions to recruit and hire competent coaches and also sign talented free agents and veteran players to both temporary and long-term contracts (table A8).

Based on his team's performances since 1993, Alexander is the league's tenth best owner as of 2015. For these reasons, he ranked relatively high among the other thirty franchise owners:

> There were two huge swings and misses by the Houston Rockets in the summer of 2015: failing to sign players Carmelo Anthony and Chris Bosh. What this resulted in was a trip to the conference finals and a renewed love for owner Leslie Alexander. He's placed Daryl Morey in charge of the franchise and the results have spoken for themselves. Whether it's the analytics or not, the Rockets are finding players to plug in and play with their rotations and they're winning. Alexander isn't the best owner in the state of Texas, and he may not be in the Top 5 of NBA owners, but he's one of the best compared to the rest. That seems like a backhanded compliment—which sort of is—but Alexander is someone the Rockets might not be the same team without.[20]

After firing head coach Kevin McHale and then releasing his replacement, J. B. Bickerstaff, the Rockets had a vacancy for the 2016–17 season. With a young star in James Harden on the roster, they should have been able to bring in the best coach available. The majority opinion of people in basketball said that Jeff Van Gundy was the best coach available followed by ex-Indiana Pacers coach Frank Vogel. Yet somehow, both of them seemed not to have a chance. Instead, franchise owner Les Alexander got involved and hired Daryl Morey to be general manager and make personnel decisions from the coaches to the fifteenth guy on the roster. If that's Morey's job, then he needed to decide on the next head coach and not be the owner's choice.[21]

Team Financials

Based on financial data published by *Forbes* magazine about NBA teams in early 2016, the Rockets' estimated market value was $1.5 billion, revenue $237 million, operating income $74 million, gate receipts $75 million, debt-to-value 7 percent, and players expenses $85 million. Among only WC teams, Houston was fourth (market value), second (revenue and operating income), third (gate receipts), tied for eleventh with the Spurs (debt ratio), and fifth (players expenses). Within the SWD, the club had the highest amounts except for players expenses, and along with San Antonio, the lowest debt percent (table A9).

In comparison to those of twenty-nine other teams, the Rockets' data ranged in rank from third in both revenue and operating income to a tie for twenty-third in debt-to-value. According to these results, this Houston-based team is an above-average, large-market, and profitable business enterprise from a financial perspective and with sufficient cash flow to continue operating as a franchise in the league for many years.

From 2011 to 2015, the Rockets' payroll among WC teams ranged in rank from fourth in 2015 ($89.7 million) to thirteenth in both 2011 ($57.0 million) and 2012 ($57.3 million). Within only the SWD, the club had the smallest payroll in the group during the 2011–2013 seasons, fourth from the top in 2014 ($71.8 million), and highest at $89.7 million in 2015 (table A10).

In comparison to payrolls of all NBA teams, Houston's was chronologically twenty-fourth in 2011, twenty-seventh in 2012, twentieth in 2013, fifteenth in 2014, and fifth in 2015. Based on these amounts, the Rockets increased their payroll each season to become more competitive and qualify for and win more games in postseasons. To that end, this was a productive strategy because it resulted in four playoff appearances and a conference final series in 2015.

Based on their player salary commitments, salary cap holds, and other variables through the NBA's 2017–18 season, the Rockets added some significant future pieces and locked up their franchise star long term. This, in turn, sent a statement to the league that the Rockets will not be the same as teams like the Thunder and Kings, whose stars are (or will be) the subject to constant trade rumors. While cap flexibility may be more limited going forward, as former head coach Kevin McHale used to say, "cap flexibility" never scored a point or grabbed a rebound. Expectations are for many more points, rebounds, and wins from star player James Harden and his new crop of teammates.[22]

Toyota Center

Opened in 2003, the $202 million, 18,300-seat Toyota Center hosts games of the NBA Rockets and American Hockey League Houston Aeros, and from 2003 to 2007, the WNBA Houston Comets. When built, the arena featured such things as a wide variety of concessions; clean, distinct, wide, and brightly lit concourses with white being the dominant hue; two levels of red-colored seats sandwiching two levels of suites on the sidelines; a scoreboard hanging above center ice/court with its lower portion a four-sided video screen and its upper portion having an eight-side LED board that showed most of the graphics and in-game statistics.

In addition to these features, club seating exists along the sidelines of the lower seating bowl. Fans in these areas have exclusive access to their own club concourse at the top of the seating bowl, which is separated from the main concourse that rings the exterior of the building. Within the Toyota Center, the Rockets hang their NBA championship banners from 1994 and 1995 along with retired numbers of players like Calvin Murphy, Clyde Drexler, and Moses Malone.

Among venues of other WC teams as of early 2016, the Toyota Center ranked as the fourteenth oldest, sixth most expensive to build, and third in value. With respect to those of all NBA clubs, the Rockets' home is twenty-fifth (age), fourteenth (construction cost), and sixth (value). Based on the data, the team actually plays its home games in a relatively modern and attractive facility with plenty of amenities for fans to enjoy. These, in turn, generate money for the franchise from operations in Houston (table A11).

In the 2011–2015 NBA seasons, the FCI for a family to attend a Rockets regular-season game at the Toyota Center ranged from a low of $271 in 2011 to a high of $376 in 2015. With respect to games of all NBA teams, the Rockets each year in Houston were consecutively tied for nineteenth with the Jazz in 2011, fourteenth in 2012 ($299), tenth in 2013 ($336), eighth in 2014 ($369), and ninth in 2015 (table A12).

To reveal specific costs for a recent season in the NBA, the Houston's FCI in 2015–16 was about 2 percent higher than in 2014–15. Listed from most to least in amount by item for one person, the team's tickets averaged $67–$68, a cap between $18 and $19, parking one vehicle $15, single beer $7–$8, hot dog $6, and a soft drink from $4 to $5.

Among other teams in the conference's SWD, they had rankings and FCIs from most to least as follows: Spurs twelfth at $325; Mavericks twentieth at $281; Grizzlies twenty-seventh at $223; and Pelicans twenty-eighth at $221. Consequently, Rockets fans paid less at games in the Toyota Center than those of eight other NBA clubs in their arenas.

The cheapest ticket cost $10 for a fan to watch a Rockets home game in 2015–16. This was about $6 or approximately 63 percent less than the league's average for a cheap seat. However, since the club's FCI was $37 above the amount of a typical NBA team, a family of four purchased tickets and enjoyed a basketball game in Houston at a small premium relative to the majority of arenas within the league. These costs and prices, in turn, were set by the Rockets organization to earn revenue and maximize profit from their operations.

In its annual ranking of all thirty NBA game-day experiences as of 2016, the *Stadium Journey* rated the Toyota Center tenth. The venue's relatively high rank was explained as follows:

> The atmosphere inside the Toyota Center is beyond entertaining whether it's Clutch the Rockets Bear pulling a prank on an unsuspecting fan, the Rockets Power Dancers drawing all eyes on the court, the Red Rowdies raising the decibel level, or undeniable talent like James Harden. All things considered, Toyota Center is one of the top sports venues nationwide and worthy of a visit from sports fans of all kinds.[23]

Meanwhile, the homes of other SWD teams were ranked third (Spurs' AT&T Center); twelfth (Mavericks' American Airlines Center); nineteenth (Pelicans' Smoothie King Center); and twenty-second (Grizzlies' FedExForum).

Business Highlights

Besides regular-season and postseason games, NBA franchises are involved in—and affected by—community events and business-related affairs, news, and projects. The following are a few of them for Houston's popular, successful, and from a financial perspective, above-average professional basketball team.[24]

First, the Rockets hired gaming industry marketing executive Scott Andrews in 2012 to be their new chief strategy officer. Andrews, who had no previous front-office professional sports experience, was hired just weeks after Chris Dacey resigned after five years as chief strategy officer. Prior to starting with the Rockets, Andrews worked for ten months as chief marketing officer at the M Resort in Las Vegas. Also, he held various marketing positions for Harrah's Entertainment for nearly a decade after earning his MBA from the Tuck School of Business at Dartmouth College. In his new job with Houston, Andrews was primarily responsible for the basketball franchise's business analysis and development.

Second, before eliminating the Dallas Mavericks from the NBA playoffs in Game 5 of the league's 2015 WC playoffs, the official Twitter account of the Rockets sent out a tweet that angered some people and it cost one employee a job. The tweet in question included a gun emoji pointed at horse emoji—presumably representing the Mavericks, whose mascot is a horse. The emojis were accompanied by the text, "Shhhhh. Just close your eyes. It will all be over soon." Did emoji animal rights groups complain and have this tweet deleted?

Third, the Rocket's regular-season television broadcast rights holder ROOT SPORTS made the team's games available to over 200,000 new households throughout Texas, Louisiana, and Arkansas. With the addition of 400-plus zip codes to the broadcast territory in 2015, more Rockets fans in the Austin, Corpus Christi, Waco-Temple-Bryan, San Antonio, Shreveport, Lafayette, and Baton Rouge areas could watch games. The expansion also introduced Rockets television coverage to the San Angelo, Texas area. The NBA defines team broadcast territories. As a result, certain zip codes within the San Antonio, Austin, and Baton Rouge Designated Market Areas were not able to receive ROOT SPORTS' Rockets game broadcasts since those areas fall within other teams' protected territories.

Fourth, thousands of fans attended their first Rockets home game, thanks to the generosity of the team's players. Through the "Rockets for Youth" Ticket Program, players purchased tickets so that children and families—who might not otherwise have the opportunity—could experience the excitement of a home game. The following players, for example, had sponsored tickets in the "Rockets for Youth" sections: Jon Barry for Barry's 3-Point Bombers; Tracy McGrady for McGrady Bunch; Rafer Alston for Rafer's Ballers; and Yao Ming for Yao's House.

Fifth, an NBA franchise can start with a structure and then hand-pick talent that conforms to that structure. Or it can first accumulate the talent, and then build a structure around it. Whereas San Antonio and Miami choose the first strategy, Houston goes talent first. This is not because the Rockets believe structure isn't important. It's an expression of the Rockets' desire to find inefficiencies in the NBA marketplace. Innovation and a defiance of convention drive the Rockets. Data is king—and efficiency the prince. In other words, there is a transactional approach to team-building, in some part a reflection of their owner, Les Alexander, who made his fortune buying and trading equities. In some sense, this outlook is diametrically opposed to the "buy-develop-hold" approach in San Antonio. Yet, it also allows Houston to pivot quickly and recover from its mistakes.

Memphis Grizzlies

Born in 1978 and raised in Silicon Valley, Robert Pera established his first computer services company while attending high school. While there, he played on the school's basketball team and after graduation attended the University of California-San Diego (UC-SD). He graduated from UC-SD with a Bachelor's of Science in electrical engineering and a Bachelor's of Arts in Japanese language and then completed his Master's in electrical engineering with an emphasis on digital communications and circuit design.

After finishing his education, Pera secured a job at Apple Inc. where he tested the company's Wi-Fi devices to ensure compliance with Federal Communications Commission standards for electromagnetic emissions. When bosses at Apple ignored his idea of increasing power sources of Wi-Fi devices to facilitate Internet access into areas that telephone and cable companies did not reach, Pera decided to build his own low-cost, high performance Wi-Fi module. In early 2005, he left Apple and formed Ubiquiti Networks, which became very successful.

During October 2012, Memphis Grizzlies owner Michael Heisley sold his team to Pera. Building on the successes of his predecessor, Pera made significant investments into the franchise, bolstering its business and basketball operations. Experiencing some success, the club won fifty-six games in its 2012–13 season and appeared in the WC finals. However, the team has never won a division or conference title as of early 2016 (table A8).

According to website fansided.com, Pera was the twelfth best owner in the league as of 2015. The following comments are why he ranked in that position:

> The Memphis Grizzlies were a team on the rise a few years ago, but then they canned head coach Lionel Hollins and moved on. At the time, when Memphis failed to renew the deal of Hollins, it appeared they were pulling the same boner that has since sunk the Denver Nuggets. Instead, the Grizz are one of the best teams in basketball and are surging towards the future and being a better team. Owner Robert Pera is among the generation of hot young owners who are taking their franchise as serious as Madden players take running a franchise in that game. It's not a total NBA2K experience, but Pera knows not only how to field talent and pay for them, but he's rallied the fans in Memphis around the team. Memphis isn't a professional sports haven, but love for the Grizzlies is something Pera has singlehandedly helped create through talents of his own and the talents of others.[25]

Team Financials

Based on recent financial information published in *Forbes* magazine on NBA franchises, the Grizzlies' estimated market value was $780 million, revenue

$147 million, operating income $10 million, gate receipts $27 million, debt-to-value 22 percent, and players expenses $81 million. Among fourteen other WC teams as of early 2016, Memphis ranked thirteenth (market value, operating income and gate receipts), tenth (revenue), second (debt ratio), and tied for sixth with the Kings (players expenses). Within only the SWD, the team's amounts were third or fourth in the group except for being lowest in operating income and gate receipts but highest in its debt-to-value percent (table A9).

In comparison to all NBA clubs, the Grizzlies' data ranged in rank from a tie for fourth place with the Detroit Pistons in their debt ratio to twenty-fifth in market value. Given these results, Memphis is a below-average business enterprise as an NBA franchise and from a financial perspective because of such things as its location, fan base, historical record, and other geographic and sport-specific factors.

From 2011 to 2015, the Grizzlies' payroll among WC teams varied in rank from third in 2013 ($72.1 million) to tenth in 2012 ($62.9 million). Within only the SWD, however, the club had the highest payroll in the group in 2013, third in 2011 ($70.5 million), 2012 and 2015 ($83.3 million), and second at $74.1 million in 2014 (table A10).

In comparison to payrolls of all NBA teams, Memphis's was chronologically ninth in 2011, twenty-first in 2012, sixth in 2013, tenth in 2014, and eleventh in 2015. Based on these amounts, the Grizzlies increased their payroll from 2012 to 2015 to become more competitive and qualify for and win more games in postseasons. To that end, this was a productive strategy because it resulted in five consecutive playoff appearances and competing in a conference final series in 2013.

The Grizzlies signed point guard Mike Conley to a five-year, $153-million deal in mid-2016 that ranks as the richest in NBA history by total value. Conley's deal was also the first contract over $100 million with an annual salary average of at least $30 million. His contract is yet another sign of the NBA's new financial reality thanks to the salary cap's one-year jump from $70 million to $94 million. The deals for Conley and Chandler Parsons (four years, $94 million) are good for the Grizzlies, who have historically struggled to lure and keep sought-after free agents. It's a good thing the team and its fan base is happy, too, because they are now locked into a core for at least three seasons.[26]

FedExForum

Opened in 2004 and shaped like a pyramid, the $250 million, 18,500-seat FedExForum is a distinctive venue located on the riverfront and adjacent to the historic Beale Street entertainment district. When built, a large glass atrium lobby existed inside the door of the main concourse with a backlit movie theater-type marquee running along the inside fascia. On the right is a glassed-in basketball court, where visitors could walk in during the day and watch the team practice. A large team store was on the left called "Grizzlies Den," and also a sports bar named "Jack Daniels Grill."

What makes the venue unique, special, and gives its distinctive character is the meticulous effort to celebrate the history of music, Memphis style, through a collection of murals, displays, and signage. Concourse areas are themed according to Blues, Jazz, Gospel, Soul, and current Memphis music. In keeping with the music theme, there are cool concession canopies, many of which look like old-style 1950s diners.

Among arenas of other WC teams as of early 2016, the Grizzlies' was the fifteenth oldest, fifth most expensive to build, and thirteenth most valuable. In comparison to all NBA venues, the FedExForum ranked twenty-sixth (age), tenth (construction cost), and twenty-fifth (value). According to this data, Memphis plays its home games in a relatively modern and unique facility with plenty of amenities for fans to enjoy and provide cash flows for the franchise (table A11).

In the 2011–2015 NBA seasons, the FCI for a family to attend a Grizzlies regular-season game at the FedExForum ranged from a low of $192 in 2011 to a high of $223 in both 2014 and 2015. With respect to the cost at home games of all NBA teams, the Grizzlies' each year were consecutively thirtieth in 2011, twenty-eighth in 2012 ($213), 2013 ($212) and 2014, and twenty-seventh in 2015 (table A12).

To reveal specific costs for a recent season in the NBA, Memphis's FCI in 2015–16 was the same as in 2014–15. Listed from most to least in amount by item for one person, the team's tickets averaged $31–$32, a cap $18 and parking one vehicle $15, single beer between $7 and $8, and a hot dog and soft drink each $4.

Among other teams in the conference's SWD, they had rankings and FCIs from most to least as follows: Rockets ninth at $376; Spurs twelfth at $325; Mavericks twentieth at $281; and Pelicans twenty-eighth at $221. Consequently, Grizzlies fans paid less at games in the FedExForum than those of twenty-six other NBA clubs in their arenas.

The cheapest ticket cost $7 for a fan to watch a Grizzlies home game in 2015–16. This was about $9 or approximately 56 percent less than the league's average for a cheap seat. Since the club's FCI was $116 less that of a typical NBA team, a family of four purchased tickets and enjoyed a pro basketball game in Memphis at a large discount relative to the majority of arenas within the league. These costs and prices, in turn, were set by the Grizzlies organization to earn revenue and maximize profit from their operations.

In its annual ranking of all thirty NBA game-day experiences as of 2016, the *Stadium Journey* rated the FedExForum only twenty-second best. Its relatively low rank was explained as follows:

> Memphis is a college basketball town and the Grizzlies are a secondary tenant, much as they were in Vancouver with the Canucks the local lords. What this means is that the team is always trying to sell more tickets, rather than entertain the fans that are there. During breaks, you are as likely to hear an ad for upcoming games or a ticket promotion as to have t-shirts fired into the crowd.[27]

Business Highlights

Besides regular-season and postseason games, NBA franchises are involved in—and affected by—community events and business-related affairs, news, and projects. The following are a few of them for Memphis's low-valued, small-market, and from a financial perspective, below-average professional basketball team.[28]

First, when the Grizzlies added eight seats between the benches and the scorer's table for its 2011–12 season, they found only one buyer for the new locations. Harrah's Casino took the four next to the visitors' bench to use as a perk for high rollers. At $850 a game—or almost $75,000 a pair for a typical full season—they were priced far higher than the $590 a game they charged for tickets on the opposite side of the floor, a steep price for relocation. So the team started offering the seats for $950 per game in packages of five games. They sold a few to sponsors and suite holders. But they still were left with plenty of openings, especially for softer games. When the lockout settled and the season started, demand picked up.

Second, the Grizzlies signed a deal with Spotlight Ticket Management during early 2012 to offer its premium seat buyers more control and data from the use of their tickets. Spotlight said it had thirty-seven professional sports teams as clients. Specific financial terms of the Grizzlies' one-year deal with the company were not disclosed. They made the ticket-tracking system available to all suite holders, who accessed the software from a Spotlight website portal and paid an unspecified fee to the ticketing company.

Third, the Grizzlies unveiled the uniforms they are wearing at a game on the Martin Luther King holiday on January 16, 2017. Every inch of the black uniforms has a specific meaning related to Martin Luther King Jr. and his assassination in Memphis. In 2017, the National Civil Rights Museum (NCRM) will commemorate the fiftieth anniversary of the assassination. The uniforms were unveiled during a special forum held at the NCRM called "A Bridge of Opportunity." The FedExForum featured Grizzlies minority owner Pitt Hyde, head coach David Fizdale, and the team's veteran small forward Vince

Carter. The uniform's piping design replicates the railing surrounding the exterior walkways and balconies of the historic hotel and museum. The sea foam color accents, numbers, and piping are pulled directly from the doors at rooms 306 and 307, where Dr. King spent his last moments on April 4, 1968.

Fourth, the Grizzlies Foundation and Memphis community TEAM UP to increase the number of youth with access to quality mentors invested in preparing them for success in college, a career, and life. Besides a youth mentoring partnership, the programs include a training institute, youth sports partnership, and a team mentor service. Collectively, these surround young people with adults who are committed to their success, facilitate positive identity development, inspire self-confidence, and reinforce the skills of hard work, determination, and goal achievement. Moreover, the programs build durable relationships over time and offer youth those personal and professional networks that translate into pathways out of poverty.

Fifth, although they play in the NBA's second smallest market, the Grizzlies have been a big beneficiary of the league's 2011 collective bargaining agreement. The deal more than tripled the amount of revenue-sharing funds transferred to low-revenue teams. The Grizzlies receive a check of more than $20 million a year, helping the franchise earn an operating profit after years of losses. Despite their small-market status, the Grizzlies made the playoffs six consecutive years including the conference finals in their 2012–13 season.

New Orleans Hornets/Pelicans

Born in 1927 in New Orleans, Louisiana, Tom Benson served in the U.S. Navy and in 1948 graduated with an accounting degree from Loyola University of New Orleans. After finishing school, he worked as an automobile salesman at the city's Cathey Chevrolet but then moved to San Antonio in 1956 to revive a poorly performing dealership.

Granted a minority interest in the business, Benson became full owner of Tom Benson Chevrolet in 1962. As an owner of several dealerships, he became wealthy by investing profits from his automobile businesses in local banks. He eventually purchased several small Southern banks and formed Benson Financial, which he sold to Norwest Corporation in 1996.

Two years after taking ownership of the Hornets franchise in 2010, the NBA sold it to Benson for approximately $340 million. His ownership of the Hornets and NFL Saints meant the two small-market franchises were locally owned and work as partners in their efforts to attract corporate sponsorships. As a result, Hornets fans expected a better product on the court.

Renamed Pelicans, the club appeared in one playoff during its 2012–2015 seasons. Among owners of fourteen other WC teams as of early 2016, Benson's Hornets/Pelicans tied for eleventh with zero division titles, tied for eighth in conference titles, and tied for sixth in league championships. With respect to all clubs in the NBA, New Orleans tied for nineteenth (division titles), for fifteenth (conference titles), and for tenth (NBA championships). Because of these and other results, Benson has not been a successful owner of the franchise (table A8).

According to a sports website, Benson is the seventeenth best NBA team owner as of 2015. Some reasons for his relatively low rank are as follows:

> It's been a rough year for Tom Benson, as his mental capacity has been openly called into question and control of both the Saints and Pelicans were almost yanked from him. He's not the best owner in sports, but his team is starting to turn things around in a big way. Monty Williams being fired by Dell Demps was a blemish thanks to how shady things went down. But Benson has put a dictator in power in his front office, and one that has lured Alvin Gentry to town to groom superstar center Anthony Davis into the next MVP candidate. It's hard to say Benson deserves credit for Davis' talents, but basketball is starting to rival football in New Orleans and that's something that Benson is allowing to happen.[29]

Team Financials

According to recent financial data published in *Forbes* magazine for NBA teams, the Pelicans' estimated market value was $650 million, revenue $142 million, operating income $19 million, gate receipts $30 million, debt-to-value 19 percent, and players expenses $80 million. With respect to those of fourteen other WC teams, New Orleans ranked fifteenth (market value), thirteenth (revenue), eleventh (operating income and gate receipts), third (debt ratio), and tied for eighth with the Warriors (players expenses). Within only the SWD, the Pelicans' amounts were fourth or fifth but their debt/value placed second to the Grizzlies' 22 percent (table A9).

Among the data of all NBA clubs as of early 2016, Benson's team ranged in rank from eighth in its debt ratio to thirtieth in market value. Based on these results, the Pelicans are a below-average and inferior NBA franchise from a financial perspective and struggle to earn enough income from gate receipts and other sources to operate efficiently while trying to compete and win titles and championships.

From 2011 to 2015, the Hornets/Pelicans' payroll among WC teams had differences in rank from fifth in 2014 ($73.9 million) to eighth in 2012 ($63.5 million) and 2013 ($66.1 million). Within the SWD, however, the club had the fourth highest payroll in the group at $65.4 million in 2011, third in 2012–2014, and fifth at $82.5 million in 2015 (table A10).

In comparison to payrolls of twenty-nine other NBA teams, New Orleans's was chronologically fourteenth (2011), eighteenth (2012), seventeenth

(2013), eleventh (2014), and thirteenth (2015). Based on these amounts, the team reduced its payroll from 2011 to 2012 but then increased it from 2013 to 2015 in order to become more competitive and qualify for postseasons. To that end, this was not a productive strategy because the Pelicans appeared in only one playoff series and lost in the conference's first round.

Do they build through the draft or play only for the 2016–17 season? From the outside, the ledger seems to tilt heavily toward patience. Not only has ownership witnessed the pitfalls of a get-rich-quick approach firsthand, but player Anthony Davis is locked into a second contract with paychecks, and thus a salary-cap number that reflect his star status. Even if the deal remains a bargain at 25 percent of the league's cap—and not the 30 they'd be on the hook for if Davis makes an All-NBA team and triggers the Rose Rule clause—the need increases for inexpensive talent to join the likes of players Tim Frazier and Quincy Pondexter.

Smoothie King Center

Opened in 1999, the $114 million, 18,000-seat New Orleans Arena—renamed Smoothie King Center (SKC) in 2014—is an octagon-shaped building, originally reminiscent of America West Arena, with its south side serving as the building's main entrance. There is a second entrance on the west side of the building. Both entrances are built with massive glass facades which soar to the top of the building. At night the gray facades are brightly floodlit, but the exterior of the building is devoid of any marquee or identification signage, and this lends to sort of a bland appearance.

People enter the arena on the ground floor, walk through a small lobby, and from there a long escalator takes them high up to the main level. The concourses are colored pale gray, off white, and pale turquoise, with terrazzo tile flooring and recessed lights in the ceiling. Concession canopies pick up the color scheme, and again, the decor looks very bland and austere, although bright and new. Regarding the seating bowl, seats are divided into lower and upper levels, divided by a separate suite level.

In addition to a separate suite level and concourse, lower-level seats between the baselines are designated as club seating. Tickets there provide access to a separate club concourse, which is located below the lower-level main concourse. This exclusive area basically consists of north and south club lounges with bar service, concession stands, and table seating. The two lounges are connected via a narrow and austere corridor.

In a long-term lease agreement with the state of Louisiana, the team is bound to the arena through 2024. The new agreement relieved the state from the burden of giving the club any financial subsidies—a potential savings of nearly $70 million—and shifted the responsibility of generating additional revenue to the franchise by making capital improvements whereby the team can earn additional monies through various methods such as redesigned seating areas and advertising.

Among those of fourteen other WC teams as of early 2016, SKC tied for seventh in age and placed tenth in construction cost and fifteenth in value. With respect to all NBA arenas, SKC tied for fourteenth (age) and ranked twenty-third (construction cost) and twenty-eighth (value). Given these results, the Pelicans' home is neither new nor of great value compared to buildings such as the Mavericks' American Airlines Center and the Clippers' and Lakers' Staples Center (table A11).

In the 2011–2015 NBA seasons, the FCI for a family to attend a Hornets/Pelicans regular-season game at the New Orleans Arena/SKC ranged from a low of $208 in 2013 to a high of $221 in both 2014 and 2015. With respect to fan costs at arenas of all NBA teams, the Hornets/Pelicans each year were consecutively twenty-sixth in 2011 ($217), twenty-seventh in 2012 ($220), twenty-ninth in both 2013 and 2014, and twenty-eighth in 2015 (table A12).

To reveal specific costs for a recent season in the NBA, New Orleans's FCI in 2015–16 was the same as in 2014–15. Listed from most to least in amount by item for one person, the team's tickets averaged $30–$31, a cap $20 and parking one vehicle $15, single beer $7, and a hot dog and soft drink each $4.

Among other teams in the conference's SWD, they had rankings and FCIs from most to least as follows: Rockets ninth at $376; Spurs twelfth at $325; Mavericks twentieth at $281; and Grizzlies twenty-seventh at $223. Consequently, Pelicans fans paid less at games in SKC than those of twenty-seven other NBA clubs in their arenas.

The cheapest ticket cost approximately $8 for a fan to watch a Pelicans home game in 2015–16. This was almost $8 or about 50 percent less than the league's average for a cheap seat. Since the club's FCI was $118 less that of a typical NBA team, a family of four purchased tickets and enjoyed a basketball game in New Orleans at a considerable discount relative to the majority of arenas within the league. These costs and prices, in turn, were set by the Pelicans organization to earn revenue and maximize profit from their operations.

In its annual ranking of all thirty NBA game-day experiences as of 2016, the *Stadium Journey* rated SKC as nineteenth best. Its below-average rank was explained as follows:

> A trip to the Smoothie King Center for a New Orleans Pelicans game has almost everything a traveling fan could ask for: an elite NBA player in action (Anthony Davis), non-stopped area entertainment, excellent concessions, a variety of

> drink options, and the perfect host city: New Orleans. The Pelican experience extends far beyond simply taking in on-court NBA action. There are endless opportunities for great food and entertainment before and after the game.[30]

Business Highlights

Besides regular-season and postseason games, NBA franchises are involved in—and affected by—community events and business-related affairs, news, and projects. The following are a few of them for New Orleans's low-valued, small-market, and from a financial perspective, below-average professional basketball team.[31]

First, a private settlement reached in the case *Benson vs. Rosenthal* expects to allow franchise owner Tom Benson to substitute cash and promissory notes for much of the non-voting Pelicans and Saints shares in the assets he assigned to Renee, Rita, and Ryan LeBlanc. Announced June 17, 2016, the settlement hinges on both the NBA and NFL approving the alteration and essentially allowing Benson to use the teams as loan collateral. But even with that approval, the future of his two franchises is far from clear.

Second, trustees for the embattled heirs of Tom Benson valued his NFL Saints at between $1.5 billion and $1.65 billion—around twice his own estimate—and they valued the NBA Pelicans at three to four times more than did Benson. Those figures, disclosed recently for the first time in court filings, took center stage in a scheduled five-day trial between Benson and the two trustees, whom he sued for blocking his attempt to strip the teams from trusts he established for his estranged heirs.

Third, the NBA's deal to sell the Hornets to NFL Saints owner Tom Benson for (approximately) $340 million (in 2012) was a break-even result for the league. According to sources familiar with the sale, the Hornets posted an $18 million loss in 2011 but were able to stop the financial bleeding after cutting player payroll while greatly increasing full-season ticket sales from 6,000 to more than 10,000 and boosting sponsorship revenue. Though the NBA had sustained an operating loss on the team, the league was made whole by its deal with Benson.

Fourth, the Pelicans announced in October 2015 that Rouses would be the official grocer of the club for the NBA's 2015–16 season. The partnership was highlighted by a series of bimonthly sweepstakes, as well as the "Year of the Uniform" game-day giveaway series for fans. Rouses and the Pelicans teamed with various vendors throughout the season to host two contests in local Rouses locations each month. Prizes included Pelicans memorabilia and experiences. Fans checked out the sweepstakes in-store and in Rouses's weekly circular and register to win via in-store display or a mail-in form.

Fifth, Pelicans president Dennis Lauscha spoke publicly on the team's in-house podcast show in July 2016 and emphasized a need for the franchise to return to the playoffs. The Pelicans' upper management has mainly been silent since the team closed out their 2015–16 season with a dreadful 30–52 record after making the playoffs in 2014–15. A report by the *Sports Business Journal* ranked the Pelicans last among NBA teams in audience size for their televised games on Fox Sports New Orleans—averaging 7,000 households per game. The Pelicans ranked twenty-third in the league in attendance—averaging 16,793 in forty-one games played at SKC—but drew bigger crowds on the road at 17,851 per game.

San Antonio Spurs

Born in 1948 in Peoria, Illinois, Peter Holt lived in San Antonio, Texas, as a child before moving to Corpus Christi. After graduating from high school there, he served in the U.S. Army for two years and was awarded a Silver Star, three Bronze Stars, and a Purple Heart from his tour of duty in Vietnam.

After being discharged from the Army, Holt went to California where he worked for an investment banking house and also became involved in a bar and restaurant business. Then in 1983, he moved to Corpus Christi to work at his father's Caterpillar dealership. Peter diversified the dealership's markets, which greatly increased sales. Four years later, he and his father purchased Holt Machinery Company in San Antonio, reuniting the original Caterpillar dealership that his great uncle started in 1933. Peter expanded the company's Texas presence by purchasing Darr Equipment Company of Dallas, a Caterpillar dealer in the Dallas/Fort Worth Metroplex.

During 1996, Holt led a partnership group—composed of twenty-two members—and purchased the Spurs franchise from B. J. "Red" McCombs for $76 million. He became majority owner after acquiring additional shares from Gaylord Entertainment. In March 2016, Spurs Sports & Entertainment announced that Holt retired as the organization's chairman and chief executive officer with his wife Julianna responsible for both roles. Peter remains on the company's board of managers and continues as part of the ownership group while Julianna became the team's governor on the NBA's board of governors.

Among owners of WC teams as of early 2016, Holt's Spurs ranked second in winning twelve division and six conference titles, and also five league championships. In comparison to all owners of NBA teams, Holt's clubs tied for second with Micky Arison's Miami Heat in number of division titles and with Jerry Reinsdorf's Chicago Bulls in conference titles, and placed third in NBA championships. Thus, Peter Holt has been a successful leader of the Spurs for more than twenty years (table A8).

Team Financials

According to recent financial data published in *Forbes* magazine about NBA teams, the Spurs' market value was an estimated $1.15 billion, revenue $170 million, operating income $31 million, gate receipts $59 million, debt-to-value 7 percent, and players expenses $76 million. With respect to fourteen other WC teams, San Antonio ranked sixth (market value and revenue), fourth (operating income), tied for fourth with the Clippers (gate receipts), tied for eleventh with the Rockets (debt ratio), and tied for tenth with the Lakers and Suns (players expenses). Within only the SWD, San Antonio had the same debt percent but smaller amounts than the Rockets and more than the Grizzlies and Pelicans except for players expenses (table A9).

In comparison to all NBA clubs, the Spurs were tenth in market value, twelfth in revenue, eighth in operating income, tied for eighth in gate receipts, tied for twenty-third in debt-to-value, and tied for eighteenth in players expenses. From a financial perspective, San Antonio is an above-average franchise and a successful business enterprise relative to other members of the league.

From 2011 to 2015, the Spurs' payroll among WC teams ranged in rank from second in 2012 ($69.7 million) to eleventh in 2014 ($69.4 million). Within the SWD, however, the club had the highest payroll in 2012, second in the group at $73.4 million in 2011 and at $87.8 million in 2015, fourth highest at $63.8 million in 2013, and smallest in 2014 (table A10).

In comparison to payrolls of twenty-nine other NBA teams, San Antonio's was chronologically sixth (2011), seventh (2012), nineteenth (2013), eighteenth (2014), and seventh (2015). Based on these amounts, the team reduced its payroll in 2012 and 2013 but then increased it in 2014 and 2015 to become more competitive and qualify for postseasons. To that end, this was a productive strategy because the Spurs appeared in five playoff series and won a championship in 2014 after losing the finals in the previous season.

AT&T Center

Opened in 2002, the 18,500-seat SBC Center—renamed AT&T Center in 2006—is a midsized, multipurpose sports and entertainment facility located on the Freeman Coliseum Grounds. Besides the Spurs, it hosts games of the WNBA San Antonio Silver Stars and AHL San Antonio Rampage plus other activities including musical concerts, high school graduations, and community events.

Among arenas of other WC teams as of early 2016, the AT&T Center tied for twelfth with the Thunder's Chesapeake Energy Arena in age and also ranked seventh in construction cost and sixth in economic value. In comparison to those of all NBA clubs, the Spurs' home tied for twenty-third (age) and was fifteenth (construction cost) and eleventh (value). Therefore, San Antonio plays its home games in a relatively modern facility with plenty of amenities to generate revenue from gate receipts for the franchise (table A11).

In the 2011–2015 NBA seasons, the FCIs for a family to attend a Spurs regular-season game at the AT&T Center ranged from a low of $319 in 2011 to a high of $340 in 2014. With respect to those of all NBA teams, the Spurs' fan costs each year were consecutively tied for eighth in 2011, ninth in both 2012 ($330) and 2013 ($339), tenth in 2014, and tied for eleventh at $325 in 2015 (table A12).

To reveal specific costs for a recent season in the NBA, San Antonio's FCI in 2015–16 was between 4 and 5 percent lower than in 2014–15. Listed from most to least in amount by item for one person, the team's tickets averaged $54–$55, a cap $30, single beer $5–$6, parking one vehicle and a hot dog each $5, and a soft drink $2 to $3.

Since the club's FCI was $14 less that of a typical NBA team, a family of four purchased tickets and enjoyed a basketball game in San Antonio at a discount relative to the majority of arenas within the league. These costs and prices, in turn, were set by the Spurs organization to earn revenue and maximize profit from their operations.

In its annual ranking of all thirty NBA game-day experiences as of 2016, the *Stadium Journey* rated AT&T Center as the third best. Its relatively high rank was explained as follows:

> The atmosphere for a Spurs game is one of the best in all sports. This may be due to the fact that the Spurs are San Antonio's only team in the four major sports leagues. As you enter AT&T Center, you'll get the festival feel that San Antonio has showcased to many tourists throughout the city. The Spurs have one of the best fan bases in the NBA, and the energy and excitement during the game is far superior to many other NBA arenas.[32]

Business Highlights

Besides regular-season and postseason games, NBA franchises are involved in—and affected by—community events and business-related affairs, news, and projects. The following are a few of them for San Antonio's midmarket, popular, and from a financial perspective, above-average professional basketball team.[33]

First, the Spurs moved forward in mid-2014 with an aggressive relaunch of their YouTube channel to boost digital presence. The proposed overhaul called for the creation of a wide variety of content and the addition of staff dedicated solely to building and operating the team's YouTube channel, including the hiring of a program director and talent.

Second, the Spurs' market was 55 percent Hispanic in 2013 with 33 percent of the team's season ticket base being Hispanic and about 45 percent of its individual game buyers. Yet, the club had few marketing initiatives targeted specifically at the Hispanic market, instead incorporating cultural touch points more broadly. The team reached Hispanics primarily through a general market approach such as a thirty-second spot on television that stressed family values and other things.

Third, the Spurs led the NBA in local television ratings during their 2014–15 season by posting an average of 8.09 on FS Southwest or 9 percent higher than the previous year. The increase in the team's ratings came on top of a 15 percent gain during the 2013–14 campaign in which the Spurs had the league's second-highest rating.

Fourth, the Spurs franchise completed a $110 million renovation of AT&T Center for the 2015–16 season that included new seats, video boards, and fourteen theater boxes. And in November 2015, the club expanded its corporate sponsor reach to Le Locle, Switzerland, by securing an agreement with Swiss watchmaker Tissot.

Fifth, an examination of head coach Gregg Popovich's management style and strategy reveals five lessons that can benefit leaders from all areas of business. These lessons are: be willing to adapt; make tough decisions for the benefit of the team; learn how to deal with multiple cultures and personalities; be resilient; and care about company culture.

NOTES

1. Two books about NBA franchises and their histories are Frank P. Jozsa Jr., *National Basketball Association Strategies: Business Expansions, Relocations, and Mergers* (New York: Springer, 2016) and Connie Kirchberg, *Hoop Love: A History of the National Basketball Association* (Jefferson, NC: McFarland, 2007).

2. For team performances and other information, see such websites as http://www.nba.com, http://www.basketball-reference.com, and http://www.sportsencyclopedia.com.

3. The article is Ian Miller, "Mavericks Tumble to 22nd in ESPN's Future Power Rankings," http://www.mavsmoneyball.com, cited September 1, 2016.

4. The reference is William Case, "Ranking the Greatest Franchises in NBA History," http://www.listicled.com, cited August 8, 2016.

5. Chad Ford and Kevin Pelton, "Future NBA Power Rankings: Full Category Rankings," http://www.espn.go.com, cited August 3, 2016.

6. See Daniel Zillmer, "All 30 NBA Franchises Statistically Ranked by All-Time Greatness," http://www.fansided.com, cited June 6, 2016.

7. One source to read is Max Croes, "James Harden is to Blame for the Rockets Coaching Problems," http://www.thedreamshake.com, cited September 3, 2016.

8. "Future NBA Power Ranking: Full Category Rankings."

9. The recommended reading is Chris Holmes, "All-Time NBA Franchise Rankings, 2015–16 Edition," http://www.greyflannelsuit.net, cited August 15, 2016.

10. See T. J. Hatter, "The Ten Worst Franchises in NBA History," http://www.uproxx.com, cited September 7, 2016.

11. Chad Ford and Kevin Pelton, "Future Power Rankings: Who Will Rise in the Next Three Years?" http://www.espn.go.com, cited June 5, 2016.

12. Reference Justin Verrier, "Pelicans Back at a Crossroads: Trade the No. 6 Pick or Build for the Future?" http://www.espn.com, cited September 15, 2016.

13. "Ranking the Greatest Franchises in NBA History."

14. "Future NBA Power Rankings: Full Category Rankings."

15. "Mark Cuban Biography," http://www.biography.com, cited September 15, 2016.

16. Josh Hill, "NBA Owners Power Rankings: Who is Best Owner in Basketball?" http://www.fansided.com, cited July 8, 2016.

17. "Fan Cost Index," http://www.teammarketingreport.com, cited August 1, 2016.

18. See, for example, Paul Baker, "2016 NBA Arena Experience Rankings," http://www.scout.com, cited August 1, 2016.

19. For the Mavericks' business highlights, references are: Candace Carlisle, "Mark Cuban Confirms Deal, Offers Details on New Mavs Facility," http://www.bizjournals.com, cited September 15, 2016; Tim MacMahon, "Mark Cuban: Warriors Being the Bad Guy Will be Good for the NBA," http://www.espn.com, cited September 16, 2016; Erik Fernandez, "Dirk Nowitzki Mocks Donald Trump in Fake Ad Campaign," http://www.huffingtonpost.com, cited September 16, 2016; "Coast to Coast," http://www.sportsbusinessdaily.com, cited September 17, 2016; Kurt Badenhausen, Mike Ozanian, and Christini Settimi, "The Business of Basketball," http://www.forbes.com, cited June 27, 2016.

20. "NBA Owner Power Rankings: Who is the Best Owner in Basketball?"

21. Yoni Pollak, "Rockets: Leslie Alexander Making Costly Mistake," http://www.houseofhouston.com, cited September 17, 2016.

22. A reading is David Weiner, "Houston Rockets Salary Cap Update, 2016 Offseason Edition," http://www.rockets.clutchfans.net, cited September 18, 2016.

23. "2016 NBA Arena Experience Rankings."

24. John Lombardo, "Houston Rockets Bet on Casino Industry Executive to Fill Chief Strategy Position," http://www.sportsbusinessdaily.com, cited September 15, 2016; Stephen Douglas, "Houston Rockets' Twitter Put Down Mavericks With Gun and Horse Emoji," http://www.thebiglead.com, cited September 17, 2016; "Root Sports Expands Access to Rocket Games," http://www.nba.com, cited September 18, 2016; "Community Begins at Home . . . Games," http://www.nba.com, cited September 18, 2016; Kevin Arnovitz, "Which NBA Team Are You?" http://www.espn.com, cited September 18, 2016.

25. "NBA Owners Power Rankings: Who is the best Owner in Basketball?"

26. Eric Freeman, "Mike Conley and Grizzlies Agree to the Biggest NBA Contract Ever," http://www.sports.yahoo.com, cited September 19, 2016.

27. "2016 NBA Arena Experience Rankings."

28. Grizzlies business news includes Bill King and John Lombardo, "The Actions on the Floor," http://www.sportsbusinessdaily.com, cited September 19, 2016; "Grizzlies Make Spotlight Available to Suite Holders," http://www.sportsbusinessdaily.com, cited September 19, 2016; Michael Sheffield, "Grizzlies Unveil MLK Day Uniforms," http://www.bizjournals.com, cited September 20, 2016; "Memphis Grizzlies Foundation," http://www.grizzliesfoundation.org, cited September 20, 2016; Kurt Badenhausen, Mike Ozanian and Christini Settimi, "The Business of Basketball," http://www.forbes.com, cited June 27, 2016.

29. "NBA Owners Power Ranking: Who is the Best Owner in Basketball?"

30. "2016 NBA Arena Experience Rankings."

31. For the Pelicans' business highlights, see Bruce Schoenfeld, "With Settlement, Future of Franchises Remains Far From Clear," http://www.sportsbusinessdaily.com, cited September 20, 2016; Daniel Kaplan, "Team Valuations Show Big Gap in Benson Suit," http://www.sportsbusinessdaily.com, cited September 20, 2016; "Sale Allows NBA to Break Even on Hornets," http://www.sportsbusinessdaily.com, cited September 21, 2016; John Reid, "Pelicans President Dennis Lauscha: 'We Have to Win in Order to be Relevant,'" http://www.nola.com, cited September 22, 2016.

32. "2016 NBA Arena Experience Rankings."

33. See San Antonio's business news at "Spurs to Refresh YouTube Channel," http://www.sportsbusinessdaily.com, cited September 21, 2016; Bill King, "Spurs Use Cultural Touch Points to Hit Mark," http://www.sportsbusinessdaily.com, cited September 21, 2016; Kurt Badenhausen, Michael Ozanian, and Christini Settimi, "The Business of Basketball," http://www.forbes.com, cited June 27, 2016; "San Antonio Spurs Finish 2014–15 NBA Season No. 1 in Local TV Ratings," http://www.nba.com, cited September 22, 2016; Lorne Chan, "New AT&T Center Welcomes San Antonians Back Home," http://www.nba.com, cited September 23, 2016; Justin Bariso, "5 Business Lessons From Gregg Popovich and the San Antonio Spurs," http://www.linkedin.com, cited September 24, 2016.

Conclusion

Chapters 1–3 and 4–6 of *National Basketball Association Franchises* reveal how teams in, respectively, Eastern Conference (EC) and Western Conference (WC) divisions each performed in regular seasons and postseasons of the league. To highlight and report their historical progress and success as franchises from a financial perspective, the chapters also contain data and other business-related information and topics from the literature about them while located within their local in addition to regional sports market.

TEAM PERFORMANCES

To compare and analyze the historical performances of five teams each within three divisions of the EC and also WC as of the NBA's 2015–16 season, table 1.1 contains some interesting but provocative results. More specifically, it depicts the variation in number of seasons and playoffs, division and conference titles, and league championships across six groups based on the leadership of their owners, coaches' decisions, and talents of players on the roster.

First, led by the dominant Boston Celtics with fifty-three and New York Knicks with forty-two, Atlantic Division (AD) teams appeared in the most playoffs while those in the Southeast Division (SED) were in fewest as of the league's 2015–16 season. Despite twelve regular seasons, the SED's Charlotte Bobcats/Hornets qualified for only three playoffs, which is the same number as the AD's four-year-old Brooklyn Nets. For various reasons, some SED teams and also a Northwest Division (NWD) club like the twenty-seven-year-old Minnesota Timberwolves experienced several losing seasons and therefore had little opportunity historically to advance in the playoffs, win their conference title, and then compete for a championship.

Table 1.1. NBA Teams, Performances by Division, Selected Seasons

	Seasons	Playoffs	Titles		
			Division	Conference	Championship
Eastern Conference					
Atlantic Division	218	139	50	18	21
Central Division	243	138	42	17	11
Southeast Division	158	88	25	10	4
Western Conference					
Northwest Division	158	95	26	6	1
Pacific Division	212	112	42	20	13
Southwest Division	150	101	30	12	8

Note: Divisions are listed alphabetically by conference. NBA is National Basketball Association. Championship is a league title. Number of Seasons, Playoffs, and total Titles are self-explanatory.
Source: See websites such as http://www.basketball-reference.com, http://www.nba.com, and http://www.sportsencyclopedia.com.

Second, although AD teams as a group ranked first in winning fifty division titles and also twenty-one NBA championships, they finished a close second to those in the Pacific Division (PD) in total number of conference titles. Because of such superstars as Jerry West, Kareem Abdul-Jabbar, Magic Johnson, Shaquille O'Neal, and Kobe Bryant, the Los Angeles Lakers won eighteen and the Celtics nine of them.

Third, besides the AD's Celtics and PD's Lakers, the most successful teams in each division as of 2015–16 included the Central Division (CD) Chicago Bulls, SED Miami Heat, NWD Portland Trail Blazers, and SWD San Antonio Spurs. Each of these clubs had won more than 50 percent of its regular-season games and except for the Trail Blazers, more than ten titles.

Fourth, according to data in the chapters, the least productive teams thus far by division have been the AD's Brooklyn Nets, CD's Indiana Pacers, SED's Charlotte Bobcats/Hornets, NWD's Minnesota Timberwolves, PD's Los Angeles Clippers, and SWD's New Orleans Hornets/Pelicans. While their all-time winning percentage is below 50 percent, they struggle periodically to get enough local fans to purchase tickets and attend home games.

Fifth, ranked from first to sixth in winning percentage, the most competitive divisions have been the SWD (.523) and then the NWD (.516), AD (.496), CD and PD (each .495), and SED (.469). In addition, SED and AD teams appeared in the least and most number of playoffs, respectively, at 88 and 139. These results occurred, in part, because of such things as their number of seasons in the league, interdivisional rivalries, coaches and players, and locations.

FINANCIAL RESULTS

In contrast to the performances of NBA teams in three divisions of each conference, table 1.2 exposes them from a financial perspective. In other words, they are sports franchises whose economic objective is to earn maximum profits while playing regular-season games at their and opponents' arenas, and if successful, competing in postseasons. Given information in the table, following are highlights of their financial results of late 2015/early 2016.

First, as denoted in column two of the table, PD teams are the most valuable of the groups and then those in the AD, CD, SWD, SED, and NWD. Sequentially, the large-market Knicks, Lakers, Bulls, Celtics, and Clippers each had amounts that exceeded $2 billion while the five least valuable included the small-market Pelicans, Bucks, 76ers, Timberwolves, and Hornets. Their current stadium deals were important factors in differences between the financial worth of the former and latter franchises.

Second, net of stadium revenues used for debt payments, the group of AD and then PD and SWD clubs had the highest revenue from their operations. The former division was led in revenue by the Knicks and Nets, PD by the Lakers and Warriors, and SWD by the Rockets and Spurs. Besides ticket sales at home games in their venues, big-city teams also earn a lot of money from such things as advertising, apparel, and other products sold in stores owned by the franchise within their arena, and also from memorabilia, merchandise, and parking.

Table 1.2. NBA Teams, Average Financial Data by Division, 2015

	Value	*Revenue*	*OI*	*GR*	*D/V*	*PE*
Eastern Conference						
Atlantic Division	1,576	199	39	63	11	80
Central Division	1,153	167	27	38	17	78
Southeast Division	947	150	13	37	17	78
Western Conference						
Northwest Division	875	149	18	34	9	77
Pacific Division	1,705	195	47	59	11	115
Southwest Division	1,096	174	31	47	12	82

Note: Divisions are listed alphabetically by conference. NBA is National Basketball Association. Value is based on the current stadium deal (unless new stadium is pending) without deduction for debt (other than annual stadium debt). Revenue is net of stadium revenues used for debt payments. Operating Income (OI) is earnings before interest, taxes, depreciation, and amortization. Gate receipts (GR) include income from club seats. Debt/Value (D/V) is percent and includes ballpark debts. Players Expenses (PE) contains benefits and bonuses. Value, Revenue, OI, GR, and PE are each in millions of U.S. dollars.

Source: Kurt Badenhausen, Michael Ozanian, and Christina Settimi, "The Business of Basketball," http://www.forbes.com, cited June 27, 2016.

Third, the Lakers ($133 million), Knicks ($108 million), and Bulls ($67 million) had the most operating income in the league. Interestingly, the Nets incurred a $5 million loss operationally because of relatively high players' salaries, disappointing attendances at their home games, and simply too many expenses before payments for interest, taxes, depreciation, and amortization. In comparison, the EC's Nets, Hawks, Hornets, and Wizards, and WC's Trail Blazers, Kings, and Grizzlies were inefficient and each failed to earn more than $10 million.

Fourth, gate receipts are primarily based on attendances and the range of ticket prices at home games. While gate receipts were highest for the group of AD and PD franchises, NWD teams each had less than $50 million. Furthermore, because of apathetic fans and problems with hometown organizations supporting their local team, the SED's Hornets and Hawks and CD's Pacers and Pistons also earned relatively small gate receipts. Rather than attend pro basketball games, perhaps sports fans in these metropolitan areas preferred to spend a significant portion of their disposal income on, respectively, events of the National Football League (NFL) Carolina Panthers and Atlanta Falcons and/or Major League Baseball (MLB) Braves, and NFL Indianapolis Colts and Detroit Lions and/or MLB Tigers.

Fifth, including benefits and bonuses, players expenses were highest for the group of teams in the PD and lowest for those in the NWD. While amounts of the PD's Clippers and Kings each exceeded $80 million, they were below $70 million for both the NWD's Nuggets and Jazz. After finishing with average to below-average regular-season records and despite differences in their expenses, three of these four clubs did not make the playoffs in the NBA's 2015–16 season because of players' injuries and lack of talent on the roster, coaches' failure to motivate them, and other issues involving trades and retirements. As denoted in table 1.3 teams in all divisions had higher average payrolls from the 2014–15 to 2015–16 season especially in the CD (25 percent) but not the AD (3 percent).

Besides data on team performances in table 1.1 and financial results in tables 1.2 and 1.3, other interesting business information is how much families typically paid to attend NBA games during the league's 2011–12 to 2015–16 seasons. Besides tickets and payments for a cap, parking a vehicle, and purchasing a program, a Fan Cost Index consists of expenditures at games for beer, soft drinks, and a hot dog.

For groups of teams by division, families paid, on average, most to be at home games played by AD clubs and least for those of SWD teams. More specifically, the highest average costs across five NBA seasons were Knicks games at Madison Square Garden ($652) and lowest for the Bobcats/Hornets at Time Warner Cable Arena ($206). These amounts, in turn, affected each

Table 1.3. NBA Teams, Average Payrolls by Division, 2011–2015 Seasons

	2011	*2012*	*2013*	*2014*	*2015*
Eastern Conference					
Atlantic Division	65	73	76	72	74
Central Division	58	63	64	68	85
Southeast Division	65	66	65	66	75
Western Conference					
Northwest Division	59	63	64	67	73
Pacific Division	68	69	67	72	80
Southwest Division	68	62	66	72	83

Note: Divisions are listed alphabetically by conference. NBA is National Basketball Association. Amounts are in millions of dollars for the league's 2011–12 to 2015–16 seasons.
Source: "NBA Salaries," http://www.hoopshype.com, cited June 29, 2016, and "NBA Season Team Salary Listings," http://www.eskimo.com, cited June 29, 2016.

franchise's market value, revenue, operating income, gate receipts, and perhaps other variables (table 1.4).

To conclude, EC teams played the most seasons and playoffs and also won more division and conference titles and also championships than those in the WC. Among divisions in each conference, AD and PD clubs, respectively, were most successful in winning titles compared to teams in the EC's CD and SED, and others in the WC's NWD and SWD. With respect to parity in NBA team performances, the EC had greater inequality or deviations—less parity—in number of seasons, playoffs, division titles, and championships than the WC but not in the distribution of conference titles among its divisions.

In comparing financial results across divisions in the EC and WC, AD clubs ranked first in average revenue and gate receipts as did PD clubs in

Table 1.4. NBA Teams, Average Fan Cost Indexes by Division, 2011–2015 Seasons

	2011	*2012*	*2013*	*2014*	*2015*
Eastern Conference					
Atlantic Division	395	400	412	418	419
Central Division	284	298	305	313	309
Southeast Division	270	278	285	289	303
Western Conference					
Northwest Division	273	287	295	298	297
Pacific Division	342	349	374	386	416
Southwest Division	262	276	283	293	285

Note: Divisions are listed alphabetically by conference. NBA is National Basketball Association. Amounts are in hundreds of dollars for divisions in the league's 2011–12 to 2015–16 seasons.
Source: "Rod Fort's Sports Business Data," https://sites.google.com, cited July 1, 2016, and "NBA FCIs," http://www.teammarketingreport.com, cited July 1, 2016.

average market value, operating income, and players expenses, while CD and SED franchises tied in their average debt-to-value percentages. Regarding parity between conferences from a financial perspective, the EC had larger deviations—less equality—among its divisions in average revenue, gate receipts, and debt-to-value percentages while average market values, operating income, and players expenses varied more between divisions in the WC. In other words, the conferences had significant differences financially especially in their divisions' average market values and players expenses but not in the amounts of average revenue, operating income and gate receipts, or debt ratios.

Lastly, there were larger deviations—less parity—in average payrolls among EC divisions than those in the WC during the 2012–13 to 2015–16 seasons. In 2011–2012, however, the variation in average payrolls was slightly greater among WC divisions because of differences in players' salaries including their benefits and bonuses. Regarding the parity of average Fan Cost Indexes, EC divisions as a group had larger deviations—more inequality—than those in the WC from the 2011–12 to 2014–15 season but not in 2015–16, in part due to a relatively large increase in prices at home games of the Golden State Warriors.

Appendix

Table A1. Eastern Conference Teams, Historical Performances, Selected Seasons

				Titles		
Teams	*Seasons*	*W%*	*Playoffs*	*Division*	*Conference*	*Championship*
Atlantic Division						
Boston Celtics	70	.588	53	30	9	17
Brooklyn Nets	4	.463	3	0	0	0
New York Knicks	70	.493	42	8	4	2
Philadelphia 76ers	53	.501	33	8	5	2
Toronto Raptors	21	.438	8	4	0	0
Central Division						
Chicago Bulls	50	.522	34	9	6	6
Cleveland Cavaliers	46	.464	20	5	3	1
Detroit Pistons	59	.485	33	9	5	3
Indiana Pacers	40	.497	23	6	1	0
Milwaukee Bucks	48	.510	28	13	2	1
Southeast Division						
Atlanta Hawks	48	.502	32	5	0	0
Charlotte Bobcats/ Hornets	12	.386	3	0	0	0
Miami Heat	28	.520	19	12	5	3
Orlando Magic	27	.490	14	5	2	0
Washington Wizards	43	.448	20	3	3	1

Note: Teams are listed alphabetically by division as of their 2015–16 or simply 2015 season. Seasons include the Basketball Association of America (BAA) 1947–1949 and National Basketball Association (NBA) 1950–2015 seasons. The W% is win-loss or winning percent. This table excludes BAA and NBA teams at their previous sites: New York Nets (1977) and New Jersey Nets (1978–2012); Syracuse Nationals (1950–1963), Fort Wayne Pistons (1949–1957), Tri-Cities Blackhawks (1950–1951), Milwaukee Hawks (1952–1955), and St. Louis Hawks (1956–1968); Chicago Packers (1962), Chicago Zephyrs (1963), and Baltimore Bullets (1964–1973). The Charlotte Bobcats were renamed Hornets in the NBA's 2014–15 season.

Source: "NBA and ABA Team Index," http://www.basketball-reference.com, cited June 25, 2016, and "Historical Moments," http://www.sportsecyclopedia.com, cited June 25, 2016.

Table A2. Eastern Conference Teams by Division, History—Principal Owners

	Principal Owners			*Team Titles*		
Team	*Name*	*Year*	*Price*	*Division*	*Conference*	*NBA*
Atlantic Division						
Boston Celtics	Wycliffe Grousbeck	2002	360	6	2	1
Brooklyn Nets	Mikhail Prokhorov	2010	365	0	0	0
New York Knicks	James Dolan	1997	300	1	1	0
Philadelphia 76ers	Joshua Harris	2011	287	0	0	0
Toronto Raptors	Larry Tanenbaum	1998	400	4	0	0
Central Division						
Chicago Bulls	Jerry Reinsdorf	1985	16	8	6	6
Cleveland Cavaliers	Dan Gilbert	2005	375	4	2	1
Detroit Pistons	Tom Gores	2011	325	0	0	0
Indiana Pacers	Herbert Simon	1983	11	6	1	0
Milwaukee Bucks	Wes Edens/Marc Lasry	2014	550	0	0	0
Southeast Division						
Atlanta Hawks	Tony Ressler	2015	730	0	0	0
Charlotte Hornets	Michael Jordan	2010	175	0	0	0
Miami Heat	Micky Arison	1988	33	12	5	3
Orlando Magic	Richard DeVos	1991	85	5	2	0
Washington Wizards	Ted Leonsis	2010	551	0	0	0

Note: Teams are listed alphabetically by division. Year is when principal owners acquired the team. Price is in millions of dollars. The NBA is National Basketball Association. Team Titles were won since Year of principal owners.

Source: Kurt Badenhausen, Mike Ozanian, and Christini Settimi, "The Business of Basketball," http://www.forbes.com, cited June 27, 2016, and "NBA and ABA Team Index," http://www.basketball-reference.com, cited June 25, 2016.

Table A3. Eastern Conference Teams, Financial Data by Division, 2015

Teams	*Value*	*Revenue*	*OI*	*GR*	*D/V*	*PE*
Atlantic Division						
Boston Celtics	2,100	181	57	56	8	69
Brooklyn Nets	1,100	220	−5	63	15	99
New York Knicks	3,000	307	108	128	0	88
Philadelphia 76ers	700	124	13	21	21	60
Toronto Raptors	980	163	23	48	12	87
Central Division						
Chicago Bulls	2,300	228	67	72	2	87
Cleveland Cavaliers	1,100	191	24	52	18	87
Detroit Pistons	850	154	16	22	22	71
Indiana Pacers	840	138	19	20	18	75
Milwaukee Bucks	675	126	11	24	26	71
Southeast Division						
Atlanta Hawks	825	142	7	30	30	67
Charlotte Hornets	750	142	3	24	20	82
Miami Heat	1,300	180	20	67	7	89
Orlando Magic	900	143	35	34	17	66
Washington Wizards	960	146	2	31	14	89

Note: Teams are listed alphabetically by division. Value is based on the current stadium deal (unless new stadium is pending) without deduction for debt (other than annual stadium debt). Revenue is net of stadium revenues used for debt payments. Operating Income (OI) is earnings before interest, taxes, depreciation, and amortization. Gate receipts (GR) include income from club seats. Debt/Value (D/V) is percent and includes ballpark debts. Players Expenses (PE) contains benefits and bonuses. Value, Revenue, OI, GR, and PE are each in millions of U.S. dollars.

Source: Kurt Badenhausen, Michael Ozanian, and Christina Settimi, "The Business of Basketball," http://www.forbes.com, cited June 27, 2016.

Table A4. Eastern Conference Teams, Payrolls by Division, Selected Seasons

Team	*2011 (R)*	*2012 (R)*	*2013 (R)*	*2014 (R)*	*2015 (R)*
Atlantic Division					
Boston Celtics	78.7 (1)	71.9 (5)	70.5 (5)	61.9 (11)	77.1 (7)
Brooklyn Nets	NA	83.0 (1)	102.8 (1)	88.1 (1)	88.0 (2)
New York Knicks	63.3 (8)	78.6 (3)	88.1 (2)	80.9 (3)	73.4 (10)
Philadelphia 76ers	66.0 (7)	67.2 (6)	53.3 (15)	53.5 (15)	64.5 (14)
Toronto Raptors	53.6 (13)	66.6 (8)	69.6 (7)	79.9 (4)	71.3 (13)
Central Division					
Chicago Bulls	68.9 (5)	74.2 (4)	71.0 (4)	66.8 (8)	87.6 (3)
Cleveland Cavaliers	50.9 (14)	53.3 (15)	66.6 (9)	81.8 (2)	108.3 (1)
Detroit Pistons	70.6 (3)	63.0 (11)	61.8 (11)	64.1 (10)	85.8 (4)
Indiana Pacers	43.9 (15)	66.5 (9)	66.6 (8)	74.4 (6)	71.6 (12)
Milwaukee Bucks	60.1 (10)	61.6 (12)	55.3 (14)	57.1 (14)	73.8 (9)
Southeast Division					
Atlanta Hawks	70.6 (4)	66.6 (7)	58.2 (12)	58.4 (13)	71.6 (11)
Charlotte Bobcats/Hornets	57.9 (11)	57.4 (14)	63.0 (10)	66.0 (9)	76.8 (8)
Miami Heat	76.2 (2)	83.0 (2)	80.7 (3)	75.6 (5)	85.7 (5)
Orlando Magic	68.5 (6)	66.3 (10)	56.7 (13)	59.0 (12)	62.3 (15)
Washington Wizards	54.7 (12)	58.0 (13)	70.3 (6)	73.4 (7)	83.0 (6)

Note: Teams are listed alphabetically by division. NBA is National Basketball Association. Although rounded to millions of dollars, equal payroll amounts in the table were actually different totals and not tied such as the Detroit Pistons and Atlanta Hawks in the league's 2011–12 season. Rank (R) is relative to other teams in the conference. NA is not applicable since the New Jersey Nets—whose payroll actually ranked ninth at $60.8 million—and not the Brooklyn Nets played in the 2011 season. The Charlotte Bobcats were renamed Hornets in the league's 2014 season.

Source: "NBA Salaries," http://www.hoopshype.com, cited June 29, 2016, and "NBA Season Team Salary Listings," http://www.eskimo.com, cited June 29, 2016.

Table A5. NBA Arenas, Eastern Conference Teams by Division, 2015

Arena (Team)	*Age*	*Owner* *Private*	*Public*	*Cost*	*Value*
Atlantic Division					
Air Canada Centre (Raptors)	18	X		175	259
Barclays Center (Nets)	5		X	845	554
Madison Square Garden (Knicks)	6	X		1,000	907
TD Garden (Celtics)	22	X		160	352
Wells Fargo Center (76ers)	21	X		217	80
Central Division					
Bankers Life Fieldhouse (Pacers)	18		X	183	152
BMO Harris Bradley Center (Bucks)	29	X		90	76
Palace of Auburn Hills (Pistons)	29	X		70	145
Quicken Loans Arena (Cavaliers)	23		X	152	248
United Center (Bulls)	23	X		175	629
Southeast Division					
American Airlines Arena (Heat)	18		X	213	308
Amway Center (Magic)	7		X	380	155
Philips Arena (Hawks)	18		X	213	198
Time Warner Cable Arena (Hornets)	12		X	265	132
Verizon Center (Wizards)	20	X		260	186

Note: Arenas are listed in alphabetical order by division. Except for Madison Square Garden (MSG)—which was extensively renovated during 2011–2014—the Age column is number of years from when these arenas opened to the NBA's 2015–16 or simply 2015 season. Owner is self-explanatory. Cost is the initial construction cost in millions of dollars including renovations of MSG. Value is the portion of each franchise's estimated market value in millions of dollars attributable to a team's arena.

Source: "Present National Basketball Association Arenas," http://www.basketball.ballparks.com, cited June 27, 2016; Kurt Badenhausen, Mike Ozanian, and Christini Settimi, "The Business of Basketball," http://www.forbes.com, cited June 27, 2016; "NBA and ABA Team Index," http://www.basketball-reference.com, cited June 25, 2016.

Table A6. Eastern Conference Teams, Fan Cost Indexes by Division, 2011–2015 Seasons

Team	*2011 (R)*	*2012 (R)*	*2013 (R)*	*2014 (R)*	*2015 (R)*
Atlantic Division					
Boston Celtics	392 (4)	420 (4)	434 (4)	444 (4)	419 (4)
Brooklyn Nets	NA	365 (5)	382 (5)	404 (5)	404 (5)
New York Knicks	608 (1)	643 (1)	659 (1)	676 (1)	676 (1)
Philadelphia 76ers	263 (10)	260 (10)	266 (9)	278 (8)	275 (9)
Toronto Raptors	319 (5)	316 (6)	321 (6)	289 (7)	323 (7)
Central Division					
Chicago Bulls	393 (3)	426 (3)	456 (3)	477 (2)	477 (2)
Cleveland Cavaliers	275 (7)	287 (8)	271 (8)	271 (9)	274 (10)
Detroit Pistons	257 (11)	254 (11)	262 (11)	261 (11)	215 (14)
Indiana Pacers	208 (14)	212 (14)	227 (14)	232 (14)	257 (12)
Milwaukee Bucks	289 (6)	313 (7)	309 (7)	325 (6)	325 (6)
Southeast Division					
Atlanta Hawks	238 (12)	233 (13)	240 (13)	245 (13)	255 (13)
Charlotte Bobcats/Hornets	203 (15)	203 (15)	203 (15)	212 (15)	212 (15)
Miami Heat	423 (2)	445 (2)	472 (2)	468 (3)	465 (3)
Orlando Magic	275 (8)	265 (9)	263 (10)	263 (10)	263 (11)
Washington Wizards	212 (13)	246 (12)	249 (12)	258 (12)	322 (8)

Note: Teams are listed alphabetically by division. Although rounded to hundreds of dollars, equal payroll amounts in the table were actually different totals and not tied such as the Cleveland Cavaliers and Orlando Magic in the league's 2011 season. Rank (R) is relative to other teams in the conference. Not Applicable (NA) since the New Jersey Nets—actually ranked ninth at $272—and not Brooklyn Nets played in the NBA's 2011 season. The Charlotte Bobcats were renamed Hornets in the league's 2014–15 season.
Source: "Rod Fort's Sports Business Data," https://sites.google.com, cited July 1, 2016, and "NBA FCIs," http://www.teammarketingreport.com, cited July 1, 2016.

Table A7. Western Conference Teams, Historical Performances by Division, Selected Seasons

				Titles		
Teams	*Seasons*	*W%*	*Playoffs*	*Division*	*Conference*	*Championship*
Northwest Division						
Denver Nuggets	40	.484	24	7	0	0
Minnesota Timberwolves	27	.391	8	1	0	0
Oklahoma City Thunder	8	.616	6	5	1	0
Portland Trail Blazers	46	.535	32	5	3	1
Utah Jazz	37	.554	25	8	2	0
Pacific Division						
Golden State Warriors	45	.467	15	4	3	2
Los Angeles Clippers	32	.398	9	2	0	0
Los Angeles Lakers	56	.613	49	28	18	11
Phoenix Suns	48	.546	29	6	2	0
Sacramento Kings	31	.424	10	2	0	0
Southwest Division						
Dallas Mavericks	36	.510	21	3	2	1
Houston Rockets	45	.531	29	5	4	2
Memphis Grizzlies	15	.488	9	0	0	0
NO Hornets/Pelicans	14	.466	6	1	0	0
San Antonio Spurs	40	.621	36	21	6	5

Note: Teams are listed alphabetically by division. Seasons include the Basketball Association of America (BAA) 1947–1949 and National Basketball Association (NBA) 1950–2015 seasons. NO is New Orleans. The W% is win-loss percent. The table excludes BAA and NBA teams at their previous sites: Seattle Supersonics (1968–2008); New Orleans Jazz (1975–1979); Philadelphia Warriors (1947–1962) and San Francisco Warriors (1963–1971); Buffalo Braves (1971–1978) and San Diego Clippers (1979–1984); Minneapolis Lakers (1949–1960); Rochester Royals (1949–1957); Cincinnati Royals (1958–1972); Kansas City-Omaha Kings (1973–1975); Kansas City Kings (1976–1985); San Diego Rockets (1968–1971); Vancouver Grizzlies (1996–2001). The New Orleans Hornets were renamed Pelicans in the NBA's 2013–14 season.

Source: "NBA and ABA Team Index," http://www.basketball-reference.com, cited June 25, 2016, and "Historical Moments," http://www.sportsecyclopedia.com, cited June 25, 2016.

Table A8. Western Conference Teams by Division, History—Principal Owners

	Principal Owners			*Team Titles*		
Team	*Name*	*Year*	*Price*	*Division*	*Conference*	*NBA*
Northwest Division						
Denver Nuggets	Stanley Kroenke	2000	202	3	0	0
Minnesota Timberwolves	Glen Taylor	1995	89	1	0	0
Oklahoma City Thunder	Clayton Bennett	2006	325	5	1	0
Portland Trail Blazers	Paul Allen	1988	70	4	2	0
Utah Jazz	Gail Miller	2009	NA	0	0	0
Pacific Division						
Golden State Warriors	Joe Lacob	2010	450	2	2	1
Los Angeles Clippers	Steve Ballmer	2014	2,000	0	0	0
Los Angeles Lakers	Jerry Buss	1979	20	18	16	10
Phoenix Suns	Robert Sarver	2004	404	3	0	0
Sacramento Kings	Vivek Ranadive	2013	534	0	0	0
Southwest Division						
Dallas Mavericks	Mark Cuban	2000	280	2	2	1
Houston Rockets	Leslie Alexander	1993	85	2	2	2
Memphis Grizzlies	Robert Pera	2012	377	0	0	0
New Orleans Pelicans	Tom Benson	2012	340	0	0	0
San Antonio Spurs	Peter Holt	1996	76	12	6	5

Note: Teams are listed alphabetically by division. The Buss family trust actually owns the Lakers following Jerry's death in early 2013. The NA means not applicable since Gail Miller inherited the team when Larry Miller died in 2009. Year is when principal owners acquired the team. Price is in millions. NBA is National Basketball Association. Team Titles were won since Year of principal owners.

Source: Kurt Badenhausen, Mike Ozanian, and Christini Settimi, "The Business of Basketball," http://www.forbes.com, cited June 27, 2016, and "NBA and ABA Team Index," http://www.basketball-reference.com, cited June 25, 2016.

Table A9. Western Conference Teams, Financial Data by Division, 2015

Teams	*Value*	*Revenue*	*OI*	*GR*	*D/V*	*PE*
Northwest Division						
Denver Nuggets	855	140	26	26	0	64
Minnesota Timberwolves	720	146	15	19	14	76
Oklahoma City Thunder	950	157	20	48	15	87
Portland Trail Blazers	975	157	4	42	11	94
Utah Jazz	875	146	27	36	9	67
Pacific Division						
Golden State Warriors	1,900	201	57	77	13	80
Los Angeles Clippers	2,000	176	20	59	0	92
Los Angeles Lakers	2,700	304	133	98	1	76
Phoenix Suns	1,000	154	21	35	18	76
Sacramento Kings	925	141	4	29	25	81
Southwest Division						
Dallas Mavericks	1,400	177	24	45	8	90
Houston Rockets	1,500	237	74	75	7	85
Memphis Grizzlies	780	147	10	27	22	81
New Orleans Pelicans	650	142	19	30	19	80
San Antonio Spurs	1,150	170	31	59	7	76

Note: Teams are listed alphabetically by division. Value is based on the current stadium deal (unless new stadium is pending) without deduction for debt (other than annual stadium debt). Revenue is net of stadium revenues used for debt payments. Operating Income (OI) is earnings before interest, taxes, depreciation, and amortization. Gate Receipts (GR) include income from club seats. Debt/Value (D/V) is percent and includes ballpark debts. Players Expenses (PE) contains benefits and bonuses. Value, Revenue, OI, GR, and PE are each in millions of U.S. dollars.

Source: Kurt Badenhausen, Michael Ozanian, and Christina Settimi, "The Business of Basketball," http://www.forbes.com, cited June 27, 2016.

Table A10. Western Conference Teams, Payrolls by Division, Selected Seasons

Team	*2011 (R)*	*2012 (R)*	*2013 (R)*	*2014 (R)*	*2015 (R)*
Northeast Division					
Denver Nuggets	58.5 (11)	64.0 (7)	65.6 (9)	56.7 (15)	72.5 (9)
Minnesota Timberwolves	56.8 (14)	63.1 (9)	67.5 (6)	69.2 (12)	72.2 (10)
Oklahoma City Thunder	59.9 (9)	67.4 (5)	70.1 (5)	79.7 (2)	96.5 (2)
Portland Trail Blazers	64.3 (8)	58.4 (12)	62.5 (12)	71.6 (9)	61.6 (15)
Utah Jazz	59.3 (10)	66.9 (6)	56.9 (14)	60.2 (14)	63.0 (14)
Pacific Division					
Golden State Warriors	57.1 (12)	69.6 (3)	71.4 (4)	73.2 (7)	93.6 (3)
Los Angeles Clippers	66.7 (6)	69.4 (4)	72.4 (2)	84.2 (1)	97.0 (1)
Los Angeles Lakers	87.9 (1)	99.9 (1)	77.0 (1)	70.1 (10)	72.1 (11)
Phoenix Suns	79.9 (2)	53.3 (15)	55.0 (15)	62.1 (13)	70.0 (13)
Sacramento Kings	48.9 (15)	54.3 (14)	62.4 (13)	73.8 (6)	70.6 (12)
Southeast Division					
Dallas Mavericks	76.3 (3)	61.5 (11)	67.2 (7)	74.9 (3)	75.3 (8)
Houston Rockets	57.0 (13)	57.3 (13)	63.3 (11)	71.8 (8)	89.7 (4)
Memphis Grizzlies	70.5 (5)	62.9 (10)	72.1 (3)	74.1 (4)	83.3 (6)
NO Hornets/Pelicans	65.4 (7)	63.5 (8)	66.1 (8)	73.9 (5)	82.5 (7)
San Antonio Spurs	73.4 (4)	69.7 (2)	63.8 (10)	69.4 (11)	87.8 (5)

Note: Teams are listed alphabetically by division. NBA is National Basketball Association. Amounts are rounded to millions of dollars each season. Rank (R) is relative to other teams in the conference. New Orleans (NO) Hornets were renamed Pelicans in the league's 2013 season.

Source: "NBA Salaries," http://www.hoopshype.com, cited June 29, 2016, and "NBA Season Team Salary Listings," http://www.eskimo.com, cited June 29, 2016.

Table A11. NBA Arenas, Western Conference Teams by Division, 2015 Season

		Owner			
Arena (Team)	*Age*	*Private*	*Public*	*Cost*	*Value*
Northwest Division					
Chesapeake Energy Arena (Thunder)	15		X	89	195
Virint Smart Home Arena (Jazz)	26	X		94	168
Moda Center (Trail Blazers)	22	X		262	207
Pepsi Center (Nuggets)	18	X		160	153
Target Center (Timberwolves)	27	X		104	118
Pacific Division					
Oracle Arena (Warriors)	51		X	121	455
Sleep Train Arena (Kings)	29	X		40	156
Staples Center (Clippers)	18	X		400	387
Staples Center (Lakers)	18	X		400	537
Talking Stick Resort Arena (Suns)	25		X	90	201
Southwest Division					
American Airlines Center (Mavericks)	16		X	420	352
AT&T Center (Spurs)	15		X	186	301
FedExForum (Grizzlies)	13		X	250	140
Smoothie King Center (Pelicans)	18		X	114	117
Toyota Center (Rockets)	14		X	202	408

Note: Arenas are listed in alphabetical order by division. NBA is National Basketball Association. Age is number of years from when these arenas opened to the NBA's 2015–16 season. Owner is self-explanatory. Cost is the initial construction cost in millions including renovations. Value is the portion of each franchise's estimated market value in millions attributable to a team's arena.

Source: "Present National Basketball Association Arenas," http://www.basketball.ballparks.com, cited June 27, 2016; Kurt Badenhausen, Mike Ozanian, and Christini Settimi, "The Business of Basketball," http://www.forbes.com, cited June 27, 2016; "NBA and ABA Team Index," http://www.basketball-reference.com, cited June 25, 2016.

Table A12. Western Conference Teams, Fan Cost Indexes by Division, 2011–2015 Seasons

Team	*2011 (R)*	*2012 (R)*	*2013 (R)*	*2014 (R)*	*2015 (R)*
Northwest Division					
Denver Nuggets	295 (7)	326 (5)	319 (8)	322 (7)	316 (8)
Minnesota Timberwolves	225 (13)	261 (12)	273 (12)	281 (11)	281 (11)
Oklahoma City Thunder	280 (8)	278 (9)	295 (10)	295 (10)	296 (9)
Portland Trail Blazers	296 (6)	296 (8)	308 (9)	317 (8)	319 (7)
Utah Jazz	271 (11)	276 (10)	280 (11)	275 (13)	275 (13)
Pacific Division					
Golden State Warriors	252 (12)	260 (13)	324 (6)	336 (6)	471 (2)
Los Angeles Clippers	322 (3)	369 (2)	395 (2)	435 (2)	437 (3)
Los Angeles Lakers	514 (1)	518 (1)	542 (1)	541 (1)	545 (1)
Phoenix Suns	346 (2)	333 (3)	344 (3)	341 (4)	341 (5)
Sacramento Kings	277 (9)	268 (11)	268 (13)	280 (12)	286 (10)
Southwest Division					
Dallas Mavericks	311 (5)	321 (6)	321 (7)	312 (9)	281 (12)
Houston Rockets	271 (10)	299 (7)	336 (5)	369 (3)	376 (4)
Memphis Grizzlies	192 (15)	213 (15)	212 (14)	223 (14)	223 (14)
New Orleans Hornets/Pelicans	217 (14)	220 (14)	208 (15)	221 (15)	221 (15)
San Antonio Spurs	319 (4)	330 (4)	339 (4)	340 (5)	325 (6)

Note: Teams are listed alphabetically by division. Although rounded to hundreds of dollars, equal payroll amounts in the table were actually different totals and not tied such as the Utah Jazz and Houston Rockets in the league's 2011 season. Rank (R) is relative to other teams in the conference. The New Orleans Hornets were renamed Pelicans in the NBA's 2013 season.

Source: "Rod Fort's Sports Business Data," https://sites.google.com, cited July 1, 2016, and "NBA FCIs," http://www.teammarketingreport.com, cited July 1, 2016.

Bibliography

Aisher, Josh. "The Ten Best NBA Teams of All Time." http://www.cheatsheet.com, cited 3 June 2016.

Alesia, Mark. "CIB Signs Off on Pacers' $50 Million Practice Facility." http://www.indystar.com, cited 24 July 2016.

Anzilotti, Eillie. "How the NBA's Progressivism is Helping it Thrive." http://www.theatlantic.com, cited 1 July 2016.

Arnovitz, Kevin. "Which NBA Team Are You?" http://www.espn.com, cited 18 September 2016.

Axson, Scooby. "Forbes: Hornets Owner Michael Jordan Now a Billionaire After Increasing Stake in Team." http://www.forbes.com, cited 12 August 2016.

Badenhausen, Kurt, Mike Ozanian, and Christini Settimi. "The Business of Basketball." http://www.forbes.com, cited 27 June 2016.

Baker, Paul. "2016 NBA Arena Experience Rankings." http://www.scout.com, cited 1 August 2016.

Bailey, Ethan. "NBA Preseason Power Rankings: How Each Team is Looking in Preseason." http://www.bleacherreport.com, cited 13 June 2016.

Bariso, Justin. "5 Business Lessons From Gregg Popovich and the San Antonio Spurs." http://www.linkedin.com, cited 24 September 2016.

Benson, Lee. "About Utah: Former Utah Jazz CEO Greg Miller is Back in the Briar Patch." http://www.desertnews.com, cited 8 August 2016.

Bieler, Des. "Milwaukee Bucks' Tax Information Released by Employee Who Fell for Email Scam." http://www.washingtonpost.com, cited 27 July 2016.

"Blazers, Heat Renew Season Tickets Via App." http://www.sportsbusinessdaily.com, cited 15 August 2016.

Bleau, Max. "Atlanta Hawks Work to Promote Diversity After Divisive Scandal." http://www.atlantamagazine.com, cited 4 August 2016.

Bontemps, Tim. "Kevin Durant and the Warriors Dream Team May Become a Salary Nightmare Next July." http://www.washingtonpost.com, cited 28 August 2016.

Borchers, Callum. "Celtics Bow to History to Draw Fans." http://www.bostonglobe.com, cited 9 July 2016.

Broughton, David. "Bucks Lead Way in NBA Phone Sales Survey." http://www.sportsbusinessdaily.com, cited 27 July 2016.

Broyles, Abby. "We Shouldn't be Subsidizing Their Payroll,' State Program Funds OKC Thunder, Other Big Companies' Payroll, Amid Budget Crisis." http://www.kfor.com, cited 28 July 2016.

Buhler, John. "10 Best NBA Front Offices." http://www.fansided.com, cited 21 August 2016.

Canzano, John. "Canzano: Portland Trail Blazers All About the Business of Basketball." http://www.oregonlive.com, cited 28 August 2016.

Carlisle, Candace. "Mark Cuban Confirms Deal, Offers Details on New Mavs Facility." http://www.bizjournals.com, cited 15 September 2016.

Carlock, Catherine. "Celtics Join Bruins With New Facility at Boston Landing." http://www.bizjournals.com, cited 9 July 2016.

Carter, Aaron. "Sixers Partners Invest in Crystal Palace." http://www.articles.philly.com, cited 14 July 2016.

Case, William. "Ranking the Greatest Franchises in NBA History." http://www.listlicled.com, cited 8 August 2016.

"Cavaliers First in NBA to Require Automatic Renewal." http://www.sportsbusinessdaily.com, cited 21 July 2016.

Chan, Lorne. "New AT&T Center Welcomes San Antonians Back Home." http://www.nba.com, cited 23 September 2016.

Chandler, Adam. "NBA Lets in Advertising, 6.25 Square Inches at a Time." http://www.theatlantic.com, cited 14 July 2016.

"Clippers Announce Partnership With American Airlines." http://www.nba.com, cited 2 September 2016.

"Coast to Coast." http://www.sportsbusinessdaily.com, cited 17 September 2016.

Cohen, Ben. "The NBA's Rich Get Richer." *Wall Street Journal* (1 July 2016): D8.

Colangelo, Jerry, and Len Sherman. *How You Play the Game: Lessons For Life From the Billion-Dollar Business of Sports* (New York, NY: Amacom, 1999).

"Community Begins at Home . . . Games." http://www.nba.com, cited 18 September 2016.

Connelly, Courtney. "Atlanta Hawks Chief Marketing Officer Talks the State of Diversity for Women in Sports Today." http://www.blackenterprise.com, cited 17 August 2016.

Coro, Paul. "Phoenix Suns Likely to Hold $13 Million Cap Space for Later." http://www.azcentral.com, cited 8 September 2016.

Cortsen, Kenneth. "Guest Blog: Miami Heat and the Role of Brand Positioning." http://www.kennethcortsen.com, cited 20 August 2016.

Croes, Max. "James Harden is to Blame for the Rockets Coaching Problems." http;//www.thedreamshake.com, cited 3 September 2016.

Dahlgren, Luke. "Power Rankings: NBA Arenas." https://fansided.com, cited 10 July 2016.

Davis, Scott. "Indiana Pacers Just Dumped Their Head Coach and Kicked Him on the Way Out." http://www.businessinsider.com, cited 24 July 2016.

Delevett, Peter. "How Vivek Ranadive Beat Out Steve Ballmer to Buy Sacramento Kings." http://www.mercurynews.com, cited 6 September 2016.
"Denver Nuggets Community Ambassadors." http://www.nba.com, cited 7 August 2016.
"Detroit Pistons." http://www.nba.com, cited 2 July 2016.
"Detroit Pistons Partner With Grow Detroit's Young Talent to Support Mayor Mike Duggan's Summer Youth Jobs Program." http://www.nba.com, cited 23 July 2016.
DiNapoli, Jessica. "The Case of a Dead Oil and Gas Mogul Takes an Unexpected Turn, and it Involves the Oklahoma City Thunder." http://www.businessinsider.com, cited 20 August 2016.
Dineen, J. K. "Warriors Win Judgement in Fight Over SF Mission Bay Arena." http://www.sfgate.com, cited 1 September 2016.
Ding, Kevin. "A Family Divided: Unrest Growing in Buss Family as Lakers Struggle to Rebuild." http://www.bleacherreport.com, cited 7 September 2016.
Douglas, Stephen. "Houston Rockets' Twitter Put Down Mavericks With Gun and Horse Emoji." http://www.thebiglead.com, cited 17 September 2016.
Dyer, Mike. "Cleveland Cavaliers Announce Preseason Games in Cincinnati and Columbus." http://www.cincinnati.com, cited 22 July 2016.
Eanes, Zachery. "Events D.C. Increases Price Tag for Wizards Practice Facility." http://www.bizjournals.com, cited 25 August 2016.
Eis, Easy. "The Bulls Are Still a Massive Success When it Comes to Making Money." http://www.blogabull.com, cited 16 July 2016.
Falk, Aaron. "Utah Jazz: Advocacy Group Opposes LHM Proposal for Arena Tax Breaks." http://www.sltrib.com, cited 5 August 2016.
"Fan Cost Index." http://www.teammarketingreport.com, cited 1 August 2016.
Fernandez, Erik. "Dirk Nowitzki Mocks Donald Trump in Fake Ad Campaign." http://www.huffingtonpost.com, 16 September 2016.
Fisher, Eric. "Celtics, Raptors Offer Dynamic Pricing Through StratBridge." http://www.sportsbusinessdaily.com, cited 9 July 2016.
Fisher, Eric. "Teams Continue to Shake up Ticketing Industry." http://www.sportsbusinessdaily.com, cited 14 July 2016.
Fisher, Eric. "Teams Put Pressure on Ticket Brokers." http://www.sportsbusinessdaily.com, cited 2 September 2016.
Flood, George. "Indiana Pacers Will Meet Denver Nuggets at NBA Global Games London in 2017." http://www.ibtimes.co.uk, cited 1 August 2016.
Ford, Chad, and Kevin Pelton. "Future NBA Power Rankings: Full Category Rankings." http://www.espn.go.com, cited 3 August 2016.
Ford, Chad, and Kevin Pelton. "Future Power Rankings: Who Will Rise in the Next Three Years?" http://www.espn.go.com, cited 5 June 2016.
Fortier, Sam. "Portland Columnist Suspicious Paul Allen Will Move Trail Blazers to Seattle." http://www.seattlepi.com, cited 25 July 2016.
Frauenheim, Ed. "What Business Can Learn From the Golden State Warriors." http://www.fortune.com, cited 1 September 2016.
"Fred Hoiberg—Chicago Bulls." http://www.business.iastate.edu, cited 15 July 2016.
Freeman, Eric. "Mike Conley and Grizzlies Agree to the Biggest NBA Contract Ever." http://www.sports.yahoo.com, cited 19 September 2016.

Fromal, Adam. "Future Power Rankings for the 2016 NBA Lottery Teams." http://www.bleacherreport.com, cited 15 July 2016.

"Gillian Zucker Replaces Andy Roeser." http://www.espn.com, cited 5 September 2016.

Goldman, Stuart. "Detroit Pistons Keep Fans Updated With Real-Time Email." http://www.athleticbusiness.com, cited 23 July 2016.

"Grizzlies Make Spotlight Available to Suite Holders." http://www.sportsbusiness-daily.com, cited 19 September 2016.

Groves, Roger. "Why the NBA Will Have Better Profit Growth Than the NFL." http://www.forbes.com, cited 1 July 2016.

Hanna-Riggs, Scott. "ESPN Insider's Future Power Rankings: Phoenix Suns 4th Worst in NBA." http://www.valleyofthesuns.com, cited 28 June 2016.

Hatter, T. J. "The Ten Worst Franchises in NBA History." http://www.uproxx.com, cited 7 September 2016.

Heisler, Mark. "Heisler: From Bad to Worse to Vivek: Top 10 Worst Owners in NBA." http://www.dailynews.com, cited 8 September 2016.

Hill, Josh. "NBA: Five Arenas That Need to be Torn Down Now." http://www.fan-sided.com, cited 15 July 2016.

Hill, Josh. "NBA Owners Power Ranking: Who is Best Owner in Basketball?" http://www.fansided.com, cited 8 July 2016.

"Historical Moments." http://www.sportsecyclopedia.com, cited 25 June 2016.

Holmes, Chris. "All-Time NBA Franchise Rankings, 2015–16 Edition." http://www.greyflannelsuit.net, cited 15 August 2016.

Holmes, Chris. "The 10 Worst NBA Franchises, 2013 Edition." http://www.grayflan-nelsuit.net, cited 6 August 2016.

"Hornets Announce Grant Thornton LLP to Become Team's Official Accounting Firm." http://www.nba.com, cited 18 August 2016.

"How The Orlando Magic Prosper With Analytics Despite Relatively Small Market." http://www.sporttechie.com, cited 21 August 2016.

Hughey, Angela. "Phoenix Suns Become First NBA Team to Sign the UNITY Pledge." http://www.openaz.com, cited 3 September 2016.

"Indiana Pacers: Using Data to Grow Fan Loyalty." http://www.umbel.com, cited 24 July 2016.

"Jazz offers Fans Chance to Sell Rights to Tickets." http://www.sportsbusinessdaily.com, cited 6 August 2016.

"Jeanie Buss: Los Angeles Lakers." http://www.concordia.net, cited 6 September 2016.

Jozsa, Frank P., Jr. *National Basketball Association Strategies: Business Expansions, Relocations, and Mergers* (New York, NY: Springer, 2016).

Jozsa, Frank P., Jr. *The National Basketball Association: Business, Organization and Strategy* (Hackensack, NJ: World Scientific, 2011).

Kaplan, Daniel. "Kroenke to Offer Plan to Comply With NFL Rules." http://www.sportsbusinessdaily.com, cited 26 July 2016.

Kaplan, Daniel. "Team Valuations Show Big Gap in Benson Suit." http://www.sportsbusinessdaily.com, cited 20 September 2016.

Karantzoulis, Mark. "How the Bulls Should Use Wade." http://www.chicagonow.com, cited 9 July 2016.

Karp, Hannah. "Sports Teams Try New Game: Scalping Tickets." *Wall Street Journal* (15 June 2016): B1–B2.

"Kevin Durant to Sign With Warriors." http://www.espn.com, cited 5 August 2016.

"Kim Stone, Miami Heat/American Airlines Arena." http://www.sportsbusinessdaily.com, cited 18 August 2016.

King, Bill. "Spurs Use Cultural Touch Points to Hit Mark." http://www.sportsbusinessdaily.com, cited 21 September 2016.

King, Bill, and John Lombardo. "The Actions on the Floor." http://www.sportsbusinessdaily.com, cited 19 September 2016.

Kirchberg, Connie. *Hoop Love: A History of the National Basketball Association* (Jefferson, NC: McFarland, 2007).

Kirchen, Rich. "Milwaukee Bucks' Owners Borrow $174 Million to Finance Their Share of Arena Costs." http://www.bizjournals.com, cited 27 July 2016.

Kornhauser, Jacob. "Ranking Every NBA Arena From Worst to First." http://www.ranksports.com, cited 13 July 2016.

Lacoste, Johnathan. "How the CMO of the Sacramento Kings Makes Game Day an Interactive Experience." http://www.inc.com, cited 7 September 2016.

"Laying the Groundwork for the NBA in Toronto." http://www.nba.com, cited 8 June 2016.

Lee, William. "Pathetic Knicks Drawing Pathetic Ratings for MSG." http://www.dailyknicks.com, cited 13 July 2016.

Lefton, Terry. "Hospital Names Nets' New Practice Facility." http://www.sportsbusinessdaily.com, cited 10 July 2016.

Levy, Dan. "How in the World Will the Sixers Get to the NBA Salary Floor." http://www.billypenn.com, cited 14 July 2016.

Lewis, Daniel C. "Nuggets Climb to 20th Overall in ESPN Future Power Rankings." http://www.denverstiffs.com, cited 5 August 2016.

Ligaya, Armina. "Bell Goes for Slam Dunk in Battle for Subscribers With Raptors Reality Show." http://www.business.financialpost.com, cited 16 July 2016.

Lombardo, John. "Blazers Win NBA Promo Award." http://www.sportsbusinessdaily.com, cited 27 August 2016.

Lombardo, John. "Cavs Clean Up at NBA Sales Awards." http://www.sportsbusinessdaily.com, cited 19 July 2016.

Lombardo, John. "Chicago Bulls: Engaging the Fans." http://www.sportsdailybusiness.com, cited 17 July 2016.

Lombardo, John. "Control Supply to Heat Up Demand." http://www.sportsbusinessdaily.com, cited 18 August 2016.

Lombardo, John. "Houston Rockets Bet on Casino Industry Executive to Fill Chief Strategy Position." http://www.sportsbusinessdaily.com cited, 15 September 2016.

Lombardo, John. "Hugo Boss Likes the Look." http://www.sportsbusinessdaily.com, cited 12 July 2016.

Lombardo, John. "In Rebranding, the Bucks Aren't Stopping Here." http://www.sportsbusinessdaily.com, cited 26 July 2016.

Lombardo, John. "Nets, Kings See Global Opportunity." http://www.sportsbusinessdaily.com, cited 10 July 2016.

Lombardo, John. "Picking a Shamrock: Indiana Pacers Hire Marketing Firm to Help Them Bring in National Sponsors." http://www.sportsbusinessdaily.com, cited 25 July 2016.

Lombardo, John. "Sixers Quadruple Sales Staff, Add to Executive Ranks." http://www.sportsbusinessdaily.com, cited 13 July 2016.

Lombardo, John. "Suns, Verizon Team for a Tech 'Wonderland.'" http://www.sportsbusinessdaily.com, cited 1 September 2016.

Lombardo, John. "What a Difference a Year Makes for the Hawks." http://www.sportsbusinessdaily.com, cited 16 August 2016.

Lombardo, John. "Wolves Get Creative in Efforts to Sell Late Addition to Home Schedule." http://www.sportsbusinessdaily.com, cited 10 August 2016.

"Longtime Timberwolves, Lynx CEO Rob Moor Steps Down." http://www.espn.com, cited 18 August 2016.

"Los Angeles Lakers: A Secure, Future-Proof, Fan-Friendly Video Archive." http://www.ironmountain.com, cited 4 September 2016.

"Los Angeles Lakers Sign Chinese Olympian Yi Jianlain." http://www.bbc.com, cited 6 September 2016.

Mackay, David. "Trail Blazers Climb High in ESPN Future Power Rankings." http://www.blazersedge.com, cited 7 August 2016.

MacMahon, Tim. "Mark Cuban: Warriors Being the Bad Guy Will be Good for the NBA." http://www.espn.com, cited 16 September 2016.

Mahoney, Brian. "Knicks Fire Fisher, Name Rambis Interim Coach." http://www.nba.com, cited 12 July 2016.

"Mark Cuban Biography." http://www.biography.com, cited 15 September 2016.

McClusky, Mark. "Techies Are Trying to Turn the NBA Into the World's Biggest Sports League." http://www.wired.com, cited 1 July 2016.

Mikash, Zack. "Forbes Paints a Murky Financial Picture for the Denver Nuggets." http://www.denverstiffs.com, cited 15 August 2016.

McIntyre, Brett. "What Business Leaders Can Learn From the Cleveland Cavaliers Championship." http://www.business.com, cited 18 July 2016.

"Memphis Grizzlies Foundation." http://www.grizzliesfoundation.org, cited 20 September 2016.

Miller, Ian. "Mavericks Tumble to 22nd in ESPN's Future Power Rankings." http://www.mavsmoneyball.com, cited 1 September 2016.

Moore, Matt. "It's Robert Sarver vs. Millennials as the Phoenix Suns Hit Rock Bottom." http://www.cbssports.com, cited 6 September 2016.

Muehlhausen, Jim. "The NBA's New Business Model: Air Ball." http://www.businessmodelinstitute.com, cited 1 July 2016.

Mullen, Liz. "Delta Air Lines Signs Multiyear Deal With Lakers." http://wwwsportsbusinessdaily.com, cited 3 September 2016.

Muret, Don. "Getting the Signal." http://www.sportsbusinessdaily.com, cited 20 July 2016.

Muret, Don. "Magic Selects VenueNext for App." http://www.sportsbusinessdaily.com, cited 22 August 2016.

Muret, Don. "MSG Rolling Out New Premium Areas." http://www.sportsbusinessdaily.com, cited 12 July 2016.
Muret, Don. "Teams Pour More Money, Tech Into Preview Centers." http://www.sportsbusinessdaily.com, cited 6 September 2016.
Naveau, James. "Bulls' TV Ratings Down Nearly 30 Percent in 2015–16 Season." http://www.nbcchicago.com, cited 17 July 2016.
"NBA and ABA Team Index." http://www.basketball-reference.com, cited 25 June 2016.
"NBA Arenas." http://www.nbaarenas.com, cited 4 September 2016.
"NBA Board of Governors Approves Sale of Nets to Prokhorov." http://www.nba.com, cited 4 June 2016.
"NBA Board of Governors Formally Approves Nets Relocation to the Barclays Center in Brooklyn." http://www.barclayscenter.com, cited 5 July 2016.
"NBA Contract Index." http://www.basketball-reference.com, cited 21 July 2016.
"NBA FCIs." http://www.teammarketingreport.com, cited 1 July 2016.
"NBA Front-Office Rankings: 2015." http://www.espn.go.com, cited 23 July 2016.
"NBA Honors Magic for Top Local Promotion." http://www.sportsbusinessdaily.com, cited 23 August 2016.
"NBA Kings to Package USSA Sponsorship Deals With Its Own." http://www.sportsbusinessdaily.com, cited 7 September 2016.
"NBA Salaries." http://www.hoopshype.com, cited 29 June 2016.
"NBA Season Team Salary Listings." http:www.eskimo.com, cited 29 June 2016.
"NBA Surpasses One Billion Likes and Followers on Social Media." http://www.pr.nba.com, cited 1 July 2016.
"NBA Team Salaries." http://www.basketball-reference.com, cited 14 August 2016.
"NBA Teams." http://www.basketball-reference.com, cited 1 July 2016.
Neely-Cohen, Maxwell. "NBA Twitter is Changing the Way We Watch Sports." https://newrepublic.com, cited 1 July 2016.
"Nets, Kings See Global Opportunity." http://www.sportsbusinessdaily.com, cited 6 September 2016.
"Nets Owner Mikhail Prokhorov Has Company Searched in Russia." http://www.nbafeeds.com, cited 11 July 2016.
"New Logo for Toronto Raptors by Sid Lee." http://www.underconsideration.com, cited 16 July 2016.
"New Seats, Signs for Wolves." http://www.sportsbusinessdaily.com, cited 15 August 2016.
"New York Knicks." http://www.nba.com, cited 5 June 2016.
Nieboda, Sarah. "Meet the Marketer Behind the Raptors' #WetheNorth Campaign." http://www.canadianbusiness.com, cited 16 July 2016.
"Novant Lands Spot on Hornets' Floor." http://www.sportsbusinessdaily.com, cited 12 August 2016.
"On the Portland Trail Blazers, the Looming Salary Cap and the Curious Case of Moe Harkless." http://www.blazersedge.com, cited 3 August 2016.
Ourand, John, and John Lombardo. "New Deal to Give Celtics Stake in RSN." http://www.sportsbusinessdaily.com, cited 9 July 2016.

Ourand, John, and John Lombardo. "Settlement Puts Nets Games on YES Net Through 2031–32." http://www.sportsbusinessdaily.com, cited 10 July 2016.

"Philadelphia 76ers Franchise Index." http://www.basketball-reference.com, cited 6 June 2016.

Pollak, Yoni. "Rockets: Leslie Alexander Making Costly Mistake." http://www.houseofhouston.com, cited 17 September 2016.

Ponciano, Jonathan. "Los Angeles Clippers May Leave Staples Center for Westside." http://www.labusinessjournal.com, cited 5 September 2016.

"Present National Basketball Association Arenas." http://www.basketball.ballparks.com, cited 27 June 2016.

Price, Greg. "Lakers Rumors: Is there Cap Space to Sign Russell Westbrook in 2017?" http://www.ibtimes.com, cited 5 September 2016.

Quirk, James, and Rodney D. Fort. *Pay Dirt: The Business of Professional Team Sports* (Princeton, NJ: Princeton University Press, 1992).

Reid, John. "Pelicans President Dennis Lauscha: 'We Have to Win in Order to be Relevant.'" http:/www.nola.com, cited 22 September 2016.

Rice, Shawn. "Charlotte Hornets and Michael Jordan Losing NBA All Star Game Due to Anti-Gay Legislation." http://www.business2community.com, cited 11 August 2016.

Rivas, Keith. "Lakers Jersey Ads: Which Companies Should Sponsor Los Angeles in the Future?" http://www.lasportshub.com, cited 7 September 2016.

Robbins, Josh. "Losing Has Forced the Magic to Upgrade as a Business." http://www.orlandosentinel.com, cited 21 August 2016.

Rocco, Matthew. "Wizards Owner Ted Leonsis: Millennials Are Changing Sports on TV." http://www.foxbusiness.com, cited 23 August 2016.

"Rod Fort's Sports Business Data." https://sites.google.com, cited 1 July 2016.

"Root Sports Expands Access to Rocket Games." http://www.nba.com, cited 18 September 2016.

Roper, Eric. "Target Center renovation Clears Final Hurdle From Minneapolis City Council." http://www.startribune.com, cited 20 August 2016.

Rossman-Reich, Philip. "Orlando Magic Rise 10 Spots in ESPN Future Power Rankings." http://www.orlandomagicdaily.com, cited 9 August 2016.

Sakamoto, Bob. "Reinsdorf Buys Bulls." http://www.articles.chicagotribune.com, cited 10 July 2016.

"Sale Allows NBA to Break Even on Hornets." http://www.sportsbusinessdaily.com, cited 21 September 2016.

"San Antonio Spurs Finish 2014–15 NBA Season No. 1 in Local TV Ratings." http://www.nba.com, cited 22 September 2016.

"SBA at the Washington Wizards." http://www.gwsba.org, cited 25 August 2016.

Scaletta, Kelly. "NBA Power Rankings: The Ultimate All-Time Ranking of Every NBA Franchise." http://www.bleacherreport.com, cited 12 August 2016.

Schnurman, Mitchell. "What Texas Businesses Can Learn From the Oklahoma City Thunder's Gun Activism." http://www.dallasnews.com, cited 21 August 2016.

Schoenfeld, Bruce. "Limited Owners, Unlimited Expectations." http://www.sportsbusinessdaily.com, cited 2 September 2016.

Schoenfeld, Bruce. "With Settlement, Future of Franchises Remain Far From Clear." http://www.sportsbusinessdaily.com, cited 20 September 2016.
"Sentient Jet Named Official Private Jet Partner of the Atlanta Hawks." http://www.businesswire.com, cited 17 August 2016.
"790 The Ticket and Miami Heat Extend Broadcast Partnership." http://www.entercom.com, cited 21 August 2016.
Shea, Bill. "Detroit Pistons Business Scorecard Improves." http://www.crainsdetroit.com, cited 22 July 2016.
Sheffield, Michael. "Grizzlies Unveil MLK Day Uniforms." http://www.bizjournals.com, cited 20 September 2016.
Singh, Satbir. "Raptors in Good Hands With or Without Tim Leiweke." http://www.hoopshype.ca, cited 18 July 2016.
Smith, Aaron. "Flint Gets $25 Million From Detroit Pistons and a Local Bank." http://www.money.cnn.com, cited 22 July 2016.
Smith, Keith. "The Maximum Available 2016 Cap Space for ALL 30 NBA Teams, Version 2.0." http://www.basketball.realgm.com, cited 4 September 2016.
"Social Experiment." http://www.sportsbusinessdaily.com, cited 2 September 2016.
Soper, Taylor. "Sacramento Kings Will Host a Startup Pitch Contest During an NBA Game." http://www.geekwire.com, cited 8 September 2016.
Soshnick, Scott. "NBA's Brooklyn Nets to Cut Ticket Prices 24% Next Season." http://www.bloomberg.com, cited 11 July 2016.
Spanberg, Erik. "How Team Paved Way for Beloved Brand's Return." http://www.sportsbusinessdaily.com, cited 12 August 2016.
"Sports Marketing Alumnus Scores a Career With the Indiana Pacers." http://www.ferris.edu, cited 23 July 2016.
"Spurs to Refresh YouTube Channel." http://www.sportsbusinessdaily.com, cited 21 September 2016.
Stein, Len. "Thunder, Spurs and Heat NBA Fan Favorites in Brand Keys 2016 Sports Fan Loyalty Index." http://www.brandkeys.com, cited 1 July 2016.
Stejskal, Sam. "NBA Owners Tom Gores, Dan Gilbert Partner to Bring MLS Team to Detroit." http://www.mlssoccer.com, cited 24 July 2016.
"Steve Ballmer's for Local TV." http://www.sportsbusinessdaily.com, cited 5 September 2016.
"Steve Schwartzman Likes the New York Knicks." http://www.thetrustedinsight.com, cited 12 July 2016.
Surdam, David G. *The Rise of the National Basketball Association* (Urbana, IL: University of Illinois Press, 2012).
Sutton, Bill. "How Inclusiveness Allows OKC to Think Big in a Small Market." http://www.sportsbusinessdaily.com, cited 25 August 2016.
Swaney, Paul. "2015 NBA Arena Experience Rankings." http://www.scout.com, cited 15 August 2016.
"The National Basketball Academy: Denver Nuggets." http://www.nba.com, cited 5 August 2016.
"The National Basketball Association Racial & Gender Report Card." http://www.tidesport.org, cited 1 July 2016.

"The Phoenix Suns Create 'People First' Employee Experiences With UltiPro." http://www.tucson.com, cited 5 September 2016.
"The Secret to Social Media Success—From the Atlanta Hawks Playbook." http://www.sportsbusiness.solutions.com, cited 10 August 2016.
"Thunder Sells Out '12–13 Season Tickets, Starts Wait List." http://www.sportsbusinessdaily.com, cited 11 August 2016.
"Thunder, Spurs and Heat NBA Fan Favorites in Brand Keys 2016 Sports Fan Loyalty Index." http://www.brandkeys.com, cited 1 September 2016.
"Top 20 Greatest NBA Teams Ever." http://www.espn.go.com, cited 1 June 2016.
"Toronto Raptors." http://www.nba.com, cited 10 June 2016.
"2015 Front-Office Rankings: Owners." http://www.espn.go.com, cited 14 July 2016.
"Utah Jazz Team Payroll." http://www.basketball-reference.com, cited 27 August 2016.
Verrier, Justin. "Pelicans Back at a Crossroads: Trade the No. 6 Pick or Build for the Future?" http://www.espn.com, cited 15 September 2016.
Vivlamore, Chris. "Hawks Owner Wants Great Franchise—and That Means a Championship." http://www.myjac.com, cited 13 August 2016.
"Warriors Honored for Sales/Marketing." http://www.sportsbusinessdaily.com, cited 3 September 2016.
"We Are Bulls Prep." http://www.chicagobullscollegeprep.noblenetworks.org, cited 18 July 2016.
Weiner, David. "Houston Rockets Salary Cap Update, 2016 Offseason Edition." http://www.rockets.clutchfans.net, cited 18 September 2016.
"WGL and Washington Gas Join Forces With Wizards." http://www.wglholdings.com, cited 24 August 2016.
"WGU and Utah Jazz Award Three Students Tuition for One Year, 4/15/14." http://wgu.edu, cited 10 August 2016.
White, Jared. "What is Next for the Los Angeles Clippers?" http://www.nbalead.com, cited 20 August 2016.
"Wolves, Lynx Announce New Practice Facility, Partnership With Mayo Clinic." http://www.nba.com, cited 20 August 2016.
Zillmer, Daniel. "All 30 NBA Franchises Statistically Ranked by All-Time Greatness." http://www fansided.com, cited 6 June 2016.

Index

About the Author

A former college and semiprofessional athlete with an undergraduate degree in accounting, Master's degrees in business administration and economics, and a doctorate in economics, Frank P. Jozsa Jr. is the author of several books on team sports in professional baseball, basketball, and football, and another on intercollegiate sports programs at American colleges and universities. His memoir, *A Hoosier's Journey: Athlete, Student, Teacher, and Author*, was published by Dog Ear Publishing in 2011.

Besides books, Jozsa has written several articles published in journals, magazines, and newspapers. His dissertation—"An Economic Analysis of Franchise Relocation and League Expansion in Professional Team Sports, 1950–1975"—was completed in 1977 at Georgia State University in Atlanta, Georgia. After teaching undergraduate and graduate courses in economics, finance, and statistics for more than three decades, Jozsa retired from Pfeiffer University in 2007.

www.ingramcontent.com/pod-product-compliance
Lightning Source LLC
Chambersburg PA
CBHW051219230926
51612CB00007B/33